1997
Year B

AN ALMANAC OF PARISH LITURGY

SOURCEBOOK

FOR SUNDAYS AND SEASONS

Peter J. Scagnelli

Liturgy Training Publications

ACKNOWLEDGMENTS

The liturgical texts from the proposed sacramentary that have been included in this book are not authorized for liturgical use. The pastoral introductions and adaptations of the introductory rites, which were included for purposes of information, may not be implemented or used to modify the present authorized form for the celebration of the eucharist. Although the members of the National Conference of Catholic Bishops have approved these texts, some of them have been modified for the United States and none of them have yet been submitted to the Apostolic See for confirmation. Only after they have received the requisite confirmation may they be published and used for liturgical celebrations.

Pastoral introductions, bibliographical notes and prayers from the revised missal are copyright © 1995, International Commission on English in the Liturgy, Inc. (ICEL). Reprinted with permission.
All rights reserved.

Texts taken from the Italian sacramentary, *Messale Romano,* copyright © 1983, Libreria Editrice Vaticana, are translated by Peter J. Scagnelli.

Sourcebook for Sundays and Seasons, 1997, copyright © 1996, Archdiocese of Chicago: Liturgy Training Publications, 1800 North Hermitage Avenue, Chicago IL 60622-1101; 1-800-933-1800, FAX 1-800-933-7094.
All rights reserved.
Printed in the United States of America
ISBN 1-56854-122-8
SSS97

The Gospel of Mark is at the heart of 1997; here the evangelist is portrayed with his traditional symbol, the winged lion. The symbol of each evangelist has been seen to portray the opening lines of the gospel. Mark begins by quoting Isaiah: "I send my messenger before you to prepare your way: a herald's voice in the desert, crying, 'Make ready the way of the Lord, clear him a straight path'" (Mark 1:2–3). Possibly because the lion was known as the king of the desert, it became Mark's symbol.

CONTENTS

RESOURCES
vii

ADVENT
1

CHRISTMAS
27

WINTER ORDINARY TIME
61

LENT
89

TRIDUUM
121

EASTER
153

SUMMER AND FALL ORDINARY TIME
181

Foreword

WELCOME to *Sourcebook for Sundays and Seasons 1997!* Wait 'til you see what we have in store for you this year! If you are new to the *Sourcebook,* you are about to discover a treasure chest of information, instructions, ideas and good common sense. If you are one of *Sourcebook*'s longtime friends in the work of liturgical renewal, thanks for your confidence in us.

■ WHAT'S NEW? The newest thing about this year's *Sourcebook* is also one of the oldest things: the author. Peter J. Scagnelli is this year's author and, God willing, will lead us through 1998 and 1999 as well. Long-time *Sourcebook* readers may recognize Peter as the author of the very first *Sourcebook*s in the late 1980s. A native of Boston, Peter is currently working on a doctorate in liturgical theology. He has served as parish priest and diocesan worship office director, and he still serves as a member of various committees of the International Commission on English in the Liturgy (ICEL). In addition to being a priest and liturgist, Peter is a linguist and translator—you may have sung some of his hymn texts, translated from Latin. Peter is also a very funny guy, and his humor definitely comes through in his writing.

Large portions of *Sourcebook* have been rewritten this year so Peter could introduce you to some of the riches that have come from the revision of the sacramentary. Although the new book is still to come (we don't know exactly when), we have included pieces from it, most notably the Pastoral Introductions prepared by ICEL.

You may notice the absence of the scriptural collect prayers that have been a feature of *Sourcebook* for the last several years. These prayers, prepared by ICEL for the revision of the sacramentary, have been approved by the bishops of the United States and are awaiting confirmation from Rome. While that is in process, ICEL has asked that we not publish these prayers again.

If you would like to encourage the approval of these prayers and the rest of the sacramentary revisions, you may write to Cardinal Antonio Maria Javierre Ortas, Prefect, Congregation for Divine Worship and the Discipline of the Sacraments, Via Rusticci 13, 00193 Rome, Italy.

A small, but we think useful, addition has been made at the end of each seasonal section. One or two pages designed for making notes (or doodling, if that's your style) have been provided. You might consider using these pages to record the decisions you make for this year's seasons. *Sourcebook '97* can then serve as a reference for next year's planning. Let us know if you find it helpful.

■ WHAT'S THE SAME? This year's *Sourcebook* is similar in many ways to the 1996 book. The basic design of the sections and pages has been kept. Rita Corbin's artwork again graces the cover and inside of this year's book. Rita has worked in religious and liturgical art for many years. You may be most familiar with her work from *The Catholic Worker.*

Rosie Kelly, a calligrapher who lives and works in the Chicago area, made the words and music of the Christmas and Epiphany proclamations into works of art.

Because *Sourcebook for Sundays and Seasons* evolves much as an almanac does, the work of many previous authors and compilers remains a part of this book. The hands of Larry Mick, Jerry Galipeau, G. Thomas Ryan, Peter Mazar, Mary Beth Kunde-Anderson, David Anderson, Barry Moorehead, Neil Kraft and Anthony DiCello all may still be detected herein. *Sourcebook* is all the richer for their contributions over the years, and so, we hope, is your parish's liturgical life.

■ WHO BRINGS IT ALL TOGETHER? Many people work hard and long to move this book from being a stack of papers (a big stack!) and a couple of floppy disks to being the book you are reading. Copy editing and general editorial assistance was provided by Pedro A. Vélez. Liturgy Training Publication's graphics department takes all these words and makes them into a thing of beauty. Jane Kremsreiter designed the 1991 book. Mary Bowers made some modifications to the original design and Ana Aguilar-Islas designed the cover. They've all moved on from LTP, but it's nice that their work is here to remind us of them. M. Urgo did the layout for this year's book, and Mark Hollopeter did the typesetting.

Work on the 1998 book has already begun, but we are interested in hearing your comments and suggestions at any time.

Victoria M. Tufano
Editor

Welcome!

WELCOME to *Sourcebook for Sundays and Seasons* of the liturgical year 1997. For nourishment at the table of God's word, this is the year the lectionaries call Year B. As Catholic Christians turn to Year B in the Roman Lectionary, most other English-speaking Christians will turn to Year B in the Revised Common Lectionary, inspired by and derived from the Roman one. Not yet in full communion sacramentally, we will nevertheless be in communion with each other scripturally on every Lord's Day.

THE ORDER OF THE WORD

It is not exactly precise to call Year B "the Year of Mark," though for most of the Sundays, Mark's gospel provides the framework within which we will read the holy books of the First Testament (what is usually called the Old Testament). We will, however, occasionally depart from Mark: Twice during Advent we will turn to the Gospel of John for a deeper encounter with the message of John the Baptist and to Luke for the story of Mary's encounter with the messenger of God. During Lent and Eastertime and in high summer, as rural folks in the Northern Hemisphere bless God for amber waves of ripening grain, we will turn again from Mark to John for a five-week reflection on the bread of life.

The cycle called Year I determines the first weekday scripture in the numbered weeks outside major seasons. Between Christmastime and Lent, that cycle gives us the Letter to the Hebrews. After Pentecost, the wisdom of Sirach and the pathos of Tobit ease us into summer. Then we break from Israel's wisdom to hear Paul instructing the church at Corinth. We spend most of the summer with the Torah, Joshua, Judges and Ruth. Later, as school, parish and social commitments call us back from the "lazy, hazy days," the lectionary returns to Paul's encouragement and admonition to the early communities, which for all the differences of time and culture sound really not so different from ourselves! In many places, leaves will be turning as we turn the Bible's pages back to the prophets of Israel's postexilic period. Finally after another few weeks of Paul, the lectionary signals the end of the liturgical year, bidding us consider the end of the ages in light of Solomon's wisdom, the Maccabees' fidelity and Daniel's perseverance. Through all these long weeks, of course, the gospels will be steadily counting out the rhythm of our days: first Mark, then Matthew and finally Luke.

THE SHAPE OF THE SEASONS

The ordered reading of scripture in the assembly, recovered and revised at Vatican II and shared now in a broad ecumenical consensus, is an important element in the evolution of that whole mix we call the liturgical year. Its cycles, in turn, intersect with the others in which the people of God live. "Sacred" and "secular" meet in Christ and are transformed through him, with him, in him. Thus early Christians had no difficulty adorning their churches not only with icons of Mary and the saints but with the signs of the zodiac as well! Medieval Latin missals begin and end each month's calendar with poems about the weather and carefully note, next to a saint's name, "the Sun moves into Capricorn today." Preaching in the fifth century, Leo the Great made the bold assertion that "all that was visible of the Redeemer has passed over into the sacraments." For Leo, sacraments "included festivals and the entire liturgical complex" (Thomas J. Talley, *Reforming Tradition*, 138). The liturgical year is thus simply the story of salvation, proclaimed unceasingly, Sunday by Sunday, year by year, "as we wait in joyful hope for the coming of our Savior Jesus Christ."

Therefore, as in every year, the shape of 1997 is sculpted by the Christ who stands at the year's center: the crucified, dead and risen Christ of the Triduum's Pasch. With Easter about as early as it ever gets, the liturgical rhythm of 1997 looks like this:

6 WEEKS: *Advent – Christmas – Epiphany:*
December 1, 1996 — January 12, 1997

5 WEEKS: *Ordinary Time:*
January 13 – February 11, 1997

13 WEEKS: *Lent – Easter – Pentecost:*
February 12 – May 18, 1997

28 WEEKS: *Ordinary Time:*
May 19 – November 29, 1997

A few times this year the Lord's Day is superseded by another commemoration: once at summer's beginning (June 29: Peter and Paul), again at summer's end (September 14: The Holy Cross), and twice in November (November 2: All Souls;

 and November 9: Dedication of the Lateran Basilica). But these latter two observances go well with the eschatological tone of that month's liturgy.

OLD AND NEW

Like 1997 itself, this latest *Sourcebook* stands in continuity with *Sourcebook*s gone before it. Much within these pages will—and should!—look and sound and be familiar to regular *Sourcebook* users. What ever made us think that the liturgy had to change constantly? No human community can function effectively or long endure if it has to fashion anew, at the dawn of each new day or the beginning of each new year, the ritual patterns by which it lives and moves and orders its being.

But like this new year, this new *Sourcebook* will—and should!—be somewhat different from its predecessors. What ever made us think that the liturgy could never change? Everything alive changes. "To live is to change," wrote Cardinal Newman (toward his ninetieth year!), "and to live long is to have changed often." Liturgy has lived a very long time and changed more often than the last 400 years of our history would have led us to believe.

When, at last, we close *Sourcebook 1997* on November 29, 1997 (the last day of the last week in Ordinary Time), it will probably not be very different from the way we close 1997 on New Year's Eve a month later. Some things we will plan to do again, only better. Other things we will resolve never to try again! We will reflect on the steady things that work so well from year to year. We will think of new things tried that gave God glory and seemed to engage the community's prayer. We will recall other things tried that surely gave God glory, if only because of our good faith and good will, but that simply didn't "work" in this time and space. We may even plan to share next year some few new treasures set aside this time because of prudent judgment or fear of failure. But all in all, please God, it will be another year of grace: a year in which to know the joy and challenge of being in communion with a universal church, whose heritage is rich and whose resources for liturgy are incomparable; a year to experience as well the responsibility of serving a local community where the risen Christ becomes flesh and blood in word, worship and witness.

■ SOME THINGS OLD, SOME THINGS (SORT OF) NEW: Count on finding again in these pages each season's images and character and detailed practical suggestions for translating all that into a lively and prayerful experience.

Each calendar entry offers a lot of information packed into a small space. The date, day of the week (except for Sundays, which are marked with a sun, and the days of Triduum, which are marked with a three-pronged symbol) and the day's liturgical title are given.

The first line (in small print) next to the date gives the lectionary number for the day's readings; if a number appears in brackets [ ], it indicates the new number for the same readings in the revised lectionary, which may or may not be available by the time this *Sourcebook* is published or during the time it is in use. On the same line, a set of parentheses may appear with the initials LMC and a number or range of numbers; this indicates the readings that may be selected from the *Lectionary for Masses with Children*. This lectionary has its own numbering system; it also does not provide readings for every day. Those who are planning liturgies with children can, in many cases, choose from several sets of readings. The color indicates the liturgical color for the season, feast or obligatory memorial.

Solemnities, feasts and obligatory memorials are printed in bold next to the date. Optional memorials (with their appropriate liturgical colors) and civil celebrations that are marked liturgically appear in italics below the date.

■ SOME THINGS (REALLY) NEW, SOME THINGS BORROWED: Throughout this book you will find many references to ICEL. This acronym (pronounced *eye*-sul) stands for the International Commission on English in the Liturgy, a body established in 1963 by the bishops of many English-speaking countries to prepare the liturgical texts used in those countries. It is governed by these bishops and made up of scholars from many disciplines (liturgy, scripture, sacramental theology, classics, English literature and church music) who work to provide both translations and new texts. Some of ICEL's most recent work is featured in this year's *Sourcebook*.

■ PASTORAL INTRODUCTIONS: These introductions do officially and formally what *Sourcebook* has tried to do over the years: gather into one place all appropriate canonical legislation, ceremonial notes and pastoral common sense. They were prepared by ICEL for the revised sacramentary, and the bishops of the United States have voted to include these in the new sacramentary. Because they are prepared for all the English-speaking countries, these introductions do not incorporate the several adaptations that will be made by the United States, Canada and the other nations, and they have yet to be submitted to Rome for confirmation. The text presented here will prepare readers for what is coming. The Pastoral Introduction for each season serves as the basis for the *Sourcebook* notes that follow. For Ordinary Time, the Pastoral Introduction: Order of Mass is explored: "transitional rites" during Winter Ordinary Time (introductory, preparation and concluding rites), the liturgy of the word and eucharist during Summer/Autumn Ordinary Time.

■ BIOGRAPHICAL NOTES AND FESTAL INTRODUCTIONS: The new ICEL sacramentary will provide a brief note for each memorial (both obligatory and optional), solemnity and feast. They are carefully and concisely written. Those for solemnities are included in this *Sourcebook*.

■ RESOURCES ON THE INTERNET: In the 1970 New American Bible translation, Isaiah (25:7) promises that the Lord will "destroy . . . the web that is woven over all nations." Revelation prays for "new heavens and a new earth." Perhaps the Lord has given us a "new web" not of destruction but of communication—the World Wide Web! This new area is a potentially rich resource but at the present time most unstable. Web sites change constantly, and contents change frequently! Large online services (America Online, CompuServe, Prodigy) have Catholic folders with postings of various topics including liturgy. But the sites listed in *Sourcebook* are on the World Wide Web. Not all are of immediate interest, but many, once accessed, provide "links" to related sites. These are best accessed through Netscape or another web browser; the most productive approach is to do a net search using the keyword "liturgy." Happy surfing! Net surfers, let us know of helpful sites you discover, so that we can include them in this expanding section for future *Sourcebook*s.

SOME THINGS BLUE (OR BLEW AWAY)

■ FESTAL INSERTS FOR EUCHARISTIC PRAYER II: These texts from previous *Sourcebook*s no longer appear. The new sacramentary by ICEL provides festal inserts only for Eucharistic Prayer III, and these complement and contrast those long used with Eucharistic Prayer I. On solemnities and feasts, communities should choose Eucharistic Prayer I or III, rather than Eucharistic Prayer II, which was intended originally for Ordinary Time.

■ SCRIPTURE-RELATED OPENING PRAYERS: *Sourcebook* first presented these collects in *Celebrating Liturgy Supplement/Sourcebook 1987*. These were translations from the Italian Missal of 1983. So popular were these that the Uniting Church of Australia included them in their official liturgical books! Some made their way into the Presbyterian Church's new *Book of Common Worship*. Meanwhile ICEL was drafting its own three-year cycle. As these went out to the English-language conferences of bishops, LTP's *Sourcebook* dropped the translations in favor of these new texts. As noted in the foreword to this book, these prayers have been approved by the bishops of the United States and many other English-speaking countries. We look forward to their confirmation by Rome.

Liturgy Training Publications will be publishing newly composed, though unofficial, scripture-related prayers and newly translated collects from the Italian sacramentary with lectionary references to both the Roman Lectionary and the Revised Common Lectionary, general intercessions derived from the day's readings, introductions to the Lord's Prayer and invitations to holy communion in a new publication: *Prayers for Sundays and Seasons*. It will be published in three volumes (for Years A, B and C). The Year B volume will be available in the fall of 1996.

A PERSONAL NOTE

Finally, I am grateful to Gabe Huck, director of LTP, who asked me to do the first *Sourcebook* years ago, for renewing that invitation, and to Vicky Tufano for her tireless encouragement and persevering good humor in bringing the project to completion. The foreword names many people who shaped *Sourcebook* over the years and on whose good work we continue to build. Liturgy Training Publications invites your insights to help fashion better *Sourcebook*s for the future. Thanks to confreres and colleagues in the parochial and monastic communities of the past, and the academic world of the present, for liturgical insights graciously shared and charity of the faith freely given. Most especially, thanks to a beloved family at home and cherished friends in the "secular city." Your hospitality and goodness reflect to me the face of the loving and welcoming Christ.

This year's *Sourcebook* is dedicated to Sister Doris Levesque, of the Sisters of the Presentation of Mary in Manchester, New Hampshire. Sister Doris and I were coworkers in the Office of Worship for the diocese of Providence, where her organizational skills and unfailing charity made up for my lack of both! I respectfully offer *Sourcebook for Sundays and Seasons 1997* as a sincere, though inadequate, tribute of gratitude and admiration to her.

At the turn of the century, a weary biblical scholar, Alfred Loissy, observed the state of preaching in his homeland and wryly marveled, "Every Sunday, thirty thousand sermons are preached in France—and still the people believe!" *Sourcebook*'s goal is be the servant of the servants of the church's liturgy, that the whole assembly may increasingly find it not only our *duty* but our *delight* to offer thanks and praise. To this end, you'll find *Sourcebook for Sundays and Seasons 1997* a reliable guide for traveling well-worn paths and an insightful scout for blazing new trails, a companion on the journey, a conspirator in the adventure.

> Praise be given to the maker
> of the seasons' yearly round:
> Father, Son, and Holy Spirit—
> Source, Sustainer, Lord of life—
> as the ever-turning ages
> roll to their eternal rest.
>   John Patrick Earls, OSB
>   (© 1990 Order of St. Benedict)

Peter J. Scagnelli

Bibliography

EACH community needs to keep up-to-date with the vast world of liturgical literature. Many parishes have found it helpful to elect or appoint someone to serve as a librarian who contacts publishing houses, gets on mailing lists and devises a proposed budget for this project.

What follows is a very basic listing of a few titles that some communities, ministers and planners have found useful. These abbreviations are used:

CB: Catholic Book Publishing Co.
CCCB: Canadian Conference of Catholic Bishops
LP: The Liturgical Press
LTP: Liturgy Training Publications
USCC: United States Catholic Conference

RITUAL BOOKS

I. The Roman Missal

A. *Sacramentary.* 1985 (CB, LP).

Complementary volumes:

Eucharistic Prayer for Masses for Various Needs and Occasions. A new, officially approved eucharistic prayer. Includes four thematic variations. Form I: The Church on the Way to Unity; Form II: God Guides the Church on the Way of Salvation; Form III: Jesus, Way to the Father; Form IV: Jesus, the Compassion of God (1996; CB, LP).

Sacramentary Supplement. Includes propers for saints added to calendar since 1985 sacramentary; Proclamation of Birth of Christ; Proclamation of Date of Easter on Epiphany; Reception of Holy Oils (1994; CB, LP).

Collection of Masses of the Blessed Virgin Mary. Volume I: Sacramentary (only volume needed in most communities); Volume II: Lectionary (needed only at Marian shrines) (1992; CB, LP).

Book of the Chair. Texts used at presider's chair on Sundays and solemnities (LP).

Forthcoming:

Two-volume sacramentary from ICEL. Revised translations from Latin, many original texts. No date for publication has been set.

B. *Lectionary for Mass* (U.S. edition). New American Bible (NAB). Available in one-volume editions; loose-leaf editions; separate volumes of yearly cycles, Sundays and solemnities (1970; various publishers).

Lectionary for Mass (Canadian Revision). New Revised Standard Version (NRSV). Sundays, Solemnities (1992); Weekdays, Sanctoral (2 volumes, 1994). Ritual and study volumes (CCCB).

Complementary volumes:

Lectionary for Masses with Children. Contemporary English Version. Ritual and study volumes (1993; LTP, LP, CB).

Introduction to 1981 Latin revision of the lectionary. English translation in LTP's *The Liturgy Documents.*

Book of Gospels. Excerpts from 1970 NAB lectionary (1985; CB).

Revised Common Lectionary from The Consultation on Common Texts. The Protestant adaptation of the Roman three-year lectionary (Nashville: Abingdon Press, 1992).

Forthcoming:

Revised lectionary for the United States. No date for publication has been set.

C. *Sunday Celebrations in the Absence of a Priest.* For use in the United States (1994; CB).

Sunday Celebrations of Word and Hours. For use in Canada. Extensive pastoral notes face difficult questions raised by this rite and present carefully crafted rites for celebration. More extensive and creative resources than U.S. edition (1995; CCCB).

II. *The Liturgy of the Hours.* (1975; 4 vols., CB; 2 vols., Daughters of Saint Paul).

Complementary volumes:

Christian Prayer. One-volume excerpt (1977; CB).

Shorter Christian Prayer. A simplified, pocket-size edition (1987; CB, LP).

Supplement. New memorials for the U. S. (1987; CB).

Psalms for Morning and Evening Prayer. Psalm translations by ICEL, arranged in four-week psalter, pointed for chanting. Hard and soft cover (1995; LTP).

The Psalter. Complete edition of ICEL's psalm translations. Hard and soft cover (1995; LTP).

Proclaim Praise. Simplified edition for communal use (1995; LTP).

III. *The Roman Ritual.* A library of volumes, usually one per sacrament or rite.

A. *Rite of Christian Initiation of Adults.* Restored catechumenate for adults and children of catechetical age. U.S. edition includes rites for those already baptized, combined rites and regulations for the United States. Ritual and study editions (1988; CB, LP, LTP, USCC; Canadian edition: CCCB).

Complementary volume:

The Book of the Elect (LP).

B. *Rite of Baptism for Children.* (1970; CB, LP). Canadian edition includes rites arranged for use within Mass and outside Mass and a slight revision of 1970 text for inclusive language (CCCB).

C. *Rite of Marriage.* (1970; CB, LP, Ave Maria Press). Canadian edition includes suggested texts for rite of reception at entrance, table and anniversary blessings, other supplementary texts (CCCB).

Forthcoming:

Revised translation based on new Latin edition. No date for publication has been set.

D. *Order of Christian Funerals.* U.S edition. Ritual and study editions (1989; CB, LP, LTP). Canadian edition includes thematic wake services with music; appendices with additional prayers; norms for cremation; and ritual directives for funeral liturgy in the presence of the ashes (Canada received an indult to make this possible) (CCCB).

Complementary volumes:

Vigils and Related Prayers. Excerpts from complete rite (1989; LTP).

Rites of Committal. Excerpts from complete rite (1989; LTP).

Book of the Names of the Dead (1991; LTP).

E. *Rite of Penance:* 1975 (CB). Sanctuary and reconciliation-room sizes.

F. *Pastoral Care of the Sick.* Includes rites of anointing and viaticum. Sanctuary and pocket sizes (1983; CB, LP; LTP has an abridged edition in Spanish and English).

Complementary volumes:

Ritual for Lay Persons. Rites for holy communion and pastoral care of the sick and dying; all rites that may be led by a layperson in the absence of a priest or deacon (LP).

Communion of the Sick (LP).

G. *Holy Communion and Worship of the Eucharist Outside Mass* (1976; CB).

Complementary volume:

Order for the Solemn Exposition of the Holy Eucharist. Includes exposition over one or several days; liturgy of the hours during the period of exposition; eucharistic services of prayer and praise during exposition; closing celebration (two forms: with Mass, outside Mass); scripture readings, litanies, music resources (LP).

H. *Rites of Religious Profession* (1988; LTP).

I. *Book of Blessings.* Orders of blessings, prayers and pastoral rites once published separately (1989; CB, LP).

Complementary volumes:

Shorter Book of Blessings (1989; LP).

Catholic Household Blessings and Prayers. First attempt since *A Manual of Prayers* (Baltimore Council, 1888) to provide a standard prayer book for the country (1988; USCC).

IV. *The Roman Pontifical.* Rites normally celebrated by a bishop. Blessing of Oil and Consecration of Chrism included in sacramentary. Rites for confirmation and church dedication are published separately and should be in every liturgical library.

A. *Roman Pontifical,* part I. Now outdated rites of initiation; confirmation, institution of readers and acolytes, ordination rites, several blessings of persons (abbot/abbess, consecration to a life of virginity) (1978; ICEL).

B. *Rite of Confirmation.* Excerpted from fuller pontifical (1977; USCC).

> Canadian edition incorporates helpful notes from *Ceremonial of Bishops* (CCCB).
>
> Forthcoming:
>
> The ICEL revision of Rome's revised ordination rites. No date for publication has been set.

C. *Dedication of a Church and Altar.* Resource for parishes undergoing renovation or construction; useful for parishes preparing yearly anniversary (1989; USCC).

V. Other Official Books:

Ceremonial of Bishops. An official compilation of rubrics, with liturgical and historical orientation to feasts, seasons and services, and emendations made since the ritual books were published. Notes useful for charting liturgical celebrations in every parish (1989; LP).

> Forthcoming:
>
> *Ceremonial for Parish Churches.* No date for publication has been set.

DOCUMENTATION

Code of Canon Law (Canon Law Society of America, 1983) contains a significant amount of legislation pertaining to the celebration of the liturgy.

Documents of Christian Worship: Descriptive and Interpretive Sources, James F. White, ed. (Louisville: Westminster, John Knox, 1992). Traced from the beginning (scripture, fathers, councils) and across the traditions (Jewish, Catholic, Orthodox, Anglican, Reformed), and grouped by "area": space, time, sacraments, word, etc. A look within but beyond Roman Catholicism to where we have all come from and what we have in common, as well as where we differ.

Documents on the Liturgy, 1963–1979: Conciliar, Papal and Curial Texts (LP; 1982). Translation and compilation of everything official. Massive index makes this a goldmine of information.

The Liturgy Documents: A Parish Resource, third edition (LTP; 1991). Most recent translations of Roman liturgical documents, along with documents of the Bishops' Committee on the Liturgy.

GENERAL OVERVIEW

John Fenwick and Bryan Spinks, *Worship in Transition: The Liturgical Movement in the Twentieth Century* (New York: Continuum, 1995). This is meant to give a sense of historical context to those engaged in the liturgical enterprise at the end of the twentieth century. Written by two Anglicans from England, this concise and comprehensive volume gives us a sense of the liturgical movement beyond Roman Catholicism and outside the United States. A particularly helpful chapter is entitled "Snapshots of the Movement in North America."

James White, *Roman Catholic Worship: Trent to Today* (Mahwah: Paulist, 1995). Like the authors of the preceding volume, White feels that before plunging into the task at hand, liturgical planners and ministers need to know something of the movement with which they stand in continuity. This book provides that orientation from the Catholic experience.

COMPENDIA

Days of the Lord: The Liturgical Year. 7 volumes. (LP, 1990–1994). In-depth commentary on the riches of the liturgical year, and companion to the sacramentary, lectionary and *Liturgy of the Hours.*

Peter Fink, SJ (ed.), *The New Dictionary of Sacramental Worship.* A vast theological and pastoral resource, whose entries run the gamut from theological, to practical liturgical, including the pastoral dimension and the insights of the social sciences.

Mary Ellen Hynes, *Companion to the Calendar* (LTP, 1993). Daily and seasonal guide to saints and mysteries that make up the Christian calendar, with additional notes on the calendars of Jews and Muslims and the national days of the United States and Canada.

Kevin Irwin's trilogy (now all from LP):

> *Advent & Christmas: A Guide to the Eucharist and Hours,* 1986.

Lent: A Guide to the Eucharist and Hours, 1985.

Easter: A Guide to the Eucharist and Hours, 1991.

A.G. Martimort, et al., *The Church at Prayer,* 4 volumes but especially volume 4: The Liturgy and Time (LP, 1986; one volume edition, 1993). See especially the essays by Pierre Jounel on Sunday and the year.

Adrien Nocent, *The Liturgical Year.* 4 volumes. (LP, 1977). One of the architects of Vatican II's reform takes us Sunday by Sunday and season by season through the church's liturgy and lectionary.

Pius Parsch, *The Church's Year of Grace.* 5 volumes. (LP, 1957 and various editions). While commenting on the old calendar, these volumes still offer enormous assistance to readers.

LTP's Sourcebook Series: Texts of all kinds from across the centuries to enliven the various days and the seasons' overall development.

An Advent Sourcebook, O'Gorman, Thomas, ed., 1988.

A Christmas Sourcebook, Simcoe, Mary Ann, ed., 1984.

A Lent Sourcebook: The Forty Days, Baker, J. Robert, Evelyn Kaehler and Peter Mazar, eds., 1991 (2 vols.).

A Triduum Sourcebook, revised edition, Henderson, J. Frank, et al., eds., 1996 (3 vols.).

An Easter Sourcebook: The Fifty Days, Huck, Gabe, Gail Ramshaw and Gordon Lathrop, eds., 1988.

A Sourcebook about Christian Death, Sloyan, Virginia, ed., 1990. For November or for the period of mourning after death.

A Baptism Sourcebook, Baker, J. Robert, Larry J. Nyberg and Victoria M. Tufano, eds., 1993.

A Liturgy Sourcebook, Huck, Gabe, ed., 1994.

A Marriage Sourcebook, Baker, J. Robert, Kevin Charles Gibley, Joni Reiff Gibley, eds., 1994.

RESOURCES ON THE INTERNET

The URL's given below were accurate at the time of *Sourcebook*'s going to press. Because of the evolving nature of this resource, always work with your web browser to do a "net search" using the keyword "liturgy." Even those sites that do not at first appear relevant to the specific aspect of liturgy for which you are searching may provide "links" to other sites that may be helpful.

1. Order of Saint Benedict

    http://www.osb.org/osb/gen/topics/liturgy/index.html

    Links from this site: Liturgical Texts; Liturgical Commentary; Liturgy Resources; Liturgy Discussion List; Liturgical Sites: Calendar, Divine Office, Early Christian Online Encyclopedia; Lutheran Church; Liturgical Press; Liturgiewissenschaft Tübingen (Dr. Gabriele Winkler); Liturgiewissenschaftliche (German liturgical sites).

2. Notre Dame Center for Pastoral Liturgy

    http://www.nd.edu/~ndcpl/

3. Liturgical Studies

    http://www.music.princeton.edu/chant_html/liturg.html

4. Catholic Sites

    http://www.cs.cmu.edu/Web/People/spok/catholic/worship.html

5. Liturgical Press, Michael Glazier Books, Pueblo Books

    http://www.csbsju.edu/litpress/index.html

6. OCP (Oregon Catholic Press)

    http://www.ocp.org/

7. CICI Internet Directory

    http://catholic.net/RCC/Indices/index.html

8. Internet Lists Relating to Topics in Religion

    http://sys1.pitts.emory.edu/boblist.html

9. Home page for the Writings and Witness of Father Alexander Schmemann

    The late Father Schmemann spent many years at Saint Vladimir's Seminary in Crestwood, NY, forming generations of

Orthodox parish priests and theologians. Someone has thoughtfully gathered a number of his writings at this web site, which is well worth the visit.

http://www.berea.edu/Publication/Schmemann.html

Addresses of Publishers

Abingdon Press
201 8th Street South
Nashville TN 37203

Augsburg Publishing House/Fortress Press
426 South 5th Street
Box 1209
Minneapolis MN 55440

Canadian Conference of Catholic Bishops
90 Parent Avenue
Ottawa, Ontario K1N 7B1, Canada

Catholic Book Publishing Company
77 West End Road
Totowa NJ 07512

Center for Pastoral Liturgy
PO Box 81
Notre Dame IN 46556

Church Hymnal Corporation
800 Second Avenue
New York NY 10017

Cokesbury
PO Box 801
Nashville TN 37202

Crossroad Publishing Company
575 Lexington Avenue
New York NY 10022

Daughters of St. Paul
50 St. Paul's Avenue
Boston MA 02130

GIA Publications
7404 South Mason Avenue
Chicago IL 60638

Michael Glazier, Inc.
(now part of The Liturgical Press)

HarperCollins Publishers
10 East 53rd Street
New York NY 10022

International Committee
on English in the Liturgy (ICEL)
1522 K Street NW
Suite 1000
Washington DC 20005-1202

The Liturgical Conference
8750 Georgia Avenue – Suite 123
Silver Spring MD 20910-3621

The Liturgical Press
PO Box 7500
Collegeville MN 56321-7500

Liturgy Training Publications
1800 North Hermitage Avenue
Chicago IL 60622-1101

National Association
of Pastoral Musicians (NPM)
225 Sheridan Street NW
Washington DC 20011

New Dawn Press
PO Box 13248
Portland OR 97213-0248

Oregon Catholic Press (OCP)
5536 NE Hassalo
Portland OR 97213

Oxford University Press
200 Madison Avenue
New York NY 10016

Pastoral Press
PO Box 1470
Laurel MD 20725 1-800-976-9669

Paulist Press
992 Macarthur Boulevard
Mahwah NJ 07430

Pueblo Publishing Company
(Now part of The Liturgical Press)

St. Vladimir's Seminary Press
575 Scarsdale Road
Crestwood NY 10707

The Seabury Press
c/o Harper and Row Publishers, Inc.
10 East 53rd Street
New York NY 10022

United States Catholic Conference (USCC)
3211 Fourth Street, NE
Washington DC 20017-1194

World Library Publications (WLP)
3815 North Willow Road
Schiller Park IL 60176

ADVENT

The Season
Orientation / 3
ICEL Pastoral Introduction: Season of Advent / 4
Perspective on Advent / 5
Purpose of the Season / 6
Presentation of the Season / 7
Celebration of Advent Masses / 10
Preparing the Parish / 12
Taking It Home / 13
Other Ritual Prayers and Sacraments / 14
The Worship Environment / 15
The Calendar
December 1 – December 24 / 16
Liturgical Texts
Texts for the Eucharistic Assembly / 23

Orientation

The Cat only grinned when it saw Alice. It looked good-natured, she thought. Still, it had *very* long claws and a great many teeth, and so she felt that it ought to be treated with respect.

"Cheshire-Puss," she began rather timidly, as she did not at all know whether it would like the name. However, it only grinned a little wider. *Come, it's pleased so far,* thought Alice, and she went on. "Would you tell me, please, which way I ought to go from here?"

"That depends a good deal on where you want to get to," said the Cat.

"I don't much care where—" Alice began.

"Then it doesn't matter which way you go," said the Cat.

"Just so long as I get *somewhere*," Alice added as an explanation.

"Oh, you're sure to do that," said the Cat, "if you only walk long enough."

Lewis Carroll, *Alice in Wonderland*

REMEMBER that exchange between Alice and the Cheshire Cat? If it seems too frivolous a way to begin our journey through the liturgical year 1997, consider the similarities between Alice's dilemma and that of the average person setting off on the great adventure of liturgical preparation and planning.

Each of us begins with all of Alice's simplicity and goodwill. But it's only a matter of time before we're confronted with a confusion not so very different from Alice's. But, we may protest, having lived and worshiped in the household of the faith, perhaps for many years, surely we have the advantage of knowing our way through the liturgical labyrinth better than Alice knew the mysterious paths of Wonderland!

In some ways this is true. Vatican II's call to "full, conscious and active participation" restored *to the whole people of God* that "to which [we] . . . have a right and obligation by reason of [our] baptism" (*Constitution on the Sacred Liturgy*, 14).

This universal call to be a living part of the celebrating assembly is basic. But the specific ministry of liturgical planning and preparation demands something more. It is a particular call to accept the responsibility of knowing the community's heritage as intimately as possible in order to serve the community's prayer as well as we can. Lest there be any temptation to elitism, we usually arrive—quickly!—at the humbling realization that, standing before the rich treasure of the church's liturgy, we are very much like Alice in Wonderland.

Our questions are virtually the same as hers: Which way should we go? Even more basically, *Where* are we going?

The analogy doesn't end with the questions: The half-friendly, half-frightening Cheshire Cat, alternately visible and elusive, is an apt image for the liturgical ideals and directives that chart the course of our work. Now you see them, now you don't! Here, there and everywhere! The sacramentary opens with a jungle of introductory

material scattered through several documents. The *Introduction to the Lectionary,* the commentary on the calendar and the *Ceremonial of Bishops* should all be consulted. The *Liturgy of the Hours* (4 volumes) has fine seasonal texts. And don't forget the host of nonofficial publications—like this one! The very wealth of material gives the same message Alice picked up from the Cheshire Cat: The liturgical year deserves to be treated with respect!

Who could possibly pull together all the information about the liturgical year? And how do we keep the general picture in focus, while trying to zero in on details?

At last, an official resource has been proposed as an integral part of the sacramentary revision project of the International Commission on English in the Liturgy (ICEL). Pastoral Introductions have been prepared for each liturgical season and for the whole order of Mass as well. Their specific purpose is twofold: to gather into one place all the pertinent material of which planners and presiders need to be aware for a well-prepared celebration and to offer solid suggestions that are both faithful to the tradition and appropriate for contemporary worship.

In directing the energies of planners, this *Sourcebook* has always pointed first of all toward the official liturgical books, especially the sacramentary and the lectionary. These are the fruits of the universal church's liturgical reform at Vatican II and therefore are the community's principal resources for celebration. They have always been the source for the official texts of prayers and readings. Now, in the "second generation" of liturgical books, they provide even more. Besides the words and rubrics of worship, they are giving us theological orientation and practical information.

The International Commission on English in the Liturgy is proposing that these Pastoral Introductions appear in the sacramentary itself, before the Mass formularies. This is entirely appropriate. To borrow the title of Kevin Irwin's handbook on liturgy, the *texts* are being placed *in context.* Before the words we need to use, we will have the theological and liturgical orientation necessary to use them well. To help planners and presiders get to know this new and welcome resource, *Sourcebook 1997* is giving these Pastoral Introductions "pride of place" at the beginning of each seasonal section. Thus we present them just as ICEL intends to in the new sacramentary.

Read each introduction all the way through as a complete seasonal unit. Then refer back to them, as the *Sourcebook* develops its own suggestions. Our commentary follows the outline of the Pastoral Introduction, and specific references are indicated by the abbreviation PI, followed by the number of the paragraph being cited. Before turning to ICEL's Pastoral Introduction for Advent, let's return to Alice's story for a final thought on liturgical planning and preparation:

> [Alice] tried another question. "What sort of people live about here?"
>
> "In that direction," the Cat said, waving its right paw round, "lives a Hatter, and in *that* direction," waving the other paw, "lives a March Hare. Visit either you like—they're both mad."
>
> "But I don't want to go among mad people," Alice remarked quickly.
>
> "Oh, you can't help that," said the Cat. "We're all mad here. I'm mad. You're mad."
>
> "How do you know I'm mad?" said Alice.
>
> "You must be mad," said the Cat, "or you wouldn't have come here."

There comes to everyone who serves the community in liturgical ministry a day, meeting or difference of opinion that prompts one to ask, "Are they mad? Am I mad? Are we *all* mad?" As every scriptural vocation story indicates, a certain "holy madness" is required before responding—or volunteering!—to serve the God of holiness or, for that matter, the holy people of God!

Planning begins, continues and concludes with prayer. As we head into the Wonderland of the liturgy, let us pray!

> Direct our actions, Lord, by your holy inspiration
> and carry them forward by your gracious help,
> that all our works may begin in you
> and by you be happily ended.
> We ask this through Jesus Christ our Lord.
>   (Thursday after Ash Wednesday
>   ICEL translation, 1994)

ICEL Pastoral Introduction: Season of Advent

1 In the course of the year, the church unfolds the whole mystery of Christ from the incarnation and nativity to the ascension, Pentecost and the

expectation of the blessed hope of the coming of the Lord. The season of Advent, at the conclusion of the calendar year and the beginning of the church's year, embraces both ends of this cycle. Advent begins with Evening Prayer I of the First Sunday of Advent and ends on 24 December, before Evening Prayer I of Christmas.

2 In some parts of the church where baptism was once celebrated at Epiphany, the 40 days prior to it were devoted to ascetical preparation, and Advent took on several of the liturgical features of Lent. Now, however, "it is no longer considered a penitential season but a time of joyful expectation."

3 Advent has a twofold character. It is the season to prepare for Christmas, when Christ's first coming is remembered, and it is the "season when that remembrance directs the mind and heart to await Christ's Second Coming at the end of time. For these two reasons, the season of Advent is thus a period for devout and joyful expectation."

4 This twofold character is reflected in the two stages of Advent, each with its own special focus expressed in the corresponding preface of the eucharistic prayer. From the first Sunday to 16 December, the liturgy expresses the eschatological expectation of Advent, the watchfulness of God's people looking forward to the time when Christ will come "again in glorious majesty," and "we shall at last possess in its fullness the promise for which we dare to hope." From 17 December until Christmas Eve, the texts proper to each day prepare us more directly to celebrate the Lord's birth, "our hearts filled with wonder and praise."

5 Advent is not simply a preparation to commemorate the historical event of Christmas nor primarily an expectation of the Parousia but is rather an anticipation or a beginning of the celebration of the integral mystery of the Incarnation, the Advent and the Epiphany of the Son of God in flesh and in majesty. The Christian community lives in an "interim" time between two historical events: the coming of Christ in the flesh and his coming in glory at the end of time. The church is called to be strong in faith "as we wait in joyful hope for the coming of our Savior, Jesus Christ."

- The use of violet in Advent suggests a state of unfulfilled readiness and should no longer be regarded as an expression of penitence. It serves to set off the joyful white of Christmas with greater dramatic effect.

- For the same reason, music in Advent may be more restrained, for example, in the use of the organ and other instruments. The Gloria is not used as the opening rite in Advent, not because it is a penitential season but so that the hymn of the angels may resound with greater freshness on Christmas Night.

- In all three years of the lectionary cycle, the focus of each Sunday is clearly identifiable: on the first Sunday, the return of the Lord; on the second, John the Baptist's call to conversion; on the third, the relationship of John to Jesus; on the fourth, Mary and the events immediately preceding Christ's birth.

6 Advent, as a period of expectation and preparation, is closely related to, yet distinct from, the feast of Christmas for which it prepares. This can create a certain tension in those places where the weeks before Christmas are exploited for commercial purposes or where social celebrations of the feast are anticipated in schools and places of work.

- Popular devotions should respect the nature and character of Advent and should be consistent with the themes presented in the *Lectionary for Mass* and the *Sacramentary* volume of the *Missal*. Songs, carols and devotions which focus on the Nativity itself are out of place in Advent, especially before 17 December.

- Where they are the custom, the Advent wreath and the Jesse tree, which help to sustain an expectant orientation toward Christmas, can assist the liturgical celebration and may be associated with the celebration of Mass.

- Vigils, services of light and celebrations of reconciliation may be very effective in fostering a sense of watchfulness and prayer and in disposing the community to a more fruitful participation in the Masses of Advent.

Perspective on Advent

THE International Commission on English in the Liturgy's (ICEL) Pastoral Introduction to Advent begins by setting the complete picture before us. Planners and presiders need such a clear vision of the broad perspective to keep the particular focus from becoming blurred. The liturgical year is an unfolding of the whole mystery of Christ (PI, 1) from incarnation to glorious

return. Planning specific seasons within this whole mystery must keep in mind this interrelated nature of the various seasons. Advent cannot be planned and celebrated in isolation from Christmas. Advent-Christmas points toward the paschal mystery, which is most intensely focused in the Triduum. The Triduum itself celebrates in several movements the whole mystery: passion, death, resurrection and glorification of the Lord. This, in turn, impels the church to bear witness in the Spirit until that blessed hope is fulfilled in the Lord's glorious return.

Such a broad perspective is the best safeguard against the temptation to "historicize" the liturgical year (PI, 5), the well-meaning but misdirected attempt to "re-live" salvation history. The verb used in the Pastoral Introduction is significant: The mystery *unfolds*. The mystery is placed before us as an invitation, drawing us into its beauty and power this year, every year. The community is not just "going in circles" through a recurring cycle. The image instead is that of a spiral: Year by year, we who celebrate the liturgical year are drawn deeper and deeper (or higher and higher) into the mystery and toward the mystery's fulfillment: undying life at the banquet of the Lamb.

Advent's place in this unfolding is expressed well (PI, 1, 2): "the conclusion of the calendar year and the beginning of the church's year . . . embracing both ends of the cycle." The death of the old year and the end of Ordinary Time suggest images of the coming kingdom: the inevitability of death, the certainty of judgment, the equally "sure and certain hope" of resurrection, reunion with the community of saints gone before us and the "blessed hope" of the coming of Christ the King whose reign is service, forgiveness, true peace. These images from the end of Ordinary Time dovetail with the beginning of Advent and offer an opportunity for the community to move into winter's darkness with the light of paschal glory.

Purpose of the Season

ADVENT'S motif, after Vatican II's reform, is "devout and joyful expectation" (PI, 3). A historical note provides a reason for the somewhat penitential mood some remember associating with Advent: It served as a second Lent in places preparing for baptisms at Epiphany. Within this single mood, however, is a twofold movement, each of which is expressed well by the preface corresponding to each phase of the season.

The words with which we pray have an immense potential for forming the community in a liturgical spirituality. As the old axiom says: *Lex orandi, lex credendi*—What we pray expresses and forms what we believe.

Thanks to the lectionary, most communities have grown familiar with the biblical set of Mass texts. But there is another set of texts that complements the biblical ones. These are less known but are a rich resource for preaching, prayer and spiritual formation. They are known officially as *euchological texts*. This word (which will recur in this year's *Sourcebook*) combines two Greek words: *euché* ("prayer") and *lógos* ("speech"). Literally, then, they are the language of the church's prayer. The euchological texts are subdivided into the *major* euchology (complex prayers such as prefaces, eucharistic prayers, solemn blessings) and the *minor* euchology (collects, also called opening prayers; prayers over the gifts; prayers after communion; prayers over the people and the psalm prayers of the *Liturgy of the Hours*).

If the scriptures are the *word of the Lord*, the euchological texts may be thought of as the *word of the church,* formed over time within the various local communities and appropriated for use by the whole church. While the revealed word of scripture is considered "closed," the euchological treasure of the church is something to which each generation contributes. Although Eucharistic Prayers II through IV are based on previous models, the post–Vatican II sacramentary also features contemporary eucharistic prayers (for reconciliation and for Masses with children) as well as a number of newly composed prefaces that represent our generation's contribution. Since its inception, this yearly *Sourcebook* has presented another euchological contribution unique to our age: scripture-related collect prayers, some of them original English texts prepared by ICEL, others translated from the 1983 Italian sacramentary. These have now been collected in a separate book, *Prayers for Sundays and Seasons* (LTP).

The *General Instruction of the Roman Missal* (GIRM) recognizes the potential of these texts as a preaching resource:

> The homily is an integral part of the liturgy and is strongly recommended: It is necessary for the

nurturing of the Christian life. It should develop some point of the readings *or of another text from the Ordinary or from the Proper of the Mass of the day* (GIRM, 41, emphasis added).

As does the Pastoral Introduction, *Sourcebook* will have occasion to refer to the prefaces as a rich source of theological and liturgical insight for the various seasons and feasts.

Presentation of the Season

IT is hard to improve on the description of Advent contained in PI, 5. This should appear in every parish bulletin and be part of any ongoing parish liturgical education program. Quoting Advent Preface II, the text presents all Christian life as a kind of "advent," the community living in an "interim" time between Christ's coming in flesh and Christ's coming in glory. Within this context, three elements of Advent's celebration are presented: color, music and the word of God.

COLOR

"Unfulfilled readiness" expresses nicely the meaning of the darker vestments of Advent. Providing a prelude to the "dramatic effect" of Christmas brightness is an insightful way to differentiate the color's purpose in Advent from its penitential use during Lent (PI, 5). There is no mention of the blue color that has become popular in recent years and continues to elicit inquiries not only at local diocesan liturgical offices but also at the Bishops' Committee on the Liturgy and at LTP!

While the *Lutheran Book of Worship* and the Presbyterian *Book of Common Worship* suggest purple or blue, the Roman color remains violet. Suggestions for differentiating one violet from another, Advent from Lent, have varied widely. Some suggest a dark bluish-violet (the color of the winter sky in some places) for Advent but for Lent the royal or "Roman" purple (in accord with the passion hymn, *Vexilla regis,* the royal banners forward go). The Canadian liturgical calendar suggests just the opposite:

Blue vestments are not approved for use at any time in Canada. To differentiate the Advent season from the Lenten, some parishes use violet-shaded (reddish-purple) vestments during Advent and darker-shaded purple vestments in Lent (*Liturgical Calendar 1994–1995,* 72).

An interesting discussion of liturgical colors from an Episcopal perspective, but with ecumenical dimensions, is presented in Howard E. Galley's *The Ceremonies of the Eucharist* (Cambridge MA: Cowley Publications, 1989). As a matter of historical fact, until the sixteenth-century Council of Trent (and well beyond that in parts of France), liturgical color schemes varied widely from diocese to diocese. Various sequences coexisted, from a very basic distinction of festive/nonfestive, to the more formal sequence still in use today, taken over almost unchanged from the Tridentine Missal.

Some liturgists claim that before Trent standardized the scheme, northern European churches used a darker blue-violet during Advent and a royal purple during Lent. Ingenious reasons are given for this, among them the theory that northern dyes were made from dark berries indigenous to that climate, while Mediterranean dyes were made from shellfish for a more "reddish" purple.

Medieval vestment catalogues are fascinating, even humorous. One English diocesan visitation records a country parish that boasted a fine set of "mouse-coloured tunicles" for deacon and subdeacon. A scholarly footnote informs us that this almost certainly means grey, because the field mice of that rural region were grey, not brown like city mice!

Galley's approach to the blue/purple question is helpful:

The principal argument for the use of the white-red-violet-green sequence today, however, is not its origin but the fact that it has become an ecumenical usage. As the most widely used scheme in Anglicanism, the official scheme of the Roman rite and the ordinary use of the Lutheran churches, it can rightly be seen as a treasure the liturgical churches hold in common. It is, therefore, the use recommended. . . (45).

With regard to the [blue alternative for Advent], it can only be said that the sharing of a liturgical color does not make two seasons alike. Christmas and Easter are very different seasons—yet the color for both is white. There is, moreover, nothing to prevent a parish from having two sets of violet vestments, an elaborate set for use in Advent and a very simple set for Lent. . . . A predominantly

blue frontal is appropriate for Advent and complements nicely many violet vestments. A lenten frontal, if used, should reflect the austerity of the season. In many places [remember, he is speaking of Episcopal churches], an unadorned frontal of unbleached linen or fabric of a similar color and texture can give the altar a look of great simplicity (44–45).

The best approach seems to be two distinctly different sets of violet, one for each season. At the very least, older-style violet vestments cluttered with appliqué nails, crown-of-thorns and other passion designs are clearly inappropriate during Advent. Just as inappropriate are the "bargain" vestments from catalogue firms that feature sewn-on Advent wreaths complete with burning candles! The association of light blue with Our Lady causes that shade to over-identify the season with Mary. While she is a principal figure in the scriptures of late Advent, she is not the only biblical personage associated with this season.

MUSIC

The official ordo published in Rome bans the use of the organ as a solo instrument during the liturgy in Advent, except on the Third, *Gaudete* ("Rejoice"), Sunday. The Pastoral Introduction, however, reflects contemporary use in English-language countries, noting simply that "music in Advent may be more restrained." A positive, nonpenitential reason for this suggested restraint is offered. Like the dramatic effect of joyful white vestments on Christmas after the violet of Advent, the hymn of the angels ("Gloria") will "resound with greater freshness" on Christmas night (PI, 5).

The characteristic musical "tone" of Advent, then, should not duplicate the austere tone of Lent but should be a somewhat subdued tone that communicates the preparatory nature of the season, blending expectation with a gradually increasing joy as the festal season approaches.

■ GATHERING: The importance of a characteristic introductory ritual for Advent will be discussed later on in this section. But reflect now on the music that will begin the Advent eucharist. Apart from an impressive array of contemporary texts, the traditional Advent hymnody of the Catholic and Reformed churches is quite extensive. Some melodies are in minor keys, creating a sense of haunting beauty and profound longing. Other major-key melodies, carol-like and gently rhythmic, express another dimension of the season. Thus the music chosen for the season ideally will reflect the many facets of Advent, eliciting various moods and reflections from our hearts. There is likewise an exceptional aesthetic beauty and theological depth to many traditional Advent texts.

The season is too brief for learning very many hymns, and the restrained quality of the liturgy noted above suggests caution lest the Mass be overloaded with musical selections. The pieces chosen should be "deep" enough to be worthy of the season.

Chant pieces work particularly well with minimal or no accompaniment and so are most appropriate for the tone of Advent. Recent arrangements of many traditional pieces incorporate handbells for chord clusters at the end of each phrase. For instance, consider Katherine Crosier's arrangement of "O come, O come, Emmanuel" (GIA). This arrangement (choir, assembly and handbells) is intended as a processional and may also provide a link between Advent and Christmas by serving as an introductory piece to a pre-Mass program of carols at the Christmas midnight or late evening Mass. Handbells with chant creates an effect of prayerful dignity and peaceful contemplation, perfect for the tone and tenor of Advent. Bells also help the assembly to keep pitch!

Oregon Catholic Press (OCP) offers a number of suitable choices, including "The King shall come when morning dawns," a beautiful Kentucky Harmony tune with which the fine eschatological text "O holy city seen of (by) John" is also associated. The haunting, Advent-style melodic line could be introduced by a solo instrument (flute or oboe) or single solo organ stop. World Library's *We Celebrate* hymnal includes a lovely contemporary setting of "Conditor alme siderum" by Melvin Farrell, "O Lord of Light" (#809).

Oregon Catholic Press also offers "You clouds of heaven, open wide," a rework of the ancient "Rorate coeli" text, which *The Collegeville Hymnal* (Liturgical Press) presents with the original, supremely "Advent" chant setting and the English and Latin texts. Effective use of this chant might employ a few select men's, women's or alternating voices. These ancient texts and chants not only support the sound of the season but connect present-day assemblies to the rich heritage of the past.

■ RESPONSORIAL PSALM: So desirous is the church that the responsorial psalm be sung that three options are always available: the proper psalm assigned to the day in the lectionary; the seasonal psalms assigned to the season (#175 in the lectionary); and a common responsorial refrain (#174 in the lectionary), with verses of the proper psalm for the day.

The seasonal responsorial psalms and common refrains try to capture the central tone of a season. Advent's refrain sounds the timeless cry of longing, "Come, O Lord, and set us free." Sung with each Sunday's proper psalm, this refrain would express well our longing for salvation.

Psalms 25 and 85, two classic psalms of poignant longing and confident trust, are the seasonal psalms provided for Advent: "To you, O Lord, I lift my soul," and "Lord, let us see your kindness." Choose a memorable and melodic setting to become the text and melody known "by heart," shaping the community's sung prayer for the whole season. Some recommended musical settings for Psalm 25:

- Marty Haugen, "To you, O Lord," *Psalms for the Church Year* (GIA, G-2664)
- Rawn Harbor, "Psalm for Advent," *Lead Me, Guide Me,* #500 (GIA)
- Howard Hughes, "To You I lift up my soul," *Psalms for Advent* (GIA, G-1905) or *Lead Me, Guide Me,* #499 (GIA)
- David Isele, "To You, O Lord," *Psalms for the Church Year* (GIA, G-2662)
- Robert E. Kreutz, "Come, O Lord," *Psalms and Selected Canticles* (OCP)
- Scott Soper, "To You, O Lord," (OCP, 8979-CC)
- Christopher Willcock, "To You, O Lord," *Psalms for Feasts and Seasons* (Liturgical Press)
- Paul Lisicky, "You are my guide," *Psalms for the Church* (World Library Publications, 6204)
- Ruth Artman, "To You, O Lord," *Sing Out: A Children's Psalter* (WLP, 7190)

Some settings for Psalm 85:

- J. Robert Carroll/J. Gelineau, "Lord, let us see your kindness," *Worship Lectionary/Accompaniment/Cantor Book,* #770 (GIA)
- Michael Connolly, "I will hear what God proclaims," (GIA, G-2401)
- Marty Haugen, "Let us see your kindness," *Psalms for the Church Year* (GIA, G-2664)
- Christopher Willcock, "Lord, let us see your kindness," *Psalms for Feasts and Seasons* (Liturgical Press)
- Jack Miffleton, "Come, O Lord, and set us free," *Sing Out: A Children's Psalter* (WLP, 7190)

■ GOSPEL ACCLAMATION: Twenty-one verses from scriptures and ancient liturgical sources provide gospel acclamations for Advent weekdays, a treasury of seasonal themes for daily prayer (found in the lectionary with each Sunday's readings and at #193 and #202). Proper to late Advent are the revered "O Antiphons," borrowed and abridged from Evening Prayer of the week before Christmas. These are powerful expressions of Israel's and the church's longing for salvation. Their ecumenical importance cannot be overstated. They incorporate the principal titles and themes of the prophetic messianic tradition and were universally preserved by the churches of the Reformation. If the complete version is being sung at parish evening prayer, there is no reason why it could not also serve as the gospel acclamation at Mass, provided that the people are able to join in an Alleluia refrain before and after the antiphon. Besides the well-known metrical version, "O come, O come, Emmanuel," there are several vernacular adaptations of the ancient, well-beloved chant from the *Antiphonale Monasticum* (GIA). Three suggested settings of gospel acclamations for Advent are:

- John Schiavone, *Gospel Acclamation Verses for Advent* (GIA, G-2110)
- ICEL *Lectionary Music* (GIA, G-2626)
- David Haas, *Advent Gospel Acclamation* (OCP, 8732)

■ EUCHARISTIC PRAYER: Some musicians unify the Advent-Christmas seasons musically, while at the same time differentiating them, by a creative use of the same set of acclamations. For instance, acclamations are sung in unison during Advent with no added instrumental or choral parts, save perhaps a single wind instrument as at the gathering song. Instrumental embellishments are added for the Christmas season.

Others favor an unadorned Advent setting and completely different, festive acclamations for Christmas. Highly recommended is Richard Proulx's *Missa Emmanuel* (GIA, G-3489), based on "O come, O come, Emmanuel," for cantor, choir and congregation. Its familiarity facilitates participation, an important consideration in parishes that may have a holiday influx of visitors and strangers. For the same reason, Christopher Walker's *Glastonbury Eucharistic Acclamations* (OCP, 7165) are suitable for Advent-Christmas, the assembly repeating each line after the cantor.

- COMMUNION RITE: Historically, the Roman rite opts for psalms with antiphons as chants for the gathering, preparation of the gifts and communion rite. Vatican II's official chant manual, *The Simple Gradual*, prescribes Psalm 85 for the communion procession during Advent. If not used as a common responsorial psalm during the liturgy of the word, it would be most appropriate here. Marty Haugen's setting, "Lord, make us turn to you" (*Gather*, #37) effectively captures the spirit of the season. Other refrain-style choices are Haugen's "My soul in stillness waits" (GIA, G-3331), based on the "O Antiphons," or Jacques Berthier's "Wait for the Lord" (Taizé; GIA, G-2778).

A fitting Advent communion processional is any responsorial-style setting of the Magnificat. James Chepponis' version (GIA, G-2302) has an easy refrain for the assembly, with verses for one or two cantors.

As a practical consideration, learning Psalms 25 and 85 provides two convenient choices for Advent Evening Prayer (Vespers). The *General Instruction of the Liturgy of the Hours* permits divergence from the officially prescribed psalmody to facilitate community participation. Incorporating the Magnificat into the assembly's repertoire during Advent provides several benefits: The late Advent scriptures celebrate Mary's role in salvation history; the Magnificat is appropriate for Marian feasts throughout the year; and the assembly has learned a Magnificat for celebrations of Evening Prayer.

WORD OF GOD

- PATTERN OF SCRIPTURAL TEXTS: The Pastoral Introduction points out the clearly identifiable scripture focus of each Sunday in all three cycles of the lectionary (PI, 5). For Year B, the Year of Mark, the outline, using the terms of the Pastoral Introduction, breaks down like this:

First Sunday: the Return of the Lord. Mark 13:33–37. Stay awake! You do not know when the Lord is coming.

Second Sunday: John the Baptist's Call to Conversion. Mark 1:1–8. Prepare the way of the Lord.

Third Sunday: the Relationship of John to Jesus. John 1:6–8; 19–28. Among you stands one you do not know, the one who comes after me.

Fourth Sunday: Mary and the Events Immediately Preceding Christ's Birth. Luke 1:26–38. The annunciation to Mary: You shall conceive and bear a son.

The Pastoral Introduction does not specifically mention the other scriptures, but the prophetic and apostolic readings sound clearly the twin Advent themes of challenge and comfort:

First Sunday: Isaiah 63:16–17, 19; 64:2–7. You are the potter, we the clay, the work of your hands; 1 Corinthians 1:3–9. Jesus will strengthen you to the end and make you blameless on that day.

Second Sunday: Isaiah 40:1–5, 9–11. Comfort my people. Like a shepherd he feeds the flock; 2 Peter 3:8–14. We await a new heavens and a new earth where the justice of God will be at home.

Third Sunday: Isaiah 61:1–2, 10–11. The Spirit of the Lord is upon me. Justice and peace shall spring up among the nations; 1 Thessalonians 5:16–24. Rejoice always. May the God of peace make you perfect for the coming of the Lord.

Fourth Sunday: 2 Samuel 7:1–5, 8–11, 16. The Lord says to David: It is I who will establish a house for you; Romans 16: 25–27. The mystery hidden for ages is now revealed—and to the Gentiles!

If the liturgy of the word is introduced by a brief introductory word from the presider (as at the Easter Vigil), or even by the lector (although the Easter Vigil approach is preferable, the lector reading only scriptural texts), being aware of the thread that connects these readings is a good preliminary step. The four introductions of the season should be prepared at the same time, viewing each week from the perspective of the whole season.

The prophetic readings, especially the long passages from Isaiah, demand a lector's best efforts and all the assistance provided in LTP's *Workbook for Lectors and Gospel Readers*. The epistle passages need to be read in that tone of confident trust and eager expectation with which each was first written.

Celebration of Advent Masses

THE Pastoral Introduction does not offer specific suggestions for every part of Mass. Nor does the sacramentary, with the exception of assigning each preface to a particular phase of Advent. Nevertheless, some ritual practices and textual choices might help to establish and maintain a seasonal tone. The suggestions that follow have proved helpful in pastoral practice and are in keeping with the spirit of the season.

INTRODUCTORY RITES

■ RITUAL STRUCTURE: An advertisement for the latest business fashions admonishes young job-seekers: "You have fifteen seconds to make a good impression. They may never read your résumé!" First impressions stick. Beginnings are crucial. How much more so the beginnings in the beginning season! But before planning how the Advent liturgies will begin, planners should look at the introductory rites throughout the liturgical year. This will help maintain a broad perspective within which to determine each particular season's distinctive opening rites. In other words, creating an outline of the other seasons' introductory rites may itself suggest the Advent pattern.

It is hard to imagine an Advent introductory rite that does not include some reference to the Advent wreath. It is just as hard to remember that, in most English-speaking Catholic churches, the presence of the Advent wreath dates only from the time of Vatican II! It is not difficult to account for the almost instant and universal popularity of the Advent wreath. Here is a richly symbolic visual that is also a highly successful symbol: It needs no explanation, is best served by few words, and admits of any number of equally acceptable and effective forms of arrangement. Peter Mazar's excellent *To Crown the Year* (LTP, 1995) provides extensive reflections and suggestions on the creation and use of this visual. But some cautions are in order. In its notes on the Advent wreath, the *Book of Blessings* (BB) (#1510, 1512) expresses two concerns: *Visually* the wreath should not compete with the setting for the eucharist; *ritually* it should not compete with the rest of the liturgy.

These concerns should be taken seriously. In fact, the *Book of Blessings* (chapter 47) places the blessing and lighting of the Advent wreath on the First Sunday of Advent either after the general intercessions, in a separate celebration of the word or during Evening Prayer.

Still it should be possible to make the introductory rite of the first and subsequent Advent Sundays unique, while at the same time not being overly verbose or overshadowing the liturgy of the word. One possibility:

- Advent chant
- processional cross and ministers gathered under wreath with assembly facing wreath
- Advent greeting and brief introduction
- chanted litany (candles are lit now if they were not lit before the liturgy)

Cantor: The Spirit and the church cry out: Come, Lord Jesus!

All: Come, Lord Jesus! (Melody: any "Lord, hear our prayer")

Cantor: All who await his appearance pray: Come, Lord Jesus!

All: Come, Lord Jesus!

Cantor: The whole creation pleads: Come, Lord Jesus!

All: Come, Lord Jesus!

- chant resumes, ministers process
- presider chants opening prayer at chair

■ BEGINNINGS BEFORE BEGINNINGS: As always, everything should be in readiness well before most of the assembly arrives. Nothing kills the Advent spirit of quiet, contemplative longing more surely than distracted ministers busily putting things in place and scrambling to establish order just before the liturgy begins. By the time most people arrive, no ministers should be in sight, except perhaps those involved in necessary hospitality.

■ MODIFIED PENITENTIAL RITE: Although *Sourcebook* provides prayers to conclude a modified penitential rite (page 24), many would question the wisdom of having, in effect, two opening prayers. One precedent is the pre-Tridentine rite (especially in England), which sometimes featured a procession before the principal Mass. Stational stops at font, shrine or rood screen consisted of a sung verse, response and collect before resuming the procession to the sanctuary.

Whatever introductory rite is established ought to be maintained from year to year, with minimal modification as may seem necessary.

CONCLUDING THE LITURGY OF THE WORD

■ DISMISSAL OF THE CATECHUMENS: Catechumens present in the assembly should be sent forth with words of dismissal that allude to the hopes and longings of the community, which they increasingly share (see sample text on page 24.)

■ GENERAL INTERCESSIONS: ICEL's Pastoral Introduction: Order of Mass, considered during Ordinary Time, offers specific instructions for the general intercessions that might well be looked

 at now even before the Advent texts are prepared. Remember that the intercessions need not be fresh each week. Some might be repeated throughout Advent, augmented by a variable weekly petition that corresponds to the day's scriptures or to current local and global concerns. See page 25 for a sample invitation to prayer. Liturgy Training Publication's *Prayers for Sundays and Seasons* offers models for each week.

LITURGY OF THE EUCHARIST

As noted above, each phase of Advent is characterized by a proper preface to signal varying emphases, first eschatological, then more incarnational. The eucharistic prayer chosen might be one less frequently heard during the rest of the year. One choice permitted is Reconciliation II, which neatly ties both emphases together. First it proclaims Christ as "the word that brings salvation, the hand you stretch out to sinners, the way that leads to your peace." Later it envisions the banquet of the kingdom at which are gathered "people of every race, language and way of life." If ICEL's proposed sacramentary revision is accepted, there will also be an Advent interpolation for Eucharistic Prayer III.

The seasonal texts on page 25 suggest possible Advent alternatives for the invitation to the Lord's Prayer and invitation to communion. If chosen, these are used at every Mass throughout the entire season, repetition permitting them to become words the assembly comes to know "by heart."

CONCLUDING RITES

A seasonal dismissal of the eucharistic ministers bearing the eucharist to the homebound is suggested on page 25.

The blessing and dismissal of the entire assembly should likewise be seasonal and stable throughout Advent. In its report to the conferences of bishops, ICEL noted that "recurring criticism" of the solemn blessings pointed to "their frequent wordiness, the imbalance among the three members that lead up to the trinitarian blessing and the difficulty in cuing the congregation to the response 'Amen' after each of the separate statements of blessing." Of course, the best way to cue the congregation's "Amen" is to chant the blessing!

Preparing the Parish

THE Pastoral Introduction summarizes well the twofold dilemma confronting First World communities trying to live Advent in the late twentieth century: commercial exploitation in the marketplace and social celebrations at school and work that anticipate Christmas (PI, 6). Here we come face to face with the tension that centers on the contrasting concepts of "the world" that the scriptures (especially the Johannine scriptures) give us. "Do not love the world," 1 John tells us, "or the things in the world." He goes on to list them: "carnal allurements, eye-catching enticements, the life of empty show." At the same time, the Gospel of John tells us that "God so loved the world that he gave his only Son."

No purpose is served, and much ill will can ensue, if the church's response is one of strident criticism or condemnation of merchants, advertisers or the culture. Most business people are simply trying to make a living. The Christian presumption must surely be in favor of the basic good will of those who buy and sell and celebrate. There is certainly a place for gentle warnings of the danger we all face: an excessive consumerism that measures love by purchases and limits celebration to spending. Some parishes may tap into the resources of groups that help Third World countries and the poor in our own country through celebrating "an alternative Christmas." The parish's liturgists should cooperate with or even initiate community efforts to coordinate religious education and social service resources toward the care of those with special needs at this season. The liturgical ministry embraces any project that helps focus on the positive meanings beneath customs the wider culture may seem to have taken over for its own ends.

For instance, that holiday longing to do something special for someone else (perhaps a surprise!), while exploited by advertisers, still reflects God's surprise gift to the world in Jesus and can be an inspiration to do something special for the poor, with whom Jesus so identified himself. Christmas lighting displays, viewed with the eyes of faith, can remind us of Jesus, the Light of the World, and challenge us as his disciples to "let our light shine." Songs of peace on earth can prompt action to foster peace. Parties and feasting can remind us to share God's gifts not only with friends and family but with all who hunger, not only physically but emotionally, too, during a season when bereavement or wounded relationships can weigh heavily on fragile hearts. A delicate balance is needed to confront false or distorted values of the culture, while still recognizing and building on the deeper truth and basic goodwill from which our holiday customs spring. Most people sense the need to recover the basic meaning of Christmas. Practical and positive guidance on how to do that, rather than criticism and condemnation, will do much to relieve the pressure and stress that can mar these holidays for so many.

Taking It Home

To "sustain an expectant orientation toward Christmas" the Pastoral Introduction suggests the use of the Advent wreath and the Jesse Tree (PI, 6).

■ THE JESSE TREE, A GIVING TREE: A recent adaptation of the Jesse Tree custom is an Advent "Giving Tree" on which are hung cards listing gifts for people in need. Parishioners take the cards home at the beginning of Advent and return the gifts near the end of the season for distribution at Christmas. This custom helps us realize the deeper purpose of gift-giving. It links Christmas shopping to the Christian love that should mark all who follow the One whose birth at Bethlehem is God's enduring gift to us. The Giving Tree is best placed in the entryway or some location other than the sanctuary, lest the simplicity of Advent decor be compromised.

■ HOME ADVENT WREATH: While increasingly associated with parish decor and worship, it is important to remember that the Advent wreath began as a home custom. It offers an excellent way to link Sunday worship, both visually and verbally, with daily prayer and Christmas preparation in the home. To make it easy to observe the custom, many parishes stock Advent candles and wreath forms, which a youth group, religious education program or parish prayer group can sell on the last weekends of Ordinary Time. A Family Advent Day on the First Sunday of Advent, with activities for various age groups and an educational program about Advent's history, scriptures, themes and customs can be a helpful way to set the parish clock to the new season. A brief midday prayer could open an afternoon gathering featuring an Advent hymn sing, making household Advent wreaths, ideas for Advent prayers and mealtime rituals.

■ ADDITIONAL RESOURCES: Liturgy Training Publications provides a number of items designed to facilitate the church-household link. Each year a large poster calendar presents the liturgical year as a great wheel of color. The *Companion to the Calendar* by Mary Ellen Hynes is filled with information about particular seasons and saints. Its material on the "O Antiphons" (pages 4–6) is too good to miss.

Fling Wide the Doors, with the art of Steve Erspamer, is an exceptionally beautiful adaptation of the traditional Advent calendar. *Welcome, Yule!* is a program of Sunday handouts that provide a tangible way to join weekend worship with daily reflection and witness. Like LTP's Advent calendar, these handouts unify the observance of Advent and Christmas. In years past, these handouts have included household blessings for important Advent moments: inaugurating the home Advent wreath, baking holiday cookies, lighting the Christmas tree, blessing the nativity scene and so forth. Even in the absence of these handouts, the parish bulletin ought to provide texts for such prayer. Advent-Christmas meal prayer cards from LTP may be used with the handouts or on their own as a way to provide words for a natural setting within which to have household or individual prayer.

Keeping Advent and Christmastime is a pocket booklet with a handy prayer format and texts for use at several times throughout the day. *Take Me Home* has pages for children and families for the beginning of Advent, St. Nicholas, Our Lady of Guadalupe, St. Lucy and the "O Antiphons" of Advent's final week.

An Advent Sourcebook is one of LTP's invaluable compilations of texts gleaned from a wide variety of liturgical texts both Christian and Jewish, from scriptural passages, as well as from secular literature.

Other Ritual Prayers and Sacraments

LITURGY OF THE HOURS: Vatican II's *Liturgy of the Hours* is a treasury of hymns, scriptural texts, readings from early Christian writers and saints of all centuries, and intercessory prayers. Several "hours" are celebrated in the course of the day. The two principal "hours" mark daybreak and nightfall, Morning Prayer (Lauds or Praise) and Evening Prayer (Vespers). The texts celebrate God's gifts of light and darkness and are a perfect way to sanctify the course of the day.

- **LESSONS AND CAROLS:** This traditional service is something of a hybrid, combining elements from Vespers and Vigils. The Episcopal *Book of Occasional Services* (Church Hymnal Corporation) has both Advent and Christmas formats for a Festival of Lessons and Music.

- **BLESSING THE ADVENT WREATH:** This is another good way to celebrate a service of light with Evening Prayer. As we have noted, the *Book of Blessings* (chapter 47) suggests Evening Prayer I of the First Sunday of Advent as an appropriate time to bless the Advent wreath and light its first candle. Modified to include these elements, Evening Prayer would look like this:

  - introduction *(not a lucernarium)* and hymn
  - psalmody
  - reading (perhaps Isaiah as in BB, #1526)
  - homily, silence (response)
  - gospel canticle (Magnificat)
  - intercessions (BB, #1530) and Lord's Prayer with proper introduction as in BB, #1531
  - prayer of blessing (BB, #1532 or #1533)
  - lighting of first candle
  - concluding rite (BB, #1534)

  Another approach, if the parish usually begins Evening Prayer with a *lucernarium,* is to use the prayer of blessing from the *Book of Blessings* and light the first candle at the start of the celebration. Then the first Advent candle becomes the light praised in hymn and thanksgiving. In subsequent weeks, the Advent candles would be used at Evening Prayer for this *lucernarium.*

- **COMMUNAL PENANCE:** Though not officially a penitential season, Advent is an appropriate time to seek peace within and around oneself. The preaching of the prophets and John the Baptist are highlights of the Advent scriptures, and these summon us to a conversion that prepares the world and ourselves for the Lord's unexpected yet certain coming. Communal celebrations of reconciliation will want to use elements from a complete Advent service in appendix II of the *Rite of Penance*. As with all the liturgies of Advent, careful use of darkness and lighting will provide the mood of the season in a powerful, nonverbal way.

- **COMMUNAL ANOINTING OF THE SICK:** Sundays in Ordinary Time, especially those with scriptural healing stories, would seem best for communal anointing services. If celebrated during Mass on an Advent Sunday, the special ritual Mass is not permitted. One of the scripture passages from the *Pastoral Care of the Sick* may be used, perhaps as a second reading, though the readings of the day may be just as suitable.

- **FUNERALS:** Funeral Masses are not celebrated on Advent Sundays or on the Solemnity of the Immaculate Conception, which this year is celebrated on December 9. Maintain the spirit of the Advent season by making sure that the Advent wreath is lighted and by choosing the Isaiah and Revelation readings from among those provided for funerals. These offer a consolation of eschatological hope and promise to the bereaved that are especially Advent in tone. Psalms 25 and 85, two of the common psalms for Advent, are most suitable as responsorial psalms, and the acclamations at the gospel and in the eucharistic prayer should be those used at the Advent Sunday Masses. Other traditional Advent music, especially those whose texts are eschatological, express well the intensity of human longing for redemption proper to Advent and to funerals. They are also generally well known to diverse congregations and visitors from other churches.

- **MARRIAGE:** The *Rite of Marriage* (#11) directs those preparing couples for marriage to advise them about the "special nature" of Advent and Lent. This is a polite way of suggesting that we help people see how contrary to the spirit of both seasons the celebration of marriage is. The presumption is that during Advent the whole community is caught up in a sense of "devout and joyful expectation," while during Lent the catechumenal journey toward initiation and the communal commitment to conversion will absorb everyone's time and energy. Nevertheless, legitimate circumstances may require the celebration of marriage during these seasons, and those minimally involved in community worship or completely removed from it may wish to be married during these times. How the community deals with such delicate and personal issues may vary from place to place. But the church's liturgical sense presumes that these marriages are the exception, not the rule. Safeguarding the primacy of the season, official norms require that on Advent Sundays (and on the Solemnity of the Immaculate Conception), all the Mass texts must be those of the current Advent day. It will probably be neither desirable nor even possible to alter the parish's Advent decor to accommodate wedding decorations, and at all liturgical gatherings, including weddings and funerals, the appropriate number of candles should be lit in the Advent wreath.

■ RITE OF CHRISTIAN INITIATION OF ADULTS: The rites of acceptance into the order of catechumens or of welcoming candidates are not appropriate for the First Sunday of Advent. Such scheduling usually indicates the desire to compress a multiyear catechumenate into a nine-month school year. This is largely ineffective for proper formation of catechumens. The Advent liturgy is meant to be somewhat quiet and focused to sustain a mood of expectancy and watchful prayer. Powerful rites of acceptance and welcoming are better celebrated on Sundays in Ordinary Time, where they will not distract from the community's focus but actually capture it. Liturgies of the word and other prayers celebrated with catechumens and candidates outside the Sunday assembly should be prepared with Advent in mind, and these people should be joyfully welcomed into the prayer experiences of this important season.

The Worship Environment

TWO of LTP's newer publications will prove indispensable for seasonal planning. Used together, these volumes provide an almost complete "theory and practice" resource for those whose special ministry and challenge it is to prepare the setting in which the assembly does its liturgy.

■ THE SACRISTY MANUAL: This book by G. Thomas Ryan, published in 1994, is a wealth of material, a first-rate manual that needs to be present in every sacristy, at home with the ordained ministers and ready at hand for anyone leading the team entrusted with arranging the material items for worship. Decorators will need to consult this book over and over again.

Under the heading "Advent" one will find two entries. The first discusses the Advent wreath briefly but follows this with an extensive and practical note about candle lighting (pages 147–149). The second is part of a precisely organized, practical "Checklist for Liturgical Seasons and Feasts." The Advent notes discuss season, vesture and decorations (pages 185–86).

■ TO CROWN THE YEAR: DECORATING THE CHURCH THROUGH THE SEASONS: Destined to become the parish decorator's daily companion, Peter Mazar's masterpiece is a one-volume encyclopedia, liturgy course and illustrated practical manual all rolled into one. Spend a lot of time in the autumn with the fine introductory section, "Getting Started," pages 2–39. Then look at Advent itself, pages 176–228.

■ MODERATION: Officially, a moderation similar to that affecting the music program is recommended also for the adornment of the worship environment during Advent (*Ceremonial of Bishops*, #236). While taste cannot be legislated, surely some balance can be struck between an over-decoration that anticipates Christmas and an austerity more appropriate to Lent. Any attempt to communicate visually the growing anticipation of the Advent season as it progresses should be done subtly, the model for this increase being the small but significant change of lighting one more candle on the wreath each week.

Whatever is done, this year's occurrence of Christmas on a Wednesday might permit an outdoor and even indoor decorating party to take place on Sunday afternoon before Vespers.

CALENDAR

December

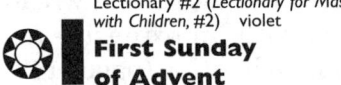

Lectionary #2 (*Lectionary for Masses with Children,* #2)   violet

First Sunday of Advent

■ ADVENT'S FIRST EVENINGS: According to the Pastoral Introduction, the season's motif is light within darkness; its mood one of watchfulness and prayer. Suggestions of "vigils and services of light" as prayerful ways to mark the season offer possibilities for an enhanced celebration of the darkest parts of this first weekend of Advent: the two evenings, "First Vespers" (Saturday evening's introduction to the Lord's Day) and "Second Vespers" (Sunday evening's closing of the Lord's Day).

No parish could or should try to do everything or overload the schedule in such a way as to leave staff and ministers in a state of total exhaustion. Nevertheless, in planning the schedule for this first weekend of Advent, arrangements should be made to mark both evenings' darkness with special gatherings for prayer. Subsequent weekends would not have as full a schedule as this first weekend but one that still offers more than is the case during Ordinary Time.

■ THE END TIME: Advent always begins with that Great Conclusion, which will also be the Great Beginning! The end of time marks the beginning of each lectionary cycle. These days of early twilights direct our thoughts toward the dawn of the eternal "day of the Lord." History bears witness to increased concern and speculation about the end of the world at the close of each millennium. Such preoccupation can lend itself to what theologians label quietism: a passive waiting for time to run its course and for God's work to be accomplished.

But this year's evangelist, Mark, permits no true disciple to sleep during the master's absence. Christian waiting is focused and purposeful. Mark's Jesus invokes the image of faithful stewardship: "Each servant has been given a particular task . . . and the doorkeeper is to be on watch." Heaven and earth may pass away but the Lord's words will not. And since speculation about the when and how of the world's culmination is futile, the faithful steward is to be busy translating the gospel's words into deeds. Creative and industrious use of the spiritual gifts given, the riches of "speech and knowledge of every kind," is Paul's challenge to the Corinthians and to us (second reading). Thus, as Isaiah puts it, waiting and working go hand in hand. Then the Lord who is surely coming will "meet us gladly doing what is right" (first reading).

■ BLESSING THE WREATH: The *Book of Blessings* (#1509) notes that the Advent wreath may be blessed during Mass, during a celebration of the word or at Evening Prayer. The first two forms are presented in BB, #1517ff. This *Sourcebook* provides an alternate blessing during the introductory rites of Mass on page 23.

■ TODAY AND THE WEEK AHEAD: Those preparing general intercessions and bulletin notes will want to remember that today is World AIDS Awareness Day, sponsored by the World Health Organization, and the anniversary of Rosa Parks' refusal to move to the back of the bus. The Advent prophets' call for justice in preparing the way of the Lord makes it especially appropriate to pray for those who are deprived of human rights, those who struggle for social justice, those who suffer from AIDS and those who care for them.

Many HIV/AIDS ministries host ecumenical or interfaith prayer services as a way of lifting up the role of pastoral and spiritual care. Since 1990, AIDS Interfaith New York has sponsored "An Interfaith Service of Hope and Remembrance." For information, contact them at 175 Ninth Avenue, New York NY 10011 (212-627-7759) or the American Association for World Health, 1129 20th Street NW, Suite 400, Washington DC 20036 (202-466-5883).

Friday is the optional memorial of St. Nicholas, a special day in many families. The parish may want to give a small gift to children after Mass on Sunday to connect with home observances of St. Nicholas and to remind children of the true origin of Santa Claus.

Preface for Advent I (P-1), with its eschatological emphasis, is used until December 16.

MON 2 Advent Weekday

#175 [176] (LMC, #172–175)   violet

Today's readings and psalm speak of the gathering of all nations from east and west into the unity and peace of God's kingdom.

Eucharistic Prayer for Reconciliation II envisions the day when God will "gather people of every race, language and way of life to share in the one eternal banquet." Its vivid eschatological vision and portrayal of Christ's redemptive mission makes this prayer appropriate throughout the season. Among the many victims of civil strife for whom we might pray today, American Catholics should certainly recall the witness unto death of Maura Clarke, Ita Ford, Dorothy Kazel and Jean Donovan, who were murdered in El Salvador on this date in 1980.

DECEMBER

TUE 3 #176 [177] (LMC, #172–175) white
Francis Xavier, presbyter, religious, missionary
MEMORIAL

How well today's saint incarnates today's scriptural message! Isaiah's comforting vision of the peaceable kingdom follows from his challenging portrayal of God (and, we hope, of God's ministers and people) as devoted to equity and justice for the meek of the earth. The opening prayer links Francis Xavier's missionary ardor with the evangelizing zeal that should mark each of us. When the disciples return from their mission, Jesus rejoices that, despite its rejection by the "wise and learned," God's plan has found a home among earth's lowly ones. Such a message, so early in the season, should give impetus to parish preparations for a Christmas outreach to those in need within the community and beyond it.

The general intercessions could mention the well-being of Christians in India and throughout the Far East, the apostolates of any local Jesuit or Xaverian communities and the labor of missionaries throughout the world. The saint's opening prayer replaces the Advent weekday one. The general intercessions could conclude with the Advent one or one from the Masses titled "For the Spread of the Gospel," with the shorter ending, "We ask this through Christ our Lord."

WED 4 #177 [178] (LMC, #172–175) violet
Advent Weekday

John of Damascus, presbyter, religious, doctor of the church, optional memorial/white. ▪ Today's optional memorial, the first of the liturgical year, provides an occasion for reviewing parish policy on observing these days. The *General Calendar,* supplemented by proper calendars of nation, diocese and religious community, establishes memorials that must be observed. Whenever an *optional* memorial occurs, especially during Advent or another season, the decision is local. Detailed norms for choosing prayers are in chapter VII of the *General Instruction of the Roman Missal;* for selecting readings in chapter IV of the *Introduction to the Lectionary.* This approach may be helpful when the community does not have a special devotion to the saint whose optional memorial it is:

1) Respect the primacy of the season. Keep the seasonal color. Use acclamations the parish has learned for the season.

2) Respect the integrity of the lectionary. During major seasons optional memorials should not displace the appointed texts. Even in Ordinary Time, there should be no interruption of continuous readings from the books assigned.

3) Integrate the saint's commemoration. While the saint's opening prayer may replace that of the season, it could also be transferred (with shorter ending) to conclude the general intercessions. This permits an explicit mention of the saint to follow the homily, during which some aspect of the saint's life, witness or even writings may be related to the day's scriptures.

For instance, in today's seasonal scriptures Isaiah prophesies the Lord's destruction of death and gathering all people to the feast on the holy mountain (first reading); Psalm 23 follows, then Christ's feeding of the multitudes. John of Damascus fed God's people through his theological commentary and poetic prayer.

THU 5 #178 [179] (LMC, #172–175) violet
Advent Weekday

The lovely heroine of the old musical challenged her suitor, "Don't speak of stars shining above, if you're in love, show me!" Advent in general, and today's scriptures in particular, say the same thing: Deeds, not words! Or better, words into deeds! The Lord is a rock but not for the nation that brags about being founded on "Judeo-Christian principles," only for the nation that acts righteously by caring for its poor and needy.

FRI 6 #179 [180] (LMC, #172–175) violet
Advent Weekday

Nicholas, bishop, optional memorial/white. ▪ Children, brides, sailors and pawnbrokers, as well as Greece, Sicily and Russia have more than made up in the strength of their devotion to Nicholas whatever weaknesses there are in the hard historical data concerning him! Though his memorial is optional in the Roman Calendar, the Eastern churches mention him in virtually every divine liturgy.

Today's remembrance of Nicholas' legendary compassion coincides beautifully with the assigned scriptures: Isaiah's vision of earth's tyrants torn down and the lowly lifted up; the gospel's portrayal of Jesus as divine physician to the afflicted. The weekend around Saint Nicholas day might be a perfect time for those communities that can do so to sponsor a children's party—especially for children whose prospects for a merry Christmas may be as dim as these long winter nights.

▪ HANUKKAH: Tonight marks the beginning of an eight-day festival of lights for our Jewish neighbors. Hanukkah celebrates fidelity to the covenant in the face of tyranny and forced cultural assimilation (see 1 and 2 Maccabees). Remember the sensitivity necessary in relating Christianity to Judaism in preaching and teaching, especially at this time of the

DECEMBER

year and during the Triduum. Helpful materials are available. Consult the Bishops' Committee on the Liturgy's *God's Mercy Endures Forever* and two resources from LTP: *When Catholics Speak about Jews* and, especially helpful in religious education programs, *Teaching Christian Children About Judaism*.

SAT 7 #180 [181] (LMC, #172–175) white
Ambrose, bishop, doctor of the church
MEMORIAL

Ambrose's influence on both the universal and local church is immeasurable. To this day the liturgy celebrated in and around Milan carries Ambrose's name. Similar to the Roman rite in many ways, the Ambrosian rite has its own calendar (six Sundays of Advent, Lent's beginning with ashes on the First Sunday of Lent), its own Order of Mass (peace greeting at the conclusion of the liturgy of the word) and its own Liturgy of the Hours (featuring numerous hymns and writings of Ambrose himself). The Ambrosian rite, reformed according to the decrees of Vatican II but maintaining its cherished distinctiveness, celebrates the church's unity in diversity.

8 #5 (LMC, #5) violet
Second Sunday of Advent

John the Baptist makes his debut today, echoing the call of Isaiah from centuries before, and calling us centuries later to repentance. At its heart, though, the call to conversion is one of comfort and hope. The Spirit's baptism is meant to elicit not the terror of retribution but the consolation of good tidings. The Lord whose advent demands the reconstruction of our hearts speaks tenderly, casts out fear and gathers us into his arms for the journey home. While Peter's second letter reminds us that the day of the Lord will be sudden in its dawning and severe in its consequences, the same author begins and ends that passage by exulting in the patience of the Lord, who wants none to perish, and who promises new heavens and a new earth.

■ ADVENT PENANCE SERVICE: These scriptures and the mood they evoke on this Second Sunday of Advent make this weekend a perfect time to announce pre-Christmas penance services. Many parishioners would surely appreciate a bulletin insert with information on parish celebrations of penance (communal and individual) and perhaps some texts associated with the rite: an Advent examination of conscience and new forms of the act of contrition.

MON 9 #689 (LMC, #429) white
The Immaculate Conception of the Virgin Mary
SOLEMNITY

This feast had its origin in the East as the "Conception of Mary by Saint Anne." It spread through the West during the Middle Ages as the "Immaculate Conception" and was extended to the entire Western church in the eighteenth century. The feast celebrates Mary, preserved from sin from the moment of conception. She is the first fruits of her Son's redemption and a prophetic model of what the church is called to be (© ICEL).

In addition, this feast is of particular importance in the United States. By the time European immigrants began arriving in this country in large numbers, the Immaculate Conception was already a popular feast. The renowned explorer Father Marquette is especially famous for his devotion to it. Eight years before the papal proclamation of the dogma (Pius IX, 1854), the bishops of the United States declared Mary patron of the nation under this title. It is providential that a newer Marian feast, occurring this year in the same week, is the gift of newer immigrants to our country.

Ironically this "patronal feast" seems to attract and multiply confusion! A longstanding confusion labels the virgin birth of Jesus an "immaculate conception." (A confusion that is reinforced, unfortunately, by the use of the annunciation gospel!) More recent confusion focuses on the feast's status as a holy day of obligation, and this year's confusion intensifies in the transfer of the solemnity from Sunday. Put briefly: The observance moves forward to Monday, but the Mass obligation does not. Still, today's liturgy should be celebrated in a way that keeps the Advent spirit while giving ample attention to the seasonally appropriate presence of Mary.

■ MAINTAIN THE ADVENT SPIRIT: The angel's challenging message and Mary's faith-filled response match Advent's mood of joyful expectation. Much of the Advent Sunday worship elements, therefore, could stay the same. The penitential rite and the acclamations at the gospel and during the eucharistic prayer could fittingly be those already chosen for Advent. The alternative opening prayer in the present sacramentary links the feast to the season.

Use the Advent formulary in the Common of the Virgin Mary to conclude the general intercessions. The special preface for the day could be followed by Eucharistic Prayer III or Eucharistic Prayer II for Reconciliation, whichever text is the customary Advent Sunday choice.

■ DISTINCTIVE FESTAL ELEMENTS: Although detailed clarification should wait for the homily, brief introductory words after the greeting could focus the subject of the feast. The ICEL note given above could be adapted.

The sung Gloria might be a setting that offers a foretaste of Christmas. The general intercessions should make room for a petition for the dignity and rights of all the people of the United States, being sensitive in relating past immigrations to that of the present. Another might be for the aspirations of women throughout our culture and society. Floral and candle arrangements near the image of Mary are especially appropriate, although attention to this image is fitting throughout the season. Consider Marian music appropriate to Advent: "She will show us the Promised One," "Behold a virgin bearing him," "The Angel Gabriel from heaven came" and "O Holy Mary" (Owen Alstott, OCP, 8724). The Marian antiphon traditionally prescribed for Compline during Advent is the "Alma redemptoris mater," particularly beautiful in its simple tone.

Today's preface is a fine summary of doctrine and images. It deserves not only to be heard but to be seen as well, perhaps as a boxed text in the parish bulletin or with some artwork in a worship program. The solemn blessing printed with today's texts in most editions of the sacramentary has been updated for inclusive language in the *Book of Blessings* (solemn blessing #20 in appendix II). Its use is optional, however, and the Advent seasonal blessing would also be appropriate today.

TUE 10 #182 [183] (LMC, #172–175) violet
Advent Weekday

Move Monday's unused Isaiah reading to today because today's repeats Sunday's. Although the first readings and gospels are "matched" during Advent, Monday's first reading has points of contact with Tuesday's gospel. The blossoming of the desert; the healing of the sick; the creation of a royal highway to salvation, freed from ravenous beasts: These images of things saved and nothing lost correlate well with the gospel text of the Good Shepherd.

Today is the anniversary of the death of the Cistercian monk and spiritual writer Thomas Merton. Some of his best writing, even before Vatican II, was on the liturgy.

WED 11 #183 [184] (LMC, #172–175) violet
Advent Weekday

Damasus I, pope, optional memorial / white. ■ The God of Israel, the mighty One, lifts up the burdened and gives them eagles' wings. Jesus bids those wearied by life's heavy burdens to come to him and shoulder his easy yoke. Today's scriptures thus recall not only the strength given by God to those who bear witness in persecution but those within the community and beyond who should be the recipients of our preferential love and solicitude, especially during Advent.

THU 12 #707–712 (LMC, #447–451) white
Our Lady of Guadalupe
FEAST

■ THE IMAGE: Mary appears on the *tilma,* or cloak, as a young *mestiza,* a woman of Amerindian and European heritage. Thus she is affectionately called *la Morenita,* "the little brown one." Because she appears as a *mestiza,* Guadalupe presents God's "yes" to the native people of the Americas. She is an image of holiness and dignity with which the native and mestizo peoples of the Americas identify.

La Morenita is pregnant, for she wears the blue band traditionally worn by Aztec women who were with child, and on her womb appears a flower, the Aztec symbol for new life and a new era. Like the church during Advent, she is also awaiting the birth of Christ who will usher in a new era of peace and justice for those long oppressed by the arbitrary power of the strong.

■ CELEBRATION: A large, growing Hispanic population has enriched the church in the United States with its rich devotional and cultural life. Today's feast celebrates not only a wonderful image and the marvelous story of its origins but the nearness of God experienced in the unity-in-diversity of God's people. Parishes not fortunate enough to have a Hispanic presence might consider publicizing celebrations of local parishes with Hispanic communities, so that everyone may take part in the fiestas those assemblies may have planned for today. *Take Me Home* by LTP describes some Guadalupe customs and menu items. Such food and festivity will introduce a welcome exuberance into the otherwise subdued joy of Advent.

DECEMBER

- **LECTIONARY:** Today's scriptures are to be taken from the Common of the Virgin Mary. Preserve a link to Advent by choosing a first reading from the prophetic passages (three from Isaiah, one each from Micah and Zechariah). Be careful choosing the gospel. While Luke is appropriate to Advent, lectionary reading #712.3 (annunciation) was just used on December 9. The visitation gospel, #712.4 is prescribed for December 21, but since that date is a Saturday this year, it may go unheard if there is no Saturday morning Mass. In that case, use this gospel with its mention of Mary's "hastening into the hill country" today. The Song of Songs for December 21 is a good match as first reading. Or consider the brief gospel #712.9, "Blest are those who hear the word and keep it." This calls to mind Augustine's remark that Mary had "conceived Christ in her heart before she conceived him in her womb."

- **SACRAMENTARY:** Today's presidential prayers, issued after the 1985 edition of the sacramentary, can be found in *Sacramentary Supplement* (Catholic Book Publishing Company, 1994). In choosing a Marian preface, remember that there are three in the sacramentary. The first (sometimes numbered P-56) is traditional, celebrating Mary who gave us Christ, "for ever the light of the world." This is certainly an Advent sentiment. The second (P-57) echoes Mary's Magnificat. A little-known third preface (hidden in the back of the present sacramentary, appendix X, #4, Mary, Mother of the Church), summarizes Mary's role in salvation history and her link to the continuation of that history in the life of the pilgrim people of God today. The solemn blessing, the same suggested for December 9, may be used at any celebrations this day, eucharistic or otherwise.

FRI 13 — #185 [186] (LMC, #172–175) red
Lucy, virgin, martyr
MEMORIAL

With a name meaning "light," Lucy is the perfect Advent saint! Many of the rich traditions surrounding Lucy's Day take inspiration from the beautiful Advent gospel of the wise and foolish bridesmaids (Matthew 25:1–13). Today's readings present the Advent contrast very clearly: the challenge of attending to what is "for your own good . . . the way you should go"; the comfort of "prosperity . . . success . . . offspring." As always, Jesus sheds Advent's light on the crux of the problem: We are often obstinate children, refusing any message that challenges our complacency. Seeing that more clearly may be the first step toward embracing the challenge and attaining the comfort.

SAT 14 — #186 [187] (LMC, #172–175) white
John of the Cross, presbyter, religious, doctor of the church
MEMORIAL

The Carmelites, whom John worked to reform, have always traced their spirit to the prophetic call, contemplative and active, of the great Elijah. Interestingly enough, today's seasonal readings highlight his fiery zeal, which Jesus relates to the mission of another John: John the Baptist. The reference to suffering as the path to glory for Elijah, the Baptist and Jesus offers an opportunity to link not only today's saint with the season but the Advent season itself with Lent-Easter. Liturgical tradition and authentic spirituality always link the incarnation with the paschal mystery.

15 — #8 (LMC, #8) violet or rose
Third Sunday of Advent

How wonderful it must have been to know the sung prayers of the liturgy well enough to identify a Sunday simply by the first word of its entrance song! Some of that tradition remains in the traditional name for this Third Sunday of Advent: *Gaudete* ("Rejoice") Sunday. Let the music chosen for today continue that heritage.

The first reading announces a year of salvation from the Lord. The responsorial psalm brings both testaments together with a refrain from Isaiah and verses from Mary's Magnificat. The second reading is filled with rejoicing and focuses on the eschatological culmination of joy in the completion of God's work in us "at the coming of our Lord Jesus Christ."

- **SACRAMENTARY:** The present translation of both the opening prayer and the prayer after communion contains "birthday" as an imprecise translation for the Latin "day of birth." There is an important difference. The forthcoming translation rectifies this:

> Gracious God,
> your people look forward in hope
>   to the festival of our Savior's
>   birth.
> Give us the strength to reach that
>   happy day of salvation,
> and to celebrate it with hearts full
>   of joy (© ICEL).

Although the rubrics do not permit the second Advent preface until Tuesday (December 17), this Sunday's gospel is our second encounter with John the Baptist, whose memory is kept in that preface.

DECEMBER

MON 16 — Late Advent Weekday
#187 [188] (LMC, #172–175) violet

The first phase of Advent draws to a close today, and the lectionary obliges with readings that provide a perfect bridge into the second phase. God's Spirit is upon the seer Balaam, "whose eye is clear": "How lovely your tabernacles, O Jacob, your encampments, O Israel . . . I see him, but not now; I behold him, but not near — a star shall come out of Jacob, and a scepter shall rise out of Israel!" (Numbers 24). Jesus shrouds himself in mystery, leaving acceptance of his authority a matter of personal choice for those with eyes, like Balaam's, sharp enough to see.

- **PREPARATION FOR ADVENT'S SECOND PHASE:** Consider providing a simple publication that provides for each of these days the scripture references, "O antiphon" and daily collect.

- **LAS POSADAS:** The Advent novena, *Las Posadas* ("the inns"), begins tonight. It commemorates the journey of Mary and Joseph from Nazareth to Bethlehem and is popular in much of Latin America and the Philippines. This novena's customs, especially the processions at night or early dawn, weave together Advent's prayerful vigilance, the virtue of hospitality and the commitment to social justice so critical to our times and so appropriate to this season.

TUE 17 — Late Advent Weekday
#193 [194] (LMC, #172–175) violet

O SAPIENTIA
As the church enters the second phase of Advent today, subtle variations might signal the change of mood. The greeting used since the First Sunday of Advent might give way to one suggested in the Italian, Spanish and Portuguese sacramentaries: "The Lord, who is coming to save us, be with you all." An optional penitential rite on page 24 has appropriate invocations drawn from the preface, which is used from today until Christmas, Advent II (P-2). The "O Antiphons" begin tonight at Vespers, sung before and after the Canticle of Mary (Magnificat). At Mass they occur in a slightly abbreviated form as the gospel acclamation verses (lectionary, #202). The hymn "O come, O come, Emmanuel" presents a metrical version well known to all. With an appropriate Alleluia refrain, it may also serve as the gospel acclamation. Be sure to begin today with verse 2 ("O Come, thou Wisdom"), and take care to use the appropriate verses as the days unfold. Three other settings are Marty Haugen's "My soul in stillness waits" (GIA, 2652), "Let the King of Glory come" by Michael Joncas and the chant adaptation in *Worship: Liturgy of the Hours, Leader's Edition*.

The scriptures begin the countdown to Christmas at the beginning of salvation's dawn, setting our feet on the tortuous path that winds from Jacob's promise to Jesus' birth. Before he dies, the patriarch gathers his sons around him. Given in full is the prediction to Judah. The long geneology with which Matthew begins his gospel is read in full today (sadly it may all be omitted at the Christmas Vigil Mass). The depth of its theology is profound.

WED 18 — Late Advent Weekday
#194 [195] (LMC, #172–175) violet

O ADONAI
"O Adonai and leader of the house of Israel . . . come and with an outstretched arm, redeem us!" To a nation whose spirit had been drained by religious apostasy and political collapse, Jeremiah spoke words of unlikely hope and daring promise. To a young man whose betrothed was inexplicably with child, the angel of the Lord offered an explanation just as unlikely and gave a command just as daring. Yet "when Joseph awoke . . . he did as the angel had commanded."

THU 19 — Late Advent Weekday
#195 [196] (LMC, #172–175) violet

O RADIX JESSE
Without rancorous criticism of the culture that surrounds us, today is an opportunity to reflect on the fact that by baptismal vows we belong to the kingdom whose Lord came into the world not to condemn but to offer salvation. Without denigrating the necessity and power of personal prayer, today presents a reminder of the privileged place accorded to liturgical prayer in the Judeo-Christian tradition. In today's scriptures an angel's visit heralds the conception of Samson who by "nazirite vow" will be consecrated to the service of God from childhood. So, too, does the angel Gabriel solemnly announce to Zechariah, at the incense psalm of Vespers, Elizabeth's conception of John, who will be under a similar vow of complete dedication to prepare for his work as herald.

FRI 20 — Late Advent Weekday
#196 [197] (LMC, #172–175) violet

O CLAVIS DAVID
Answer quickly, O Virgin. Reply in haste to the angel. . . . Answer with a word, receive the word of God. Speak your own word, conceive the divine Word. Breathe a passing word, embrace the eternal Word (Bernard, "Homily in Praise of the Virgin Mother").

In the days before Vatican II, Advent had only three proper Masses. Today's Mass was one of

DECEMBER

those. It was known as the "Golden Mass" *(missa aurea)*. Beginning with the beautiful introit *Rorate coeli* ("Bedew us, O heavens, from above"), it proclaimed the Isaiah prophecy and the annunciation to Mary. In the post–Vatican II liturgy, today's Mass forms one movement in a whole suite of Masses featuring messianic prophecies and annunciation narratives. Together with tomorrow's visitation story, it presents an appropriate setting in which to honor Mary's role in salvation history by preaching, prayer and song.

SAT 21 — Late Advent Weekday
#197 [198] (LMC, #172–175) violet

O ORIENS

Peter Canisius, presbyter, religious, doctor of the church, optional memorial ▪ "O Dayspring, splendor of eternal light, and sun of justice!" This is the perfect antiphon for the day of the winter solstice! In the first reading (surely the Song of Songs should be the option chosen) the bridegroom hastens across the hills toward his beloved. Into the hill country hastens Mary, pregnant with the Christ, to be of service to Elizabeth and to magnify the Lord. Because tomorrow's gospel is replaced by Sunday's scripture, it may be joined to today's passage.

☼ 22 — Fourth Sunday of Advent
#11 (LMC, #172–175) violet

O REX GENTIUM

▪ LECTIONARY: Year B of the lectionary features a gospel passage of the annunciation to Mary, which has been heard twice already this Advent, on Immaculate Conception and last Friday. This is no problem if we follow the lectionary principles and look at this gospel in light of the other two readings. The context of today's readings highlights the establishment, beyond anyone's imagination to envision, of the Davidic dynasty. "I took you. . . . I have been with you. . . . I will make your name great. . . . The Lord himself will make you a house." That house will be one whose guestlist will be inclusive, says Paul in the second reading: "the mystery . . . kept secret for the ages . . . now disclosed . . . to all the Gentiles."

These thoughts point to a possible emphasis for this weekend: Mary's faith-filled response is the dawn of salvation not just for her, not just for the children of the covenant, but for all!

▪ SACRAMENTARY: The first opening prayer, a free translation of the old Angelus collect, clearly links the incarnation and the paschal mystery of Christ and, especially appropriate to this year's lectionary, mentions explicitly the angelic message. If not used as the opening prayer, it could fittingly end the general intercessions. The alternative prayer in the present sacramentary has a clear Marian reference. Although the rubrics prescribe the second Advent preface, there is an official annunciation preface (P-44). In the *Collection of Masses of the Blessed Virgin Mary,* that preface has been revised for inclusivity (P-2).

▪ CHRISTMAS SCHEDULE: With Christmas only two days away, everyone should be able to remember the schedule, although an attractively printed outline will help. Some parishes continue the custom of mailing the schedule out with late Advent-Christmas greetings from the staff. A printed schedule permits the comments at the end of the liturgy to be not a rehash of the schedule but a brief description of the events, some of which may not be familiar: First Vespers on Christmas Eve, the Office of Readings or Vigils preceding a Midnight or late evening Mass, and the post-Mass social gathering for holiday food and drink, which is customary in many cultures.

MON 23 — Late Advent Weekday
#199 [200] (LMC, #172–175) violet

O EMMANUEL

John Kanty, presbyter, optional memorial. ▪ Liturgical norms for this penultimate day of Advent permit only a brief commemoration of the saint. If commemorated, he should be mentioned in the introduction to the liturgy. The opening prayer may be that of the season or saint, the unused prayer transferred to conclude the general intercessions. These might include prayers for Poland, for all who teach and learn in universities, specifically for college students traveling home or newly arrived for Christmas break.

The scriptures today and tomorrow set forth the birth of John the Baptist and the return of Zechariah's speech in his beautiful canticle.

TUE 24 — Late Advent Weekday
[morning] #200 [201] (LMC, #172–175) violet

"The appointed time has come: God has sent his Son into the world" (entrance antiphon at Mass). "Today you will know the Lord is coming, and in the morning you will see his glory" (invitatory refrain, *Liturgy of the Hours*). "Behold, all things are now completed, which were spoken of by the angel concerning the Virgin Mary" (monastic office).

TEXTS FOR THE EUCHARISTIC ASSEMBLY

INTRODUCTORY RITES

Greeting

From the Christ who was, who is and who is to come:
grace, light and peace be with you all.

Advent Wreath Lighting

For an alternative wreath lighting, see page 11.

Presider: In the silence of watchful hearts,
and in the longing of expectant prayer,
let us prepare the way of the Lord.

Silence

Presider: The Spirit and the church cry out:
All: Come, Lord Jesus!
Presider: All those who await his appearance pray:
All: Come, Lord Jesus!
Presider: The whole creation pleads:
All: Come, Lord Jesus!

Appropriate number of candles is lit. Entrance chant and procession to chair resume; opening prayer is prayed.

—*Lutheran Book of Worship*

or

In devout and joyful expectation,
let us call out to the Christ,
who is our salvation.

Silence

FIRST SUNDAY OF ADVENT
You came to turn the hearts of all
to love of God and neighbor:
Lord, come and save us.
You come to enrich us with gifts of grace
and knowledge:
Lord, come and save us.
You will come on a day we cannot know
and your words will endure:
Lord, come and save us.

The first candle is lit.

Almighty God, give us grace to cast away the works of darkness and put on the armor of light, now in the time of this mortal life in which Christ came among us in great humility; that in the last day, when he shall come again in glorious majesty to judge the living and the dead, we may rise to life immortal with him who lives and reigns for ever and ever.

—*Book of Common Prayer (BCP)*

Entrance chant (or instrumental music) and procession to chair resume; opening prayer is prayed.

SECOND SUNDAY OF ADVENT
You came as herald of the good tidings
of God's mercy and might:
Lord, come and save us.
You come to baptize in the Holy Spirit a
people to be your own:
Lord, come and save us.
You will come to establish a new heavens
and earth where righteousness will be
at home:
Lord, come and save us.

Two candles are lit.

Merciful God, you sent your messengers the prophets to preach repentance and prepare the way for our salvation. Give us grace to heed their warnings and forsake our sins, that we may greet with joy the coming of Jesus Christ our Redeemer, who lives and reigns for ever and ever.

—*BCP*, adapted

Entrance chant (or instrumental music) and procession to chair resume; opening prayer is prayed.

THIRD SUNDAY OF ADVENT
You came as God's anointed
bringing good news to the oppressed:
Lord, come and save us.
You come to stand among us
as the one we long for but do not know:
Lord, come and save us.
You will come as the God of peace
to accomplish our sanctification:
Lord, come and save us.

Three candles are lit.

Eternal God, you sent John the Baptist to prepare the way for the coming of your Son. Grant us the wisdom to see your purpose and openness to hear your will, that we, too, may prepare the way for Christ who is coming in power and glory to establish the kingdom of peace and justice and who is Lord for ever and ever.

—*Lutheran Book of Worship*, adapted

ADVENT: TEXTS FOR THE EUCHARISTIC ASSEMBLY 23

Entrance chant (or instrumental music) and procession to chair resume; opening prayer is prayed.

FOURTH SUNDAY OF ADVENT
You came as Son of David
    to establish the kingdom of God:
Lord, come and save us.
You come as Son of Mary
    to be Emmanuel, God-with-us:
Lord, come and save us.
You will come as Son of God
    to bring creation to fulfillment:
Lord, come and save us.

Four candles are lit.

Stir up your power, O Lord, and with great might come among us; and, because we are sorely hindered by our sins, let your bountiful grace and mercy speedily help and deliver us. We ask this through Christ our Lord.
    —BCP

Entrance chant (or instrumental music) and procession to chair resume; opening prayer is prayed.

or:

FIRST SUNDAY OF ADVENT
After the homily, use the blessing for the wreath found in the *Book of Blessings,* #1517–1519.

SECOND SUNDAY OF ADVENT
As we light the Advent wreath, let us pray that God's power may prepare our hearts and our world for the advent of the kingdom, the dawning of God's day of righteousness and peace.

Two candles are lit in silence. Presider then proclaims the opening prayer.

THIRD SUNDAY OF ADVENT
As we light the candles of our Advent wreath, let us pray that God's radiant splendor will bring the light of hope to those shadowed by oppression and enlighten our eyes to behold Christ in others.

Three candles are lit in silence. Presider then proclaims the opening prayer.

FOURTH SUNDAY OF ADVENT
As we light our wreath on this final Sunday of Advent, let us pray that we, like Mary, may welcome the mystery of Christ's coming into our lives and so become instruments of the coming of God's reign in all its fullness.

Four candles are lit in silence. Presider then proclaims the opening prayer.

Penitential Rite

[My brothers and sisters:]
coming together at the table of word and
    eucharist,
let us be alert to the advent of God
and prepare the way by turning from sin,
embracing justice and finding comfort in the
    Christ who promises peace.

FIRST SUNDAY OF ADVENT THROUGH
DECEMBER 16

Form Cii in the sacramentary or:

You came as redeemer to announce glad
    tidings of salvation:
Lord, have mercy.
You come as shepherd to gather and feed
    your people:
Christ, have mercy.
You will come as judge to establish a new
    heaven and earth:
Lord, have mercy.

DECEMBER 17–24
Messiah announced by the prophets and
    long-desired of earth:
Lord, have mercy.
Child borne in the Virgin's womb and
    awaited with love:
Christ, have mercy.
Lamb heralded by John and proclaimed
    as Savior:
Lord, have mercy.

LITURGY OF THE WORD

Dismissal of Catechumens

My dear friends: With the assurance of our loving support, this community sends you forth to reflect more deeply on the word we have shared. Our Advent prayer is that God bless you with every spiritual gift and strengthen you with the comfort of glad tidings, so that in due time you may share fully at the Lord's table and be found blameless on the day when Christ comes in glory.

General Intercessions

Invitation to prayer

The advent of our God heralds the dawn of a new heaven and earth where righteousness and peace will be at home. Let our prayer give voice to the longings of all the human race for the coming of God's reign in our midst.

LITURGY OF THE EUCHARIST

Introduction to the Lord's Prayer

In joyful expectation of the dawning of the
    day of the Lord,
let us lift up our [hands and our] voices to
    pray as Jesus taught us:
Our Father . . .

Invitation to Communion

Behold the Lamb of God, who takes away
    the sins of the world;
the Savior whose coming will be the dawn
    of righteousness and peace.
Blessed are those called to the banquet
    of the Lamb.

CONCLUDING RITE

Dismissal of Eucharistic Ministers

Go forth in peace to the sick and homebound of our community, bearing the word of life and the body of Christ together with the assurance of our love and concern. Be to our brothers and sisters heralds of glad tidings and ministers of Christ's abiding presence.

Dismissal

Go in peace to prepare the way of the Lord.

NOTES

CHRISTMAS

The Season

Orientation / 29
ICEL Pastoral Introduction: Season of Christmas / 30
Perspective on the Season / 31
Purpose of the Season / 34
Presentation of the Season / 35
Preparing the Parish / 41
Taking It Home / 41
Other Ritual Prayers and Sacraments / 41
The Worship Environment / 42

The Calendar

December 25 – January 12 / 43

Liturgical Texts

Texts for the Eucharistic Assembly / 52
Texts for a Christmas Vigil / 53
Texts for a New Year's Vigil / 54
Proclamation of the Birth of Christ / 56
Proclamation of the Date of Easter / 58

Orientation

THE pastor said to the music director, "Thank heaven the preparation of the gifts doesn't take very long—even with incense! That means we can leave out the 'myrrh' verse. It's so depressing and doesn't fit in at all with the spirit of the season!" He was referring to "We three kings":

> Myrrh is mine: its bitter perfume
> Breathes a life of gathering gloom;
> Sorrowing, sighing, bleeding, dying,
> Sealed in the stone cold tomb.

This anecdote met with general agreement on the part of diocesan musicians gathered for a post-Christmas social, several folks heartily concurring with the pastor's judgment. Some pointed out approvingly that most new hymnals had judiciously "amended" another well-known carol, "What child is this?"

But the authentic spirit of the liturgy sides with the *Lutheran Book of Worship,* which retains the original words:

> Nails, spear shall pierce him through,
> The cross be borne for me, for you;
> Hail, hail the Word made flesh,
> The babe, the son of Mary.

The issue here is not a Scrooge-like desire to keep Christmas from being too enjoyable. At stake is the power of the gospel! The term *paschal mystery* embraces all that Christ did for humanity's salvation. This includes the events we celebrate at Christmastime, though we do not usually associate them with the passion and the cross. The infancy stories are undoubtedly some of the loveliest scenes ever enshrined in the human heart. The most tender songs and loveliest art have fashioned them into a cherished part of Christian culture. They are literally "gospel"— "glad tidings of great joy," as the angel told the shepherds.

But the gospel is not comfort only. It is challenge, too, or it is not the gospel at all! It demands a choice: acceptance or rejection. Indifference, too, is a choice: an alternate form of rejection! So Matthew and Luke, whose infancy narratives provide the principal gospels of Christmastime, are not just telling lovely stories. Though using a form that touches our deepest emotions and arouses the most poignant sentiments, the evangelists of Christ's infancy are presenting "the essential gospel story in miniature" (Raymond Brown, *An Adult Christ at Christmas,* Liturgical Press, 1978). The characters surrounding the Christ child prefigure, one and all, the cast who will be close at hand when the hour of the passion arrives: lowly shepherds, curious Gentiles, nervous authorities of the sacred and secular worlds, and, of course,

the Virgin Mother who "pondered all these things in her heart."

The task of preacher and presider, liturgy planner and music minister, is thus crucial. Our goal is to help the assembly celebrate this most lovely of liturgical seasons in such a way as to incarnate its saving power in word and song, in visual beauty and in prayerful silence. But the power of the Christmas liturgy flows ultimately from the Lord's paschal mystery. This must shine forth clearly in the mode and mood of our celebration. Drawn to the wood of the manger, we are directed toward the wood of the cross. So true is this that the ancient liturgical manuals of the Orthodox Church call Christmas and Easter by the same term: Pascha! It is this "paschal perspective" from which ICEL's Pastoral Introduction: Season of Christmas is written.

ICEL Pastoral Introduction: Season of Christmas

1 The season of Christmas begins with Evening Prayer I of Christmas and concludes with the Feast of the Baptism of the Lord, that is, the Sunday after Epiphany or after 6 January. This season celebrates the birth of Christ and his early manifestations, and the church considers it second only to the annual celebration of the Easter mystery.

2 In the earliest centuries, the church had but one feast, the weekly and yearly celebration of the paschal mystery. Soon the church began to celebrate the birth and manifestation of Christ, the sun of justice (see Malachi 4:2) and light of the world (see John 8:12). This feast coincided with the winter solstice. Since the days of Saint Leo the Great, the texts of the season have expressed the church's understanding of Christmas as more than the simple commemoration of a historical event. It is rather the celebration of a mystery, not a separate mystery independent of the paschal mystery but the beginnings of that mystery of salvation. From the first moments of his human existence, Christ was achieving humanity's redemption. The Christ who was to die and rise for us is recognized as the incarnate Son of God: "Today a new day dawns, the day of our redemption, prepared by God from ages past, the beginning of our never ending gladness."

3 A high point of the Christmas celebration is the reading of Saint John's prologue, which proclaims that "the Word was made flesh and lived among us" (John 1:14). All the readings and prayers lead up to, or echo, this conviction, proclaimed by the great councils of Nicaea, Ephesus and Chalcedon and celebrated in the Christmas liturgy as the "holy exchange," whereby "we come to share in the divinity of Christ, who humbled himself to share in our humanity."

4 The church celebrates the one true light, the light that banishes darkness.

- The Christmas image of light, of night giving way to day, is reinforced by the sequence of the Mass texts. Texts are provided for Christmas Masses in the evening (vigil), at midnight, at dawn and during the day. The texts of these several celebrations are meant to be used at the actual time of day indicated by the titles of the celebrations.

- The Gloria is inspired by the song of the angels at the birth of Christ (see Luke 2:14). On Christmas night it is heard for the first time since the beginning of Advent. On this occasion above all others it should be sung by the whole assembly with joy and festive fervor.

- Eucharistic Prayer I has an interpolation that may be inserted after the Sanctus on Christmas and during its octave.

- Symbols of the triumph of light over darkness and of life over death, for example, in some places candlelight and evergreens, are traditionally used to decorate the church and assist devotion.

- The rich images of new light and new life provide many creative possibilities for decorating the church in harmony with the local culture and traditions. The symbol of light recalls the Christian celebration of Easter and helps to link the incarnation with the paschal mystery of salvation. The symbol will be expressed differently in the Northern Hemisphere, where Christmas occurs at the winter solstice, and the Southern Hemisphere, where it coincides with the height of summer.

- The manger scene can be of great assistance to all in recalling the story and the circumstances of Jesus' birth in history and in rekindling a sense of wonder and simplicity. By its design or location, however, it should not displace or overshadow the signs of the Lord's real presence and activity in word and sacrament, in the assembly and in its ministers.

5 Christmas has its own octave, during which the feasts of Saint Stephen (26 December), Saint

John (27 December) and the Holy Innocents (28 December) are celebrated. These saints are seen as having a particular relation to the Christmas mystery and were traditionally honored as "companions of Christ." The Sunday occurring within the octave is celebrated as the feast of the Holy Family.

6 The octave day itself, 1 January, is observed as the Solemnity of Mary, Mother of God, and like the Fourth Sunday of Advent it highlights the role of the Blessed Virgin Mary in the incarnation and manifestation of the Lord. It also recalls the conferral of the name of Jesus. In some places people seek God's blessing for the year that begins on this day.

7 In the Eastern churches the Solemnity of the Epiphany was the original feast of Christ's birth. When adopted by the West, it became a celebration of the revelation of God's eternal plan of salvation in Christ, manifested as "the light to enlighten all nations" and represented traditionally in the story of the Magi. From early times it was associated also with a commemoration of the Lord's baptism when he was anointed as Messiah and revealed as God's Son.

- The Epiphany is celebrated on 6 January or, wherever it is not observed as a day of obligation, on the Sunday falling between 2 and 8 January.
- The custom of keeping Christmas decorations until Epiphany has been celebrated helps to show that Christmas and Epiphany are but two aspects of the same feast. It would be even more appropriate to extend this custom through the celebration of the Baptism of the Lord, the close of the season of Christmas.

8 The Baptism of the Lord is now celebrated separately on the Sunday after 6 January. (In those places where the Epiphany is transferred to the Sunday falling on 7 or 8 January, the Baptism of the Lord is celebrated on the following Monday.) The Baptism of the Lord brings to a close the Christmas season and recalls the opening of Jesus' public mission and ministry. The voice from the cloud acknowledging Christ as the beloved Son of God ushers the church into Ordinary Time and its weekly proclamation of the life and teaching of the Lord.

Perspective on the Season

THE Pastoral Introduction's presentation of the Christmas season can best be described as inclusive. Its intent is to keep the broad sweep of the whole liturgical year in clear perspective, even while focusing on the specific season at hand. Thus the Christmas season is considered within the setting of the paschal mystery. But even the season's immediate content is set forth in terms far more inclusive than those we commonly use when thinking about Christmas.

SETTING

The term paschal mystery occurs three times in the first two paragraphs. Sunday has been described as a "little Easter." Historical reality points in the opposite direction: Easter is a big Sunday! Sunday, the first Christian feast day, is the *weekly* Pascha. Easter is the *yearly* Pascha (see *Proclamation of the Date of Easter*, page 58). Then there evolves the "*winter* Pascha" (in Schmemann's wonderful expression): "the beginning of our never ending gladness" (PI, 2). From the first moments of the Child's human existence, we see in the flesh that redemptive love of God that will be fully revealed only on the cross. Reminding us that this season is "not a separate mystery independent of the paschal mystery," the Pastoral Introduction affirms Raymond Brown's insight that Christmas is a proclamation "in miniature" of the whole gospel.

Modern research into the origins of the liturgical year intensifies this link between the winter and spring paschas, between Christmas and Easter. This overthrows a theory we've all assumed to be unassailable fact. Supported by an impressive amount of research, the preeminent scholar of the Christian calendar, Thomas J. Talley, states the challenge:

> For two hundred years it has been popular to say that Christmas is a Christian adoption and adaptation of the Roman pagan festival *Dies natalis solis invicti,* the birthday of the invincible sun. That was not a festival of great antiquity at Rome. It was established on 25 December, the traditional (but inaccurate) winter solstice date, by the Emperor Aurelian in the Year of our Lord 274. Those who seek to base Christmas on this festival seldom give full weight to its late institution (Thomas J. Talley, *Reforming Tradition,* 132).

It is highly unlikely, says Talley, that a persecuted minority would so wholeheartedly adopt a pagan god's feast! Furthermore, newly analyzed documentation shows Christmas being observed in North Africa well before Constantine became emperor. If Christians did not come up with December 25 as the birth of Christ by "baptizing" a pagan feast, where did it come from?

Talley's research shows that early Christians wanted to determine precisely the actual date of Christ's death. According to scripture, he suffered on 14 Nisan. Roman Christians computed the 14th day of the spring moon in that year of crucifixion to have coincided with the Roman date March 25. In Semitic tradition, patriarchs were born and died on the same date. That tradition was enhanced in Christ's case to include his conception. Texts from Augustine and others show that Christians believed Christ had been conceived and died on the same date. Counting forward, then, from the conception date of March 25, they determined his date of birth to be December 25.

There is nothing wrong with wanting to anchor ourselves in history—especially salvation history! But we need to remember that we are celebrating a mystery, not simply commemorating a historical event! Making Christmas just a remembrance or a symbolic reliving seems to make the past events more present to the imagination. But the opposite happens! The celebration is emptied of transformative power; the impact of the saving event is removed from the present. The mystery is relegated to the realm of make-believe or "let's pretend." Think, for instance, of birthday cakes and congregational renditions of "Happy Birthday, dear Jesus." However well-intentioned or warmly received, these practices blur the focus. Reflective adults—and children!—sense a trivializing of something profound.

From solid liturgy derives right belief. Good theology, in turn, leads to solid pastoral practice. And then all things work together for good. Already celebrating Christ's birth and believing his paschal mystery, Christians could see, even in the festivals of a pagan sun god, traces of the handiwork of the Lord who owns the planet, "the Sun of justice rising with healing in his wings" (Malachi 4:2). Words and silence, music and art, the elements of earth and the signs in the heavens: All are consecrated to the service of the living God.

CONTENT

The Pastoral Introduction retains the title "Season of Christmas," an expression hallowed by tradition and dear to the heart. But the description of the season's content makes it clear that we are not celebrating exclusively, or even primarily, the nativity of Christ. Rather, the whole mystery of the incarnation must claim our attention, more precisely "[Christ's] early manifestations" (PI, 1, 6–8). It's a mystery to which we can relate, as the liturgy lets Christ's days unfold very much like our own: brightened by beauty and tenderness, clouded by conflict and pain.

■ CHRISTMAS DAY/MARY'S DAY (December 25, 1996/January 1, 1997): Solemnity and octave day, child and mother, covenant and name. Two solemnities bracket an eight-day celebration, one of two "octaves" retained in the liturgical calendar (the other is Easter). Unique as his conception was, Christ's birth was remarkably like the birth of every other Jew, "born of a woman, born under the law" (Galatians 4:4). Luke presents a particularly modern image: Christ's birth occurs in the context of an empire-wide census. Reduced to the level of a statistic, the only-begotten Son, the long-desired of nations achieves instant solidarity with us who often feel like mere numbers in the database of an anonymous society. As with every birth, believing eyes see a deeper mystery at work, a providence both human and divine. Matthew traces the human descent of the mystery; John marks the divine lineage of "the hopes and fears of all the years" that meet in this particular birth.

After a considerable shuffling of names over the centuries, the octave day of Christmas has settled on a seventh-century Roman title: Mary, Mother of God. Various influences have attached other themes to this day. The Eastern church continues to designate it (as the pre-1960 Roman rite did) "Circumcision of the Lord." Episcopal and Lutheran churches celebrate the bestowal of the name Jesus. And, in the midst of the Vietnam conflict, Paul VI made this first day of the civil year a day of prayer for world peace.

■ COMPANIONS OF CHRIST/THE CHRISTMAS OCTAVE (December 26–31, 1996): The newborn Messiah's liturgical entourage consists of "saints . . . seen as having a particular relation to the Christmas mystery" (PI, 5). They appear in the Christmas octave like blood-red berries on Christmas holly, for they bore witness at the cost of suffering, in most cases even unto blood. There is Stephen (December 26), first martyr after the Lord's resurrection, whose passion is patterned on Christ's and whose final words commending his spirit and pardoning his persecutors echo those of Christ. John the Evangelist (December 27) gives his name to the gospel that celebrates Christ as word and light. And the revelation that bears John's name affirms his willingness to suffer "persecution ... and patient endurance ... because of the word of God and testimony of Jesus" (Revelation 1:9). In the Holy Innocents (December 28), "The child makes of those as yet unable to speak fit witnesses to himself.... They cannot speak, yet they bear witness to Christ. They cannot use their limbs to engage in battle, yet already they bear the palm of victory" (Office of Readings).

Two optional memorials likewise occur, the first overtaken this year by Sunday. Thomas Becket's (December 29) "murder in the cathedral" (repeated in our own age in the martyrdom of Archbishop Romero of San Salvador) has inspired pilgrimages, playwrights, poetry and even an ongoing mystery, *The Quest for Becket's Bones* (New Haven: Yale University Press, 1995). Sylvester I (December 31) was bishop of Rome when Constantine's peace gave Christians the "luxury" of internal discord. Doctrinal disputes and schism were the order of Pope Sylvester's day. With their names inscribed on the days immediately following Christmas, these saints forge a living link of fidelity and witness between the beginnings of our salvation and its consummation in the paschal mystery.

Keeping alive our communion with these friends on the calendar is only one dimension of keeping the liturgy but an important one. If we keep the liturgy, the liturgy will keep us in focus and focused on Christ, who is incarnate also in this year of grace in the lovely and the unloved of our own day.

■ HOLY FAMILY (Sunday in the Christmas Octave, December 29, 1996): Like the octave day of Christmas, this observance has had its share of assigned dates and even a period of suppression. It enters the universal calendar just before the Great Depression, coincidentally during an influx of immigration to North America. These two events placed enormous burdens on family life. Liturgists have pointed out correctly that like so many "modern" feasts (e.g., Christ the King, Joseph the Worker), this is an "idea feast," not the celebration of a saving mystery. But the feast was promoted warmly by Leo XIII, a man of articulate sensitivity to the plight of working people. And it was loved by John XXIII, a sturdy peasant who attributed his instinctively compassionate heart to the nurturing atmosphere of a strong and stable family. Perhaps these popes saw a special relevance to celebrating Christ's manifestation within a family that was not only holy but, according to the gospels, also quite human.

The three-year lectionary presents Christ's human family besieged externally by hostile forces (Year A) and beset internally by parent-child misunderstandings (Year C). This year (Year B) we meet a family strikingly like our own: going to great difficulty to comply with legal requirements. This is surely an aspect of the paschal mystery important to reflect on and to celebrate: a family filled with hopes and premonitions, potential and powerlessness, the lot of every human family.

■ EPIPHANY TO BAPTISM OF THE LORD (January 5–12, 1997):

> In second century Ephesus, the Epiphany marked the beginning of the course reading of the Gospel of John, a reading brought to its conclusion with the reading of this gospel's passion narrative at Pascha. In my own study of the origins of the Christian year I have suggested that the same was or became true of the Gospel of Matthew at Jerusalem and of the Gospel of Mark at Alexandria. The complex themeology of the Epiphany derives from the variety in the beginnings of the gospels, one or another of which, I believe, was read on the Epiphany. Matthew begins with the nativity story, including the visit of the Magi; Mark with the baptism of Jesus in the Jordan; John with both of these, perhaps, but in close connection with the wedding at Cana (Talley, 135).

In most older Latin altar missals, the woodcuts for January 6 present a triptych: adoration of the Magi, baptism at the Jordan, wedding feast at Cana. Even the new *Liturgy of the Hours* has antiphons for the gospel canticles at Morning and Evening Prayer on January 6 that unite these three events.

> Today the Bridegroom claims his bride, the church, since Christ has washed her sins away in Jordan's waters; the Magi hasten with their gifts to the royal wedding; and the wedding guests rejoice, for Christ has changed water into wine, Alleluia (Morning Prayer).

Three mysteries mark this holy day: today the star leads the Magi to the infant Christ; today water is changed into wine for the wedding feast; today Christ wills to be baptized by John in the river Jordan to bring us salvation (Evening Prayer).

The current Roman calendar separates these manifestations of Christ into three distinct observances. Epiphany and the Lord's baptism are celebrated, in most places, on the two Sundays after New Year's Day. The wedding feast at Cana appears only in the gospel of Year C.

But despite fragmentation of the single theme of Christ's manifestation into several celebrations, the unity of the season remains clear. The themes of light and light's increase are preserved carefully through Christmas' "Twelve Days" and beyond. Words and images provide a common thread, a liturgical "timeline" running through the whole season: the glory of the angelic choir over the hillside on the outskirts of Bethlehem, the star that guided the Magi, Simeon's canticle of the Child as "a light of revelation to the Gentiles," and the cloud overshadowing Jesus at the Jordan (PI, 7).

Purpose of the Season

As with Advent, so in Christmastime, the broad perspective of the season as well as its particular emphases are expressed well in the prefaces to the eucharistic prayer. Of Vatican II's many enrichments to the church's liturgical texts, the prefaces are among the most important. The Council's reform provides over five times as many prefaces as before (16 in the 1962 Tridentine Missal, over 85 in the 1970 Missal of Paul VI). Just as we can barely imagine the absence of a weekday lectionary, it is hard to remember that before the Council there were no Advent prefaces at all, only one for Christmas and another for Epiphany. Now there are three for Christmas, one for Epiphany, one for the Lord's baptism. They capsulize the theology and spirituality of the season.

Preface of Christmas I, "Christ the Light," begins immediately with a reference to John's prologue:

> In the mystery of the Word made flesh
> your glory fills the eyes of our mind . . .

Then it sings of the twofold movement God initiates in the incarnation:

> . . . seeing God made visible in Christ,
> we are caught up in love of things we cannot
>   see.

Christmas II, a new composition drawing on the homilies of Leo the Great, subtly links incarnation with paschal mystery in the title "Universal Restoration in the Incarnation." The wedding of opposites is celebrated in these beautiful lines:

> . . . the God we cannot see
> has now appeared in human form.
> The one begotten before all ages
> begins to live in time.

Christmas Preface III, drawn from ancient sacramentaries, celebrates the "Exchange in the Incarnation of the Word." This "marvelous exchange" is a series of "redemptive paradoxes":

> . . . your eternal Word assumes human frailty,
> our mortal nature takes on immortal value.

> . . . this union between God and ourselves
> makes us sharers in eternal life.

In the Northern Hemisphere, the steadily growing light in nature mirrors the growing light of salvation. The Epiphany Preface combines echoes of Christmas liturgical texts, the Magi story (Matthew) and the presentation (Luke). Christ is "the light to enlighten all nations," and

> Now that he has appeared in our mortal flesh,
> you have refashioned us in the image of his
>   immortal glory.

Finally, the Preface of the Lord's Baptism recapitulates the principal "conviction" celebrated in the Christmas season (PI, 3):

> . . . a voice came down from heaven
> to waken our faith in your Word dwelling
>   among us;

It also "ushers the church into Ordinary Time and its weekly proclamation of the life and teaching of the Lord" (PI, 8):

> . . . Christ your servant
> was anointed with the oil of gladness
> and was sent to preach the good news to
>   the poor.

Presentation of the Season

FROM the treasury of liturgical words and images that fill the Christmas season, the Pastoral Introduction directs our attention to the principal motifs of new light and new life. Our ancestors in the faith left us a great inheritance in their creative correlation of the worlds of nature and revelation. We call this "inculturation," and the Pastoral Introduction notes that the approach will vary from place to place (PI, 4). The Northern and Southern Hemispheres, for instance, must necessarily incorporate the symbol of light into the Christmas liturgy in different ways, for the winter solstice in the north coincides with the height of summer in the south. Wherever the liturgy is being planned and prepared, the challenge to the liturgist is the same: to facilitate a creative and life-giving interaction between the tradition's resources and the community's reality. The Pastoral Introduction considers a number of elements, both traditional and contemporary, that are part of this season's liturgical configuration; that listing provides a helpful outline for planners and presiders.

INTRODUCTORY RITES

Even before the words of greeting are spoken, the ritual of greeting should welcome the assembly and set the tone. Reflections on the ritual beginning of Advent Masses suggest a contrasting or complementary opening for Christmas liturgies. On Christmas Eve itself (whether early or at midnight), Mass should begin with an opening rite that echoes, but does not compete with, the uniqueness of the Easter Vigil. A suggested order of service for Christmas Eve appears in the calendar (pages 44–45). In the absence of a prescribed vigil in the Roman rite, this *Sourcebook* offers some of the Ambrosian rite's resources of texts and prayers, reminiscent of the Easter Vigil.

The United States' *Sacramentary Supplement* (New York: Catholic Book, 1994) provides a new form of *The Proclamation of the Birth of Christ* with suggestions for use at Midnight Mass or the Liturgy of the Hours. A traditional form is on page 56. At other Masses, sing a beloved Christmas carol during a solemn incensation of the altar to provide an experience of sight, sound and smell that establishes a perfect setting for words of welcome and a joyful Gloria.

■ GREETINGS: Adapted from the Spanish-language sacramentary and *Book of Blessings,* greetings appear among Christmastime texts on page 52. The first is a good keynote for the whole season, emphasizing God's manifestation in Christ. The third hearkens back to Advent's candle lighting and points toward the paschal mystery. Good ritual practice suggests that whatever is chosen should remain through the whole season.

■ PENITENTIAL RITE: Formulas appear on page 52 and also at Ciii in the sacramentary, but an option recently approved by the United States bishops (awaiting Roman confirmation) permits omission of the penitential rite whenever the Gloria is prescribed. The goal is to establish a strong ritual beginning that fits the character of the season. The Pastoral Introduction emphasizes the importance and appropriateness of the sung Gloria during Christmastime (PI, 4). Adding a penitential rite seems to interrupt the flow of festive incensation, solemn greeting and canticle of praise.

■ BLESSING AND SPRINKLING OF HOLY WATER: This rite could take place on Epiphany and the Lord's baptism, linking the two celebrations ritually and acknowledging that Epiphany once celebrated both "manifestations." Incensation and greeting remain, followed by the water blessing. In some parishes the Gloria accompanies the sprinkling of the assembly.

Some communities take the Feast of the Baptism of the Lord as an opportunity to renew baptismal vows, sprinkling with water after the homily, as on Easter Sunday. This may at first seem appropriate, but there are several reasons to hesitate. In the Roman rite, the usual place in the Order of Mass for the sprinkling with water is the introductory rite, immediately after the water blessing. These blessings refer to the water specifically as a reminder of baptism, our "passageway" to word and eucharist. On Easter, the only day on which the sprinkling takes place after the liturgy of the word, there is no water blessing because the water for sprinkling has been blessed at the Easter Vigil. A renewal of baptismal vows after the homily on the Feast of the Baptism of the Lord would require an overburdened rite: water blessing, renewal of vows

and sprinkling. Nor should anything be done on this day that might seem to lessen the uniqueness of Easter as the primary festival of initiation and baptismal renewal.

- THE COLLECTS: The opening prayers (collects) provided for the Christmas Masses reinforce "the Christmas image of light, of night giving way to day" (PI, 4). There are subtle, and not so subtle, echoes of paschal words and images. The Pastoral Introduction points out that each text is to be used at the actual time of day for which it is prescribed. This caution is based on experiences of ministerial carelessness and a past mistaken application to the sacramentary of a lectionary rubric that permits a "pastoral selection" from among the many readings of the several Christmas Masses. With the sacramentary texts, a thoughtful reading of the prayers reveals their power and beauty, and their potential usefulness as homiletic, devotional and educational resources.

CONCLUDING THE LITURGY OF THE WORD

- THE DISMISSAL OF THE CATECHUMENS: For an appropriate seasonal dismissal, see page 52. Each community will have its own program for the catechumens, formed perhaps in part by diocesan guidelines. But the *Rite of Christian Initiation of Adults* itself suggests some appropriate content:

> The instruction that the catechumens receive during this period should be of a kind that while presenting Catholic teaching in its entirety also enlightens faith, directs the heart toward God, fosters participation in the liturgy, inspires apostolic activity and nurtures a life completely in accord with the spirit of Christ (78).

While these "after dismissal" sessions are not, strictly speaking, instructional, their formative value can draw much power from the liturgy. These periods would seem to be especially suitable not only for reflecting on and praying over the biblical texts but the seasonal euchological texts as well. Direct the attention of the catechumens especially to the collects and prefaces of Christmastime as rich sources of solid theology and spirituality. Remember, too, that many Christmas carols are well known far beyond the setting of church and worship. Those familiar to the catechumens could be helpful in orienting them to this season's prayerful beauty and gospel challenge. Those that aren't familiar could be shared as an important and endearing part of the faith and family the catechumens are preparing to embrace.

- PROFESSION OF FAITH AT CHRISTMAS MASSES: Twice a year, liturgical language is highlighted by body language during the profession of faith. The words that express our faith in the incarnation are given a special, "experiential" reverence on Christmas and the Annunciation (March 25) by a genuflection during their pronouncement. In the pastoral experience of many, this genuflection just doesn't work. For one thing, no liturgical gesture can be a meaningful experience of reverence if it sneaks up on the assembly twice a year. More basically, however, the dramatic twice-yearly genuflection makes no sense if the weekly prescribed bow never happens. This seems to be the case in many parishes.

What is at stake here is not simply an insignificant rubric but a traditional Catholic — incarnational — instinct to involve the whole self, all our senses, in the act of prayer. Even where such an approach is a familiar reality, it will most likely be necessary to alert the assembly to the genuflection in a brief invitation before the profession of faith. Because the invitation to a posture of prayer is similar to that used during the solemn prayers of Good Friday, these or similar words are appropriately spoken by the deacon:

> Today, as we profess our faith together, let us genuflect at those words that enshrine our belief that the Word of God has indeed become flesh to dwell among us.

Once set to some of the most stately chants in the church's Gregorian repertoire, the profession of faith might again be sung on this feast.

- PROCLAMATION OF THE DATE OF EASTER ON EPIPHANY: The *Sacramentary Supplement* (1994) contains an optional "Proclamation of the Date of Easter on Epiphany." The *Ceremonial of Bishops* (#240) encourages observance of the custom, and this *Sourcebook* has carried a form of the proclamation yearly. Although its practical purpose predates wide availability of printed calendars, the symbolic value of the proclamation endures. The clear message of the text is that Christ's Pascha is central to the church's life in this and in every year, the fountain from which all feasts flow, the reason we pay honor to Mary and the saints as believers in whom Christ's passover mystery has triumphed. The ritual message can likewise be powerful.

The proclamation is made from the ambo. The *Ceremonial of Bishops* notes that a deacon or other minister may vest in a cope for the proclamation, giving unspoken, visual honor to the action. Especially when chanted, it serves as solemn consecration of the new calendar year.

LITURGY OF THE EUCHARIST

■ PREFACES: We have already looked at the rich theology and prayerful beauty of the Christmastime prefaces. Choose among three Christmas prefaces for the solemnity and throughout the octave (even when saints' days occur). In fact, although the Epiphany preface may be used on weekdays following that solemnity, so may the Christmas prefaces, right up to the Feast of the Baptism of the Lord. The second and third Christmas prefaces are strikingly appropriate even after Epiphany, since they celebrate restoration of unity to creation, universal salvation and the "divinization" of our human nature in Christ. These are the special scriptural themes of Epiphany week, with its selections from the First Letter of John and gospel passages about Christ's healing outreach to Israel and beyond it to the Gentiles.

On the Solemnity of Mary, Mother of God (January 1), the sacramentary specifies the Preface of the Blessed Virgin I (inserting the name of the feast, "Motherhood") or II (which incorporates phrases from the Magnificat). Since this rubric was written, a third Marian Preface has been added. See the Votive Mass of Mary, Mother of the Church, found in appendix X of the 1985 sacramentary, for a preface titled "Mary, Model and Mother of the Church."

A new source for good euchological texts is the *Collection of Masses of the Blessed Virgin Mary*. In the Christmas Season section of this volume are several Mass formularies centered around titles of Mary related to the Christmas mystery.

■ EUCHARISTIC PRAYER: Eucharistic Prayer I (the Roman Canon) has special inserts for Christmas Day, its octave and Epiphany. The use of variable seasonal prefaces with Eucharistic Prayers for Reconciliation is now permitted. Reconciliation II with one of the Christmas prefaces might be a good choice on weekdays after Epiphany. Although it is always supposed to be used with its own preface, Eucharistic Prayer IV seems appropriate on the feast of the Lord's baptism with its lyrical praise of Christ who

> lived as one of us in all things but sin.
> To the poor he proclaimed the good news
>   of salvation,
> to prisoners, freedom, and to those in sorrow, joy.

■ COMMUNION RITE: Sample texts for the introduction to the Lord's Prayer, and the invitation to communion are given on page 53.

CONCLUDING RITES

■ SENDING EUCHARISTIC MINISTERS: A seasonal text for sending eucharistic ministers to the sick and homebound is on page 53.

■ BLESSINGS: There are three solemn blessings for the Christmas season:

Christmas: ICEL's proposed revision greatly simplifies the long individual paragraphs of the Christmastime formula by fashioning an introductory sentence from their several phrases. This introduction emphasizes the darkness/light theme characteristic of Christmastime. The blessing members continue that theme, introduce a sense of the assembly's mission as "heralds of the gospel," and speak beautifully of the peace and goodwill celebrated in the carols and customs of the season.

January 1: The solemn blessing "Beginning of the Year" is obviously appropriate. Unfortunately it does not incorporate explicitly the scriptural and liturgical themes associated with the season. The solemn blessing for feasts of Mary mentions both Christ's birth and the redemption of the human race.

Epiphany: The solemn blessing for Epiphany successfully incorporates and recapitulates the seasonal themes. It mentions enlightenment of the world in Christ and our call as Christ's disciples to be a source of that light to our brothers and sisters.

■ DISMISSAL: For a seasonal dismissal, see page 53.

MUSIC

The Episcopal Church's *Hymnal 1982 Companion: Volume I* (New York: Church Hymnal Corp., 1990) quotes Richard Greene's explanation of the English word *carol:*

a direct borrowing of the Old French *carole*, which means a round dance in which the participants provide their own music by singing an alteration of a choral part, a burden (refrain) and uniform stanzas assigned to a soloist who leads the dance, the "ringleader," in fact (282).

Along with folk carols, sometimes associated with various Christmas customs, are more biblically and doctrinally oriented hymns. These retain some folk-carol "feel" and often are set to folk tunes. Familiar and beloved carols are sacramental in the deepest sense of that word. They both signify and effect the presence of Christ in the world, for they are heard at this time of the year not only as church hymnody but even as mall music. Many are truly known "by heart": A mere snippet of tune or text conjures up deepest joy or poignant pain.

■ GLORIA IN EXCELSIS: The Pastoral Introduction points out that the Gloria is an important part of the Christmas liturgy especially on Christmas night, both because the assembly has abstained from its joy throughout Advent and because it is inspired by the angels' song at Christ's birth (PI, 4). If the simplification of the introductory rites approved by the United States' bishops is confirmed by Rome, the Gloria will stand out as central to the distinctive beginning of Christmastime liturgies. The entrance procession (and perhaps a festive incensation) would lead directly into this song of praise.

"The whole assembly" should sing the Gloria on Christmas night, says the Pastoral Introduction, though there ought to be some participation whenever the Gloria is sung. Since "joy and festive fervor" are keynotes of this song (PI, 4), strength and attractiveness are musical qualities for which to look. Ideally the same setting will be used until the feast of the Lord's baptism, underscoring the unity of the season. Performance could be enhanced and musical interest sustained by vocal harmonies, handbells, flute, trumpet or whatever embellishments are available at each celebration.

The well-known "Gloria in excelsis Deo" from "Angels we have heard on high" provides an easy assembly refrain in several settings. "A Christmas Gloria" by Paul Gibson (OCP, 9551), for assembly, cantor, SATB choir, organ and trumpet in C, features imaginative use of this carol's melodic material for unison verses. Daniel Laginya's "Christmas Gloria" (GIA, G-2971) is a nice setting for cantor and congregation, as are Glorias by Benedictine composers Columba Kelly in *The Collegeville Hymnal* (Liturgical Press) and Becket Senchur's "Mass of Hope" in *The People's Mass Book* (World Library Publications). These invite creativity when used with choir and/or instruments. Richard Proulx's "Gloria for Christmastime" (GIA, G-3085) employs two-part mixed voices, cantor and congregation (with a flute/oboe obligato). Look also at the "Chant-style Gloria" with optional Christmas refrain by Howard Hughes (WLP, 8534) and Peter Jones' "Glory to God" (OCP), especially good if brass is available, and Steven Janco's "Glory to God" (WLP, 8559). Almost any setting of the Gloria can be made more festive by imaginative use of handbells and by dividing verses between the choir's men and women.

■ RESPONSORIAL PSALM: Proper psalms for solemnities and feasts are in the lectionary with the rest of the proper readings; seasonal psalms and refrains are found at #174 and #175.

Christmastime: Psalm 98, with the refrain "All the ends of the earth have seen the saving power of God," may be used throughout Christmastime. A different psalm is provided for Epiphany and the Lord's baptism, but Psalm 98 with its message of universal salvation is still appropriate. Several suggested arrangements include:

- David Haas and Marty Haugen, "All the ends of the earth" (GIA, G-2703)
- Rawn Harbor, "Psalm for Christmas," *Lead Me Guide Me* (GIA), #504
- David Isele, "All the ends of the earth," *Psalms for the Church Year* (GIA, G-2262)
- Richard Proulx and John Hirten, "Psalm for Christmas Day" (GIA, G-3631)
- Michael Joncas, "All the ends of the earth" (GIA, G-3431)
- James Marchionda, "Psalm 98," *Psalms for the Cantor*, volume II (WLP)
- Mary Kay Beall's arrangement for children (with Christmas descant) in *Sing Out! A Children's Psalter* (WLP, 7990)

Psalm 147 with the refrain "The Word of God became flesh and dwelt among us" is proposed by the new Canadian hymnal *Catholic Book of Worship III* as an alternative seasonal psalm for Christmas.

Holy Family: Psalm 128 with the refrain "Happy are those who fear the Lord and walk in his ways," a classic wedding psalm, is appropriate on a feast that celebrates the family. There are a number of arrangements; the Gelineau setting and refrain is perhaps the best known. *We Celebrate* (World Library) contains a setting by Ron Rendek (#257).

Mary, Mother of God: Psalm 67 with the refrain "May God bless us in his mercy" is an invocation of God's blessing on the new year. Consider Robert Batastini's expanded form in *Worship III* and the Canadian hymnal's variation, "O God, be gracious and bless us, and let your face shine upon us."

Epiphany: Psalm 72 with the refrain "Lord, every nation on earth will adore you" is prescribed. Many settings are available: GIA's *Worship III* offers five; *Service Music for the Mass*, vol. 1, from World Library has a setting by Noel Goemanne.

Baptism of the Lord: Psalm 29 with the refrain "The Lord will bless his people with peace" is prescribed. In the new lectionary, Year B will feature a "responsorial canticle," Isaiah 12 with the refrain "You will draw water joyfully from the springs of salvation." This currently appears in the Easter Vigil as the response to Reading V. World Library offers two fine settings, one from Donald Regan (WLP, 8529) and one from Bob Moore (WLP, 8579).

- GOSPEL ACCLAMATIONS: Verses that supplement those proper to the season's several solemnities and feasts are at #212 and #219 in the lectionary. In looking for suitable quotes to use with parish handouts, participation aids and mailings, these liturgical texts are perfect. They communicate, in a concise way and rhythmic form, the spirit of the season and can provide a good springboard for personal prayer.

- EUCHARISTIC PRAYER: Whether the parish uses the same acclamations for both Advent and Christmastime, or a set unique to each season, Advent's simplicity will undoubtedly give way to a more festive sound for Christmastime. A good way to facilitate participation, as guests and strangers join year-round participants, is to employ festive settings that feature a cantor-assembly call and response. Howard Hughes' *Mass of the Divine Word* (GIA G-2415), Christopher Walker's *Glastonbury Eucharistic Acclamations* (OCP, 7165) and William Ferris' *Music for the Banquet* (WLP, 7555) are such arrangements.

- COMMUNION RITE: Christmas is a perfect time for congregations to start singing *during* the communion procession. An abundance of seasonal selections known to all eliminates the inconvenience of carrying participation aids. The parish's favorite carols, particularly those with refrains, are especially appropriate at communion throughout the season.

WORD OF GOD

The "sequence of Mass texts," says the Pastoral Introduction, reinforces the "Christmas image of light, of night giving way to day" (PI, 4). This should be understood as referring also to the scriptural passages that span the entire season. Picture the liturgical celebration of the mystery of the incarnation as sunrise on a crystal clear morning after the winter solstice: Light breaks at dawn, rises and reaches full zenith in the noonday blaze of epiphany and the shining cloud over the Jordan.

As in Advent, parish handouts or mailings should include references to the rich array of biblical texts that grace the season. Surveys and pastoral experience testify that a growing number of people take the time to prepare for communal worship by praying with the appointed scriptures when resources are provided.

With regard to the four sets of readings for Christmas itself, a rubrical clarification is in order. The 1970 United States edition of the lectionary notes before the Vigil Mass that its readings are used "on the afternoon of December 24" but adds confusingly "before or after First Vespers of Christmas." A further rubric suggests they "may also be used on Christmas Day with a choice from one of the three Christmas Masses." The new Canadian lectionary clarifies matters. Before the Vigil Mass readings it states:

> The readings below are intended for use at the eucharist celebrated during the afternoon of December 24, before or after first evening prayer, which is a separate vigil from the celebration of the Solemnity of Christmas. For the celebration of Christmas the readings for during the night are used.

This new translation addresses a pastoral concern. The choice of Vigil Mass readings seems to presume that the assembly is still awaiting Christmas and will reconvene later that night or in the morning to hear the traditional Christmas gospel. But because the Christmas Eve Mass will be the only liturgical event for many people, a strong pastoral case can be made for proclaiming the nativity story from the Gospel

of Luke. This rubric steers our choice toward the other sets of readings. A second rubric gives wide latitude to choices for the other Christmas Masses as well:

> The texts below [referring to the three Christmas Masses] may also be used for Masses on Christmas Day. The readings from any of the Christmas Masses may be used according to the pastoral needs of each celebration.

Here, however, an important caution is in order. The prologue of the Gospel of John is an ancient choice for the principal Mass of Christmas Day. Liturgical planning needs to consider, therefore, both pastoral sensitivity and the church's wisdom in providing, for centuries before Vatican II, an ensemble of scriptural texts for this solemnity.

The second edition of the lectionary will provide complete formularies for all three years of the Holy Family and the Lord's baptism. Though the first and second readings of Year A may be used, the Year B formularies (missing from the 1970 United States lectionary) are Genesis 15:1–6; 21:1–3 (the Canadian edition adds 17:3b–5, 15–16 and 21:4–7); Hebrews 11:8, 11–12, 17–19; Luke 2:22–40 or 2:22, 39–40 (in Canada the shorter form retains 25–27, 34–35).

SYMBOLS OF NEW LIGHT AND NEW LIFE

■ CANDLELIGHT: Scriptures, collects and prefaces, as well as hymns ancient and modern, celebrate Christmas as a festival of light, the revelation of Christ, the Light of the world (John 8:12) and the Sun of Justice rising with healing in his wings (Malachi 4:2). Nonbelievers likewise celebrate, in the Northern Hemisphere's winter darkness, a festival of light and warmth in holiday feasting, revelry and gift-giving.

Parish liturgists and decorators will want to spend a lot of time with Peter Mazar's ideas on lighting, which form but one section of his insightful discussion on Christmas decorating in LTP's *To Crown the Year* (pages 230–64). While he has excellent ideas for electric lights with the Christmas tree or outdoors, Mazar advances the simple truth that it is especially hard to use Christmas lights in church:

> There are ways to use them well but even more ways to use them poorly. The worship environment is almost always better served by candles. A constellation of flickering votive candles—perhaps lining a beam or clustered in a corner—is a lot more magical and unexpected than electric lights (248).

■ EVERGREENS: Similar to candlelight as a symbol of light's triumph over darkness is the use of evergreens to denote the victory of life over death (PI, 4). In fact, many elements associated with Christmas decor point to the paschal glory associated principally with Easter. Thus the Christmas tree is a reminder of the tree of life and of the life-giving cross. Its trunk may even be considered suitable for the limbs of the Good Friday cross. The holly's thorns and blood-red berries remind us of Christ's passion, as does the red poinsettia. Wreaths are ancient symbols both of victory (Christ's paschal victory) and of the mystical union of marriage (the marriage of Christ and the church).

■ MANGER SCENE: From Christmas Eve at Assisi in 1223, to the Christmas Eves of childhood, and onward to the Christmas Eves of a new century, the crèche, or manger scene, is a touchstone of continuity and fondness. The Pastoral Introduction sees the manger as a comforting yet challenging sacramental. It reminds us, who too often glory in self-sufficiency and count too readily on wealth, that Christ's birth took place in homelessness and poverty. It can rekindle in the most sophisticated heart a sense of wonder and summon cluttered lives back to the simplicity in which God took flesh (PI, 4).

Two aspects of the manger scene call for attention, according to the Pastoral Introduction: design and location. Altar, ambo and assembly hall remain the principal focal points for celebration of the eucharist during Christmastime. The Lord's "real presence and activity" are "in word and sacrament, in the assembly and in its ministers" (PI, 4). Too grand a scope could cause the manger to overshadow the liturgy, and too prominent a setting could displace it. Basically, and in some places delicately, this means rethinking placement of the manger scene near the altar or maybe anywhere else in the sanctuary. Mazar's excellent proposals will help avoid pitfalls and, at the same time, encourage creativity (*To Crown the Year,* pages 241, 250–55).

The manger scene may be blessed at Evening Prayer on Christmas Eve or at a pre–Night Mass vigil. While the *Book of Blessings* suggests that the blessing take place after the general intercessions, the manger's location at some distance from the altar may suggest a stational stop during the entrance or recessional as an alternative.

Preparing the Parish

THE goals of parish preparation include: to offer God glory; to invite God's people to worship that is prayerful, reverent and beautiful; and to provide hospitality that is warm, inclusive and genuine. The schedule must be planned carefully, arranged thoughtfully and publicized very well. And it needs to be presented in an artistically pleasing and conveniently arranged format, printed and mailed out to the full mailing list. Perhaps a guestbook at the door during special Advent services has indicated new folks who might appreciate knowing what's going on. Attractive posters at church entrances and notices in the printed bulletin will reinforce whatever is mailed home. Without suggesting a new commercialization of the season, perhaps (as Jesus once suggested) we "children of light" can take a lesson from the resourcefulness of the "children of the world." How well the malls publicize their holiday specials! How much richer the treasures we have to share!

Taking It Home

THE DOMESTIC CHURCH: The expression "domestic church" comes from ancient Christian writers, like Saint John Chrysostom, who delighted in seeing parallels and links between the place where the community gathered officially and the homes where Christian families lived. For early believers there was an obvious relationship between the assembly's altar table, prepared for the Lord's sacrifice and supper, and the family table where the sacrifice of mutual love and care provided a feast for those united in Christ. Ideally, public morning and evening prayer, celebrated daily in church, began with prayer together at home and echoed in a family life of mutual service within and beyond the home. Early church orders even specified prayer formulae for use by believing couples at various hours of the day—and night. And often enough the very materials for the eucharist, bread and wine, were prepared and brought, week by week, by the various households who made up the local church.

While these customs may strike us as quaint, the term "domestic church" appears in the new *Catechism of the Catholic Church*. The tradition of prayer at home together is the object of renewed interest and the focus of several recent publications. Almost all families have religious customs and symbols they associate with Christmas. A number of customs that do not at first appear religious are, in fact, religious by origin or adaptation. So Christmas is a perfect time to give new impetus to the concept of household prayer and ritual. The first and most basic thing the parish liturgy team can do to assist this effort is make a number of materials more widely accessible to the community.

Start by providing a beautiful publication filled with practical ideas: *Catholic Household Blessings and Prayers* (Washington: United States Catholic Conference, 1988). The hardbound edition especially is worthy of a place of honor next to the family Bible. In the Christmas season alone are simple rites for blessing a Christmas tree, a crèche or manger scene, for blessing the New Year, the home or household on Epiphany. Seasonal table prayers are also provided. Many parishes make these prayerbooks available for purchase as Christmas gifts.

Other Ritual Prayers and Sacraments

LITURGY OF THE HOURS: If the custom of Morning and/or Evening Prayer has begun or grown during Advent, continue the momentum during the Christmas season. Depending on the size of the group, such gatherings could take place at the manger or near the Christmas tree. In fact, the blessing of these items may appropriately take place during the celebration of one of these hours. The *Liturgy of the Hours* (volume I) contains fine nonscriptural readings for all these holy days.

- COMMUNAL ANOINTING OF THE SICK: Because the major feasts of this season each have a unique focus, the ritual Mass for anointing is not permitted on Christmas, January 1 or Epiphany. At weekday celebrations with the sick, whether in small groups or the parish assembly, special readings from the rite's selection of texts could be made. For instance, as in Advent, the three Isaiah passages would work well, and the reading from 1 John and the Lucan gospel of Jesus and John the Baptist fit the spirit of the season. But why not simply use the readings appointed for the day? These are generally rich in messianic and manifestation images and would draw the sick into the image world of Christmas. The Word, who became flesh for our health and deepest healing, is present vividly in the sick, living icons of God's epiphany.

- FUNERALS: At funerals, too, consider using the readings appointed for the day, supplementing them perhaps with Isaiah or 1 John. The lectionary selections for the Christmas octave and the weekdays before and after Epiphany often present passages that lead easily to thoughts of the paschal mystery. In a church filled with Christmas decorations, it will be impossible to pretend that it is not Christmastime. Nor is there any need to do so. Homiletic artistry can join reflections on Christian death to seasonal images of light and new life, and point the assembly toward Christ's victory over death.

- MARRIAGE: Marriages on Christmas, January 1 or Epiphany must use the texts proper to these unique days. On the Feasts of the Holy Family and the Baptism of the Lord, nuptial Masses that are not parish Masses can use the full set of marriage texts; and, as noted in the *Rite of Marriage* (#11), a reading from the rite's own scripture selections can be integrated into the feast day's proper readings. The Song of Songs, 1 John and the wedding feast at Cana are traditional and beautiful both for weddings and for this time of year.

The Worship Environment

BECAUSE ICEL's Pastoral Introduction emphasizes the seasonal adornments of the worship environment during the Christmas season, this *Sourcebook* has already considered them in detail. The content of much of this discussion was inspired by Peter Mazar's reflections and suggestions in *To Crown the Year,* pages 229–64.

- WORSHIP PREPARATIONS: G. Thomas Ryan's *The Sacristy Manual* presents brief general notes on the Christmas season (pages 186–87) but also features particularly helpful and detailed outlines for Christmas Eve. Two such outlines are Vigil Service and Mass Late at Night (pages 188–89) and Epiphany Sunday: Celebration of the Eucharist (pages 190–91).

- CIVIL RESPONSIBILITY: In some places it may be necessary to consult a local fire marshal or civic regulations. Some important considerations might be: What space is needed for safe evacuation of the numbers we expect? Are cut trees and real greens allowed? On one hand, we should not give in to artificiality too easily. Nor are candles and incense optional elements in Catholic worship. We, therefore, have not only an obligation but a right to use them. But how do we place lit candles in relationship to evergreens, floral and other decorations, and to straw? If we do not like the answers we receive, and are sure that other approaches respect both liturgy and public safety, then it may be time for representatives from the parish or diocesan liturgical commission to meet with the boards or officials responsible and to see how other religious groups reconcile their worship needs and civil regulations.

- OUTDOORS: Christmas is probably one of the few times when even otherwise reticent citizens make some public display of holiday cheer. Light and evergreens, already discussed as decorations for the worship space, are used by believers and nonbelievers alike to adorn their homes. How much more fitting are they for the *domus ecclesiae,* literally "the house of the church" but more accurately, "the house of the assembly that is the church." Large and beautiful wreaths along with lights and walkway luminaries are signs of festivity and hospitality. Increasingly, people

CALENDAR

December

WED 25 #13–16 (LMC, #13) white
The Birth of the Lord (Christmas)
SOLEMNITY

An essential prelude to fruitful use of this calendar is a careful reading of the material in the previous section. It provides extensive notes about the various elements of the eucharistic liturgy on the major festivals of this season.

SETTING THE SCHEDULE

■ THEOLOGICAL, HISTORICAL AND PASTORAL PERSPECTIVES: All three perspectives are important in planning the community's Christmas schedule. Parish liturgists who attend to the insights of each perspective will serve the community's prayer well and "order" worship fruitfully on this rich solemnity. A focus on only one or another might impoverish the community's prayer or even lead it astray. By embracing all three, we both serve the community where it really is and gently suggest directions it may choose to go as it deepens its participation in the celebration of the incarnation.

Theologically, in the Christmas liturgy we celebrate "the one true light that banishes darkness" (PI, 4). *Historically,* this theological orientation, "night giving way to day," has been expressed in a developing sequence of celebrations spanning the hours from Christmas Eve to Christmas night, "reinforced" by a corresponding sequence of liturgical texts, some of which we have already examined. We heirs of the Roman rite ought to consider this rich heritage of Christmas celebrations and settings!

- For 1500 years Roman Christians have celebrated a nocturnal liturgy near a replica of Bethlehem's manger in the principal Roman basilica dedicated to Mary. An important note: The old and new Latin missals do *not* say "at midnight" but simply "at night."

- In the morning, on his way to Saint Peter's, the pope stopped for Mass at Saint Anastasia's Basilica, for December 25 was her feast day, too! This became the Mass "at dawn," and the old Missal gave the "station" as "at Saint Anastasia."

- The original Christmas Mass, "during the day," then took place at Saint Peter's, though this was moved eventually to Saint Mary Major (where the manger was), and this is the "station" given in the Missal as late as 1962.

- Based on evidence of extensive noneucharistic prayer, it is safe to assume that in addition to the three Masses there were gatherings to keep the hours.

Pastorally, we must be willing to learn from what the community has done in the past. The first question from a pastoral perspective is: What "works" in this local church? Openness and humility are essential. But there is always creative tension at work in the pastoral dimension. Essential, too, is the responsibility to educate (literally "to lead out") and move beyond the local and familiar. An informed liturgical ministry should be daring enough to offer the local church, with all patience and sensitivity, some of the treasures of the universal church's heritage.

EVENING PRAYER

When? Ideally before the (first) evening Mass. *Where?* In the main worship space, around the manger, near the Christmas tree, in a chapel (numbers may determine location). *Who?* Everyone, including planners, presiders, ministers, musicians, decorators and staff. Here is a prayerful conclusion to frantic preparations, a peaceful way to usher in the solemnity and dispose heart, soul and senses for liturgical service.

Anyone may preside: ordained, religious, layperson. Here are some variations you may add to the order of service:

- Before prayer: Once all have gathered and spent a few moments in silent recollection, the presider stands and begins.

- Call to worship: Sung dialogue on light: V. Light and peace in Jesus Christ our Lord (or even Christ our Light). R. Thanks be to God.

- Lucernarium: Candle lighting could include the lighting of the Christmas tree, or the tree could be blessed and lighted after the gospel canticle.

- Hymn: Prescribed is the anonymous sixth-century "Christe, redemptor omnium" (*Hymnal 1982,* #85).

- Psalmody: 113, 147B and New Testament canticle Philippians 2:6–11.

EARLY EVENING MASS

Paying attention to the age levels and numbers of those who participate in the early evening

Mass will be important for everything from scripture selection to procession logistics. Reality may have established this as a Mass of convenience, but there are still simple ways to enhance prayer and invite participation.

Let the space bespeak prayerful wonder and quiet anticipation. Subdued light can set a good tone. The incense of Evening Prayer (or even an informal incensing before anyone arrives) can be an olfactory invitation to enter the mystery and magic of this eve.

Official norms permit using the *Lectionary for Masses with Children* only with children apart from the assembly this night. But is this an appropriate option this evening? On Christmas Eve, children in the midst of the assembly are a living liturgical "symbol." And the Lucan nativity gospel would seem the most appropriate choice (see pages 39–40). Its power and beauty resound in any translation. There are surely other ways to make the liturgy special for children this evening without separating families or excluding adults.

Blessing the manger would be a beautiful ritual this evening, particularly if the assembly or at least the children process there with joyous song.

MASS IN THE NIGHT

Even if Midnight Mass is no longer a viable option, it is possible for a community to make Christmas Eve special by scheduling an evening Mass that is truly "in the night." Depending on parish needs, this might even replace the early evening Mass, thus establishing a subtle link with the Easter Vigil.

Soft candlelight, subdued artificial light, the scent of evergreens and incense—let these be a visual and olfactory welcome. All is in readiness well before anyone arrives. There are no ministers busily preparing books or vessels, no unnecessary sound or movement to distract from the silent wonder and prayerful silence. Parishioners may be quietly greeting each other, but that is part of the gathering, the sacramental presence of one another.

■ BEGIN WITH A VIGIL of psalmody and silence, reading and prayer scheduled up to an hour before the Mass itself. If the assembly is prepared by careful pastoral explanation for some weeks beforehand, and if the hour chosen is appropriate, many will come for the whole vigil. But people ought to feel free to arrive whenever they are able. Greeters and ushers are available to pass out tapers and indicate seating if necessary. There is something beautiful about keeping vigil in a darkened church and watching the candlelight increase as newcomers arrive. The official Roman ordo (the yearly guide for celebrating Mass and hours), the *Ceremonial of Bishops* (#238) and more recently some national sacramentaries urge this preliminary time of prayer. Here is a good way to apply to the traditional "choir concert" Vatican II's directive that all devotional gatherings be informed by the spirit and content of the liturgy.

A full Office of Readings (*Liturgy of the Hours,* vol. I, 399 and appendix I) is a challenge to most communities: three psalms, canticles and responsories. The Ambrosian rite of Milan opts for an Easter/Pentecost Vigil model, incorporating Roman material but alternating reading, silence, song and collect. This order borrows from both.

- Entrance procession: Begin with the church in semidarkness. The large Advent wreath candles lead the procession, if possible, while all carry candles. The procession pauses a few times so that light can be passed to the assembly.

  The processional song is a chant-like piece inviting participation, perhaps through a refrain. "A child is born in Bethlehem," with a haunting Gregorian melody and quietly joyful refrain, is perfect, especially a capella or punctuated by handbells.

  When the procession arrives at the altar, many candles are lit there and throughout the church (pew candles, consecration candles on the walls).

- Sung greeting: V. Light and peace in Jesus Christ our Lord (or Christ our Light). R. Thanks be to God.

- Hymn: "Of the Father's love begotten" or other quietly reflective piece.

- Thanksgiving for light: Sung by cantor, deacon or priest (page 53). As the community sings Amen, a few lights may be turned on, but ideally the vigil continues by candlelight.

- Introduction or welcome (page 52).

- Readings. Several may be chosen from this list of traditional readings. Each is followed by a psalm or a carol, and a collect (page 53).

  I. Genesis 15:1–12, 17–18 (lectionary, #373); psalm or carol ("It came upon the midnight clear"); collect.
  II. Isaiah 7:10–14 (lectionary, #10); psalm or carol ("What child is this?", "Lo how a rose e'er blooming"); collect.
  III. Isaiah 11:1–10 (lectionary, #4); psalm or carol ("From heaven above," "God rest ye"); collect.
  IV. Micah 5:1–4 (lectionary, #12); psalm or carol ("O little town of Bethlehem," "Once in royal David's city"); collect.
  V. Christmas homily of Leo the Great (*Liturgy of the Hours,* vol. I, 404).

VI. Proclamation of the Birth of Christ (traditional, page 56; revised, *Sacramentary Supplement*, 19) or: gospel of the genealogy (lectionary, #13, optional ending at v. 17).

VII. The Gloria is sung by all and continues as usual.

■ WHEN BEGINNING WITHOUT A VIGIL, two forms are possible. In the first, after the preludes and congregational/choral singing, the church remains in subdued light. Following a brief period of silence, the proclamation of the birth of Christ is sung. The lights are raised, proceeded by the entrance procession and incensation of altar, followed by greeting, the Gloria and the opening prayer.

The second form, suggested by the *Sacramentary Supplement* (19), begins with the entrance procession, greeting, introduction and singing of the proclamation. The Gloria and opening prayer follow.

Notes for Mass

■ GOSPEL: A gospel procession with incense and candles, culminating in a chanted gospel, is a particularly effective way of proclaiming the "good news of great joy" on Christmas. See *Chants for the Readings* (Joseph T. Kush, GIA, G-2114) and *Liturgical Music for the Priest and Deacon* (Columba Kelly, St. Meinrad's Archabbey, St. Meinrad IN).

■ PROFESSION OF FAITH: Remember to genuflect (see page 36).

■ ANNOUNCEMENTS: Brief and carefully chosen words of thanks to all who carried out the multiple preparations for liturgy may certainly be appropriate. But several cautions are in order: The impression should never be given that the laity helped the pastor conduct his parish. Thanks should be in the name of the entire assembly, and the assembly's participation may be gratefully acknowledged as well. Thanking the choir and musicians will be appreciated, but is not applause usually the response of a grateful audience after a fine performance? Applause may be out of place here. The thanks could conclude with a final word of Christmas wishes from the whole parish, followed immediately by the concluding rite.

EARLY MORNING MASS

Early Morning Mass

The Latin title *In Aurora* bespeaks beauty, peace, a quiet increase of light. Let these be this liturgy's characteristics. In many communities the early Mass, even if not at dawn, is sparsely attended. Remember that the demographics inform the style, tone and content of the homily, which may, therefore, be very different from that preached last night.

Since this will probably be the only Christmas Mass for many, the gospel from the night Mass might be added to the verses assigned to the dawn Mass.

While it may not be possible (but do try!) to have musicians accompany this early Mass, most assemblies will gladly join in an a capella carol or two and the acclamations.

MASS DURING THE DAY

This is not the night Mass. As at Easter, therefore, it is best not to import elements that make the night Mass special: the proclamation of the birth of Christ, for instance, or elements of the Vigil. Instead, plan enhancements that would not be appropriate for the quiet of the Vigil. Some parishes station a brass ensemble in the gathering area just inside the door to welcome people with festive music and feature a brief time of congregational carols before the liturgy begins. Additional instrumentation for these carols can also help to make the setting uniquely festive.

Because many who participate in the day Mass may have rushed from home, or may be planning later dinners, refreshments following the liturgy, with appropriate music (live or taped), may be a welcome convenience and provide the opportunity for a bit of holiday socializing.

■ SCRIPTURE: As noted, the lectionary rubrics permit the interchangeable use of four sets of Christmas readings. But the proclamation of the prologue to the Gospel of John is a venerable tradition at this Mass during the day. Its proclamation links us again to the light/darkness theme of the season. A solemn chanting of this prologue would give it the prominence the tradition claims for it; the genuflection during the Creed will reinforce in body language the central importance of the community's conviction and joy that "the Word was made flesh and lived among us."

DURING THE DAY

■ CHRISTMAS MIDDAY PRAYER: Especially when celebrated at the church or parish hall, this prayer could come from the *Liturgy of the Hours,* with familiar musical settings of one or more of the assigned psalms or with the parish's Christmas responsorial psalm in a version everyone knows ("All the

DECEMBER

ends of the earth"). A fuller passage from scripture and a concluding carol would enhance the celebration. At church this is led by a deacon or lay minister.

This Midday Prayer could lead into a festive Christmas dinner, which at church (or at home) could include neighbors, who would otherwise eat alone, and the area's homeless.

■ BLESSING OF THE MANGER SCENE: The full form of this rite (*Book of Blessings*, #1547ff.) with carols added, can be led by a deacon or lay minister.

■ TABLE PRAYER: The prayer found in the *Book of Blessings* (#1038ff, 1048) might seem too much for the average household, but if the parish is sponsoring a festive dinner, this table blessing could be celebrated and even expanded with carols and a Christmas reading or two. At home, the form in *Catholic Household Blessings and Prayers* is beautiful in its simplicity and easy to celebrate.

■ AN OPEN DOOR: If possible, leave the church open throughout the day and announce it at all Masses with an invitation to return. Some people may enjoy stopping in with their guests to show off their parish home and to spend a few moments in prayer before the manger.

CHRISTMAS VESPERS

Many people seem to welcome an opportunity to go out this evening for a breath of fresh air and a little prolongation of the holiday. The parish can offer an opportunity for communal prayer through the celebration of Evening Prayer.

The pattern established for Advent (or Sunday Vespers through the year) can continue with perhaps a more extensive lucernarium during which all the church's candles are lighted. A well-known Christmas carol would be a fitting accompaniment to this rite. Whatever psalms the assembly can sing may be used (*General Introduction of the Liturgy of the Hours*, #247). The official psalmody of Evening Prayer on Christmas prescribes one we would not ordinarily choose for a festive day, the "De profundis" ("Out of the depths"), perhaps because of the line, "with the Lord there is mercy and fullness of redemption." The prescribed New Testament canticle this evening is Colossians 1, the hymn to Christ that closes Christmas Day by linking the celebration once again to the paschal mystery: "He is the first born from the dead." The scripture passage from 1 John is likewise fitting: "What we have seen with our eyes, what we have looked upon, what our hands have touched — the word of life."

THU 26
#696 (LMC, #437 and #456–459) red
Stephen, first martyr
FEAST

The first of the *comites Christi*, "Christ's companions," most of whom sealed their witness in blood, makes his appearance today as leader of the royal child's entourage. Stephen, along with the others whose names adorn the Christmas octave, seems at first a countersign to the "peace on earth" the angels promised; but their struggles define and refine on the "comfort and joy" the carols celebrate.

FRI 27
#697 (LMC, #430 and 452–454) white
John, apostle, evangelist
FEAST

Today's first reading (also at Christmas Vespers) speaks of the historical, tangible fact of the incarnation: heard, seen, touched. The gospel connects Christmas and Pasch in the story of the empty tomb. While exegetes caution us about making connections too easily, today's saint is identified by tradition with "the disciple Jesus loved," the one who "reposed upon his breast" at the Last Supper. John's feast, therefore, after this grand holiday and at the end of a busy week, invites us to train our focus close to home, hearth and heart; to reflect on the quality of our love toward those nearest to us.

SAT 28
#698 (LMC, #439 and 456–459) red
The Holy Innocents, martyrs
FEAST

The continuation of John's first letter throughout the octave and beyond it keeps before our eyes the "light out of darkness" motif of Christmastime. Nowhere does the struggle between light and darkness seem more intense than in the suffering of children, who for world-weary adults are often the last living icons of holiness and innocence. The feast reminds us again that Christmas is not all "Silent night" and "Joy to the world." The Child is a sign of contradiction still, the one who reveals "the thoughts of many hearts."

If we look deeply into our own hearts this day with John's first letter before us, we will have to acknowledge that the roots of violence are to be found not only in far-off lands or in the hands of unscrupulous leaders but in our own sin-scarred hearts. But the incarnation has filled the world and our hearts with light, says John, for "we have an advocate with the Father, Jesus Christ, the righteous; and he is the atoning sacrifice for our sins, and not for ours

DECEMBER

only but also for the sins of the whole world." In the face of innocent suffering, and confronting our own lack of innocence, these are truths that should inspire us to take heart and face the world, ourselves and the New Year with conviction of faith and the joy of Christ-given hope.

29 The Holy Family
#17 (LMC, #14)   white
FEAST

This feast was established as part of the Christmas season in 1921 following promotion of the cult in the nineteenth century; it was linked to the octave of Christmas in 1969. The holy family of Jesus, Mary and Joseph, itself subject to the difficulties and social pressures of its time, is offered as a model of Christian family life today (© ICEL).

The bishops of the United States have approved a shorter version of the second reading, using just verses 12 to 17. This feast celebrates another aspect of the Lord's incarnation: his birth into a specific human family, with many of the trials and triumphs all families share. The feast calls for sensitivity toward real conditions that beset so many families today, wounds that can be particularly painful in the holiday season. For this reason, many pastoral people feel that a blessing of families or renewal of marriage vows is not appropriate today and could unwittingly hurt more than help.

In some parishes, however, people bring devotional objects received as Christmas gifts to be blessed. Where this custom is observed, those who bring such gifts may gather at the manger where a priest or deacon can use the *Book of Blessings* (chapter 44, shorter form for use after Mass).

MON 30 Sixth Day in the Octave of Christmas
#203 [204]   white

Today's selection from 1 John addresses all age groups in the community with a challenge to new life in Christ. It may be worth noting to the assembly that "world" in 1 John means a way of life unenlightened by the gospel, anchored in self-centeredness and sin. Contrast this to "the world" in John's gospel: "God so loved the world that he gave his only Son" (John 3:16). Though yesterday's gospel was the presentation story, today's passage presents the "Anna" part that may have been omitted if the shorter form of Sunday's gospel was used.

TUE 31 Seventh Day in the Octave of Christmas
#204 [205]   white

Sylvester I, pope, optional memorial/white. ▪ The prologue of John's gospel is featured on this last day of the year, presenting another opportunity for reflections on the incarnation, Christ as true Light of the world, the enlightenment of the baptized in Christ, and the gift of enduring love given us in the Word made flesh. Keep in mind that this is primarily a "day within the octave": If Pope Sylvester is commemorated, this takes place in the opening prayer and intercessions. A possible link to the day's gospel would be a remembrance of Sylvester's defense of Christ's divinity against the Arian heresy.

NEW YEAR'S EVE

▪ PARTIES AND PRAYER: "First night" inspires people in both directions! Parishes might consider welcoming in the new year with a vigil that may, but need not, culminate in the eucharist. While the vigil may be scheduled with an orientation to the midnight hour, some communities might prefer a time earlier in the evening, before the parties begin. Some parishes have found it popular to schedule their own "safe and sober" New Year's Eve party in conjunction with the vigil. While the *Liturgy of the Hours* has material for a vigil office of readings (vol. I, 479ff. and appendix I), the observations made for Christmas Eve are pertinent here (see page 44), and the focus is primarily on Mary's maternity. The Episcopal Church's *Book of Occasional Services* provides readings more oriented toward the sanctification of time and seeking the blessings of peace (another theme of January 1). The order of worship could be similar to that of the Christmas Eve vigil and may be adapted easily to conclude with the eucharist:

- Entrance procession: Church in semidarkness. Candle lighting during the continuation of the hymn that has accompanied the procession to the altar or lucernarium after the greeting.

- Sung dialogue: V. Light and peace in Jesus Christ our Lord, Christ our Light (or Jesus Christ, the same yesterday, today and forever). R. Thanks be to God.

- Hymn: perhaps incorporating references to Christ as "Prince of Peace."

- Thanksgiving for Light (page 54).

- Readings: Several may be chosen from this list:
  I. Exodus 23:9–16, 20–21; Psalm 111 or 119:1–8 or carol; collect (collects for each of these readings, page 54).

DECEMBER

II. Deuteronomy 11:8–12, 26–28; Psalm 36:5–10 or 89, Part I or carol; collect.

III. Ecclesiastes 3:1–15 or 12:1–8; Psalm 90 or 130 or carol; collect.

IV. Ecclesiasticus (Sirach) 43:1–22; Psalm 19 or 148 or 74:11–22 or carol; collect.

- If the eucharist follows, the Gloria and opening prayer are prayed. The liturgy of the word from the lectionary takes place as usual. The "Te Deum" might be sung after communion. If the eucharist is not celebrated, the vigil continues:

  V. 2 Corinthians 5:17–6:2; Psalm 63:1-8 or Canticle of Simeon; collect.

  VI. Hebrews 3:1–15 (16—4:13); Psalm 95; collect.

  VII. Revelation 21:1–14, 22–24; optional homily; "Te Deum" or Gloria; Concluding Prayer (Mass for Special Needs, #24).

- Solemn Blessing #3.
- Dismissal.

January

WED 1 — #18 (LMC, #15) white
Mary, Mother of God/ octave of Christmas
SOLEMNITY

The Virgin Mary was already venerated as Mother of God when, in 431, the Council of Ephesus acclaimed her *Theotokos* ("God-bearer"). Her role in the mystery of the incarnation was celebrated on this day in Rome in the seventh century but was soon eclipsed by other feasts of Mary. Restored to the liturgical calendar in 1931, and to this day in 1969, the feast celebrates from a Marian perspective the Word made flesh and so enriches the observance of the octave of Christmas and provides a solemn beginning to the New Year (© ICEL).

■ NEW YEAR'S DAY MASS: What times will best serve most people? It may be that only one Mass should be scheduled, late in the morning. Or if there was no evening Mass New Year's Eve, or no eucharist with the vigil, some who stayed out late might appreciate Mass being celebrated later on New Year's afternoon or in the early evening.

Today we celebrate the octave day of Christmas, the motherhood of Mary, the day of the Child's circumcision and naming, the beginning of the civil year and day of prayer for world peace! By judicious use of sacramentary and lectionary, by composing thoughtful intercessions and by choosing music carefully, planners can weave these several strands into the tapestry of this day's celebration. A symphony of scriptures blends notes of peace (reading I), Mary's motherhood, God's fatherhood, our adoption as free children of God in Christ (reading II) and a gentle link to the historical nativity as well (gospel).

The collect for the votive Mass "Beginning of the Civil Year" (Various Needs and Occasions, #24) would be a fitting ending to intercessions that seek peace in the church, the world, our town, our homes, our hearts. The preface of Mary, Mother of the Savior (*Collection of Masses of the Blessed Virgin Mary,* P5) keeps the focus on Christ through the scriptural imagery of the season. There is a solemn blessing for the New Year (#3). Countless hymns and carols highlight the incarnation, mother, child and the blessings of peace.

THU 2 — #205 [206] white
Basil the Great and Gregory Nazianzen, bishops, doctors of the church
MEMORIAL

Weekday assemblies could be puzzled by the gospel passages of these days before Epiphany. We are sent back into Advent, to the Jordan again, where John is baptizing. Homilists may point to this as an example of the liturgical use of time. We are not in the realm of strict chronology nor does the liturgy try to teach by leading us step by historical step. Rather, liturgical time is mystical, celebratory, richly evocative. Having celebrated the incarnation, we hear John the Baptist anew, preparing the way for the Christ, who has come and is to come, and who here and now is in our midst.

Today's memorial reminds us that in every generation Christ is present vividly among us in the lives of the saints. These two models of friendship in Christ remind us that a particularly delightful experience of divine presence is found in the love given and received in friendship. See the Office of Readings for Gregory's moving tribute to Basil.

■ SCHOOL LITURGY: Make sure the decorations are still up when the children return; and if school resumes today, this may be an appropriate day for celebrating Christmastime with them. A Christmastime celebration after vacation is far better than a "Christmas" Mass during Advent. Consult the *Leader's Manual of the Hymnal for Catholic Students* (page 74) for helpful resources.

JANUARY

FRI 3 #206 [207] white
Christmas Weekday

Children of God, as yet unrecognized by the world: That is how John's first letter describes us and the Christian movement in general. But we need to be gentle toward those near and far who seem to reject the gospel we've embraced and those who persecute it actively. Even John the Baptist did not, at first, recognize Christ. The world has to try to see him in disguise, as it were, through the flawed reflection of him that our not always faithful witness gives.

SAT 4 #207 [208] white
Elizabeth Ann Seton, married woman, religious founder, educator
MEMORIAL

The God who was manifested in the flesh long ago, in far away Palestine, was manifested closer to our own age, here in the still-young United States, in the remarkable person of Elizabeth Ann Seton. A glance at her "titles" in the calendar reminds us: She did it all! And she didn't even make it to her fiftieth birthday! Our awe increases when we hear the litany of grief and suffering that formed the lived prayer of her life. But how deeply rooted in Christ she was: We might say that in the manifold trials of her life, Elizabeth Seton truly "remained with him" in the words of today's gospel.

5 #20 (LMC, #16) white
The Epiphany of the Lord
SOLEMNITY

A striking instruction in the *Ceremonial of Bishops* tells the bishop to "see to it that this solemnity is celebrated in a proper manner." Of course, ritual Masses are not permitted today, but an unusually detailed checklist follows the admonition about "proper observance" and is incorporated into these reflections on the day's Mass.

MASS

■ INTRODUCTORY RITES: "There will be a suitable and increased display of lights." Begin before the beginning with church building and worship space illumined gloriously, proclaiming radiantly in ways beyond words the splendor of Christ's manifestation. Whatever candlelight adorned Christmastime should be present today: gathering area, altar, consecration candles, pew candles. The entrance procession could be a blaze of glory as well.

■ LITURGY OF THE WORD: The gospel, accompanied by lights and incense, may be chanted to the old simple tone. "After the singing of the gospel reading, depending on local custom, one of the deacons . . . or someone else, vested in cope, will go to the lectern (ambo) and there announce to the people the movable feasts of the current year." See page 58.

■ PRESENTATION OF GIFTS: "The custom of having a special presentation of gifts will be observed or renewed in accordance with local usage and tradition." Liturgical scholars assure us that symbolism in liturgy admits of, and even encourages, a variety of interpretations. They rightly warn against our didactic tendency to explain and define everything. The *Ceremonial*'s directive regarding a "special presentation of gifts" on Epiphany leads us into just such ambiguity.

On one hand, it hearkens to the gifts of the Magi proclaimed in the gospel. Renewing or introducing this custom raises many questions and suggests several possibilities. Who will come forward and with what? Children as well as adults should be involved. Gold could be brought forward as gifts earmarked to assist those in need. Frankincense is used later to honor gifts, altar and assembly, and may be distributed afterward for the Epiphany home blessings. What would pass for myrrh in this age? A gift destined for the homebound or the bereaved? Something associated with catechumens or penitents? Other gifts are possible: for instance, the chalk that will later be used in the home blessings just mentioned or the parish calendars to be blessed before distribution.

On the other hand, herein is the ambiguity! Just after our presentation rite comes this prayer over the gifts:

> Lord,
> accept the gifts of your church,
> which offers you today not gold,
>   frankincense and myrrh
> but the one who in these gifts is
>   proclaimed, offered and
>   received,
> Jesus Christ our Lord . . . .

JANUARY

Just a reminder that the gifts we bring for the eucharist, in their eloquent simplicity, are the vehicle for our welcoming of the greatest gift of all! Remember the proper insert for Eucharistic Prayer I in the sacramentary.

■ ADDITIONAL CONSIDERATIONS: "The invitations, comments and homily will explain the full meaning of this day with its 'three mysteries,' that is, the adoration of the child by the Magi, the baptism of Christ and the wedding at Cana" (see pages 33–34).

BLESSINGS

■ THE HOME OF THE CHURCH: Since the blessing of homes on Epiphany is a time-honored custom, why not start with the "home" where the family of God's people gather — not necessarily the church building itself, since the feast of its dedication commemorates its solemn consecration and blessing, but rather whatever building the community associates with its gatherings for business or socializing.

When the prayer after communion ends, an announcement is made, and a sung invitation (by the deacon) offered to join in the procession: V. Let us go forth in peace! R. Thanks be to God! The procession exits to a festive carol or a triumphal organ piece. Incense, cross and candles lead the way, followed by all those who were in the entrance procession and finally the whole assembly with the presider.

■ THE FAMILY HOME: *Catholic Household Blessings and Prayers* (page 126) provides a home blessing for Epiphany, a traditional custom in various ethnic groups, and a fine reminder that Christ is incarnate in the love and care we manifest to each other in our ordinary, daily lives together. The parish should provide the incentive and the simple materials that will enhance the custom and make it a joy to celebrate. One custom is to trace crosses, the initials of the "kings" and the numerals of the year over the doorway with chalk: 19 + C + M + B + 97. Legend names the kings Caspar, Melchior and Balthazar. But the initials were long ago reinterpreted by northern European Protestants who loved the custom but not the legend: CMB became *Christus mansionem benedicat*, "May Christ bless this house!"

EPIPHANY VESPERS

Epiphany Sunday night provides a wonderful setting for a parish Christmas choir concert. This could be preceded by Evening Prayer, following the outline that by now should be familiar, featuring candlelight, incense and carols for everyone to sing (one last time!). The evening could conclude with a festive parish supper or open house. And some parishes take the opportunity at this gathering to offer thanks and show appreciation to all those who worked to make Advent and Christmas a time of beautiful, glorious prayer.

MON 6 — #212 [213] white
Christmas Weekday

Blessed André Bessette, religious, optional memorial/white ▪ This week continues and concludes the reading of 1 John. Over the next few days the scriptures seem to build a bridge over which we can pass from our meditation on the incarnation into Ordinary Time. Briefly, the Johannine readings assert that rejection of false gods and profession of faith in Christ lead the disciple to confidence in God's abiding love. This love should, in turn, inspire believers to mutual love for one another. Brother André was renowned as one whose prayer could heal those who came seeking the restoration of physical and spiritual health.

TUE 7 — #213 [214] white
Christmas Weekday

Raymond of Penyafort, presbyter, religious, optional memorial/white ▪ Yesterday we heard of the healing of the crowds and today we read about the feeding of the multitude. Both aspects of Jesus' public ministry continue in the community through its service of charity and the sacramental life of its liturgy. If today's saint is commemorated, the readings are related easily to his life, for Raymond is remembered as a wise confessor and a compassionate priest.

WED 8 — #214 [215] white
Christmas Weekday

The call of 1 John to mutual love continues, and he begins today a line of reasoning that will continue tomorrow: God, whom no one has ever seen, is seen among us in our love. But even in the first days of the new year, with our brand new resolutions fresh in our minds, we know how long the path is between the real and the ideal! How comforting, then, to read in the gospel that even the disciples who were Jesus' daily companions "did not understand." To us, as to them, Jesus says, "Take heart, it is I; do not be afraid."

THU 9 — #215 [216] white
Christmas Weekday

The Christian message is so clear and straightforward: "Those who do not love a brother or sister whom they have seen cannot love the God they have not seen." The Lord for his part announces, in his inaugural homily, the theme of his preaching and the purpose of his death: "To proclaim the

JANUARY

year of the Lord's favor." That favor should reveal itself still in this year of favor through our witness, we disciples brought to life by Christ's paschal mystery.

FRI 10 #216 [217] white
Christmas Weekday

Luke's gospel shows us his favorite snapshot of Jesus: touching the untouchable, healing the marginalized and then withdrawing from the adulation of the crowds to seek the face of God in solitary prayer. As John reminds us in his first letter, "Jesus came by water and blood," and he emphasizes, "not with the water only but with the water and the blood." Baptism of water points to baptism in blood. As the Christmas season draws to a close, here is yet another link to the time of the Lord's Passover.

SAT 11 #217 [218] white
Christmas Weekday

The penultimate Mass of Christmastime summarizes the weeks just past and focuses our resolve on those just ahead. The scriptures affirm: "We know that we are God's children . . . and that the Son of God has come and has given us understanding" (1 John). Now it is time for each of us to join John the Baptist in proclaiming by the witness of our lives that "he must increase, but I must decrease" (gospel).

Some communities use this Saturday to reduce, at least somewhat, the scope of the Christmas decorations, so that tomorrow's feast may mark, even visually, a return to Ordinary Time. In preparation for tomorrow, avoid setting up a temporary font or special water display. Take care instead to make sure that the real font is suitably honored and highlighted.

12 #21 (LMC, #17) white
The Baptism of the Lord
FEAST

This feast presents a challenge: to blend elements of the Christmastime liturgies and decor with references and images to the baptismal covenant, which we live out through the days and weeks of the Ordinary Time that is now close at hand. Some parishes keep all the Christmas decorations in place, while others begin a subtle modulation out of that key in time for this Sunday. However the setting is arranged, some liturgical elements should make the link obvious: The liturgical greeting of Christmastime should be used, and the Christmastime Gloria and acclamation set should be sung one last time. Christmas carols may be wearing rather thin by now, but perhaps there could be one last hurrah for "Joy to the world" or another of the less Bethlehem-oriented ones. Musical options for this feast have increased in recent years, as various Christian communities have taken it into their calendars. The "Epiphany" section of *Hymnal 1982* (Episcopal) and the *Lutheran Book of Worship* offer some fine selections. At least two hymns make explicit the traditional connection of Epiphany, baptism and Cana: "Songs of thankfulness and praise" and "All praise to you, O Lord." Some contain fine mission-oriented verses that fit in well with the scriptures of the coming weeks and, therefore, might serve the community during Ordinary Time.

The rite of sprinkling should be used today.

Evening Prayer followed perhaps by one last round of carols, winter refreshments and maybe an "undecorating party" would be a fitting and festive way to bring Christmastime to a close. Ordinary Time begins tomorrow.

TEXTS FOR THE EUCHARISTIC ASSEMBLY

INTRODUCTORY RITES

Greeting

The peace and love of God our Father,
manifested in Christ who was born for our salvation,
be with you all.

or:

The grace and peace of our Lord Jesus Christ,
who was born for us of the Virgin Mary,
be with you all.
—*Book of Blessings, #1549,* adapted

or:

The light of Christ,
who is our peace and our salvation,
be with you all.
—*BB, #1577,* adapted

A Christmas Welcome

As we begin the celebration of this great feast, we welcome all who have come to celebrate here at _____ parish.

We welcome those who are guests from out of town or from other parish communities. It is good to have you with us.

We extend a special welcome to our college students and other young adults home for the holidays. It is a joy to see your bright and shining faces among us.

And, of course, we rejoice in all those here whose faces we see each week. It is good for all of us to be here together to celebrate the love of God revealed in the gift of the Word made flesh.

The introductory rites may take one of the following forms:

I. Rite of Blessing and Sprinkling of Holy Water

II. Penitential Rite

Gathered together to celebrate the eucharist,
let us seek the grace of Christ,
in whom the goodness and loving kindness
of God have appeared.

I confess . . . *and the prayer of absolution.*

III. Litany of Praise

Peace on earth and good will among all
are the gifts God offers us in our Savior.
Let us praise the Lord Jesus Christ.

Eternal Word, through whom all things were made:
Lord, have mercy.

True Light, enlightening all born into the world:
Christ, have mercy.

Son of God, made flesh in the womb of the Virgin Mother:
Lord, have mercy.

IV. Kyrie

You are called to the joyful salvation that this day embraces the world.
Acclaim Christ, the Word of God made flesh among us.

Lord, have mercy . . . *or Kyrie, eleison litany follows.*

V. Gloria

LITURGY OF THE WORD

Dismissal of Catechumens

My dear friends: With the assurance of our loving support, this community sends you forth to reflect more deeply on the word we have shared. Our prayer for you in this season of Christmas joy is that the mystery of the Word made flesh may strengthen your resolve to embrace Christ as your Savior and lead you to share fully with us at the Lord's table as children of God and heirs, in hope, of eternal life.

General Intercessions

Invitation to prayer

In Christ, Emmanuel, the Word made flesh, we behold God's love for us. Let us, therefore, draw near to God in prayer with the joyful confidence of those who trust in God's saving power.

LITURGY OF THE EUCHARIST

Introduction to the Lord's Prayer

The Son of God became a child among us
that we might become the children of God
   who dare to pray:
Our Father . . .

Invitation to Communion

Behold the Lamb of God, who takes away
   the sins of the world;
Emmanuel, God-with-us, Son of Mary and
   Savior of all nations.
Blessed are those called to the banquet
   of the Lamb.

CONCLUDING RITE

Dismissal of Eucharistic Ministers

Go forth in peace to the sick and homebound of our community, bearing the word of life and the body of Christ together with the assurance of our love and concern. Join their voices to our hymn in praise of God's glory and in the name of this community share God's peace with them in the gift of Emmanuel.

Dismissal

As witnesses of God's glory and heralds
   of God's peace,
go forth in joy and gladness to love and
   serve the Lord.

TEXTS FOR A CHRISTMAS VIGIL

These texts may be used in conjunction with the outline for the Christmas Vigil office given on page 44.

Thanksgiving for the Light

V. The Lord be with you.
R. And also with you.
V. Let us give thanks to the Lord our God.
R. It is right to give him [our] thanks
   and praise.

Blessed are you, O Lord our God,
for you have made our gladness greater
   and increased our joy
by sending to dwell among us
the Wonderful Counselor, the Prince of Peace.
Born of Mary,
proclaimed to the shepherds
and acknowledged to the ends of the earth,
your unconquered Sun of righteousness
gives light in darkness and establishes us
   in freedom.
All glory in the highest be to you,
through Christ, the Son of your favor,
in the abiding presence of your Spirit,
this night and forever and ever. R. Amen.
—*Book of Common Worship* (Presbyterian Church).
Text by John Allyn Melloh, SM, copyright ©1979 GIA Publications, Inc., Chicago, IL. Altered with permission. All rights reserved.

Collects

After Reading I
O God,
in Jesus the Christ
you have given Abraham a multitude
   of descendants
as countless as the stars in the sky or the
   sands of the shore.
Multiply over all the earth the wonders
   of your mercy,
that upon the darkness that envelops
   the nations
there may dawn your Sun of righteousness
   with healing in his wings:
Christ who is Lord forever and ever.
—*Mozarabic rite*

AFTER READING II
Almighty God,
you have given your only-begotten Son to
   take our nature upon him,
and to be born this day of a pure Virgin:
Grant that we, who have been born again
and made your children by adoption and
   grace,
may daily be renewed by your Holy Spirit.
We ask this through Christ our Lord.
—*Book of Common Prayer, 1549*

After Reading III
O God of justice and peace,
whose kingdom is at hand,
give us a spirit of repentance
to make us worthy of your kingdom,
that in our day justice may flourish
and conflict give way
to the peace you bestow in Christ,
who lives and reigns forever and ever.
—© *ICEL,* adapted

After Reading IV
Merciful and most loving God,
the Lord Jesus humbled himself
to exalt the whole human race;
descended into the depths
to lift up the lowly;
and took our nature of the Virgin Mary
to restore in us the heavenly image we had forfeited.
By the wonder of the incarnation
and the grace of the paschal mystery
make us cleave always to you,
that, as you have redeemed us by your goodness,
we might ever please you by our devoted service.
We ask this through Christ our Lord.
—*Gallican sacramentary,* adapted

TEXTS FOR A NEW YEAR'S VIGIL

These texts may be used in conjunction with the outline for the New Year's Eve Vigil office given on page 47.

Thanksgiving for the Light

As in the Christmas Vigil

Collects

Adapted from the Episcopal Book of Occasional Services

After Reading I
O God our Creator,
you have divided our life into days and seasons,
and called us to acknowledge your providence year after year:
Accept your people who come to offer their praises,
and, in your mercy, receive their prayers;
through Christ our Lord.

After Reading II
Almighty God, source of all life, giver of all blessing,
and savior of all who turn to you:
Have mercy upon this nation;
deliver us from falsehood, malice and disobedience;
turn our feet into your paths;
and grant that we may serve you in peace;
through Christ our Lord.

After Reading III
In your wisdom, O Lord our God,
you have made all things,
and have allotted to each of us the days of our life:
Grant that we may live in your presence,
be guided by your Holy Spirit,
and offer all our works to your honor and glory;
through Jesus Christ our Lord.

After Reading IV
Almighty Father, you give the sun for a light by day,
and the moon and the stars by night:
Graciously receive us, this night and always, into your favor and protection,
defending us from all harm and governing us with your Holy Spirit,
that every shadow of ignorance, every failure of faith or weakness of heart,
every evil or wrong desire may be removed far from us.
Then may we, being justified in our Lord Jesus Christ,
be sanctified by your Spirit, and glorified by your infinite mercies
in the day of the glorious appearing of our Lord and Savior Jesus Christ,
who lives and reigns for ever and ever.

After Reading V
Most gracious and merciful God,
you have reconciled us to yourself through
    Jesus Christ your Son,
and called us to new life in him:
Grant that we, who begin this year
    in Jesus' name,
may complete it to his honor and glory;
who lives and reigns for ever and ever.

After Reading VI
O God, through your Son you have taught
    us to be watchful,
and to await the sudden day of judgment:
Strengthen us against Satan and the forces
    of wickedness,
the evil powers of this world and the sinful
    desires within us.
Grant that, having served you all the days
    of our life,
we may come at last to the dwelling place
    your Son has prepared for us;
who lives and reigns for ever and ever.

After Reading VII
Almighty and merciful God,
through your well-beloved Son Jesus Christ,
the King of kings and Lord of lords,
you have willed to make all things new:
Grant that we may be renewed by your
    Holy Spirit,
and may come at last to that heavenly
    country
where your people hunger and thirst no more,
and the tears are wiped away from every eye;
through Christ our Lord.

PROCLAMATION OF THE BIRTH OF CHRIST

The twenty-fifth day of December. In the five thousand one hundred and ninety ninth year of the creation of the world from the time when God in the beginning created the heavens and the earth; the two thousand nine hundred and fifty-seventh year after the flood; the two thousand and fifteenth year from the birth of Abraham; the one thousand five hundred and tenth year from Moses and the going forth of the people of Israel from Egypt; the one thousand and thirty-second year from David's being anointed king; in the sixty-fifth week according to the prophecy of Daniel; in the one hundred and ninety-fourth Olympiad; the seven hundred and fifty-second year from the foundation of the city of Rome; the forty second year of the

56 CHRISTMAS: PROCLAMATION OF THE BIRTH OF CHRIST

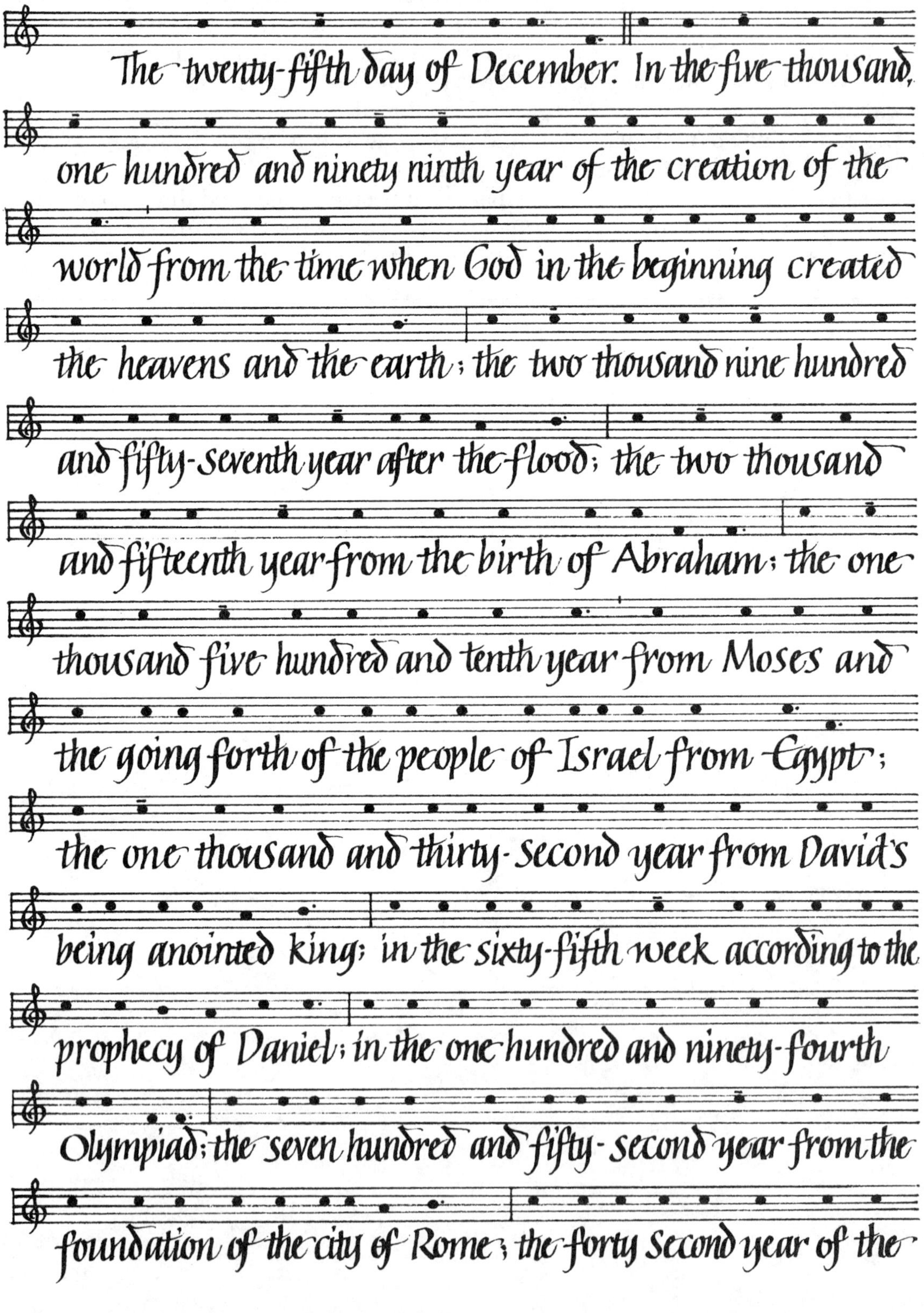

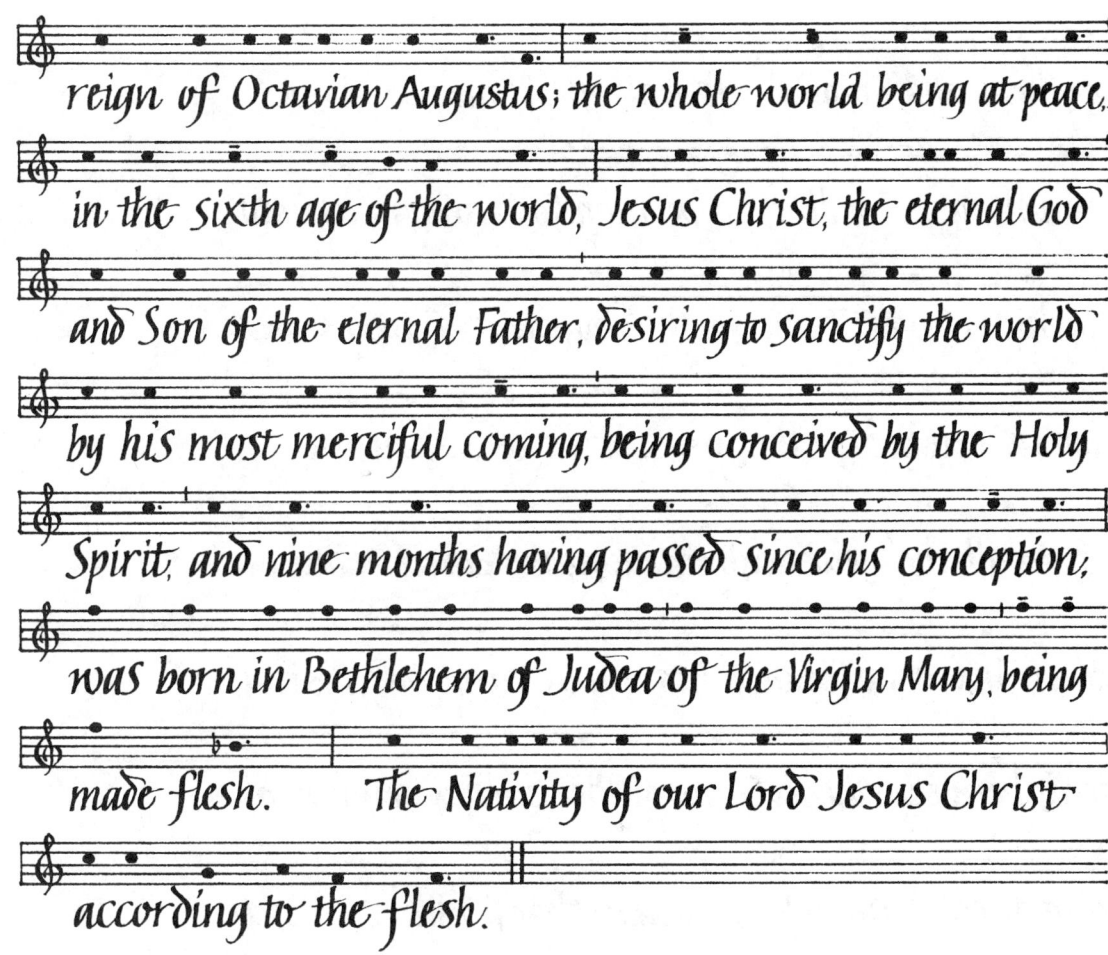

Suggestions for using the Christmas proclamation:

This is a traditional rendering of the Christmas proclamation, taken from the entry for December 25 in the ancient martyrology. It may be sung at the beginning of the Midnight Mass. It should be done without explanation, with great simplicity and reverence in the silence and darkness as the assembly keeps vigil.

Acolytes with lighted candles might accompany the cantor to the ambo or another appropriate place in front of the assembly. The cantor may indicate with a gesture that the assembly is to stand; when all are standing, the proclamation begins. The tradition calls for the assembly to kneel after the words "having passed since his conception..." and to rise before "The nativity of our Lord..." The cantor should stop at both times to allow this to take place. The acolytes and other ministers should know beforehand so that they can model for the assembly the kneeling and the rising.

When the proclamation is concluded, the entrance rites of Midnight Mass—which have truly begun with this chant—can continue with song.

Text copyright © 1989, United States Catholic Conference (USCC), 3211 Fourth Street NE, Washington DC 20017-1194. All rights reserved. Text was prepared by Rev. Richard Wojcik. Chant adapted from the original chant by Msgr. J. T. Kush. Calligraphy by Rosie Kelly.

PROCLAMATION OF THE DATE OF EASTER

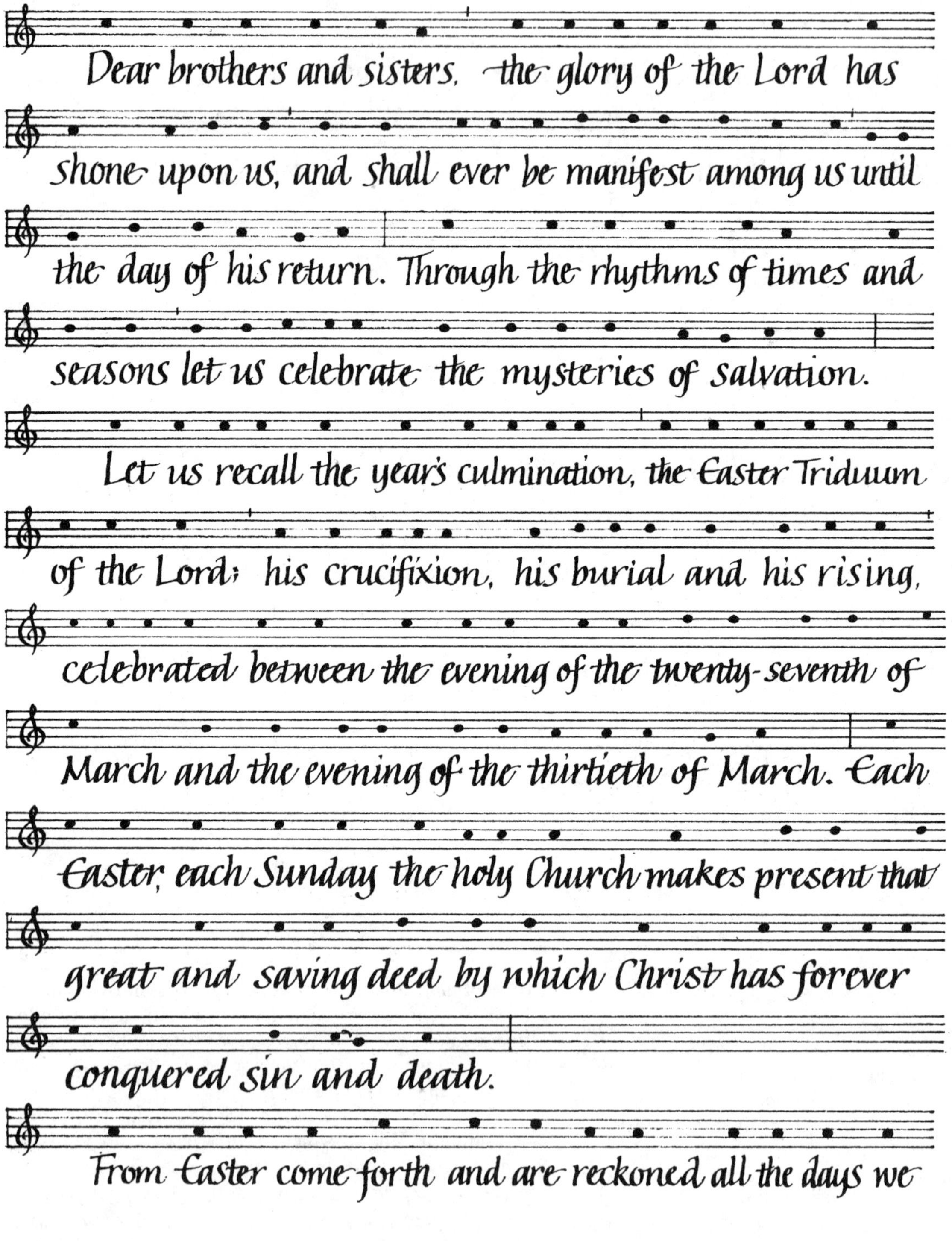

Dear brothers and sisters, the glory of the Lord has shone upon us, and shall ever be manifest among us until the day of his return. Through the rhythms of times and seasons let us celebrate the mysteries of salvation.

Let us recall the year's culmination, the Easter Triduum of the Lord: his crucifixion, his burial and his rising, celebrated between the evening of the twenty-seventh of March and the evening of the thirtieth of March. Each Easter, each Sunday the holy Church makes present that great and saving deed by which Christ has forever conquered sin and death.

From Easter come forth and are reckoned all the days we

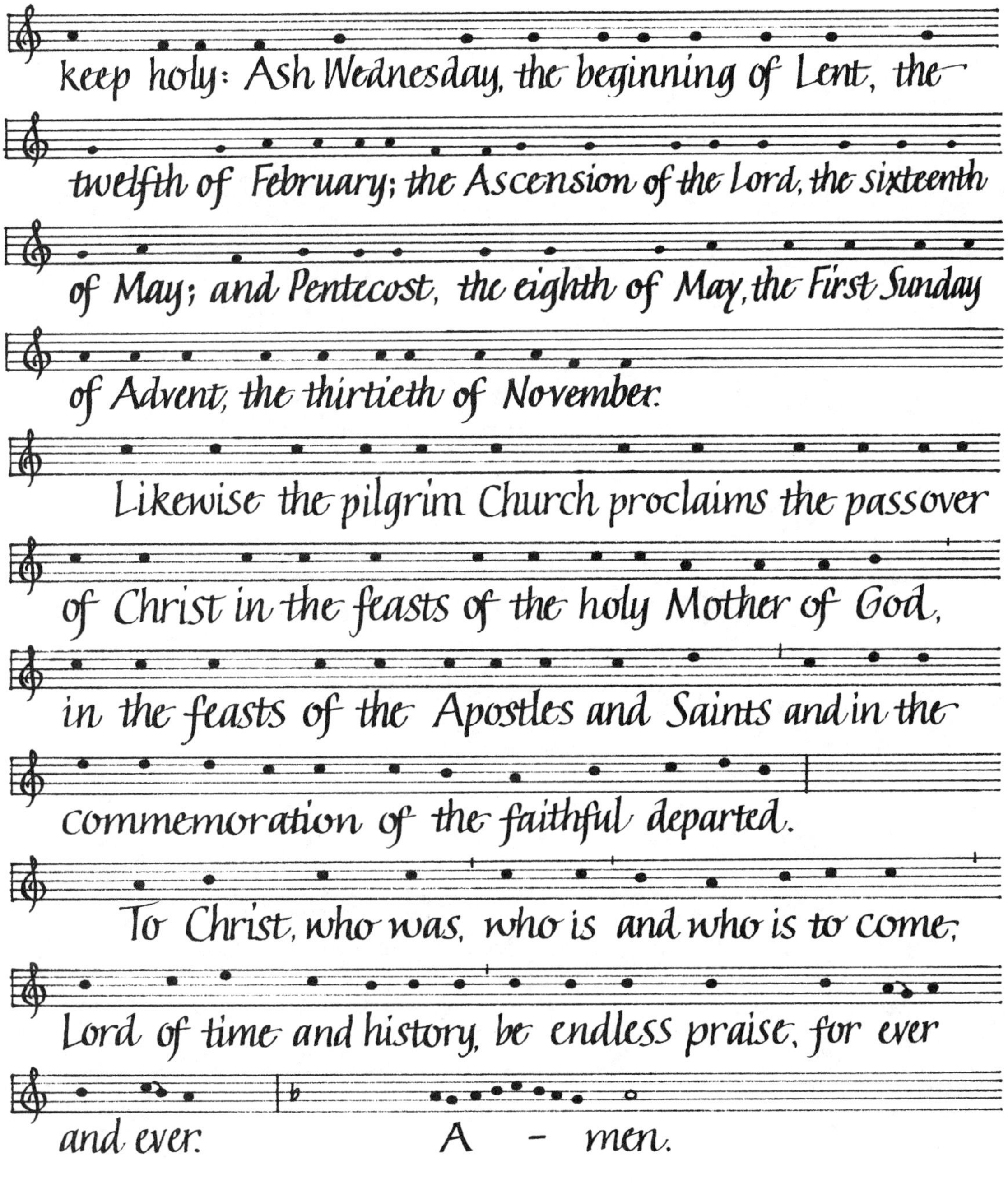

keep holy: Ash Wednesday, the beginning of Lent, the twelfth of February; the Ascension of the Lord, the sixteenth of May; and Pentecost, the eighth of May, the First Sunday of Advent, the thirtieth of November.

Likewise the pilgrim Church proclaims the passover of Christ in the feasts of the holy Mother of God, in the feasts of the Apostles and Saints and in the commemoration of the faithful departed.

To Christ, who was, who is and who is to come, Lord of time and history, be endless praise, for ever and ever. A - men.

Suggestions for using the Epiphany proclamation:

This proclamation, announcing the date of Easter and the various dates that depend on Easter, is chanted by a cantor after the gospel reading or homily on the solemnity of the Epiphany. The proclamation can be sung from the ambo with lights and incense as at the gospel. The line, "Each Easter, each Sunday, . . ." may sound like an error when chanted. The Italian sacramentary reads: "Every Sunday, as in a weekly Easter, . . ." Cantors, take note of the key change in the final lines. After a brief pause, this section should take on a different character, as the proclamation concludes with an acclamation of praise.

Text copyright © 1989, United States Catholic Conference (USCC), 3211 Fourth Street NE, Washington DC 20017-1194. All rights reserved. Calligraphy by Rosie Kelly.

NOTES

WINTER ORDINARY TIME

The Season
Orientation / 63
ICEL Pastoral Introduction: Ordinary Time / 64
Perspective on Ordinary Time / 66
Purpose of Ordinary Time / 66
Presentation of Ordinary Time / 67
Transitional Rites / 67
Liturgy of the Word / 74
Liturgy of the Eucharist / 75
Preparing the Parish / 76
Taking It Home / 77
Other Ritual Prayers and Sacraments / 77
The Worship Environment / 78
The Calendar
January 13 – February 11 / 79

Orientation

Do the names Saturninus, Emeritus and Victoria ring a bell? No? Too bad, because if they had a feast day in the liturgical calendar, it would be coming up just one month from now. On February 12, 304, these saints and their companions bore witness and suffered the consequences. It's too bad, liturgically speaking, that their names and martyrdom are not better known to the church at large. For while we've all heard of the North American martyrs and the martyrs of Uganda, these "martyrs of Abitina" have an important and moving message for the church of today. But sadly, not only are their names not widely known but neither is the reason for their execution. Stephen was put to death for bearing witness to the Lordship of Jesus. Thomas Becket in the twelfth century and Thomas More in the sixteenth gave their lives for the integrity of the church and for defending its liberty in the face of secular encroachments. In our own age, Archbishop Oscar Romero of El Salvador was slain at the altar for his prophetic denunciation of an oppressive military regime and his fearless advocacy of justice for the poor.

But Saturninus, Emeritus, Victoria and their friends? They were martyrs for Sunday! That's right, for Sunday! Let's go to the court transcript:

Thirty-one men and eighteen women arrested for illegal assembly appeared before Proconsul Anulinus in Carthage.... When the official accused them of disobeying the imperial edicts, Saturninus, a priest, answered: "We must celebrate the Lord's Day. It is a law for us." Emeritus, a lector, in whose home the community had assembled, spoke to the same effect: "Yes, it was in my house that we celebrated the Lord's Day. We cannot live without celebrating the Lord's Day." And Victoria, a virgin, proudly declared: "I attended the meeting because I am a Christian" (P. Jounel quoting a Latin hagiography in Martimort (ed.) *The Church at Prayer IV* [Collegeville: Liturgical Press, 1986], 15).

Imagine laying down your life for the Lord's Day! Some Sundays we can barely put down our newspapers or the remote control! But our attitude toward Sunday is not simply a case of bad faith or ill will. After all, we are Christians at an odd point in liturgical and human history.

On one hand, Vatican II opened to the people of God the manifold riches of the liturgy. Our liturgical prayer is communal now and in the vernacular. The Council's reforms refined the outline of the liturgical year and pruned back the sanctoral calendar. It trimmed off excess material (the Septuagesima "pre-Lent" and the Pentecost octave) and defined the nature of the major seasons through the clear explanations of the *General Instruction of the Roman Missal* and through enriched texts in the sacramentary and

lectionary. Moreover, for the first time in history all this "official" material was made widely available to the laity of the church through the preparation of people for liturgical ministries and for sharing in liturgical planning. The orientation of the liturgical books is chronological: They begin at the beginning of the liturgical year. First in the book is Advent, followed by Christmastime, then Lent, the Triduum and the Fifty Days. The orientation of educational and catechetical materials, however, is hierarchical. The most important season is presented first: the Paschal Triduum, center of the liturgical year, with its preparatory time and extended festal period. Then comes Christmas with its attendant seasons.

On the other hand, the effect of all this has been to direct our attention to the two major cycles on which the liturgical year turns, to channel our energies into planning these cycles carefully and celebrating them well. This is fine, but we sometimes forget the first holy day of all and end up neglecting the kernel from which all liturgical observance springs:

> By a tradition handed down from the apostles and having its origin from the very day of Christ's resurrection, the church celebrates the paschal mystery every eighth day, which, with good reason, bears the name of the Lord's Day or Sunday. For on this day Christ's faithful must gather together so that, by hearing the word of God and taking part in the eucharist, they may call to mind the passion, the resurrection and the glorification of the Lord Jesus and may thank God, who "has begotten them again unto a living hope through the resurrection of Jesus Christ from the dead" (1 Peter 1:3). Hence the Lord's Day is the first holy day of all and should be proposed to the devotion of the faithful and taught to them in such a way that it may become in fact a day of joy and of freedom from work (*Constitution on the Sacred Liturgy,* 106).

The text of ICEL's Pastoral Introduction: Ordinary Time keeps our focus on Sunday as Sunday, on the primacy it has in itself. It is best read with reference to various sections of the Pastoral Introduction to the Order of Mass. Together these documents help us to reflect on the care and attention with which the Lord's Day eucharist should be celebrated. This *Sourcebook,* therefore, presents the Pastoral Introduction: Ordinary Time (PIOT) in its entirety, with portions of the Pastoral Introduction: Order of Mass (PIOM) cited when relevant. Because Easter comes so early this year, the period of Ordinary Time between Christmas and Lent is extraordinarily brief. There may barely be time for the community and its ministers to catch their breath before Lent, let alone reflect on our observance of the Lord's Day! It will almost certainly be necessary to return to this section when Ordinary Time resumes after Pentecost. But these reflections are offered "in the dead of winter" (in the Northern Hemisphere, anyway) as a way of sowing some seeds that may blossom when summer leisure is finally at hand.

Remember that as we turn to these documents and the task to which they summon us, we travel with Saturninus, Emeritus, Victoria and their companions. Why not ask their intercession as we begin our journey? Chances are they are less besieged with requests for prayer than the saints whose names we all know. They may be pleasantly surprised — even downright shocked! — to hear their names called out across the centuries. And they will no doubt be pleased to know that modern-day Christians, even if not as heroically as they, are still taking the Lord's Day seriously and trying to keep it well!

ICEL Pastoral Introduction: Ordinary Time

1 The church celebrates the mystery of Christ according to the rhythm of a yearly cycle whose climax is the Easter Triduum. The seasons of Lent and Easter and, to a somewhat lesser extent, the seasons of Advent and Christmas are the most solemn times of the year. The yearly cycle is completed by the 33 or 34 weeks that comprise Ordinary Time.

2 Ordinary Time begins on the Monday after the Sunday following 6 January and continues until the Tuesday before Ash Wednesday inclusive. It begins again on the Monday after Pentecost and ends before Evening Prayer I of the First Sunday of Advent.

- The numbering of Sundays in Ordinary Time is computed in this way: The first week in Ordinary Time follows the Feast of the Baptism of the Lord. The other Sundays and weeks are numbered in order until the beginning of Lent. If there are 34 weeks in Ordinary Time, the numbering of the weeks resumes after Pentecost, even though the Solemnities of the Holy Trinity and of the Body

and Blood of Christ (transferred to the Sunday after Trinity Sunday where it is not observed as a holy day) will be celebrated on the first Sundays after the Easter season. If there are 33 weeks in Ordinary Time, the first week which would otherwise follow Pentecost is omitted.

- The transitions between seasons deserve special attention in order to enhance the rhythm of the liturgical year. After the Feasts of the Epiphany and the Baptism of the Lord, the Sunday gospels concentrate on the beginnings of the Lord's preaching. As the liturgical year draws to a close and Advent approaches, eschatological themes predominate. After the Easter season, the Solemnities of the Holy Trinity and of the Body and Blood of Christ provide a kind of transition to Ordinary Time.

3 While the other liturgical seasons have their own distinctive character and celebrate a specific aspect of the mystery of Christ, the weeks of Ordinary Time—especially the Sundays—are devoted rather to the mystery of Christ in all its aspects.

4 Ordinary Time enables the church to appreciate more fully the ministry and message of Christ. The lectionary for Mass provides a semicontinuous reading of the synoptic gospels on the Sundays in Ordinary Time in such a way that, as the Lord's life and preaching unfold, the teaching proper to each of these gospels is presented.

- For this reason the integrity of the lectionary is respected, and the homily at the Sunday eucharist normally draws upon the scriptures to open up for the assembly the mysteries of the faith and the guiding principles of the Christian life. In this way, the celebration of the mystery of Christ is connected with the everyday life and commitments of the Christian people who make up the assembly.

- Thanks to the continuity of the scriptural texts used on Sundays, the liturgy sometimes commemorates a certain aspect of Christ's life and ministry over a period of several weeks, for example, the five weeks in Year B of the lectionary when the reading of chapter six of the Gospel of John is inserted into the cycle of Mark's gospel. It can be helpful in planning the Sunday liturgy to take notice of these elements of unity.

- Sensitive selection from among the variety of texts and alternative ritual elements can assist the assembly to celebrate the various aspects of the mystery of Christ. For instance, different forms of the opening rite may be chosen. The Mass formulary for each Sunday includes opening prayers inspired by the readings of the three-year lectionary cycle. The prefaces and solemn blessings for Ordinary Time may be chosen to complement the readings. The second eucharistic prayer has an interpolation for Ordinary Time that may be inserted after the Sanctus. The variety of texts available for the weekdays of Ordinary Time is even greater. These are all found in Volume II of this edition of the Missal. [This paragraph refers to new elements that will be found in the revised sacramentary, which is awaiting approval and publication.]

- General intercessions are ordinarily included.

5 When a solemnity or a feast of the Lord or the Commemoration of All the Faithful Departed falls on a Sunday in Ordinary Time, this celebration normally takes precedence over the Sunday liturgy. Some special feasts are normally celebrated on a Sunday in Ordinary Time (the Holy Trinity, Christ the King and the Body and Blood of Christ where it is not observed as a holy day).

6 By its nature, however, Sunday excludes the permanent assignment of any other celebration to the day. While on rare occasions it may be appropriate to celebrate a ritual, votive or other special Mass on a Sunday in Ordinary Time, this should only occur when a serious need or pastoral advantage is present and at the direction of the local ordinary or with his permission.

- It may happen that special themes are proposed for the Sunday eucharist, for example, peace, Christian unity, vocations, the missions, Christian education and social justice. These intentions may be referred to in the homily when appropriate to the prayers and readings of the day's liturgy. They may be expressed in the general intercessions, mentioned at the time for announcements and reflected in the decoration of the church. But these observances do not change the liturgical calendar or displace the regular Sunday liturgy.

- Out of respect for the nature of the liturgy and in order to avoid the possibility of its being perceived as a means for promoting various worthwhile causes, it may be better to rely mostly on other means of education or exhortation concerning special themes. These could include the distribution of printed matter, the use of the church notice board or special displays, separate talks, discussions, films and the like.

- The collection of money for one of these special intentions could likewise take place outside the liturgy, for example, as the people leave the church. If money gifts are to be received during the liturgy, they should be collected at the time of the preparation of the gifts.

7 Ordinary Time provides the church with an opportunity to bring out more clearly the importance of Sunday as the first feast day of all, the weekly celebration of the paschal mystery.

- Good quality in liturgical celebration should be maintained throughout Ordinary Time, as in all

the seasons of the liturgical year. The planning and preparation of the liturgy should seek to develop consistent patterns for both ministers and the assembly as they fulfill their respective roles in the celebration of the eucharist. Such patterns can be achieved without the loss of appropriate variety in the choice of texts and ritual elements for particular celebrations. In this way liturgical ministers will be well prepared for their tasks, and the actions and objects used will have the strength and clarity of symbols that are effective.

- Vestments are green in color for Sundays and weekdays. Decorations may appropriately reflect the beauty of nature and the changes in the local natural environment.

Perspective on Ordinary Time

THE liturgical year is not about a year, it is about a week. And it is not even about a week, it is about one day, the day after the seventh, the eighth day, the Lord's Day.

Sunday's centrality is an important concept to remember as we enter into a season of the liturgical year that, from this point of view, is not a season at all!

So the Pastoral Introduction: Ordinary Time makes it clear that there is no "distinctive character" to these Sundays before Lent or to the Sundays between Pentecost and Advent. There is no focus on any "specific aspect of the mystery of Christ" (PIOT, 3). Or to cast it in positive terms, the church is stepping back and looking at the whole paschal mystery of Christ: Christ who is announced and incarnated, who is born and baptized, who preaches and teaches, heals and prays, endures a passion and death from which he rises to return to the Father and send forth the Spirit, that he might confirm the mission of the church in which he reigns until his glorious return. As the church looks at that whole Christ, the shape and sight and sound of the mystery are mediated through the lens of each week's scriptures. Over a short span of weeks, thanks to the continuity that informs the structure of the lectionary, "a certain aspect of Christ's life and ministry" may emerge with greater clarity (PIOT, 4). But the focus is never so sharp or so clearly defined as it would be in a particular liturgical season or on a specific feast.

Ordinary Time is really a "season of Sundays." The term "ordinary time" does not even appear in the Latin liturgical books. It is an attempt to convey in English a Latin term that defies translation: for example, *Dominica XII per annum*. Rendered literally as Twelfth Sunday through the year, it actually means "Sunday Number Twelve occurring during the course of the year outside the liturgical seasons." So this is not ordinary time, but ordinal, or counted, time. In the liturgical seasons we say "Sundays *of* Advent, *of* Lent, *of* Easter," but these are Sundays *in* Ordinary Time. The numbers simply help us find our way around the lectionary and sacramentary during these approximately 30 weeks, the largest slice of the yearly pie.

Purpose of Ordinary Time

THERE is no question, then, of developing a "spirituality of the season," or of imposing on this short period in winter, or longer period in summer and fall, any kind of theme or spirit. These unnamed Sundays are given to the church to enable us "to appreciate more fully the ministry and message of Christ" (PIOT, 4). Come to think of it, these Sundays only *seem* to be unnamed. They are, in fact, named for the Lord: the Lord's Day and, therefore, the day of the Lord's Supper.

Two aspects of the weekly celebration are highlighted, then, by the Pastoral Introductions to Ordinary Time and to the Order of Mass: Christ's teaching presence in the church through his living word and Christ's paschal presence through the eucharistic mystery. The first aspect, of course, directs our attention to the liturgy of the word. Through a semicontinuous reading of the synoptic gospels, in a schema shared now with almost all the Christian churches, the Sunday lectionary in Ordinary Time lets "the Lord's life and preaching unfold" (PIOT, 4). There is a discipline involved in respecting the integrity of the lectionary, but a corresponding freedom flows from observance of that discipline. By following the lectionary, the assembly is protected from the preacher's or planner's choice of favorite passages. If the admonition "normally to draw upon the scriptures" is observed, the homilist and congregation will find themselves under the judgment of a word being proclaimed that Sunday throughout the churches, including those with whom we do not yet enjoy eucharistic communion. While at times the community will delight in a "comfortable word," on other Sundays it will wrestle with hard sayings that neither it nor the homilist would have chosen to proclaim! Through the passage of these "ordinary" Sundays, week by week, year by year, "the mysteries of the faith and the guiding principles of the Christian life" are held up before us, and "the celebration of the mystery of Christ is connected with the everyday life and commitments of the Christian people who make up the assembly" (PIOT, 4).

The other aspect of Sunday liturgy in Ordinary Time is particularly evident in the liturgy of the eucharist. Freed from intense seasonal emphases on the Lord's incarnation and appearance, manifestation or passion, the paschal nature of Sunday and of Sunday's eucharist can more clearly shine through (PIOT, 7). This will be aided through a judicious choice of texts, but there is the clear appreciation that the risen Christ is mediated not only through words but through people, things, actions. Both Pastoral Introductions indicate that much needs to be done with these "components" of the Sunday celebration: People need to work on things, and things need to be worked on. Ordinary Time, especially the long period from Pentecost to Advent, may furnish the leisure and liberty to hone skills and refine practices. It may be the perfect opportunity "to develop consistent patterns for both ministers and assembly as they fulfill their respective roles," and to attend with care to the strength of liturgical objects used and the ritual actions carried out (PIOT, 7). Sunday doesn't "work" by itself; it is literally liturgy, *leitourgia,* the public work of the people of God.

Presentation of Ordinary Time

TRANSITIONAL RITES

IF the liturgy of the word and the liturgy of the eucharist are to be celebrated with all the power and potential that is theirs, then the rites that lead us to them and take us from them—the transitional rites—need to be celebrated in such a way that they accomplish their tasks graciously and well.

"Transitional" does not mean unimportant; it simply indicates that these rites bring the assembly and ministers, and the things used by the assembly and the ministers, from one place to another. It is most important that these minor rites do what they are meant to do unobtrusively and with reverent dispatch. This will help preserve the proper proportions of the liturgy's several components and enable the overall dynamic of the liturgy to thrive.

The Pastoral Introduction: Order of Mass tells us what each rite is meant to do and then how each may best accomplish its purpose. The official text is presented here to guide the community's reflections on what we are doing right now and how we might do it better in the future. Some reactions will be offered, some questions raised. But each community, reflecting on these notes in light of its own liturgical practice, will be able to conduct its own "examination of conscience."

The paragraph numbers in the quoted excerpts are those of the PIOM. The extensive footnotes to the original are omitted here, but every "must do" in the PIOM is referenced to the church's official liturgical documentation, and every "may do" is rooted in the best of contemporary scholarship and pastoral practice.

Introductory Rites

66 In the introductory rites the assembly is called together in Christ and established again as the church. The risen Lord is present in the midst of the assembly, which becomes visible as the body of Christ. Thus, the assembly itself is the first instance of Christ's presence in the liturgy. The function of these rites is to enable the community, coming together from a multiplicity of concerns and a variety of ways of life, to become aware of itself again as a gathered community, alert and ready to listen to the word and to celebrate the sacrament.

- The introductory rites are led from the chair rather than from the altar or ambo.

■ ENTRANCE PROCESSION

67 The assembly's worship begins with the opening song and procession, which help to create an ambience of celebration and a sense of identity and common purpose.

- The opening song should be such that everyone is able in some degree to join in singing it. It may consist of an antiphon and psalm or another appropriate song. When no singing is possible, the recommended antiphon may appropriately be used by incorporating it into the introductory remarks that may follow the greeting.

- A procession of ministers through and from the assembly expresses visibly the relationship of the priest celebrant and the other ministers to the congregation.

- Depending on the occasion, the procession is led by ministers carrying the censer (thurible) with burning incense, the cross and two candles. They are followed by acolytes and other ministers, then the deacon or reader carrying the book of the gospels, if it is to be used, or the lectionary. Concelebrants, the deacon of the Mass and the priest celebrant then follow. If the book of the gospels has been carried, it is placed on the altar upon arrival in the sanctuary.

68 The altar is an abiding symbol of Christ and the center of the eucharistic action.

- The priest and deacon, together with concelebrants and other ministers in the procession, bow to the altar on arrival as a sign of reverence. If a tabernacle containing the blessed sacrament is in the vicinity, they genuflect. Afterwards, the priest and deacon, and any concelebrants, then make an additional reverence to the altar with a kiss.

- On more solemn occasions, this reverence may be enhanced by the use of incense.

- After the procession and the reverencing of the altar, the priest and deacon proceed to the chair. From there the priest greets the people and leads the opening rite.

■ GREETING

69 After making the sign of the cross together, the priest and people exchange formal greetings as a mutual acknowledgment and evocation of the presence of Christ in their midst and as a prayer for his sustaining power.

- As the first dialogue between priest and people, the greeting and response should be both warm and reverent. Casual and personalized greetings that emphasize a merely human exchange and obscure the mystery of Christ's presence and action are inappropriate.

70 The Mass of the day may be introduced at this point. A very brief and well-prepared comment can help to create the appropriate atmosphere and give tone and orientation to the entire celebration.

- At this point strangers, guests and special groups may briefly be welcomed to the celebration.

- When significant numbers of children are present, they may be acknowledged and addressed directly at this point.

- Though the introduction will normally be the function of the priest, on occasion it may be fitting for the deacon or some other member of the assembly to do this.

■ COMMENTARY: This first transition rite is meant to bring us from our separate worlds and private spaces and help us to remember who we really are together: God's own people. That's a lot for this rite to accomplish, and it is remarkable how few components there are to the rite. A procession with song, a kiss of the table, a greeting: the famed "noble simplicity" of the Roman rite. But is it nobly simple in our community? And if not, why not?

Maybe we sense that no procession, no song, no greeting can "gather us and make us aware" of who we are meant to be. Perhaps that is why, in many places, we have let other things rush in to rescue the moment: "Our cantor this morning is . . . Our lector is . . . Our eucharistic ministers are . . . Please stand now and greet our celebrant, Father . . ." Well-intentioned, sincere words. But they unwittingly announce the cast members of a show we are about to watch. They unintentionally tell us that we are standing and singing not to celebrate Christ already in our midst but to greet one person whose liturgy this is in some special way. The presider, in turn, feels almost compelled to return the "good morning" greetings and then keep the informality and "warmth" going by inviting everyone to greet those around them—or make a new friend! But as Gabe Huck notes, "This rite is not about how friendly we can be with one another." He continues:

> What too often happens here is theft. The liturgy is being taken away from the assembly. The presider who wants to be so loved, so much with it, ends up acting like the liturgy is what he or she does and we enjoy. Pleasing people, making them like you, has nothing to do with presiding ("From Bed to Book: Entering into Sunday Mass," part 2, *Liturgy 90,* July 1995).

Especially in Ordinary Time, consider the most simple greeting, which is also the most ancient: *The Lord be with you.* Let any words of welcome or introduction be carefully chosen and well prepared: Spontaneous ad-libbing almost always sins by excess.

■ OPENING RITE

71 One of the following opening rites is selected. The choice may be made on the basis of the liturgical season, the feast, the particular occasion, for example, a particular ritual Mass, or on the basis of the circumstances of the assembly that gathers for the celebration. Each of the forms of the opening rite begins with an invitation by the priest. On occasion the invitation may appropriately be incorporated into the introductory remarks that may follow the greeting.

■ RITE OF BLESSING AND SPRINKLING OF WATER

72 As they assemble, the people of God are attentive to the risen Christ. In so doing, they recognize themselves as reconciled sinners and prepare to receive the gift of word and sacrament. The blessing and sprinkling of water serves as a memorial of Easter and baptism. God is thanked for intervening to save us through the medium of water and is asked to continue to give forgiveness and life.

- Because of its emphasis on Easter and baptism, it may be particularly appropriate to do the blessing and sprinkling during the season of Easter.
- If the greeting and blessing take place at the door, the priest may sprinkle the people during the entrance procession.

■ PENITENTIAL RITE

73 In the penitential rite the assembly, gathered in God's presence, recognizes its sinfulness and confesses the mystery of Christ's love. This may take one of two forms, both of which conclude with a prayer of absolution.

- The first form, once a private prayer of preparation, is a general confession that invokes the support of the communion of saints and, specifically, of the community gathered for the eucharist.
- The second form comprises verses of the penitential psalms.
- The season of Lent may be a particularly appropriate time to select the penitential rite.

■ LITANY OF PRAISE

74 The litany of praise is addressed to Christ our Redeemer. A number of models are offered for imitation and adaptation. All such adaptations should, like the models provided, focus on Christ and his mercy.

- The litany of praise is sung or recited. The verses or tropes may be sung by a cantor or choir.

■ KYRIE

75 The Kyrie is an ancient chant by which the assembly acclaims the Lord and pleads for mercy. The Roman Church adopted it from the Eastern liturgies, where it formed the response to various litanies of intercession. It may be used in English or in the original Greek.

- It is by nature a chant and, when used, is normally sung by all, alternating with the cantor or choir.

■ GLORIA

76 The Gloria is one of the church's most ancient, solemn hymns. In the West its use was originally restricted to the opening of only the most solemn eucharistic celebrations.

- The Gloria is by nature a festive hymn and is normally sung entirely, or in part, by the people.
- Its use is particularly appropriate during the seasons of Christmas and Easter.
- The Gloria may not be used on the Sundays or weekdays of Advent and Lent.

■ OTHER OPENING RITES

77 Another opening rite may be selected for particular occasions and in accord with the prescriptions of the respective liturgical books. These rites occur on certain special feasts, when the Liturgy of the Hours is combined with the Mass, or when special rites are celebrated during the Mass, for example, baptism, marriage or funeral rites. Sometimes, for example, on Passion Sunday or on the Feast of the Presentation of the Lord, when an entrance procession forms part of this opening rite itself, the opening rite follows the form given for these occasions.

■ COMMENTARY:

According to a proposed simplification of the introductory rites, approved by the United States bishops and (at this writing) awaiting Roman confirmation, only one of these components is chosen at any given Mass. The Vatican II Order of Mass appears to many scholars and pastoral ministers to string together a series of unrelated elements. This proposal attempts to prune that structure already in place at funerals, when infant baptism is celebrated at Mass, on Palm Sunday and whenever another rite begins Mass. It might be helpful to establish a seasonal approach to the choice of introductory rite, for example:

- Advent: lighting of Advent wreath and/or litany of praise
- Christmastime: sung Gloria
- Lent: penitential rite or sung Kyrie
- Eastertime: blessing and sprinkling with water
- Ordinary Time: litany of praise or varied rites

- **OPENING PRAYER**

78 The opening prayer completes the introductory rites. Through petition to God, it sets the tone of the celebration and prepares the assembly to hear the word of God.

- As the culmination of the introductory rites, an opening prayer is always used. It may be sung or said.

- When paraphrases are permitted at Masses with children, they should respect the nature of this prayer.

- After the invitation "Let us pray," all observe some moments of silence in which they place themselves in God's presence and make their personal petitions.

- The opening prayer always ends with a full trinitarian conclusion, to which the assembly responds "Amen."

- On Sundays, solemnities and feasts of the Lord, besides the prayers taken directly from the Latin text, alternative opening prayers are provided that are inspired by the appointed readings for Years A, B and C of the lectionary for Mass. A number of these prayers are also found in volume II for weekday use.

Preparation Rite

100 At the beginning of the liturgy of the eucharist the gifts that will become the Lord's body and blood are brought to the altar. This taking of bread and wine is a preparation of the gifts. It is not in itself the sacrifice or offering but a preparation for the eucharistic prayer, the great act of blessing and thanksgiving, which constitutes the church's memorial offering of Christ's sacrifice, and for communion.

101 The church encourages the faithful to bring forward, and even to provide, the elements through which Christ's offering will be made present, together with money and other gifts for the sustenance of Christ's body, especially the poor and the needy.

102 The purpose of this rite, then, is to make the altar, the gifts which are placed on it, and the assembly ready for the eucharistic offering which is to follow.

- **PREPARATION OF THE ALTAR**

103 First, the altar, the Lord's table, is prepared as the center of the eucharistic liturgy. Until this point in the celebration, with the exception of its veneration at the beginning, the altar has not been the focus of attention. It remains almost bare and unused during the liturgy of the word, which is centered at the ambo. Now the setting is prepared for the sacred meal.

- Everything indicates that a new and important stage of the liturgy is about to commence. Lighting may be directed toward the altar. A corporal is laid out of sufficient size to accommodate all the vessels that may be brought to the altar now and at the time of communion.

- The corporal, purificators and sacramentary are requisites needed for the eucharistic offering. They are not themselves offerings or gifts and are not brought up in the procession of gifts. They should be brought reverently but without ceremony from a side table, along with the cup if it will be prepared at the altar.

- Since these are preparatory tasks, they are carried out by a deacon, acolyte or other minister, or other members of the assembly.

- **PRESENTATION OF THE GIFTS**

104 It is one of the church's most ancient customs that the people themselves provided the materials for the eucharist. They also brought other foodstuffs to be blessed for their own use and for the poor. The rite of carrying up the gifts continues the spiritual value and meaning of the ancient custom. This is also the time to bring forward money or gifts for the poor and the church.

105 The procession with the gifts is a powerful expression of the assembly's participation in the eucharist and in the social mission of the church. It is an expression of the humble and contrite heart, the dispossession of self that is a necessary prerequisite for making the true offering which the Lord Jesus gave his people to make with him. The procession with the gifts expresses also our eager willingness to enter into the "holy exchange" with God: "Accept the offerings you have given us, that we may in turn receive the gift of yourself."

- The collection of money takes place first. As an integral part of the eucharistic liturgy since apostolic times, its purpose and value will be better appreciated if, after the general intercessions, the priest celebrant, ministers and people all sit and wait while the collection is taken and then made ready with the other gifts for the procession. The collection is not to be taken during the profession of faith or the general intercessions, nor should it continue during the prayer over the gifts or the eucharistic prayer. Music or song may begin with the collection and continue during the procession of gifts; it continues at least until the gifts have been placed on the altar.

- The elements of bread and wine are carried in the procession in vessels that can be seen by all the assembly. So far as is possible, the bread and wine should each be contained in a single vessel, so that priest and people may be seen to be sharing the same food and drink in the sacrament of unity.

- The gifts of bread, wine and money are carried forward by members of the congregation. It is more expressive of the assembly's identification with the gifts if the procession passes right through the assembly. The gifts are accepted by the priest, who may be assisted by the deacon and other ministers. The collection of money and other gifts is deposited near the altar or in another suitable place. The priest places only the vessels containing the bread and wine on the altar.

- Besides money, gifts in kind and other real gifts for the poor are appropriate but not token items that will be retrieved and returned to ordinary use after the celebration.

- The purpose of any music at this point is to accompany the collection, the procession and the presentation of gifts, particularly when these will occupy a considerable period of time. Sung texts need not speak of bread and wine, nor of offering. Texts expressing joy, praise, community, as well as the spirit of the season, are appropriate. Since the presentation of gifts is preparatory, instrumental music or silence may often be more effective.

■ PLACING OF THE GIFTS ON THE ALTAR

106 The formularies accompanying the placing of the gifts on the altar are based upon Jewish table prayers. They are an expression of praise of God for the creation of the world and for human collaboration in the production of bread and wine that will become the medium of Christ's presence in the midst of the assembly.

- The priest holds the vessel containing the bread slightly above the altar and blesses God. He places the bread on the altar. He then holds the cup in the same way, blesses God and places the cup on the altar.

- Since the taking of bread and wine is expressed primarily by the action, it is envisaged that normally both formularies will be uttered inaudibly during the singing or music. If there is no music, the priest may say them aloud. In this case, the people may respond with the acclamation "Blessed be God for ever." The two formularies should be seen as a unit; it should never happen that one is said inaudibly, the other aloud.

■ MIXING OF WINE AND WATER

107 In the ancient world, wine was regularly tempered with water. In time this functional practice during the eucharist came to be interpreted mystically as symbolizing either the hypostatic union or the union of Christ and the church. Both understandings are included in the formula "By the mystery of this water and wine," which is derived from an ancient Christmas collect.

- The preparation of the cup is a function of the deacon. When no deacon is present, the priest prepares the cup. The one who prepares the cup says the prayer "By the mystery" inaudibly.

- The cup may be prepared at the side table before the bread and wine are placed on the altar.

■ INCENSE

108 Incense may be used at the preparation of the gifts to honor the elements and to acknowledge the presence and action of Christ in the priest celebrant, the ministers and the rest of the assembly.

- The priest incenses the gifts and the altar. The deacon or other minister incenses the priest and the rest of the assembly.

- When the members of the assembly, including the other ministers, are incensed at this time, they stand.

■ WASHING OF HANDS

109 Though historically it may have been a practical necessity for the priest to wash his hands after assembling and arranging the elements of bread and wine and incensing them, the washing of hands was well known in early Christianity, as in Judaism, as a symbolic expression of the need for inner purity at the beginning of a religious action.

- For the sake of authenticity, this action needs to be performed with dignity and deliberation. An appreciable quantity of water is poured from a pitcher and the hands are dried with a towel.

- The words from Psalm 51, like the previous formulary "With humble and contrite hearts," are an expression of the priest's personal preparation and are not pronounced audibly.

■ PRAYER OVER THE GIFTS

110 The prayer over the gifts concludes the preparation of the gifts and points forward to the eucharistic prayer.

- The priest invites the people to pray using either the formulary "Pray brothers and sisters" or simply "Let us pray."

- The prayer may be sung or said; the assembly responds "Amen."

- After concluding the prayer over the gifts, the priest should make a distinct pause to make clear that the preparation of the gifts (the "taking") is complete and that the eucharistic prayer (the "giving thanks") is now about to begin.

■ COMMENTARY: The PIOM's notes on this second "transition" rite have been set forth here in their entirety, without comment, because ideally the rite is carried out without words. The preparation rite is ordinarily quite brief. It certainly should be so during Ordinary Time. At other times, it may be enhanced, for example, by the generous use of incense. But when read carefully, the notes make one thing clear: Whether carried out in a simple or enhanced form, the gestures should speak for themselves.

For this to happen, the gestures need to be carefully thought out and thoughtfully carried out. If what follows sounds like "fussy" attention to detail, remember that whenever words are not used, the gestures have to say it all; consider the silent artistry of ballet or mime. Gracious and graceful movements, authentic and worthy objects, eloquent silence: These are some of the elements that constitute the preparatory rite celebrated well. The questions and comments that follow, under the headings Gestures and Words, are offered as a way of getting a handle on the flow of this rite. Local practice, of course, will shape each community's particular reflection.

■ GESTURES: Is the altar "almost bare," "unused," until this moment? The altar is not a convenient bookstand for the opening prayer. The chair is the place from which the introductory rites are celebrated. If there is no one to hold the book, an unobtrusive bookstand (nothing remotely like the ambo) could be used. With the exception of the altar cloth, there should not be any linens or sound equipment in constant residence there.

The collection is an entity unto itself, with ample warrant in the Pauline letters and Justin's first-century description of the Sunday eucharist. Its existence needs no apology, but it has its place. Or rather, it has its time, which is neither before the general intercessions have ended nor after the prayer over the gifts—or, worse, the eucharistic prayer—has begun.

What is brought forward and what does it look like to the assembly? Are the vessels of a size proportionate to the worship space? Is there one vessel only for each element: a single plate of bread, a single container of wine? Elsewhere the PIOM (#140) suggests that the wine be in a clear glass vessel so that it can be seen and of a sufficiently rich color as to be recognizable as wine. If something beyond bread, wine and the monetary offering is brought forward, is it a mere "token gift" that will later be removed and returned to ordinary use, or is it a true gift for the poor or the church?

Where are things going? Do we put the money near the altar or somewhere else? Are the water cruet, the lavabo bowl and towel kept at an unobtrusive side table? Is the water mixed with the cup there, so that only the bread and cup make it to the altar table?

Once the gifts are brought to the altar table, how are they placed on it? The rubric says the presider holds them "slightly above" the altar. That means not at the same level as at the showing that follows the institution narrative, certainly not as high as during the eucharistic prayer's doxology, and not extended toward the people as at the invitation to communion. Each element, one at a time, needs to be held and placed; taking them both together will inevitably look like the doxology or invitation. The gesture needs to be prolonged enough to make the silent statement: These are being set apart for eucharist. The length of time it takes to say the blessing prayer (inaudibly) is just right. There is no need to speak out loud if the gesture is speaking for itself. The formularies are a unit; both are said aloud or both inaudibly. If the music or singing stops before the setting apart of the cup, the presider should not feel compelled to fill the ensuing silence with the blessing prayer for the wine.

If incensation is done, it is a silent way of honoring the elements for what they will become, the altar for being the table of the paschal sacrifice and meal, and the presider and assembly for Christ's presence in them and in their midst. The presider should not be incensed and then the assembly neglected, nor should the incensation be so minimal as to make the sign inauthentic.

For the washing of hands, authenticity demands more than a cruet and minipurificator. A pitcher and basin and towel are the recommended objects, dignity and deliberation the suggested attitude.

■ WORDS: At last we get to a consideration of the words—because, ideally, they come last! The first words the assembly hears is the invitation "Pray, brothers and sisters," with an appropriate gesture of invitation (extending the hands). In line with practice in some non-English countries, ICEL has recommended the option of introducing the prayer over the gifts with the simple "Let us pray," thus linking this prayer to the opening prayer and the prayer after communion.

Concluding Rites

141 After the communion rite, the Mass closes with a brief concluding rite. Its purpose is to send the people forth to put into effect in their daily lives the paschal mystery and the unity in Christ that they have celebrated. They are given a sense of abiding mission, which calls them to witness to Christ in the world and to bring the gospel to the poor.

142 The concluding rite consists of the priest celebrant's greeting and blessing, which on certain days and occasions is expanded by the prayer over the people or other solemn forms. This is followed by the dismissal and an orderly procession of the ministers and the assembly. The whole rite may be preceded by necessary but brief pastoral announcements.

- When another liturgical rite is to follow immediately, for example, the final commendation at a funeral, the entire concluding rite is omitted because these other rites will have their own form of conclusion.

■ ANNOUNCEMENTS

143 Just as the introductory comments by the priest at the beginning of the celebration may help the assembly to a better appreciation and experience of the mysteries celebrated in the eucharist, so also the pastoral announcements at the end may help the people make the transition from worship into renewed Christian witness in society. They should help people become aware of the faith life and pastoral activity of the community and invite participation in the ongoing work of the church.

- Ordinarily announcements, when required, should be brief enough for the assembly to remain standing.

- In order to respect the dignity of the ambo as the place of God's word, announcements are made from some other place.

- Announcements may be made by the deacon, by the priest if he prefers or by another member of the community chosen for this purpose.

■ COMMENTARY: These notes suggest one foundational question: Do our concluding rites, in fact, communicate a true sending forth to live what we have just celebrated: "Unity," "abiding mission," "witness," "the gospel to the poor?" To serve as transition from worship to witness, announcements need to be brief and well worded. It is not "community bulletin-board time" but a linking up of what we have just been about and something particular we need to remember to be about in the coming week. It is certainly tedious to listen to a simple reading of what we can all read for ourselves in the bulletin. For this reason, perhaps, the PIOM notes wisely that ordinarily there should be no need to sit down again.

■ GREETING

144 The greeting "The Lord be with you" helps the assembly to focus attention again on the prayerful aspect of blessing.

■ BLESSING

145 As scripture attests, all beings are created and kept in existence by God's gracious goodness. They are themselves blessings from God and should move us to bless God in return. This is above all true since the word has come in flesh to make all things holy by the mystery of the incarnation.

146 Blessings, therefore, refer first and foremost to God, whose majesty and goodness they extol, and they involve human beings, whom God governs and by divine providence protects.

- The priest celebrant is encouraged to give a more solemn form of blessing on Sundays and holy days. He may use either a solemn blessing or a prayer over the people. When either of these forms of blessing is used, it is the function of the deacon, after the greeting, to invite the people to dispose themselves in reverence to receive the blessing.

- In the case of the solemn blessing, the priest extends his hands over the people as he sings or says the formula of the blessing in such a way that the assembly is clearly invited to respond with an "Amen" to each invocation. The threefold solemn blessings touch upon various aspects of a feast or of divine graciousness and often they affirm the mission of the eucharistic assembly.

- In the case of a prayer over the people, which by contrast is simpler and more general in content, the priest uses the same gesture of extending his hands over the people.

- When a bishop presides, in addition to these formularies he may use other special formularies of blessing.

- All these various forms of blessing conclude always with the trinitarian formulary, during which the priest with his right hand traces the sign of the cross over the members of the assembly as they make the sign of the cross on themselves.

■ COMMENTARY: The celebration ends as it began: with simple and strong ancient words of greeting and the gesture that reaches out and almost seems to embrace the assembly: "The Lord be

with you." Where the pre-Vatican II Missal had but one formula, the brief trinitarian one, the words of blessing now may draw on a rich treasury of solemn blessings and prayers over the people. These expanded texts often are both invocation of divine favor and mission for Christian witness. They need to be chosen carefully, pronounced reverently and accompanied by the appropriate gesture—a gesture identical to that which accompanies the invocation of the Spirit on the gifts of bread and wine.

The new ICEL translations of the solemn blessings try to elicit the assembly's response by rhythm, length and phrasing, but the best way to assure a communal "Amen" is to sing the words of blessing. Pope John Paul II did this at the Mass in the Meadowlands during his 1995 visit to the United States, drawing forth a deafening "Amen" from an assembly of over 85,000 people.

■ DISMISSAL

147 The dismissal sends the members of the congregation forth to praise and bless the Lord in the midst of their daily responsibilities.

- It is the deacon's role to say or sing the dismissal, which should be done in a way that invites the people's response.

- The response "Thanks be to God" is a statement of grateful praise for encountering the risen Christ in the assembly's worship.

- Beginning at the Easter Vigil and up to and including the Second Sunday of Easter, the double Alleluia is added to the dismissal and the response. It is also added on Pentecost.

- Dismissal formularies should reflect the sacredness of the ritual. Casual remarks or secular forms of farewell are out of place as they distract from the dignity of the rite.

- The priest celebrant and deacon kiss the altar if they are near it at the time of the dismissal or pass it as they leave.

- After giving the proper reverence to the altar, the ministers ordinarily leave in the same order in which they entered at the beginning of the celebration.

- If they have not left earlier, ministers who are to bring communion to the sick may take their place immediately before the concelebrants in the procession.

- The procession may be accompanied by a song of praise, seasonal hymn, appropriate instrumental music, or even, on some occasions, silence. A recessional song is always optional, even for solemn occasions.

■ COMMENTARY: Note here again the caution against casual farewells. This is not a pitch for stuffiness but a reminder, as in the notes on the introductory rites, that we are about serious business here. As liturgist Aidan Kavanagh once remarked, "Don't tell me to leave the eucharist and have a nice day! Christians have hardly ever left the eucharist just to go out and have a good day—some went out to bear witness unto death!" Warmth and sincerity can be communicated in a formal dismissal, a strong, confident, purposeful sending forth for mission. And there will be time at the door or at a gathering time after Mass for exchanging more informal and personal greetings. Note that for the procession out, there are alternatives to a closing song.

LITURGY OF THE WORD

The PIOM emphasizes the unity of the Mass, word and eucharist so intimately related "as to form one act of worship" (#79). Many elements constitute the flow of the liturgy of the word, and the PIOM notes that "care is necessary so that the many human words and elements do not obscure the divine word itself" (#81). An examination of the ritual elements of the liturgy of the word and liturgy of the eucharist, and more detailed reflections on their celebration, will appear in the next section of Ordinary Time. Here we will look at the ministry of the lector.

■ LECTOR: In simple but awesome words, the PIOM summarizes the ministry of reader:

> In proclaiming the word of God, readers exercise their responsibility in mediating the presence of Christ. God speaks to the assembly through [the readers], and the impact of God's message will depend significantly on their conviction, their preparation and their delivery (16).

The lectionary's primary challenge to the reader is in the sheer scope of the readings selected. The full spectrum of biblical literary genres is represented in every cycle of the lectionary's readings: historical narratives, psalm poetry, prophetic oracles, parables in both testaments, theological expositions, apocalyptic visions. The reader's goal is to proclaim the content of the text accurately, in a tone and style befitting the particular genre.

To accomplish this, it is not sufficient to know the text. The reader needs to know the context as well. And that context is itself multifaceted. There is the biblical context (Where does the lectionary's excerpt come from?), the liturgical context (Where in the liturgical calendar is this passage prescribed and how should this placement color the proclamation?) and the immediate context (What does this assembly need to hear?).

A number of resources are available to help the reader, among them LTP's *Workbook for Lectors and Gospel Readers,* which contains biblical, liturgical and technical assistance as well as the scriptures for Sundays and solemnities in two translations: the New American Bible (approved for use in the United States) and the New Revised Standard Version (approved for use in Canada). Some practical suggestions are offered in the PIOM, the most obvious being multiple readers for the liturgy of the word. The reasons bear serious consideration:

- Multiple readers will involve more people in an active liturgical ministry.
- A different reader for each reading can assist the assembly's appreciation of the varying genres and contexts of the different passages.
- Although the ideal is to sing the psalm, when this is not possible, a different reader for the psalm will help the assembly to respect the rhythm of proclamation and response which is proper to the liturgy of the word.

■ YEAR B: GOSPEL OF MARK IN ORDINARY TIME: Mark's gospel is the shortest of the gospels and the only synoptic without an infancy narrative. For these reasons, Mark is little used in Advent-Christmas and is supplemented in summer Ordinary Time by John 6, the discourse on the bread of life. But if Mark is brief, he is also blunt! One question dominates Mark's gospel: Who do you say that I am? This question, and Peter's confession of faith in response, is the heart and turning point of the gospel, a question that will be answered, surprisingly, in Mark's passion account, by the most surprising character! Because Mark wants us to decide who Jesus is for us, one way of approaching the gospel's structure, and that of Ordinary Time, is to see it as a progressive revelation of the mystery of Jesus' person. Some of Mark's concerns are strikingly contemporary (see D.E. Nineham, *Pelican Gospel Commentary,* Penguin Books):

- an effort to explain how the Messiah could end up in disgrace, dying as a criminal. Jesus' messiahship is thus to be understood as a suffering that is prelude to glory.
- an explanation of why Jesus' identity as Messiah was not often claimed by Jesus nor recognized by others. Jesus is presented as keeping his identity secret and forbidding others to reveal it till the end of the gospel. Scholars call this "the messianic secret." It may also be based on Jesus' own desire not to be identified as a military or political messiah.

- a view of Jesus as God's agent against the powers of evil, the one who begins the great and final battle with the evil powers. Hence Mark's emphasis on miraculous cures and exorcisms, and on Jesus' conflict with human opponents who are seen as agents of the evil powers.

LITURGY OF THE EUCHARIST

■ PREFACES: The liturgy of the eucharist on Sundays in Ordinary Time has been enriched with a number of significant texts. We often forget that prior to Vatican II there was only one preface used on all these Sundays.

But now there are, in the Latin edition of the Missal, eight prefaces for these Sundays in Ordinary Time, drawn from ancient sources. In the process of translation, many language groups have added to this collection. The new ICEL edition of the sacramentary also will have an additional preface of the Lord's Day, expressing more fully, and in beautifully lyrical language, the rich nature of the Lord's Day.

Each of the Sunday Ordinary Time prefaces celebrates in a general way "the whole mystery of Christ," which is, as we have seen, the only "theme" of these Sundays. There are, however, some particular emphases. For instance, the first four deal with salvation history through Christ's paschal mystery. The fifth focuses on creation, a time-honored theme of the Lord's Day. According to Genesis, the first day was the day God began the work of creation. This becomes the day of the new creation, for Jesus rose from the dead "early on the first day of the week." The sixth preface reflects another dimension of the Lord's Day, its "eschatological" thrust toward the day of the Lord's return. The seventh preface pictures salvation as the fruit of Christ's obedience, and the eighth sees the church's unity as springing from the unity of the Godhead within the Trinity. The original text, the ninth preface, contains a particularly rich summary of the theology of the Lord's Day.

While one or another of these prefaces may resonate more obviously with a given scriptural theme, there is really no need to try to match preface to Sunday. On the other hand, all liturgical choices should be made thoughtfully; they

should never result from simply moving the ribbons around! There should be some effort to use all the prefaces over a period of time. But repetition is the essence of ritual. It may be very appropriate to choose one particular preface for use over a span of Sundays. This will be especially important if a text is referred to in preaching and if Sunday is made the subject of some catechesis during Ordinary Time.

Technically, there are two more prefaces for use on the Lord's Day, since Eucharistic Prayer II may and Eucharistic Prayer IV must be used with their respective prefaces. Also, from Sundays 17 to 21, when John 6 on the bread of life is read, the prefaces of the Holy Eucharist I and II might be appropriate.

Preparing the Parish

WITHIN the general designation "Ordinary Time," there are special kinds of movements discernible. Each of the synoptic gospels has a particular kind of inner dynamism determined by the purpose of the evangelist and revealed in the movement of his unique narrative. Ordinary Time, now and after Pentecost, is a perfect opportunity to begin a systematic study of the gospel of the given year. Group Bible studies have the benefit of the explosion of resources in Catholic and ecumenical scriptural studies, many of them geared specifically to the lectionary. The publishers listed on page xv will gladly provide catalogues and reference aid.

■ COUNTDOWN TO LENT: We have already noted the importance of attending to the liturgy's "transitional rites," if the major parts are to stand forth with clarity and strength. The same is true with regard to the year itself. The Pastoral Introduction: Ordinary Time mentions the final weeks of Ordinary Time as a time when the scriptures (and nature, in the Northern Hemisphere) turn our thoughts toward the End Time and the day of the Lord's return. After Pentecost, the Solemnities of the Holy Trinity and of the Body and Blood of Christ are a kind of easing back into Ordinary Time, when Sunday will stand forth most clearly as the day of the Father's first creation, the Son's re-creation in the resurrection, the Holy Spirit's "creation" in the first gathering of the infant church.

But these weeks after Epiphany and the Lord's baptism are proposed as a transition period of their own. The gospels of these weeks "concentrate on the beginnings of the Lord's preaching" and wider aspects of his ministry. This year those weeks are few. Lent can "sneak up" on planners and presiders (not to mention parishioners) just finishing their celebration of the Lord's incarnation. It may be useful, then, to present these Sundays, in preaching and program, as a transition from Advent-Christmas to Lent-Easter. In response to Christ's manifestation, we renew our baptismal covenant and place our own gifts and ministries at the service of the coming kingdom.

Among the ways that kingdom comes in our own day and in our own locale is in the journey of the catechumens, which becomes the journey of all of us "returning" to the font from which we were reborn. It may be an appropriate time for the commissioning of people in the various ministries and for the renewal—spiritual and technical—of those already serving in the parish ministries.

■ INTEGRITY OF SUNDAY: As the original holy day of the Christian community, Sunday, even in Ordinary Time, is not just another day looking for a theme, title, designation or slogan. Sunday is rich enough in meaning and content all by itself. The Pastoral Introduction has good, practical suggestions for making sure Sunday is perceived this way (PI, 6). Place special intentions in the places where they appropriately belong: in the homily if the readings suggest the particular theme, in the general intercessions, in the announcements at the conclusion of Mass, in the decoration of the church, if this can be artistically and tastefully done. Consider other means of educating the assembly and eliciting its support: distribute well-prepared and informative printed materials; use the church notice board or prepare a special display in a suitable place; plan a talk, film, discussion or similar gathering separate from the liturgy. Collect money for special projects outside the liturgy time, "for example, as the people leave the church."

Taking It Home

SCRIPTURES AT HOME: We have already noted the appropriateness of Ordinary Time as an opportunity to begin parish Bible study. It is also a good time of year to encourage parishioners to read the scriptures for Sunday Mass during the week prior to celebration. Printing the biblical references in the bulletin for the next Sunday enables the assembly to prepare to hear the word more fully. Adding the weekday citations permits those who cannot be present at daily eucharist to share in a "communion of the word." Groups and individuals might appreciate the availability of resources like LTP's *At Home with the Word,* which offers each week's readings and reflections on how they might be lived out. *Share the Word* (Paulist Evangelization Office) provides a similar service.

■ DOMESTIC PRAYER AND RITUAL: *Catholic Household Blessings and Prayers* (CHB) is a valuable resource for growing in a life of prayer because it provides material that teaches us to sanctify all of life in a very natural way. Awakening, opening the eyes, washing and dressing, prayer at table: Everything is here and all the seasons provided for. A resource for teaching children to pray in this way is LTP's *Blessings and Prayers,* with wonderful illustrations by Judy Jarrett.

Rely on CHB also for prayers that celebrate important days that occur this time of year: Week of Prayer for Christian Unity, Martin Luther King Day, Washington's Birthday, Receiving Blessed Candles at Home (Candlemas Day). *Take Me Home* (LTP) also has pages for Martin Luther King Day, Saint Anthony (patron of pets, January 17), the Feast of the Presentation (February 2), Mardi Gras (the "Fat Tuesday" that turns into Lent) and for Saint Valentine's Day just after Lent begins (February 14).

Other Ritual Prayers and Sacraments

LITURGY OF THE HOURS: If the community has learned to celebrate Morning and/or Evening Prayer during Advent and Christmastime, keep the momentum going, at least in some minimal way, in this brief time until Lent begins.

Some parishes have found it easier, however, to begin with regular weekday Morning or Evening Prayer, one day a week or even daily. Morning Prayer might be scheduled to precede the usual starting time of the morning Mass. Evening prayer could be scheduled in a similar way before parish meetings so that parishioners can celebrate prayer together before business. A perfect resource, solid but accessible, is LTP's *Proclaim Praise.*

Another approach to making this prayer part of parish life highlights special feasts (as well as Sundays) by celebrating Evening Prayer on those days. When daily Mass is not celebrated on some weekdays, consider using Morning and/or Evening Prayer rather than always having a communion service. This could have the effect not only of helping the assembly learn to pray in a noneucharistic prayer form but also deepening the community's sense of the eucharist's uniqueness.

Even when the hours are not celebrated, homilists and leaders of prayer will want to have access to the complete *Liturgy of the Hours* or the one-volume *Office of Readings* (Boston: Daughters of Saint Paul) for excellent nonscriptural readings. Recent Episcopal and Lutheran publications have adapted this nonbiblical "lectionary" of classics from the writings of the fathers of the church and of the saints across two thousand years.

■ WEEK OF PRAYER FOR CHRISTIAN UNITY: Each year from January 18 to 25, Christians celebrate a Week of Prayer for Christian Unity. Begun at Graymoor in Garrison, New York, as the "Church Unity Octave," it is an annual reminder to pray with and for other Christians "that all may be one . . . that the world may believe" (John 17:21). The 1997 theme, "We entreat you on behalf of Christ, be reconciled to God (2 Corinthians 5:2), underscores the importance and urgency of Christian unity. Resources in both English and Spanish are available from Week of Prayer, PO Box 300, Garrison NY 10524-0300 (914-424-3458) and the National Council of Churches, 475 Riverside Drive, Room 850, New York NY 10115 (212-870-2227). The "Order for Blessing of Ecumenical Groups" (*Book of Blessings,* #553) also may be useful when joining other Christian communities for prayer during this week.

■ BLESSINGS IN WINTER ORDINARY TIME: Beyond the liturgical blessings related to particular feasts, the *Book of Blessings* has proven to be a

rich resource for prayer for an increasing number of parishes. Some traditional blessings, such as the blessings of the sick or of articles of devotion, have survived in the devotion of the people. But the *Book of Blessings* provides an opportunity to revive customs that may have been neglected in recent years and the occasion to initiate new ways of blessing God and praying together. See, for example, the several forms for the blessing of families and of homes. Consider also inviting people to stay after Mass to receive a special blessing if they will be celebrating a birthday during the week (#340) or going away for winter holidays or ski trips (#635). If the blessing of liturgical ministers occurs during this time of the year, when the gospels proclaim the inauguration of Christ's public ministry, be sure to look at the many resources provided in part VI of the *Book of Blessings*.

The Worship Environment

A "USER FRIENDLY" BUILDING: The psalmist provides us, unwittingly perhaps, with an interesting perspective on the worshiper's relationship to the place of worship: "In your house I am a passing guest, a pilgrim like all my ancestors" (Psalm 39). In Winter Ordinary Time, parishes in colder climates should reflect on the fact that most of us "pilgrims" arrive wearing heavy coats. Consider turning unused space into a coatroom or setting up coat racks in the vestibule. Maybe ask people to use an entry through the parish hall or rectory and leave coats there. Or leave enough space in every pew to allow for a coat pile. Whatever solution works best, leave the heat on high enough for comfort, increase the number and training of ushers, and make inviting announcements explaining new procedures. To keep the building hospitable and safe, those who prepare the liturgy should cooperate with the janitorial staff in caring for walkways and entrances. Especially on snowy Sundays, many folks may need to lend a hand.

■ VESTMENTS: It can happen that a community, which otherwise expends much care and attention to liturgical celebration, leaves one of its major liturgical "signs," the vestments, at the mercy of whatever is in the closet or whatever collection the ordained ministers have assembled on their own. The Pastoral Introduction: Order of Mass has several thoughtful things to say in this regard:

> Vestments serve several functions in the celebration of the eucharist. As festal clothing, for example, they suggest the ritual and solemn character of the eucharistic banquet, and as insignia, they identify the specific function or ministry in the assembly of those who wear them (57).

The vestments can be made from any fabric that is "worthy and beautiful." Further, we are reminded that the "beauty should derive from the quality and cut of the fabric as much as from its ornamentation." Peter Mazar, in *To Crown the Year* (pages 28–31), presents some fine reflections on quality and ornamentation that deserve review, discussion and implementation. Ordinary Time is perfect for cataloguing what the parish has and what the parish needs to think about acquiring, especially for the major liturgical seasons and feasts. This schema is adapted from his suggestions:

- *White:* three sets. (1) for the Christmas season and could be worn also on Presentation, Saint Joseph, Annunciation and the Birth of John the Baptist; (2) for the Easter season and could be worn also on Transfiguration, Assumption, All Saints, also for funerals and All Souls, unless violet or black is worn; (3) for "white" days in Ordinary Time.
- *Violet:* two sets. (1) for Advent; (2) for Lent and penance services.
- *Red:* two sets. (1) deep red for Palm Sunday, Good Friday, Holy Cross, martyrs; (2) bright red for Pentecost, Ss. Peter and Paul, apostles.
- *Green:* three different sets. (1) winter Ordinary Time; (2) summer Ordinary Time; (3) fall Ordinary Time
- *Rose:* one set for the two days this color may be worn.

CALENDAR

January

MON 13 #305 (LMC, #193–227) green
Weekday

Hilary, bishop, doctor of the church, optional memorial/white. ▪ From now until the week of Ash Wednesday, with the exception of only one feast day (January 25: Conversion of Paul), the first readings will be from the Letter to the Hebrews and the gospels from the Gospel of Mark.

There is a fine introduction to the Letter to the Hebrews by Luke Timothy Johnson in *The Catholic Study Bible* (New York: Oxford University Press, 1990).

Daily worshipers might appreciate a printed overview of this letter, which will be read almost in its entirety over the next four weeks.

TUE 14 #306 (LMC, #193–227) green
Weekday

"Jesus is not ashamed to call us brothers and sisters." This is surely one of the most moving and consoling texts in all the New Testament. The healing power of Jesus reaches out in compassion to the afflicted man in the gospel and in power against the ancient enemy of humankind. Thus as we return to Ordinary Time, the scriptures remind us that it is in these very days that God in Christ embraces our reality and joins us in pilgrimage. Besides making us feel better about ourselves and our "ordinary" lives, here is a powerful call to look at others with the same compassion and sense of solidarity in pilgrimage.

WED 15 #307 (LMC, #193–227) green
Weekday

The author of the Letter to the Hebrews pictures Jesus as being tested by what he suffered and, "like his brothers and sisters in every respect." Tested by illness and healed of fever, Simon's mother-in-law transforms God's gift of her restored health into generous service of others. In the prayer-and-work pattern of his own ministry, Jesus becomes the model for all of us of a healthy rhythm of life.

THU 16 #308 (LMC, #193–227) green
Weekday

Today and tomorrow, Hebrews considers the rest to which the Christian community is called. Our weekly entering into the Lord's Day is a strange combination of entering both God's rest and God's work. It is no longer the Sabbath of old: The rest of the kingdom to come is something we journey toward while working to build up the kingdom. Christ's rest in the tomb on his Great Sabbath ushers in the eighth day of the new creation. Our Lord's Day rest frees us for the work of the liturgy. But like the work of Jesus, the healer, so our work for the kingdom is meant to bring rest and refreshment of spirit to those afflicted emotionally or physically, those who find life weary and burdensome.

FRI 17 #309 (LMC, #193–227) white
Anthony, abbot
MEMORIAL

The faith of those who brought their paralyzed friend to Jesus moves us to the depths almost 2000 years later. So does the faith of the young Anthony. Athanasius tells us that Anthony came into church just as the deacon was reading the gospel (young people today are still often late for church). But how powerfully those gospel words struck the young man just coming into liturgy! "If you wish to be perfect, go, sell your possessions, and give the money to the poor, and you will have treasure in heaven; then come, follow me" (the gospel is an option for use today, lectionary, #513). Anthony did just that! He went off into solitude "to battle the devil." Years later, when people asked him what he learned in solitude, he is said to have replied, "I no longer fear God, I love him."

We need not go to the desert to fight the devil or to discover God's love.

SAT 18 #310 (LMC, #193–227) green
Weekday

Mass of the Blessed Virgin Mary, optional memorial/white ▪ According to a tradition dating back to Charlemagne's time, on the Saturdays of Ordinary Time the votive Mass of the Blessed Virgin Mary may be celebrated. The weekday lectionary should be used: There is no need (or permission!) to abandon the semicontinuous reading of Hebrews and Mark. But there is a new collection of Mass texts that every parish should have at hand, *Collection of Masses of the Blessed Virgin Mary*, Volume I: Sacramentary (complete edition: Catholic Book Publishing, 1992). Not only are there Mass texts but a fine introduction to each of the 46 Mass formularies and prefaces. Mass #39, "Mary, Mother of Mercy," might be used today. Jesus' banquet with sinners in Levi's house reminds us that, fortunately for us, Jesus is dining with sinners still! Opening Prayer B of the formulary refers to our sinfulness and the Savior's compassion, while the Prayer over the Gifts begs that "we may show ourselves merciful to others and receive your pardon toward us."

▪ THE WEEK OF PRAYER FOR CHRISTIAN UNITY: From January 18 to 25, daily intercession at Mass and the hours should include prayer for unity. Gatherings in Unity Week that include

JANUARY

children from school or religious education should rely on LTP's *Leader's Manual of the Hymnal for Catholic Students* for prayer service ideas (page 77). The formularies for Christian Unity are in the Various Needs section of the sacramentary, #13. See page 77 for more information.

☼ 19 — Second Sunday in Ordinary Time
#65 [66] (LMC, #60) green

■ MARTIN LUTHER KING, JR.: This weekend the United States observes this prophetic preacher's birthday. Prepare well ahead of time by ordering materials for bulletin inserts and ecumenical prayer services (available also in Spanish and Vietnamese) from the National Catholic Conference for Interracial Justice (NCCIJ), 1200 Varnum Street NE, Washington DC 20017; 202-529-6480. The prayer found in *Catholic Household Blessings and Prayers* (page 195) might be used to conclude the general intercessions.

Liturgy Training Publications offers two resources for commemorating Dr. King: "Evening Prayer Commemorating the Birthday of Dr. Martin Luther King, Jr." (a special edition of LTP's periodical on black Catholic liturgy, *Plenty Good Room*) and *Amazing Days: Martin Luther King's Birthday,* a handout that can be used as a bulletin insert, with quotations, prayers and commentaries.

The call of Samuel in today's first reading and the call of the disciples in the gospel both provide an opportunity to reflect on what the cost of discipleship was in King's life and what it might need to be in our own.

MON 20 — Weekday
#311 (LMC, #193–227) green

Fabian, pope, martyr, optional memorial/red. ▪ *Sebastian, martyr, optional memorial/red.* ▪ *Civil observance: Martin Luther King, Jr.* ▪ The readings should be taken from the weekday, and they are most appropriate. The first reading reminds us that Christ, Son though he was, learned obedience through what he suffered and offered intercession with loud cries and tears to God. The nonviolent way in which Christ preached the coming of the kingdom, his steadfast refusal to be the political messiah and military revolutionary some longed for provide excellent reflections on this holiday. New wine for new wineskins: Surely racial justice and mutual respect are hallmarks of the Lord's kingdom and, sadly, dimensions of that kingdom that we Christians have yet to embrace fully.

Today is an excellent day for using prayers from the Masses and Prayers for Various Occasions: #21, For the Progress of Peoples. Alternative texts: #22, for Peace and Justice; appendix X, #6, Independence Day and Other Civic Observances. Eucharistic Prayer for Masses of Reconciliation II is especially appropriate today.

TUE 21 — Agnes, virgin, martyr
MEMORIAL
#312 (LMC, #193–227) red

For the next two weeks, the Letter to the Hebrews reflects on the high priesthood of Jesus Christ. Vatican II reminded us that, from one point of view, all the baptized share in the priesthood of Jesus, called to offer a spiritual sacrifice of praise and thanksgiving on behalf of all creation, and to offer intercession on behalf of all humankind. As Lord of the Sabbath, Jesus changes all the musts of human existence and places love of God and neighbor at the center of the law.

Is such love the center of the law by which we live our lives? Agnes is said to have pledged her love to Christ in a virginity that bore witness to the inbreaking of God's kingdom in human history. Her martyrdom is said to have resulted from such a dramatic choice that proclaimed how stunningly real the person of Christ was to her and how near the coming of his kingdom. Today would be a good day to offer Eucharistic Prayer I, in which her name has long been included.

WED 22 — Weekday
#313 (LMC, #193–227) green

Vincent, deacon, martyr, optional memorial/red ▪ Melchizedek's offering of bread and wine, as priest of God Most High and king of Salem (that is, of peace), provides the author of Hebrews with a parallel to Jesus, whose priesthood is based not on familial descent but on appointment by God. The link, these many centuries later, to the signs we use in our assembly's eucharist should move all of us deeply.

■ ANNIVERSARY OF ROE V. WADE: The day on which the nation (pro and con) remembers the Supreme Court decision needs some recognition, but it should not take over the Mass. In the gospel Jesus asks, "Is it lawful to do good or to do harm on the Sabbath, to save life or to kill?" Rather than providing us with ammunition to apply labels or issue condemnations, the question might provide us with a moment to reflect on how many ways we humans can kill each other and how our commitment to life is one that embraces all life's issues and victims.

JANUARY

THU 23 #314 (LMC, #193–227) green
Weekday

The daily assembly is an especially fitting place to reflect on the power of intercessory prayer in the parish. Those who take the time, and perhaps have the leisure, to gather so frequently should be called on to consider their lives a real ministry of intercession in union with the priestly prayer Jesus forever offers in the sanctuary of heaven. Today's gospel gives us an example of the so-called "messianic secret," which forms one of the principal devices that Mark's gospel uses for focusing us on the person of Christ and the nature of his messiahship.

FRI 24 #315 (LMC, #193–227) white
Francis de Sales, bishop, religious founder, doctor of the church
MEMORIAL

It is most fitting that today's saint is remembered during the Week of Prayer for Christian Unity. He is "the gentleman saint," whose philosophy of life often is quoted in one form or another, though few actually know the source of the quote: "A spoonful of honey attracts more flies than a barrelful of vinegar." It is interesting to note that Francis de Sales' classic work on an authentic spirituality for the laity, *Introduction to a Devout Life,* is available to this day — now in paperback!

The first reading, about the new covenant, gives us the opportunity to reflect on how well we Christians, so beset by divisions and disputes, have lived the testament established for us in Christ's blood. The call of the apostles — people so different from one another yet formed by Christ into the core of his new people — should help us to celebrate Augustine's formula for church unity: "In essentials unity, in nonessentials diversity, in all things charity."

SAT 25 #519 (LMC, #247) white
The Conversion of Paul, apostle
FEAST

This feast marks the conclusion of the Week of Prayer for Christian Unity. Several saints have a secondary feast to commemorate the transfer ("translation") of the saint's remains from one place to another. Today's feast began as such a remembrance, but because the Latin *translatio* also can mean "conversion," it came to be a celebration of that famous moment on the road to Damascus. The first reading (either option) tells the story, and the gospel gives the goal of Paul's conversion. The wonderful working of God's providence in Paul's life reminds us in a powerful way that we who are Christ's disciples are, by that fact, the body of Christ. How we treat each other matters profoundly and speaks volumes — for good or ill — to those outside the community. Pray today for Christian unity and for all those on conversion journeys, not only the catechumens but those who have been away from the community and may now, and during Lent, be making a long-awaited journey home.

26 #68 [69] (LMC, #63) green
Third Sunday in Ordinary Time

■ LITURGICAL MINISTRIES: The gospels of this section of Ordinary Time speak frequently of call, service, ministry. These weeks of Ordinary Time are, for many parishes, a time to reflect on the formation and ongoing education of liturgical ministers, and maybe to make plans for their blessing as well.

The *Book of Blessings* (chapters 61 and 62) provides orders for blessing readers, servers, sacristans, musicians and ushers. "Commissioning" is used only in chapter 63 (Order for Commissioning Extraordinary Ministers of Holy Communion). Planners who wish to bless all the liturgical ministers at the same liturgy can add sections from chapters 61 and 63 of the *Book of Blessings* into the more inclusive chapter 62.

■ PREPARATION FOR CANDLEMAS DAY: The Feast of the Presentation of the Lord falls on a Sunday this year. People should be alerted this Sunday as to what the schedule will be and invited to bring candles from home that they would like to have blessed.

MON 27 #317 (LMC, #193–227) green
Weekday

Angela Merici, virgin, religious founder, educator, optional memorial/white.

■ CATHOLIC SCHOOLS WEEK: This week, which includes the optional memorial of Angela Merici and the memorial of "Don Bosco" is usually designated as Catholic Schools Week. The National Catholic Education Association provides preaching and worship suggestions for use on Sunday and a prayer service for January 31. Care should be taken to respect the integrity of the Sunday itself if either Sunday is chosen as a day to celebrate the role of the school in the local community. The role of religious education programs should also be celebrated: These programs have become "the school of Christian living" for many young people.

JANUARY

Today's saint, Angela Merici, was convinced that "disorder in society is a result of disorder in the family." How contemporary that sounds! Her solution: to form Christians who would bear witness as a kind of "secular institute" and to labor to improve social conditions by educating future wives and mothers. The gospel today presents Jesus' reminder that "a house divided cannot stand." He is referring to Satan's house and kingdom but with application to our own situation. The Christian formation of the young, by our word and example, is the best way to make the house strong and the kingdom secure.

TUE 28 — Thomas Aquinas, presbyter, religious, doctor of the church
#318 (LMC, #193–227) white
MEMORIAL

The perfect sacrifice of Christ (first reading) and the Lord's new definition of what it means to be "family" to him (gospel) coincides well with the remembrance of Thomas Aquinas. So much of what we believe concerning the eucharist, both in its dynamic sense (the Mass) and in its abiding reality (the blessed sacrament), finds eloquent expression in the writing of Aquinas. His was the gift not only of writing formal theological expositions but of being able to translate into moving poetry the doctrine his more technical writing explored. It would be a good day to sing some of the eucharistic hymns attributed to Aquinas.

WED 29 — Weekday
#319 (LMC, #193–227) green

"I will put my laws in their hearts, and I will write them in their minds," says the Lord in the first reading. In the gospel Jesus proclaims and explains the parable of the sower and the various kinds of soil that receive the seed. We are, all of us, each kind of soil from time to time, and from mood to mood. It is a good day to intercede for the parish lectors, deacons and presbyters. A good day, too, to remember not only those who are ordained to preach the word but those who sometimes offer the most challenging "homilies": catechists.

THU 30 — Weekday
#320 (LMC, #193–227) green

We often "provoke" one another but not in the way Hebrews has in mind: "Provoke one another to love and good deeds . . . encouraging one another" (NRSV). The need to be a living part of the assembly is proclaimed in this passage, as is the beautiful image of entering the heavenly sanctuary with confidence, because we are entering through Jesus, in the power of his blood and washed with pure water. It is a special day to remember in intercession the catechumens who are getting ready for their lenten journey as the elect toward the font.

FRI 31 — John Bosco, presbyter, religious founder, educator
#321 (LMC, #193–227) white
MEMORIAL

With all due respect to the Salesians (one suspects they would be the first to chuckle!), John Bosco once was asked "What would you do differently if you were to found your congregation again?" John's wry response: "I probably wouldn't do it!" Apocryphal or not, the story makes a good point. Wednesday's gospel, describing various kinds of soil, may have been discouraging. We wonder: Why can't we be good soil all the time? Why isn't there more good soil and more abundant fruit everywhere in the world—or even in the parish? Today's gospel is the other, comforting side of that coin. The seed grows and the harvest comes, we know not how, nor do we even perceive it. This is, of course, because the Farmer of the heart's field and the world's farm knows his business well! The Letter to the Hebrews also calls the community to persevere, for there is a day of reward. And the chronology Hebrews offers can be both comforting and disconcerting: That day is probably closer than we think!

■ PREPARING FOR CANDLEMAS AT SCHOOL OR RELIGIOUS EDUCATION CLASSES: Liturgy Training Publication's *Leader's Manual for the Hymnal for Catholic Students* (page 78) has a number of good, practical ideas for preparing students to take part in the principal Mass of this weekend, which celebrates the Lord's presentation and the blessing of candles.

February

SAT 1 — Weekday
#322 (LMC, #193–227) green

Mass of the Blessed Virgin Mary, optional memorial/white. ■ The readings of weekdays in Ordinary Time are not chosen for any particular correlation. Yet so often there is a coincidental relation between the two readings. Today is such a day. The Letter to the Hebrews presents its magnificent hymn to faith from chapter 11. And Jesus challenges the faith of the frightened disciples as he stills the winds and waves of the storm.

If it is desired to celebrate the Saturday memorial of the Virgin Mary, these weekday readings find an echo in two formularies from the *Collection of Masses of the Blessed Virgin Mary*: #20 cel-

FEBRUARY

ebrates Mary as the New Eve; #37 celebrates Mary as an example of hope, the virtue that accompanies faith.

■ BLACK HISTORY MONTH: Communities wishing to mark Black History Month in the liturgy may do so in the intercessions, homilies and a rich heritage of spiritual music. This observance, like so many others, expresses genuine human dreams and sentiments, but the timing is difficult to mesh with the liturgy. The saints especially revered in black Catholic communities, Peter Claver (September 9) or Martin de Porres (November 3), for example, might be especially good days for parishes to reflect on the histories of black Americans.

#524 (LMC, #252)   white

02 The Presentation of the Lord/ Candlemas Day

■ FROM THE MANGER TO JERUSALEM: The Child born in Bethlehem is presented in Jerusalem, in the city where the paschal mystery will be fulfilled. The liturgical instinct of this feast is correct, says biblical scholar Raymond Brown: "The presentation scene is an intrinsic part and, indeed, the climax of the Lucan infancy narrative." Scripturally and liturgically, it is not possible to separate the celebration of the incarnation from its fulfillment in the paschal mystery.

■ WHEN AND WHERE: Well before last week, planners and presiders will have decided when and how often to celebrate the "first form" (procession) and where to begin those introductory rites. Some communities may well be able to celebrate the full rite more than once. Others may wish to follow the Palm Sunday pattern: principal Mass(es) with the "first form," other Masses with "solemn entrance" or even a more simplified opening rite.

■ MUSIC: The incomparably beautiful processional antiphon, "Lumen ad revelationem," is easy to sing in Latin and/or English. It is used with the Canticle of Simeon and accompanies the candlelight procession. At least one Catholic hymnal (*Worship,* third edition, #1023) has an English adaptation that works quite well. Unfortunately, the best hymns for the feast appear only in the Latin *Liturgy of the Hours.* The English text of the hours has "When Mary brought her treasure." See *Hymnal 1982* and *Worship* for "O Zion, open wide thy gates" and "Hail to the Lord who comes." The *Lutheran Book of Worship* offers "In his temple now behold him." See the hymnals, too, for metrical versions of the Canticle of Simeon (the Nunc Dimittis).

■ BLESSING OF CANDLES AND PROCESSION: The order of service appears in the sacramentary and more fully in the *Ceremonial of Bishops:*

- Gathering takes place somewhere outside the place where the eucharist will be celebrated; ushers assist the assembly, providing a candle for all who gather; ministers, vested for Mass (presider may wear cope), go there for the opening.

If weather or lack of space prevents the gathering in a separate place, use the "solemn entrance" option and fill the worship place with candlelight. The procession should be an action of the whole assembly, not just a few people moving from a table with candles to the altar.

- Candles are lit while the assembly sings the proper antiphon or a hymn.
- sign of the cross, greeting, invitation by presider;
- blessing prayer over the candles;
- candles are sprinkled with water in silence;
- incense is placed in the censer;
- deacon or presider announces the procession as in the sacramentary;
- procession moves to site of eucharist, all bear lit candles and sing antiphon and Canticle of Simeon (or, if necessary, metrical version of canticle).

The rite suggests that as the procession enters the church, the entrance chant of the Mass is sung, then the Gloria. But two different pieces of music followed by a sung Gloria would make the rite unwieldy. Perhaps an opening hymn or the Gloria might be sung to mark the transition from procession to eucharist. During this song, the altar is venerated and incensed by the presider, so that when the singing and movement cease, the opening prayer may be chanted at once.

■ HOMILY: Homilists will find contemporary inspiration in Raymond Brown's *An Adult Christ at Christmas* and traditional "mystagogical" fare in the homily of Saint Sophronius in the Office of Readings.

The candles may be lit again as the assembly stands for the gospel and for the eucharistic prayer.

■ OLD PALMS FOR ASH WEDNESDAY: With Lent following close upon the Feast of the Presentation this year, the link between this feast and the paschal mystery takes on a very practical di-

FEBRUARY

mension. The parish needs ashes! And the ashes come, traditionally, from the palms of last year's procession. People should be invited to bring their old palms from home to next week's liturgy so that the ashes for Ash Wednesday may be prepared at a suitable time next weekend.

MON 3 Weekday
#323 (LMC, #193–227) green

Blase, bishop, martyr, optional memorial / red. ▪ *Ansgar, bishop, missionary, optional memorial / white.* ▪ The Order for Blessing Throats on the Feast of St. Blase (*Book of Blessings,* chapter 51) is proper to this memorial. It may be presided over by a priest or deacon, or by a layperson, male or female. The blessing can be celebrated during Mass, at its own liturgy of the word or as part of Morning or Evening Prayer (before the gospel canticle). There is no provision mentioned for celebrating this blessing on any other day. The texts make it clear that it is part of celebrating the Feast of St. Blase. "Pastoral reasons" do not warrant offering the blessing at a Sunday Mass. Although a blessing of any kind should be given gladly whenever requested, the pastoral approach urges celebration of the saint's memorial with devotion. Within that context the blessing finds its proper place as prayer; outside of the memorial there is danger rather of a sense of quasimagical protection.

TUE 4 Weekday
#324 (LMC, #193–227) green

The healings of Jesus continue in the gospel, as does the "messianic secret" proper to Mark's narrative. The Letter to the Hebrews sets the race of faith before us: A cloud of witnesses spurs us on, encouraging us by example and intercession. This may be a good opportunity to reflect on the role of the saints in our faith lives and in our personal prayer. The Catholic tradition takes the communion of saints very seriously. An authentic presentation of their role in our lives takes due note of their intercessory power to assist us but balances this by reminding us (as Hebrews does) that we keep our eyes fixed on Jesus, "pioneer and perfecter of our faith."

WED 5 Agatha, virgin, martyr
#325 (LMC, #193–227) red
MEMORIAL

Agatha is the patron of nurses. Their special and cherished work is really a ministry that might be the focus of intercession today. Moreover, J. Frank Henderson, a prominent liturgist and cancer research scientist in Canada, has frequently suggested (*Canadian Studies in Liturgy: No. 1, Holy Days: Opportunities and Challenges,* 1985, 35) that Agatha be considered patron of women with breast cancer. Today the concerns of these women can also be part of the intercessions. This might therefore be an appropriate day for communal anointing of the sick (whatever their disease) or a blessing of the sick (*Book of Blessings,* chapter 2), an order that can be led by an ordained or lay minister. The latter blessing might be scheduled this day for any support group of women or cancer patients in the parish.

THU 6 Paul Miki, religious, missionary, martyr and his companions, martyrs
#326 (LMC, #193–227) red
MEMORIAL

The martyrdom of Paul Miki, a 35-year-old Jesuit scholastic, and 25 others, mostly Japanese laypeople, some still quite young, is said to have resulted from a Spanish captain's boast that missionaries were preparing the way for Spain's conquest of Japan. An excerpt from the account of their martyrdom is found in the Office of Readings. The first reading celebrates the assembly of the firstborn; the saints' memorial provides a good reason to remind ourselves that this assembly is multiethnic and racially diverse. Our local assemblies should be also, with our witness having nothing in it of conquest and everything in it proclaiming service. The gospel speaks, too, of the call to missionary witness. Our mission field is as close as our neighborhood, our place of work or learning, indeed, at times, our own homes!

FRI 7 Weekday
#327 (LMC, #193–227) green

We are reaching the end of our reading from Hebrews and hearing final exhortations to the community then and now about the responsibilities of discipleship. The gospel presents in a most vivid way the cost of discipleship in the witness of John the Baptist. Those who come to the weekday assembly might be invited today to help with final lenten preparations. For this Sunday's liturgies, posters regarding lenten programs will need to be in place; printed materials will have to be folded and placed where they will draw attention; the Rice Bowl boxes might need to be prepared; and all nonessential materials would best be removed from book and pamphlet racks, from bulletin boards and notice areas.

SAT 8 Weekday
#328 (LMC, #193–227) green

Jerome Emiliani, religious founder, optional memorial / white. ▪ *Mass of the Blessed Virgin Mary,*

FEBRUARY

optional memorial/white. ▪ Today's readings set the weekday assembly's stage for the lenten journey that will begin next Wednesday. The Letter to the Hebrews concludes on a paschal note, celebrating Jesus as the great Shepherd brought back from the dead after sealing the eternal covenant in his blood. In the gospel, meanwhile, Jesus invites the disciples to "come apart" to a deserted place for prayer, renewal and refreshment.

Today's saint might remind us of young men and women who are far from home during their time in the service and others who are away at school. Does anyone think to send them the parish bulletin from time to time, together with a personal remembrance? This would especially be appreciated by those who may have served the assembly in liturgical ministries when they were younger or who may have been in the religious education program. Jerome reminds us, too, of those children who — perhaps with a single parent — may live in shelters near the parish. Jerome went out looking for people to help. In fact, that is how he gave his life! Here is one way the saints live on in our midst: by compelling us to "go and do likewise."

If the Saturday Mass of Mary is offered one last time before Lent, the Mother of Consolation Mass (#41) might be appropriate, given the day's scriptures.

#74 [75] (LMC, #69)   green
Fifth Sunday in Ordinary Time

The brevity of life (first reading) and the compelling nature of Christ's ministry (gospel) set the stage for the lenten journey that we are just about to begin.

▪ LENTEN ANNOUNCEMENTS, HANDOUTS AND COVENANTS: Masses on this last Sunday before Lent traditionally include many announcements and at least some handouts. The traditional lenten disciplines provide a handy way to organize our thoughts on such materials. Some parishes even provide a printed "Lenten Covenant" in a threefold brochure that outlines the schedule and suggestions for keeping the threefold discipline of prayer, fasting and almsgiving.

▪ PRAYER: *Paschal Mission 1997* is LTP's approach to a complete celebration of Lent, Triduum and Eastertime in a way that unites the seasons and the disciplines that make up the keeping of these days. *Keeping Lent, Triduum and Eastertime* is a pocket-size prayerbook from LTP for all the days of these seasons. It is also available in Spanish. *Catholic Household Blessings and Prayers* has prayers for blessing the lenten disciplines and an especially fine form of table prayer for the season. *Table Prayer Cards* for Lent-Triduum-Eastertime from LTP is an even more practical resource for use at table. Lent is on one side of the card and Easter on the other. *Proclaim Praise* is LTP's simplified form of the *Liturgy of the Hours* for marking morning, evening and night with psalmody and intercession.

▪ FASTING: Catholic Relief Service's "Rice Bowl" box is the modern successor to the lenten "mite box" of generations past, a handy way to remember the social dimension of fasting. Here is a reminder to keep the fast in solidarity with the poor and hungry throughout the world. The Rice Bowl provides a tangible, helpful way of cheerfully going without so that others can have at least the minimum of what they need.

Parish fasting meals have become very popular in some places as a way to keep the discipline in a communal way that provides for mutual support and encouragement. Friday is the best night, from the perspective of tradition, but on whatever night possible (except Sunday!), parishioners gather in the parish hall for a simple, meatless meal. Perhaps the meal is taken in silence, while scripture or spiritual reading provides "food for thought." It's a good way to involve all age-groups and to bring together the baptized and the catechumens in purposeful interaction: Seniors can help prepare, religious education students or youth group members can set up and clean up, and the parish ministers (ordained and lay) can serve!

Personal commitment could be assisted by providing parishioners with a printed brochure of suggestions. Many folks are simply swamped with work and family commitments. It's a thoughtful thing for the parish liturgists to brainstorm ideas for personal devotions and disciplines and then share these by means of an attractively prepared handout.

▪ ALMSGIVING: The Rice Bowl box has already been mentioned as a nationally promoted lenten discipline. Each diocese or parish community might have its own focus points that cry out for helpful service, either in terms of hands-on assistance or monetary, food and clothing aid.

Respecting the anonymity of those in need, parishes may wish to invite families and households, even individuals who can afford to do so, to set aside money otherwise devoted to personal comfort and entertainment to assist

FEBRUARY

a particular person or household in need.

- LENTEN MATERIALS: If there are many items to be distributed, consider providing them all in one convenient "lenten pack" for each household, with extra material available after Mass near the exits.

If such materials are provided for Lent, parishes should be sure to provide similar helps for Easter. Lent-Eastertime, like Advent-Christmas, needs to be seen as a kind of threefold, unitive affair: preparation, fulfillment and celebration.

- ALLELUIA FAREWELL: This is the last Sunday the assembly will sing Alleluia until the Easter Vigil. Alleluia banners, tapestries or scrolls, if they are nice ones that will be used again as decorations during the Easter season, can be carried out in procession at the end of the day's liturgy. In medieval times, some communities even "buried" these Alleluia scrolls or banners in the permanent "sepulchre" that was part of the decor of many a parish church. Today it might be possible to "bury" them in some container near the baptismal font, which presumably will not be used again until the Easter Vigil. The seriousness with which our ancestors in the faith observed the "fast from Alleluia" is attested to by an eleventh-century Latin farewell song: "Alleluia, dulce carmen." While there is a slightly modernized version in *Worship* (#413), the traditional text seems better suited to the lenten fast about to come. It's in *Hymnal 1982*.

Even before the end of Mass, however, the Alleluia can be sung to its rest with great fanfare at the gospel acclamation and might even be added to the dismissal in the twofold form familiar from Eastertime. If Evening Prayer is celebrated tonight, the Alleluia may be added to that dismissal as well.

- PREPARING ASHES: Another custom that prepares for Lent is burning last year's palms outdoors after the recessional or in the evening after Vespers.

MON 10 #329 (LMC, #193–227) white
Scholastica, virgin, religious
MEMORIAL

Today and tomorrow the Book of Genesis is begun in the semicontinuous sequence presented by the lectionary. Of course, the sequence is only two days long this year because of Lent. But the arrangement works out surprisingly well, since the two passages are the first creation story. Thus we are in the providential position of hearing just before Lent the same story we will hear at the beginning of the liturgy of the word during the Great Vigil of Easter. Attention could be called to this coincidence, as a way of reminding the weekday assembly that the lenten journey is, for the baptized, precisely a journey back to our beginnings, our re-creation in the waters of the font.

The Office of Readings for the memorial of Scholastica presents Gregory the Great's delightful story of how Scholastica got her twin brother Benedict to stay at her guesthouse when he was determined to go back to the monastery. It's a wonderful story about the power of prayer and the power of a woman. And isn't faith-filled prayer one of the principal disciplines of the season just before us?

TUE 11 #330 (LMC, #193–227) green
Weekday

Our Lady of Lourdes, optional memorial/white.

- LAST MASS BEFORE LENT: The first reading concludes the creation story of Genesis 1. As we prepare for the discipline of lenten fasting, it is important for us to hear the biblical assertion that "God saw all that he had made, and indeed it was very good." We forego some of the blessings of God's creation during Lent not because they are bad but because they are so good! To empty ourselves of all that we could do without has the practical consequence of leaving more for others, particularly if we join almsgiving to fasting, as all the spiritual writers (and Jesus himself) warn us that we should. And "distance makes the heart grow fonder." How much more we later appreciate things we have not had for a while. The discipline of fasting is thus not only ascetical but anticipatory as well. It is time to embark on the journey toward Easter filled with anticipation at meeting the Lord we will encounter there.

Where there is a devotion to Our Lady of Lourdes, this feast, too, should be directed toward the season that begins tomorrow. There are some fine reflections in the introductory materials to the lenten Masses in the *Collection of Masses of the Blessed Virgin Mary*.

- MARDI GRAS: The English language knows today as Shrove Tuesday, the day on which to be shriven, or absolved, of our sins in preparation for Lent. But other cultures call it Mardi Gras, Fat Tuesday or Carnivale (goodbye to the meat). This is a day to be enjoyed by all those who plan to take their lenten fasting seriously! Carnival kings and queens, bonfires, dances, clowns, magic shows, parish plays and sing-a-longs: All have served generations past as a final fun get-together before the serious business of Lent!

NOTES

NOTES

LENT

The Season
Orientation / 91
ICEL Pastoral Introduction: Lent / 92
Perspective on Lent / 94
Presentation of the Season / 96
The Environment of Worship / 96
Movement and Music / 97
Introductory Rites / 98
Liturgy of the Word / 98
Liturgy of the Eucharist / 100
Preparing the Parish / 103
Taking It Home / 103
Other Ritual Prayers and Sacraments / 104
The Calendar
February 12 – March 27 / 105
Liturgical Texts
Texts for the Eucharistic Assembly / 117
A Penitential Procession for the First Sunday of Lent / 118

Orientation

ON a warm day in early September, the students at Boston University's School of Theology were in a festive, expectant mood for the first day of the new semester. The course was "The Liturgical Year," taught by Dr. Horace T. Allen, Jr., a major contributor to the Revised Common Lectionary used by so many Protestant churches. A student had drawn a large "happy face" on the chalkboard with the message "Welcome, Liturgy People!" Waiting for the professor, another student began drawing a series of "happy faces," each depicting a liturgical season. To Advent's face she gave a broad smile and a head crowned with four Advent candles. Christmas' mouth was a large "O" — "Glooooria in excelsis Deooooo," no doubt — and angel wings protruded from invisible shoulders. Epiphany had three happy faces, and each head wore a king's crown.

Then there was "Lent." Lent's mouth was turned down in a frozen grimace denoting brute effort and tortuous fasting. Lent's forehead, of course, was smeared with a large cross of chalk "ashes."

When Dr. Allen arrived, he studied the liturgical faces for a moment, then picked up the eraser and chuckled, "You've pretty much captured the 'received wisdom' of the liturgical year. Now let's see if we can correct it!" He began by wiping the smile from Advent's face, explaining, "In the Revised Common Lectionary, and the Roman Lectionary it's based on, you'll find that Advent begins, in all three cycles, with gospels warning of Christ's return in glory. Then two weeks of John the Baptist's preaching. Countdown to Christmas or countdown to judgment? No cause for smiles there!"

Leaving the Christmas angel alone, he erased two of the Epiphany faces. "First of all," he explained, "we don't know how many Magi there were. Read Raymond Brown's *Birth of the Messiah!* Second, you've left two things out." He drew an abstract river of wavy lines and what looked like six large vessels, "Epiphany includes the Lord's baptism and Cana."

But certainly the students' biggest shock came with Dr. Allen's complete revision of the lenten "unhappy face." "Of all the errors on this blackboard," he said, "the lenten error is the worst of all." He wiped away the cross of ashes on its forehead. "Didn't Jesus say, 'When you fast, do not look gloomy like the hypocrites who disfigure their faces. . . . But wash your face and anoint your head'?" He turned the face's frown into a broad smile. "Check the lenten lectionary," he suggested, "especially the normative year, Year

A. On the First Sunday, a victorious Jesus defeats Satan and is waited on by angels. On the Second Sunday a transfigured Jesus, radiant in glory, hears the Father announce him as the beloved Son. Then on the Third Sunday a Samaritan woman finds the faith she thirsts for; on the Fourth a blind man finds sight; on the Fifth Lazarus is raised. Jesus is living water, light of the world, the resurrection and the life. There is just nothing sad about any of that!"

By this time the students were busy scribbling notes! For, despite the seeming frivolity of the "happy face" images, the exercise had been education in the most literal sense of the word. The Latin *educere* denotes both a "leading out" and a "leading beyond." In this case Dr. Allen's chalkboard corrections initiated a movement out of the popular theology imposed on the seasons by standard preaching. The class had begun moving toward the deeper insights suggested by contemporary liturgical scholarship. That journey leads beyond a well-intentioned but sometimes superficial devotional piety toward the possibility of a sacramental encounter with the living Christ, mediated to the community, among other ways, through the scriptures of the lectionary and the texts of the liturgical books.

Lent is a liturgical "place" so rich in theology and history, so filled with tradition and so shaped by memories, both ecclesial and personal, that every return journey yields fresh insight and deeper wisdom. With ICEL's Pastoral Introduction as a guide, we embark once again. Much of what we encounter will be familiar from Lents of the past. But the attentive traveler will, it is hoped, make new discoveries as well.

ICEL Pastoral Introduction: Lent

1 Lent is the season in which we "prepare joyfully for the mystery of Easter with minds and hearts renewed." In Lent, the community of faith is blessed with a spirit of loving reverence for God and of willing service to neighbor. The season of Lent begins on Ash Wednesday and concludes before the Evening Mass of the Lord's Supper on Holy Thursday.

BAPTISMAL AND PENITENTIAL THEMES

2 The liturgy of Lent is marked by two closely related themes, the baptismal and the penitential. It is a time of purification and enlightenment for the elect, those preparing to receive the sacraments of Easter initiation. In this they are helped by the local church, the whole community of the faithful who recall their own baptism and prepare for its renewal. Both the elect and the local community join together in a spirit of repentance and conversion of heart, making Lent a time of spiritual recollection for the whole church as it prepares for the celebration of Easter.

3 Therefore Lent is a time for more intense prayer and reflection and for particular attention to the word of God. This takes place above all in the Sunday eucharist. Lenten penance is not "only inward and individual but also outward and social." Prayer, fasting, almsgiving and other works of charity are the traditional ways of deepening conversion to Christ.

4 The celebration of the rite of election or enrollment of names usually coincides with the beginning of Lent. By means of this rite, the candidates for initiation are accepted for their final preparation for the sacraments of initiation. The church's acceptance of the candidates is founded on the election by God, in whose name the church acts. As a pledge of fidelity, they inscribe their names in the book containing the list of those who have been chosen for initiation.

- Sponsors and godparents, as well as catechists, priests and deacons have particular responsibilities toward the elect. They show the elect how to practice the gospel in personal and social life, sustain them in moments of hesitancy or anxiety, guide them, and bear witness on their behalf before the whole community.

- The presence of the elect in the midst of the community and their gracious dismissal from the eucharistic assembly during Lent are strong symbols of the baptismal character of the season. The celebration of the scrutinies during the parish Sunday eucharist not only heals and strengthens the elect but helps all the faithful to deepen their own conversion.

- As the season of Lent leads the elect to the sacraments of initiation, so it leads the faithful to celebrate the sacrament of penance, which restores them from sin to baptismal innocence and reconciles them to God and the church. Opportunities for communal and individual forms of reconciliation should be provided, especially toward the end of Lent.

- Because Lent is a time of preparation for the Easter sacraments, parents and godparents of infants to be baptized are also to receive appropriate formation so that the infants can be baptized on Easter Sunday, either at the Vigil or at one of the Masses during the day, or on one of the Sundays of Easter.
- A homily is recommended at weekday Masses during Lent; intercession for the elect and for sinners is especially appropriate in this season; and the Eucharistic Prayers for Masses of Reconciliation may be especially suitable.
- Music should reflect the more sober mood of Lent and thus provide a contrast with the festive music of the Easter season which follows. The Gloria is not used as the opening rite at Mass and the Alleluia is replaced by other gospel acclamations.
- The use of violet vestments and the simplicity of decoration in the church reflect the penitential nature of this season. In those places where the conference of bishops has decided that the custom be maintained of covering crosses and images in the church during the last two weeks of Lent, the crosses are uncovered after the Good Friday liturgy, and other images before the Easter Vigil.

Penitential services, the Liturgy of the Hours and devotions such as the Stations of the Cross can play a part in stirring up a spirit of repentance during the season of Lent.

THE ROLE OF THE BISHOP

5 The celebration of the Easter mystery is the high point of the church's year and is accomplished with the utmost solemnity. The intimately related seasons of Lent and Easter are therefore an eminently suitable time for the bishop as chief shepherd of the diocese to gather the flock of God's people for special liturgical celebrations. Thus it becomes clear that initiation, reconciliation and healing are essentially ecclesial acts.

- As the focal point of the church's concern for the catechumens, admission to election belongs to the bishop. The presiding celebrant for the rite is the bishop himself or one who acts as his delegate.
- Following the ancient custom of the church of Rome, the bishop is strongly encouraged to gather the faithful on Sundays or on other days during Lent, in the principal parish churches or places of pilgrimage in the diocese, to celebrate the liturgy with them.
- Toward the end of Lent, the bishop gathers the diocese to bless the oils for its ministry to catechumens and the sick and to consecrate the chrism used in the sacraments of Easter initiation and holy orders. Although presbyters may bless oil before anointing catechumens in the initiation of adults and, in case of necessity, before anointing the sick, use of the oil blessed by the bishop expresses more strongly the ministry of the whole local church. The bishop may take this opportunity to instruct the presbyters about the reverent use and safe custody of the holy oils.

THE DAYS OF LENT

6 The season of Lent leads to the Easter Triduum, which begins with the evening Mass of the Lord's Supper on Holy Thursday and ends with Evening Prayer on Easter Sunday. The final days of Lent together with the Easter Triduum make up Holy Week. Beginning on Passion Sunday (Palm Sunday) with Jesus' messianic entry into Jerusalem, Holy Week recalls the passion and resurrection of Christ.

- The Sundays of Lent, Ash Wednesday and the weekdays of Holy Week take precedence over all feasts and solemnities; only feasts and solemnities take precedence over the weekdays of Lent.

7 Ash Wednesday, a day of fast and abstinence, sets the tone for Lent through the call to turn away from sin and to be faithful to the gospel.

8 The Sundays of Lent each have a special character drawn from the gospel of the day. On the first Sunday, the church remembers how the Lord is led into the wilderness for 40 days where he is tempted, and on the second, how Christ is transfigured on the mountain. On the next three Sundays, three great Johannine passages of major importance for Christian initiation are read: the Samaritan woman at the well, the man born blind and the raising of Lazarus. While alternatives are given for Years B and C, these gospels from Year A may always be used with the other readings from Year A, especially where the elect are preparing for Easter. Finally, on the last Sunday of Lent, the account of the Lord's passion is proclaimed from one of the synoptic gospels.

9 The first readings for the Sundays of Lent present the main elements of the history of salvation from its beginning until the promise of the new covenant. The readings from the letters of the apostles have been selected to complement the gospel and the first readings and, as far as possible, to make a connection between them.

- The opening prayers and prefaces for the Sundays of Lent serve to reinforce the power of the readings for these Sundays. The scrutinies, which are

celebrated on the Third, Fourth and Fifth Sundays of Lent, draw from and build upon the gospel reading in particular for each of these Sundays. The penitential rite is particularly appropriate as an opening rite for the celebration of the eucharist in Lent.

Perspective on Lent

A SEASON OF MIXED EMOTIONS

IF the Pastoral Introduction's characterization of Lent as a "joyful season" strikes us at first as strange, how much more so these ancient words used to this very day in the Christian East:

> The lenten spring has come:
> let us receive the announcement of Lent with joy!
> For if our forefather Adam had kept the fast,
> we would not have been deprived of paradise.
> The time of Lent is a time of gladness!
> Filled with resplendent prayer and all good deeds,
> let us sing with joy ...

If that note of joy clashes with our most recent experience of Lent in the Western church, such was not always the case. In the sixth-century Rule of Benedict, as in the Byzantine texts, the call to conversion is permeated by an attitude of joy:

> The life of a monk ought to be a continuous Lent. Since few, however, have the strength for this, we urge the entire community during these days of Lent to keep its manner of life most pure and wash away in this holy season the negligences of other times. This we can do in a fitting manner by refusing to indulge evil habits and by devoting ourselves to prayer with tears, to reading, to compunction of heart and self-denial. During these days, therefore, we will add to the usual measure of our service something by way of private prayer and abstinence from food or drink, so that each of us will have something above the assigned measure to offer God of his own will with the joy of the Holy Spirit (1 Thessalonians 1:6). In other words, let each one deny himself some food, drink, sleep, needless talking and idle jesting, and look forward to holy Easter with joy and spiritual longing (chapter 49).

For Benedict, Lent was a time for the monk to live more fully the life he was supposed to be living all the time. And to live it with joy! A hundred years before, Pope Leo the Great had said almost the same thing to us "ordinary" nonmonastics:

> Dear friends, what the Christian should be doing at all times should be done now with greater care and devotion. . . . The special note of the paschal feast is this: The whole church rejoices in the forgiveness of sins. It rejoices in the forgiveness not only of those who are then reborn in holy baptism but also of those who are already numbered among God's adopted children (Sermon 6 on Lent, in *Liturgy of the Hours,* Thursday after Ash Wednesday, Office of Readings).

Here again is a call to live this special time as we should be living all the time. And again, the "special note" is joy, Lent identified as an integral part of the paschal feast. The call is to the whole community, composed then as now of those going to the font for the first time and those returning to renew their baptismal covenant. With this authentic tradition as background, the Pastoral Introduction's characterization of Lent as "joyful preparation" sounds a bit less strange.

A SEASON OF MULTIPLE ORIGINS

The earliest pre-Easter fast seems to have been only two days long! Liturgical historians generally agree that the observance of Easter Sunday represents a wedding of two independent traditions. Jewish Christians celebrated an annual Passover with a gradual "modulation" of its theme of redemption to include the triumph of Jesus, the new Paschal Lamb. This early "Easter," preceded by a day of fast, occurred on any day of the week, as did the Jewish Passover. Meanwhile, Gentile Christians assembled weekly at the close of the Sabbath to celebrate the Lord's Day with the Lord's Supper on the first day of the week. They fasted on Wednesdays and Fridays. Eventually, perhaps after Gentile bishops came to Jerusalem, these traditions melded: The annual paschal celebration was "adjusted" to take place on the nearest Lord's day, hence, "Easter" Sunday. The fixed observance of Easter on Sunday meant that the day before, Saturday, was a fixed day of fasting, now added to the already established Friday fast. This two-day preparation came to be lengthened to a week, beginning the previous Sunday: a "holy week" focused on reading the passion narratives, a practice that continued down to our own day in the pre-Vatican II Missal.

■ BAPTISMAL PREPARATION: In the Acts of the Apostles, baptism follows conversion immediately. But in the third century, at least in some places, Christian initiation had become a process accomplished in several ritual stages, as the *Apostolic Tradition* (about 215) testifies. The length of preparation is not specified nor is Easter assigned as the special occasion for baptism. Tertullian, writing around that time, extols "Passover and Pentecost (the Fifty Days)" as "a most joyful period" for baptism. But he adds that "every day is the Lord's Day; any hour, any season, is suitable for baptism. If there is a difference of solemnity, it makes no difference to the grace." Socrates, a fifth-century historian, notes a three-week fast in Rome. An eighth-century sacramentary provides three Masses for baptismal scrutinies to be held, as in the present *Rite of Christian Initiation of Adults,* on the Third, Fourth and Fifth Sundays of Lent. Scholars believe these to be remnants of the ancient three-week preparation. The gospels from the third Sunday on are taken from the Gospel of John, whose passion narrative is the focal point of the Good Friday celebration.

The Council of Nicea (325) established a common date for Easter and noted the appropriateness of a preparatory forty-day fast. But there is no mandate about how to observe this period or when to begin it. Nevertheless, within a generation of the Council, there was fasting of "about forty days" almost everywhere in the Christian world! The eventual adoption of paschal baptism almost everywhere guaranteed that the principal focus of this fast would become one of baptismal preparation.

■ THE FAST OF JESUS: But these were not the only strands being woven into the tapestry of Lent. The church of Alexandria, the ancient see of Saint Mark, had a different approach, whose influence reached far beyond its boundaries. Again, the lectionary provides the clues. Before December 25 became a nativity feast in the East, the church of Egypt considered January 6 as the date of Jesus' appearance and the beginning of the liturgical year. Thus they began on that day the sequential passages from "their" evangelist, Mark. His gospel begins with the Lord's baptism, followed immediately by desert fasting, so the Alexandrian church celebrated Christ's baptism on January 6 and began a forty-day fast like his on January 7. These 40 days were completely independent of the week-long fast before Easter. A special "secret" addition to Mark's gospel provided the Egyptian church with a reading and reason for prepaschal baptism on the Friday that ended this fast. This was followed by a special "Feast of Palms," all independent of Easter.

It seems that a "collision of customs" occurred after Nicea. In some places, the new prepaschal 40 days, counted backward from Easter toward Epiphany, ran into the post-Epiphany 40 days. Various accommodations were made. Some Celtic monastic documents dependent on the Egyptian tradition observe a "full hundred days'" fast, from Epiphany through Easter, which became a monastic attempt to reconcile both traditions. The church of Aquileia (Northern Italy) names the church of Alexandria as a "sister church" in its form of the Creed, modern scholarship supports the theory that this "Fast of Jesus" spread well beyond Egypt. This may have contributed to identifying the prepaschal 40 days with Jesus' desert fasting, and to the penitential emphasis of Lent, as adult initiation declined in the fifth and sixth centuries.

■ TO THE EVE OF VATICAN II: The Lent we knew just before Vatican II was the fruit of a long development, elaboration and fragmentation. Adult initiation disappeared early. Baptismal preparation was replaced by a preoccupation with penitence. A "mini-Lent" developed: On Septuagesima, Sexagesima and Quinquagesima Sundays (70, 60 and 50 Days before Easter), violet vestments were worn as the real Lent drew near. Because Sunday, the Lord's Day, can never be a fast day, Wednesday before the First Sunday of Lent became Lent's beginning. This provided a fast of exactly 40 days for those who were scrupulously counting.

From the Mozarabic (Spain) and Gallican (France) churches came the custom of initiating penitents into public penance by a sprinkling with ashes. In 1091, a reforming monk of the liturgically renowned Abbey of Cluny, Pope Urban II, directed all the faithful to begin Lent by this dramatic, external sign of penance and conversion. Thus *Ash* Wednesday arrived on the scene, to this day one of the most popular and well-attended days in the liturgical calendar. The latter part of Lent eventually "subdivided" as well. For two weeks of Passiontide, statues were veiled in violet; popular preaching turned from personal repentance to a preparation for Holy Week. Holy Week came to include the Triduum, whose services were "anticipated," that is, moved up from evening to morning. Imagine the "night vigil" of Easter in a sunlit church on Saturday morning, the blessing of fire, candle

and water witnessed by only a few early risers! Finally, toward noon on Saturday the church bells rang, signaling the end of a very strange Lent (as we look back on it), a season of diverse origins, contradictory influences and a most complex development!

Presentation of the Season

THE ENVIRONMENT OF WORSHIP

THE great Orthodox liturgist Alexander Schmemann spoke of the lenten "atmosphere" as a "climate" that anyone walking into church should be able to sense immediately. The liturgy begins before the beginning! For our age, used to an audio-visual environment whose signals are all-pervasive and often subliminal, the liturgy begins even before we enter the space where the liturgical beginning takes place. As with choosing texts, music and ritual patterns, so with decorations: It is best to plan out the full season, the Forty Days (Lent), the Three Days (Triduum) and the Fifty Days (Eastertime).

■ FROM OUTSIDE TO INSIDE: Attending to the worship space itself and all the details of the liturgy that will be celebrated there, establishing good ritual patterns to be repeated year after year: As important as all this is, the work is still not done! The space that leads into the place of worship must be thought of as "the beginning before the beginning."

Imagine people driving into the parking lot, walking onto the grounds and knowing immediately from what they see that, yes, Lent has begun! Imagine the journey through the parking lot, up the walkway and into the church as a kind of "procession"! Malls and marketplaces, businesses and homes do this sort of outdoor, silent announcement all the time with flags, colors, wreathes and so on. Why not the house of God, the home of God's family, the community's gathering place?

In reflecting on any decorating—outdoors and indoors—attention is again directed to Peter Mazar's important and practical guide, *To Crown the Year*: parking lots, church grounds, paths and walkways, doorways and vestibule all can announce that business as usual has been suspended and that keeping Lent is the business of the day.

■ ON THE INSIDE: Once inside, everything should say to those who enter that a new season has begun, a time of serious and sustained reflection, a time of focus and attention to the things that really matter. This is the point of lenten austerity and sobriety aimed at in the church's liturgical legislation. What may at first seem simply negative has a positive goal: for instance, the ban on flowers, except on actual festivals such as Laetare Sunday (the lenten midpoint) and solemnities (Saint Joseph, Annunciation). The goal is a visual sobriety matched by an aural one: the ban on instrumental music, festive preludes, postludes, interludes, any instrumentation except that which is needed to sustain the assembly's singing.

■ ASSEMBLY: Mazar suggests we attend to some focal points when preparing the inside worship space. The first of these is the assembly's place. Decorating this area is neither to teach nor entertain but to create "an atmosphere and a mood" (*Environment and Art in Catholic Worship*, page 100). Mazar develops the concept:

> The area high over the heads of the congregation or along the walls is usually a good area for strong decoration that signals the season. For example, a cluster of large branches . . . an array of purple or gray fabric hangings grabs people's attention when they first enter the worship space, but it does not necessarily demand attention during the liturgy (48).

Stressing the continuity of the whole paschal season (Ash Wednesday through Pentecost), he continues with suggestions for "winter-turning-into-spring," a helpful concept for decorators in many regions.

■ FONT: Many parishes postpone baptisms until the Easter Vigil, or in the case of infants, Easter Day or Eastertime. This might be signaled visually by keeping the font (and holy water fonts?) empty during Lent. But, Mazar notes, mere emptiness may be misread as simple neglect. Recent attempts at creativity have misfired badly: Sand in the holy water fonts turns them into hotel lobby ashtrays! Mazar suggests that the baptismal font be "drained, cleaned and sealed in a noble manner" before Ash Wednesday. A bold and simple cross of purple cloth placed over the font says a lot, as does putting the paschal candle away except for funerals and leaving the ambry open, empty of the chrism vessel. Maybe the Book of the Elect is kept near the font, inviting prayer for those about to be initiated.

■ CROSS: The cross, besides being a primary symbol of Christianity, is a supremely important item in Catholic worship. The community's standard, shield and coat-of-arms is borne before us whenever we move in pilgrimage formation (except, interestingly, during the Easter Vigil, when the paschal candle leads the way): the penitential procession at the beginning of Lent, the Palm Sunday procession (when the cross is, according to the sacramentary, "suitably adorned"), the veneration on Good Friday, and perhaps at the beginning of every Sunday eucharist during Lent and the rest of the year. What does the community's processional cross look like? Is it the cross that is set in the sanctuary during liturgy? Venerated on Good Friday? Should it be? Could it be? Again, *Environment and Art in Catholic Worship* (page 88) has something to say about this. So does Mazar:

> Ideally, the main cross in the worship space is the one venerated on Good Friday and the one used as the processional cross throughout the year. That way our worship space has one cross, and one cross only (67).
>
> Some parishes use a cross as a decoration during Lent.... Sometimes it is placed near the altar (where it is often redundant to the main cross).... Lent is not a six-week Passiontide. The liturgy does not focus on the passion of Christ until the final days of Lent. The tradition during Lent has been to hide the cross from view, if only to make us eager to see it once again during the Triduum. There is, however, a good, strong tradition for honoring the holy cross throughout Eastertime, because once the cross is carried into our midst on Good Friday, it is not carried out (67–68).

Clearly, the ideal is not always possible. The community's reality needs to be respected and treated with reverence. It may also need to be challenged: patiently, charitably, intelligently. Ritual is established through repetition. One year's obvious "mistake" need not be repeated for the sake of consistency!

■ VESTURE: For lenten vesture, the prescribed color is a purple or violet different from that of Advent. Some argue that the traditional lenten vesture is a somber blue-violet, almost black; some modern Lutheran publications suggest earth or ashen colors. Whatever the exact color, the goal of lenten vesture is visual austerity, simplicity, plainness. Avoid the gaudy purples of some church goods catalogues and the appliqué symbols that are busy and distracting (and often not very good art). On Laetare Sunday a dusky "old rose" (not hot pink) color may be used, and on Saint Joseph's day perhaps the Christmas whites could reappear, a visual echo of that lovely season with which he is so associated. For Palm Sunday, use the same red set reserved for the Triumph of the Cross and for Good Friday. Maybe it's the same set used on martyrs' days. But not the Pentecost set, and certainly nothing with appliqué doves!

ENTERING THE LENTEN LITURGY: MOVEMENT AND MUSIC

■ THE PENITENTIAL PROCESSION: In January 1988, the Congregation for Divine Worship in Rome issued a *Circular Letter Concerning the Preparation and Celebration of the Easter Feasts* (available in the March 17, 1988, issue [vol. 17, #40] of *Origins* or from the United States Catholic Conference's publishing office, 1-800-235-8722; ask for publication 219-5). Among its many suggestions (a number of which are incorporated into ICEL's Pastoral Introduction) was the recommendation that the community's principal Mass on this Sunday be marked by a procession beginning in a place apart from where the eucharist would be celebrated. This movement is accompanied by the litany of the saints. The letter referred to the *Ceremonial of Bishops,* #261, where this gathering and procession mark not just the First Sunday but any celebration of the eucharist during Lent at which the bishop gathers with a community of the faithful. The order of worship to be followed and suggested texts appear on page 118. Each community will have to decide whether such a procession is practical before the principal Mass on the First Sunday (or every Sunday) of Lent.

■ SIMPLE ENTRANCE: Every lenten entrance ought to establish the purposeful presence and focused attention the penitential procession is intended to establish. Good order, deliberate pace and the consciously reverent bearing of all who take part will help even the most diminished procession of ministers (and elect?) "gather" the rest of the assembly into the mood and mystery.

■ MUSIC: The music chosen to accompany whatever form this opening movement takes will

be crucial. Once again, simplicity and sobriety need not mean gloominess! For this reason, and because the most ancient Roman tradition favors the approach, a chanted antiphon or refrain rather than the usual metrical hymn might be the best way to begin. Since there are no preludes during Lent (except perhaps on the Fourth Sunday), this first chant the community hears and sings must set exactly the right tone. A perfect chant for this purpose is the traditional refrain to the Latin lenten piece, "Attende, Domine." Appearing in several translations in all the major hymnals ("Draw near, O Lord our God"; "Hear us, almighty Lord"; "Hear our entreaties, Lord," etc.), the chant is a brisk and bright Mode 5 melody, quickly learned and easily memorized. There is nothing gloomy about this unadorned and straightforward piece, whose words and melody are perfectly matched. And, like so many of these chants, it has staying power: It will bear the weight of five weeks' use.

Another option for gathering music comes from Taizé: "Adoramus Te Domine" (*Music from Taizé,* Volume I, GIA G-2433). Poetically gifted planners might write verses for each Sunday. For instance, for the First Sunday: "In the desert of repentance, adoramus te domine"; "In a land parched dry and lifeless, adoramus te domine." If Year A of the lectionary is used, at least at the Masses where the elect are present, creative verses particular to the Third, Fourth and Fifth Sundays could draw on the rich scriptural images of water/thirst, darkness/light and death/life. The music would be the same, but varied texts could draw the assembly deeper into the lenten desert of repentance as the season unfolds.

ENTERING THE LENTEN WORD: THE INTRODUCTORY RITES

■ GREETING: The sign of the cross and greeting come at the end of what may have already been an extensive rite of gathering and greeting. Words here will be brief and formal, the introduction unnecessary if one preceded the procession and minimal even if one did not! Choose one special greeting for use throughout the season. Or perhaps one text for the first four weeks and a second for use toward the end of Lent and through Holy Week.

■ PENITENTIAL RITE: The proposed simplification of the introductory rites (approved by the U.S. bishops and awaiting Rome's confirmation) suggests a choice among the sprinkling with water, the penitential rite properly so-called, and two other options, the litany of praise and the Kyrie. The sprinkling with water would hardly be appropriate during Lent as we look forward to Easter baptism and baptismal renewal. The order for the other forms follows:

Penitential Rite
- invitation to repentance
- pause for silent reflection
- "I confess" or a set of versicles and responses
- absolution: either the familiar "May almighty God have mercy on us" or the form previously used to conclude the rite of sprinkling, "May almighty God cleanse us of our sins."

Litany of Praise
- invitation to praise Christ
- invocations to Christ: form C of the penitential rite in the present sacramentary
- no absolution text; "Let us pray" and the opening prayer follow immediately

Kyrie
- invitation to praise Christ
- invocations to Christ in Greek or English ("Kyrie, eleison" or "Lord, have mercy")
- no absolution text; "Let us pray" and the opening prayer follow immediately

Whichever form is chosen, the deacon (or in the deacon's absence, the presider) intones, "Let us kneel." This formal directive to a posture for prayer will be heard again at the Good Friday liturgy. While the "I confess" is a good text for Lent, there is nothing quite as moving as singing the Kyrie in a fine chant setting. Consider Richard Proulx's "Three Plainsong Kyries" with tropes from the sacramentary (GIA, G-3162) with choral companion (G-3161). In the present sacramentary's form C of the penitential rite, invocations IV and V seem to be lenten in tone, and further texts are provided on page 117 of this *Sourcebook*.

The Gloria is omitted during Lent, except on the feast of the Chair of Peter and on the Solemnities of Saint Joseph and the Annunciation (transferred this year into the Easter season).

LITURGY OF THE WORD

The "character" of each lenten Sunday, notes the Pastoral Introduction, is "drawn from the gospel of the day" (PI, 8). Indeed, so carefully crafted is the whole lenten Sunday lectionary (all three readings in all three cycles) that even without a knowledge of Lent's history and theology, anyone carefully reading these scriptures in any year would quickly get a clear sense of the season's nature and movement.

■ FIRST SUNDAY: Each year of the lectionary presents Christ's fast and temptation. In this Year B, the Year of Mark, the temptation is mentioned with no embellishment of detail. Christ is simply in the place of solitude and danger with the wild beasts; his glory and lordship emerge victorious, for the angels waited on him. The "brackets" around this temptation and victory are the Spirit, at whose bidding Christ enters the desert sojourn and the kingdom, whose proclamation is the outcome of it. The mood of the gospel is a perfect reflection of Lent. There is a sober call to commitment: repent. But the motive for that repentance is overwhelmingly positive: The time is fulfilled, the kingdom is near, the news in which we are to believe is good!

■ SECOND SUNDAY: Again, there is a clear note of victory right at the beginning of Lent. Each year a different synoptic version of the Lord's transfiguration is proclaimed: the goodness of being in the presence of God's glory, the witness of the law and the prophets to the message of Christ, the terror, the passing of the vision, the questioning about what all of this means and what the resurrection means. That experience is our experience: glimpses of glory on mountains where we cannot stay and mountains of questions along the everyday streets we have to travel.

■ THIRD, FOURTH AND FIFTH SUNDAYS: Beginning on the Third Sunday, a decision needs to be made:

> While alternatives are given for Years B and C, these gospels from Year A may always be used with the other readings from Year A, especially where the elect are preparing for Easter (PI, 8).

If there are catechumens in the community, the decision is easy: The readings from Year A are used. But they may be used in every year in every parish.

■ SEASONAL PSALMS FOR LENT: Psalm 51 is appointed for Ash Wednesday and at least three other times in the lenten weekday lectionary. It is also used each Friday at Morning Prayer. Traditionally known as the "Miserere" (from the first word in the Latin version), settings of this classic penitential psalm have been composed in every style and appear in every major hymnal. If the parish already has a "standard" setting, which helps identify the season for the assembly, then by all means retain it. Some newer settings of Psalm 51 include:

- Psalm 51: "Be merciful, O Lord" by John Karl Kirten (GIA, G-3318)
- Psalm 51: "Be merciful, O Lord" by Steven Janco (GIA, G-3518)
- Psalm 51: "Be merciful, O Lord" by Joseph B. Smith (GIA, G-3494)
- Psalm 51 by Michael Ward (WLP, 8568)
- Psalm 51 by Michael Bedford (from *Sing Out! A Children's Psalter,* WLP, 7190)

Psalms 91 and 130 are also seasonal lenten psalms.

■ GOSPEL ACCLAMATION: According to one of Lent's oldest and most distinctive traditions, the singing of Alleluia is completely excluded from the liturgy, even on solemnities and feasts, and at ritual Masses that happen to fall in Lent. A number of acclamations substitute for the Alleluia. These appear in a variety of styles, in every major hymnal. Choose one or two settings and use them for the entire season. World Library offers two that you might consider: Charles Gardner's "Praise to you, Word of God" (WLP, 8560), a practical setting with easy-to-learn verses for cantor or choir; and Paul French's "Praise and honor to you, Lord Jesus Christ," a slightly more challenging piece.

■ GOSPEL CEREMONIAL AND PROCLAMATION: How and where the gospel is proclaimed has varied considerably among the different rites of the church over the many centuries of our history. All of us have experienced and participated in the "parts" approach to the passion gospels of Palm Sunday and Good Friday. Older Catholics may remember three clerics cantoring the passion during Holy Weeks past, and some will remember the ornate chants that could be used on certain days. In fact, adaptations of the ancient chants, with English texts, are available still (the *Passion Gospels and Chants for the Readings* from GIA). Opinion varies on the suitability of this. Some feel that one good reader ought to be able to carry the whole narrative, signaling the varying characters in the story by the subtle changes of inflection and movement that anyone well-trained in public reading would use. Some fear an overdramatization or an entertainment orientation being inflicted on a sacred text that

is, after all, a liturgical proclamation. Yet as Aelred Rosser has pointed out, regarding the passion narrative, in LTP's *Workbook for Lectors and Gospel Readers,* 1996:

> Liturgical practice through the ages, however, has preferred a group—not only because it adds variety but because it adds dynamism and power (140).

The principle might be extended to include the Johannine gospels for the Third, Fourth and Fifth Sundays of Year A. David Haas and Victoria Tufano have prepared arrangements of these gospels, faithful to the biblical texts, the narrative line kept intact but punctuated with acclamations sung by the assembly at appropriate places (GIA, G-3662). Of course, musicians could search the parish repertoire of well-known hymns to find a musical fragment to serve as an acclamation in place of those composed by Haas.

Highlight the gospels of Lent ritually by honoring their proclamation with a formal gospel procession: incense, candles, lectors (if parts will be used), deacon or presider with gospel book. Consider the custom of some Eastern rites and Western "usages," like the "Sarum use" of medieval England: Process to the center point of the main aisle, chant "The Lord be with you," and the announcement of the gospel. Lectors, if taking part, could move during the procession to other places in the church (as long as they can be heard!), accompanied by candlebearers.

■ DISMISSAL OF CATECHUMENS AND ELECT: Throughout the year, the catechumens are dismissed each Sunday after the homily. During Lent, the catechumens and those among them who have been elected for Easter baptism are dismissed. Alternative forms of the dismissal for specific occasions during Lent are in the *Rite of Christian Initiation of Adults.*

Two texts for dismissing catechumens (#67) make the spirit of the dismissal clear. Other words may be used, but any dismissal should convey concern and affection. A lenten seasonal formula is proposed in this *Sourcebook* on page 117.

■ PROFESSION OF FAITH: The profession of faith is prescribed for Sundays and for the Solemnity of Saint Joseph on March 19. Be aware that lenten initiation rites change the order of concluding the liturgy of the word: Following the initiation rites (rite of sending, rite of election, penitential rite for candidates for reception into the church, scrutinies for the elect), the catechumens and elect are dismissed. The general intercessions and the profession of faith follow.

■ GENERAL INTERCESSIONS: On Sundays when catechumenal rites take place, two different kinds of intercession happen closely together in the liturgy. Be sure to keep them distinct. Intercessions for the elect could be chanted with a sung response. Bilingual communities will want to do the intercessions for the elect in various languages, a sung refrain following each intention. After the dismissal, use a more familiar format for the general intercessions by the faithful. If there are no general intercessions after the dismissal (although we do not recommend this), intercessions for the church and the world are added to the intercessions for the elect.

LITURGY OF THE EUCHARIST

■ PREPARATION OF THE GIFTS: Since a sung refrain is suggested for both the entrance and communion processions, here is a perfect place for the assembly to offer prayer in the form of a metrical hymn. The very moment in the ritual invites reflection between the liturgy of the word, probably with its initiatory rituals, and the liturgy of the eucharist with its more intensive style of attentive prayer. Though they are associated in the Roman rite primarily with the Liturgy of the Hours, many fine metrical hymns grace the lenten season. One or two could be learned and sung throughout the season. Remember to choose music that is strong yet simple, in keeping with the austerity that preserves the focused attention proper to the lenten season.

Some pieces from our own Latin tradition ought not to be neglected. A number of them are rich in biblical and seasonal imagery, such as "Again we keep this solemn fast" and "O Sun of justice." See the *Lutheran Book of Worship,* naturally, for some wonderful lenten and passion-oriented chorales of the German tradition that might become parish standards in the years ahead.

■ LENTEN PREFACES: In contrast to the one lenten preface in use until 1970, the post–Vatican II sacramentary has 12 (P8–19), drawn from the finest resources of the universal church's rich treasury of liturgical texts and patristic homilies. As is the danger with the expanded repertoire provided by Vatican II, these prefaces can be chosen at random by the presider at the last minute. As befits Vatican II's careful provision for solid theology and pastoral variety, particular texts should be carefully and thoughtfully chosen.

- *First Sunday of Lent (P 12) / Second Sunday of Lent (P 13), Years A, B, C:* These prefaces, for use each year, focus on the gospel stories of the temptation and transfiguration respectively. The First Sunday's preface explicitly links Christ's victory with what we pray will be the fruit of our victory in him: the eternal feast of heaven. The Second Sunday's preface proclaims the Lord's approaching passion as the necessary prerequisite to glory.

- *Third Sunday of Lent (P 14), Year A scriptures only:* For use only with the gospel of the Samaritan woman, this preface draws on the ancient Mozarabic (Spanish) rite, among other sources, for a beautiful summary of the patristic interpretation of that gospel. Christ is thirsty not for water but for the woman's faith. And faith is not a vague feeling or an experience we somehow come to; it is instead a gift that Christ bestows.

- *Fourth Sunday of Lent (P 15), Year A scriptures only:* For use only with the gospel of the man born blind, this preface has been recast by ICEL in inclusive language, and the allusions to baptismal water and resurrection in Christ have been made clearer. The new text:

    By the mystery of his incarnation
    he has led the human race out of darkness
    into the clear light of faith.
    Through the fall of Adam we were born the
        slaves of sin,
    but through the waters of baptism
    Christ has raised us to new life
    as your adopted children.

- *Fifth Sunday of Lent (P 16), with Year A scriptures only:* For use only with the gospel of the raising of Lazarus, this preface expresses well the age-old interpretation of the raising of Lazarus as an image of Christian initiation and of restoration to the community through penitence for those who sin after baptism. The new ICEL version corrects the exclusive language and echoes the gospel story more literally. More importantly, it emphasizes not only the sacramental life of the church in general but the specific rites we are about to celebrate at the Easter Vigil. The new text:

    As one like us,
    he wept for Lazarus his friend;
    as eternal God,
    he called him forth from the tomb.
    In his compassion for the human family,
    Christ leads us by the Easter mysteries
    from death to new life.

- *Prefaces for the Third, Fourth, Fifth Sundays of Lent, with scriptures of Years B and C, and for weekdays of Lent:* Designated especially for Sundays that do not have a proper preface, Lenten Prefaces I and II (P 8, P 9) are for the Third through Fifth Sundays of Years B and C, unless the decision has been made to use the readings from Year A. The first preface emphasizes the joy with which the Christian people should respond to the call to cleanse their hearts. The second preface celebrates Lent as a season of grace designed to renew and purify, to reorder our priorities here and to refocus our goals on the life to come.

- *Prefaces for Weekdays:* Prefaces for Lent III and IV (P 10, P 11), titled respectively, "Fruits of Self-Denial" and "The Reward of Fasting," are ideal for lenten weekdays, especially for Fridays (a day of obligatory abstinence). The first of these, especially, is rich in scriptural allusions, especially in ICEL's revision:

    You bid us show our thanks
    through the practice of self-denial,
    that we may curb our sinful pride
    and, by sharing our bread with the hungry,
    may imitate your generous love.

- *Option during the Fifth Week of Lent: Preface of the Lord's Passion I:* This beautiful text, taken from the lenten sermons of Pope Leo the Great, is optional for use during the Fifth Week of Lent, when, as has been noted, the mood of Lent changes subtly toward an increased reflection on the passion.

- *Holy Week: Preface of the Lord's Passion II:* This last of the lenten prefaces (P 18) is a gem whose use is reserved for the last three days of the season. It bespeaks the liturgy's mystical "immediacy": The days of the Lord's life-giving death and glorious resurrection are not long ago and far away. The days "draw near"—"this is the hour."

■ "LENTEN" EUCHARISTIC PRAYERS: The eucharistic prayers used through Lent should be chosen with no less care than the prefaces. Time should never be a factor in this holy season, even when initiatory rites are being celebrated. Note the following special "inserts," technically called "interpolations," for the eucharistic prayers.

- *Eucharistic Prayer I:* Two interpolations for Masses at which the scrutinies are celebrated: at the first "Memento" ("Remember, Lord . . .") and at the "Hanc Igitur" ("Father, accept this offering . . ."). See the sacramentary, "Ritual Masses," I. Christian Initiation, 2. The Scrutinies.

- *Eucharistic Prayer for Reconciliation I and II:* These prayers are also appropriate for use during the lenten season, though there is no provision in them for inserts regarding the elect.

Reconciliation II is especially appropriate for the first four weeks of Lent, celebrating as it does Christ as "the Word that brings salvation (Sundays 1 and 2), the hand you stretch out to sinners (Sunday 3) [and] the way that leads to your peace (Sundays 4 and 5)."

Reconciliation I is especially appropriate during the fifth week of Lent and Holy Week, with its beautiful echoes of the Lord's passion: "When we were lost and could not find the way to you. . . . Before he stretched out his arms between heaven and earth. . . . He desired to celebrate the paschal feast in the company of his disciples. . . . Knowing that he was to reconcile all things in himself by the blood of his cross. . . ."

■ EUCHARISTIC PRAYER ACCLAMATIONS: The sung acclamations during the eucharistic prayer should remain constant for the lenten season, certainly for Ash Wednesday and the first four Sundays. A set that echoes the "lenten" sound should be chosen, and for this many of the old chant-style settings work well, especially adaptations of the simple and solemn Mass XVIII. When a modern setting is chosen, some parishes signify the unity of the full ninety-day season in an aural way, by using the same acclamations, keeping them in unison (and even a capella) during Lent, then adding choral and instrumental embellishments for the Triduum and Easter's Fifty Days.

■ THE COMMUNION RITE: Texts to be chosen and kept stable throughout Lent (or at least for the first four weeks) are: the introduction to the Lord's Prayer (third form particularly appropriate for Lent); the prayer for peace, if a special text is used; the invitation to the sign of peace; the invitation to holy communion; and the sending forth of the eucharistic ministers, if this is done.

■ SIGN OF PEACE: This ritual act may have become a liturgical item that we, the baptized, take for granted or, worse yet, trivialize. It ought to be celebrated with new meaning and sincerity during this holy season. One option recently approved by the United States bishops (awaiting confirmation from Rome) follows the lead of the Ambrosian rite. In this option, the sign of peace takes place after the general intercessions and before the gifts are brought forward from the assembly. This would be a particularly striking place to have the sign of peace, if the catechumens and elect have just been dismissed. They, after all, will first share in that sign during their initiation at the Easter Vigil. The location of the sign of peace should remain the same throughout the season.

■ MUSIC DURING COMMUNION: An antiphon sung by the congregation, with psalm verses by a cantor or choir, remains the Roman rite's first preference for music at this moment and the most practical arrangement for people moving forward to receive communion. When a common psalm is used consistently at the liturgy of the word, the communion procession provides an opportunity to sing the appointed psalms for the Sundays of Lent. Some may already be known to the parish. The learning load is light for the assembly, which has only to learn the refrain.

The "normative" lenten psalms (51, 33, 95, 23 and 130) contain a wide variety of themes: repentance, trust, openness to God, protection, supplication and hope. Refrain-style settings of these psalms can be found in many hymnals.

■ CONCLUDING RITES: The dismissal rite in Lent should have its own distinctive style. During the first four weeks choose #6 ("a complete change of heart") or #16 ("care for your people and purify them") or #24 ("strengthen [your children] against the attacks of the devil"). For the fifth week of Lent and for Holy Week, #17 is a traditional, "passion-oriented" prayer ("the love which our Lord Jesus Christ showed us when he delivered himself . . . and suffered the agony of the cross"). Whichever is chosen may be used on weekdays as well.

■ THE RECESSIONAL: It often comes as a surprise to people that the Roman rite's revised Order of Mass does not prescribe a recessional hymn. We have become used to singing as we end the liturgy. The final hymn serves as a kind of musical "sending-forth" or "commissioning for witness." The absence of a hymn before we leave may even strike us as odd, as if someone has forgotten something, or as if the liturgy has not been brought to proper closure. This popular expectation and impression may be precisely the reason to omit a concluding hymn during Lent!

Because absolute silence at this point may quickly degenerate into loud conversation (which would set no kind of mood at all), here might be a good place *not* to observe the lenten ban on instrumental music. A quiet instrumental version of a chant piece, such as "Audi, benigne conditor" or, later in the season "Vexilla regis prodeunt" (both available in many older hymnals), would set just the right tone for the exit of ministers and assembly.

Preparing the Parish

At the beginning of Lent over 1500 years ago, Pope Leo the Great reminded his local church in Rome:

> Dear friends: What the Christian should be doing at all times should be done now with greater care and devotion so that the lenten fast enjoined by the apostles may be fulfilled, not simply by abstinence from food but above all by renunciation of sin.

This call to reflection is as inclusive of the whole community as the Prophet Joel's cry for repentance in the scripture read on Ash Wednesday. Therefore:

- Organizations of all ages and of every purpose need to trim their yearly calendars every year to the time and tone of this season.

- Religious education needs to be tuned in to this season, as the church's living catechism, whose "scope and sequence" embrace a lifetime of learning and living.

- Social events need to be planned carefully around the precious few days of festivity that mark an easing of the lenten intensity. All through the centuries, almost every religious order and local diocese had one midlenten holiday worked in. Pick a saint!

- Fundraising needs to forget our needs and focus on others, to move beyond the parish to embrace the community and beyond that to cradle the world. Lent is our "tithe" of the year, in time and effort and income.

- Friday evening as the culmination of a day of abstinence might feature a meatless, fasting meal of soup and bread after the evening Mass and before Stations of the Cross.

Maybe this process has to begin in the spring or summer before Lent or whenever the "big calendar" is put together with dates fixed beyond changing. Planning Lent is a work that has to be done together, as seasons can only be kept together, and we can only be church together. To assist in the planning, LTP provides the *Paschal Mission* each year. It is a resource that has the potential to bring all the disciplines, the days and the disciples together. The season is too powerfully rich not to give it a try!

■ IN THE SCHOOL: Consult the *Leader's Manual of the Hymnal for Catholic Students* (pages 81–92) for models of weekday liturgy with children.

Taking It Home

In this, as in every season, *Catholic Household Blessings and Prayers* is the rich resource to have at hand. The following celebrations should be considered for use or adaptation by every household:

- Ash Wednesday: Blessing the Season and a Place of Prayer, page 132
- Blessings of the Lenten Disciplines: Fasting and Almsgiving, page 137
- Passion Sunday: Placing the Branches in the Home, page 140
- Prayers of the Triduum, page 143

■ PRAYER AT TABLE: In Lent, certainly, this is a custom to revive or intensify. *Catholic Household Blessings* has texts on page 76, and LTP has lenten mealtime prayercards (Lent on one side; Eastertime on the reverse). On the table might be a reminder of the lenten season—cross, bare branches, violet candle.

■ PRAYER ALONE: The custom of *lectio divina,* "holy reading," has been embraced by many busy Christians as an oasis of peace in a too-busy world. Lent is the perfect opportunity to begin or revive this custom. The Office of Readings, excerpted from the *Liturgy of the Hours,* is published by the Daughters of Saint Paul. It is filled with fine patristic and sanctoral writings from across the centuries and has a whole year's cycle of scripture readings as well. The two-volume *Lent Sourcebook* from LTP is a remarkable compendium of lenten scripture, homilies, poetry, reflections and prayers.

Other Ritual Prayers and Sacraments

Morning and Evening Prayer: An increasing number of parishes have begun the tradition of celebrating Vespers on Sunday evenings of Lent. This can be the basis for a tradition of regular celebration of Morning and Evening Prayer throughout the year. It may be very easy to interest at least a part of the regular weekday assembly in gathering a bit earlier

or staying a bit later around the morning and/or evening Mass times to celebrate this form of liturgical prayer.

- VIGILS: Parishes that have grown familiar with the *Liturgy of the Hours* may find the later hours of Saturday night a quiet time conducive to extended praise and reflection. The Lent-Easter volume (II) of the full *Liturgy of the Hours* contains all the material necessary for an Office of Readings-Vigils celebration.

- COMMUNAL PENANCE: Since "lenten penance is not only inward and individual but also outward and social," Lent is a most appropriate season for communal penance services (PI, 3, 4). One approach is to schedule one service early in Lent and a second closer to or at the beginning of Holy Week. Confession and absolution can take place at both services, or the focus of each service could be slightly different. The early lenten service could be primarily an opportunity to hear the word of God and a directed meditation on it, leading to an examination of conscience and the undertaking of a penance or penitential "rule" to be lived throughout Lent. The later service then becomes the occasion for confession and absolution in preparation for the Triduum. Resources for planning an order of service appear in the *Rite of Penance,* appendix II. Unfortunately, by suggesting the use of water and the veneration of the cross, these rites anticipate ritual elements best left to the Triduum. Instead, the chanting of a litany while kneeling is a traditional form of lenten penitential prayer. For a fine text, see *The Book of Common Prayer,* page 267.

- COMMUNAL ANOINTING OF THE SICK: The celebration of anointing is a sacramental way of joining the sick even more closely to the Lord's paschal mystery. Ritual Mass texts should not replace proper texts on Sundays of Lent or on March 19. The rite, however, may be celebrated within Mass even on those days. One reading from the ritual lectionary may be substituted for a lenten scripture passage.

- FUNERALS: Funeral Masses are not permitted on Sundays of Lent. The spirit of Lent can be maintained and the celebration of Christian death enhanced on weekdays by using the day's scriptures, if appropriate.

- MARRIAGES: With the pastoral sensitivity that marks Vatican II, liturgical norms permit marriages during the lenten season. But we are also required to explain to couples why the nature of Lent makes it an inappropriate season for such celebrations (*Rite of Marriage,* #11; *Ceremonial of Bishops,* #604). The ban on flowers and instrumental music seems to apply to these celebrations as well. Pastorally, all policies need to be arrived at with broad discussion and free exchange of ideas, and implemented with charity and understanding.

- BAPTISMS AND CONFIRMATIONS: The *Circular Letter Concerning the Preparation and Celebration of the Easter Feasts* (#27) emphasizes the inappropriateness of baptism and confirmation during Holy Week. That observation goes for Lent as well. As with weddings, a pastorally sensitive policy should defer baptisms, ordinarily, until the Easter Vigil, Easter Day or Eastertime.

- STATIONS OF THE CROSS: Stations of the Cross on Fridays is a time-honored tradition in many parishes and a newly revived custom in many others. Recent publications offer a variety of formats and emphases for this devotion. While venerable and fitting, the "Stabat Mater" is not mandatory at Stations. The "Vexilla regis" is available in a number of modern translations, set to the ancient chant (*Worship,* #435), and is a powerful hymn celebrating the triumph of the cross. Another option is the chanted Agnus Dei of Mass XVIII. This is a fine opportunity to blend some of our rich heritage of Latin chant into our public prayer.

CALENDAR

February

WED 12 #219 [220] violet
Ash Wednesday

■ DAY OF FAST AND ABSTINENCE:
Ash Wednesday, a day of fast and abstinence, sets the tone for Lent through the call to turn away from sin and to be faithful to the gospel (PI, 7).

Since this is true, the parish may wish to provide in advance a helpful approach to keeping the day. Suggestions could embrace all aspects of the observance and point out practical ways to make Ash Wednesday the keynote for a lenten season of spiritual growth and renewal.

Ash Wednesday Mass

There should be no burning of palms as part of today's liturgy. In fact, nothing "extra" should be added to this liturgy whose symbol is ashes, not fire, and whose tone is sober simplicity. Traditionally, ashes are placed on our foreheads in the form of a cross, "branding" us again with the sign of baptism, reminding us that Lent is a time of baptismal renewal. Because the ashes are the symbolic focus for today's worship, give them visual prominence. Set up a pedestal in the sanctuary, in the midst of the assembly, or near the font or entrance if all can turn and face it. Dignified vessels used for the ashes should be reserved for this once-a-year purpose only. The ashes may remain visible as part of the seasonal decor or as a feature of a "seasonal corner." See the preparation notes for Ash Wednesday in *The Sacristy Manual* (G. Thomas Ryan, LTP, 1993), pages 194–95.

■ INTRODUCTORY RITES: The opening song should be strong and stately, and perhaps a capella. "Attende Domine," for instance, is a good choice. Like the official introit chant of the sacramentary, it extols God's mercy. Some Taizé Kyries are appropriate as well.

Choose suitable words for the greeting (see page 117). Perhaps the greeting and the opening prayer, which on this day follows the greeting immediately, may be chanted.

There is no penitential rite today. The ritual with ashes is today's penitential rite.

■ LITURGY OF THE WORD: The ritual we are about to celebrate, like the season we are about to undertake, can be empty formalism without the corrective and directive notes sounded by these excellent passages, especially the gospel.

No matter how pressed for time you are, take the time to sing Psalm 51, the Miserere, today. This is the community's processional chant as we move toward the Easter festival.

Today's gospel acclamation verse is the invitatory from the *Liturgy of the Hours*. Like Psalm 51 it, too, is one of Lent's time-honored theme songs: If today you hear God's voice, harden not your hearts.

For inspiration, preachers might turn to the *Liturgy of the Hours*, volume II, Office of Readings for Ash Wednesday. Clement's Letter to the Corinthians says so well what we all need to hear at the beginning of this season.

■ BLESSING AND GIVING OF ASHES: There is no formal introduction to the ritual. Since it follows the homily, perhaps it was felt that the homily would provide the necessary introduction. Homilists might adapt the brief words found in the *Book of Blessings* (#1663) or the somewhat lengthier introduction in the *Book of Common Prayer* (#264) as a way of concluding their homilies and follow this with the invitation to prayer found in the sacramentary.

■ MUSIC: For the distribution of ashes, choose processional music that does not require hymnal or worship aid. Hymns are generally not useful here. Lucien Deiss' (World Library, *People's Mass Book*) "My soul is longing for your peace" (Psalm 131) or "Grant to us, O Lord," (Ezekiel and Jeremiah) would work well. The refrain of "Give us, Lord, a new heart" by Bernadette Farrell (OCP, #7104) is lovely and easily coupled with verses of any psalm that speaks of trust and conversion (Psalms 25, 62 and 130) chanted to Tone 14 by Joseph Smith (*Lead Me, Guide Me*).

■ GENERAL INTERCESSIONS: These conclude the rite, reaching as always beyond the community and linking the community's prayer, fasting and almsgiving to the needs of the wider human family.

■ LITURGY OF THE EUCHARIST: The suggested preface for this day is Lent IV, but Lent III is also most suitable since it speaks of self-denial as a form of expressing thanks and of the social dimension of Lent. If Eucharistic Prayer III is used, remember ICEL's new lenten insert for this text. Reconciliation II is also a good eucharistic prayer with which to begin the season.

FEBRUARY

Distribution of Ashes outside Mass

The complete order for blessing and distributing ashes apart from Mass is in the *Book of Blessings* (chapter 52). This may be done in church or with a gathering of the sick (as in a nursing home) and may be led by a priest, deacon or layperson, either male or female (a layperson uses ashes already blessed). There is no provision any longer for distribution of ashes apart from communal prayer and the proclamation of some scripture. For liturgies celebrated with children, consult the *Leader's Manual of the Hymnal for Catholic Students* (page 81).

THU 13 — Thursday after Ash Wednesday
#220 [221] (LMC, #176–184)   violet

On these few days before the First Sunday of Lent, the church sets forth the disciplines and attitudes that form our approach to life from now until Easter. Both scripture readings sound the note of choice: the way of life (Deuteronomy), the way of the cross (the gospel).

FRI 14 — Friday after Ash Wednesday
#221 [222] (LMC, #176–184)   violet

Day of abstinence / Cyril, religious, missionary, and Methodius, bishop, missionary / optional memorial. • Today's scriptures are perfect for this first of the lenten Fridays, all of them days of abstinence. Our fast must be the kind of fast acceptable to the Lord! And Isaiah tells us what that means in no uncertain terms: We are to fast from our own self-centeredness to become more deeply attuned to the needs of others.

SAT 15 — Saturday after Ash Wednesday
#222 [223] (LMC, #176–184)   violet

Isaiah's call to conversion continues, again a call to shift the focus of our attention from self to others. The call of Levi parallels this, making the social nature of conversion clear. Levi invited all his friends — his fellow sinners, that is — to meet the Lord. Is there a missionary outreach to our lenten observance, or have we come to think of Lent as a time for personal spirituality only? How will renewing Christians in this community seek out alienated or apathetic neighbors who should be here. "If you really believe so much in Catholicism," the Mormon missionary asked, "why hasn't a Catholic ever come to my door to talk to me about it?" Hmm. Good question. Certainly parishes that have no catechumens or elect or candidates seeking full communion this year might want to reflect early in Lent why that might be, and what steps might be taken to make next Lent different.

16 — First Sunday of Lent
#23 (LMC, #19)   violet

As the ancient beginning of Lent, before the addition of Ash Wednesday and its weekdays, this Lord's Day features several special elements.

■ PENITENTIAL PROCESSION: Rome's 1988 *Circular Letter* on Lent, Triduum and Eastertime (#23) suggests the penitential procession (*Ceremonial of Bishops*, #261) in all communities today. An extensive description is on page 97; texts on page 118. See the notes on pages 196–98 of *The Sacristy Manual*.

■ RITE OF SENDING: See *The Sacristy Manual*, pages 199–200. Most dioceses celebrate the rite of election at the cathedral and perhaps at an additional location when the diocese covers a lot of territory. The parish rite then becomes the rite of sending the catechumens for election and candidates for the call to continuing conversion (see *Rite of Christian Initiation of Adults*, #111 for catechumens, both adults and children; #438 for baptized candidates; and #536 for catechumens and candidates together).

Testimony by godparents should express to the assembly what God has done in the lives of the elect. If not using the formulary given in the rite, godparents should avoid listing achievements and focus instead on God's action in the lives of the elect during their long initiation journey.

Appropriate music is in David Haas' *Who Calls You by Name*, volume 1 (GIA); musicians might also contact diocesan planners to see what is being used at the cathedral, so that using some of the same music can link parish and cathedral celebrations.

MON 17 — Lenten Weekday
#224 [225] (LMC, #176–184)   violet

Seven Founders of the Order of Servites, religious / optional memorial. • Because Lent is the period of final preparation for the elect, the arrangement of the lenten lectionary has always been of crucial importance. Enshrined within those scriptures, even in the pre–Vatican II Missal, were the lessons considered most important for assimilation by the elect before their initiation could take place. Reflecting this ancient catechetical dimension, the current lenten lectionary does not present "continuous" readings as during most of the liturgical year. Instead, there are daily "thematic couplets" — a first reading and gospel passage closely related

FEBRUARY

to each other. Moreover, the antiphons at the gospel canticles of Morning and Evening Prayer likewise quote the day's scriptures.

Today's Leviticus passage itemizes, in great detail, the demands of justice toward one's neighbor. This reading from Israel's Torah is linked to the last judgment gospel in Matthew, where Jesus teaches that the judgment we will receive hinges on our practical care for those in need.

TUE 18 — Lenten Weekday
#225 [226] (LMC, #176–184) violet

The beautiful passage from Isaiah pictures God's word descending as rain and flowering in an abundant harvest of holiness. The gospel defines further the fruit to be expected: the prayer formed in the heart of the Son and placed by him on the lips of his disciples in every age. But note the "lenten" postscript that Jesus adds: Without the link to mutual forgiveness, no prayer is acceptable and our own sins are retained.

WED 19 — Lenten Weekday
#226 [227] (LMC, #176–184) violet

Today Jonah figures in both scripture readings: in the first, as a prophet heeded; in the second, as a warning to us to heed a prophet even greater than Jonah. Though only the briefest portion of Jonah is prescribed, this is a good day to read the whole thing (it isn't very long). Early in Lent we do well to rejoice that God's love has found us, especially a God, Jonah tells us, whose love embraces the multitude "who do not know their right hand from their left — not to mention all the animals!" (Jonah 4:11). The arms stretched out on the wood of the cross have portrayed that love for us in an image as vivid as life and death.

THU 20 — Lenten Weekday
#227 [228] (LMC, #176–184) violet

Today is the only time the church reads from the moving book of Esther, the basis of the Jewish feast of Purim. The extermination of the Jewish people, plotted by the wicked Haman, is sadly not a mere memory but a horror made real in our own time. May we never forget! But Esther's radical trust in God's power to save is Israel's stronghold then and now. Today's gospel bids us, who are beset by spiritual foes, to pray with the same undaunted courage and persistence.

FRI 21 — Lenten Weekday
#228 [229] (LMC, #176–184) violet

Day of abstinence / Peter Damian, bishop, religious, doctor of the church / optional memorial. • On this day of lenten discipline, the scriptures remind us that personal conversion to God is inseparable from reconciliation with our brother and sister.

SAT 22 — The Chair of Peter, apostle
#535 (LMC, #263) white
FEAST

Peter's confession of faith is followed, in Matthew's gospel, by the Lord's prediction of the passion, words that Peter did not want to hear! This drew the famous rebuke, "Get behind me, Satan!" For Peter, as for every disciple, the following of Jesus is not a path free from pain. Celebrating this ancient feast of unity with the bishop of Rome gives us an opportunity to embrace the church's long history of light and darkness, of sanctity and sin, as our own history.

☉ 23 — Second Sunday of Lent
#26 (LMC, #22) violet

The transfiguration of the Lord is celebrated twice in the course of the liturgical year, once in summer as a feast of its own and once on a Sunday oriented toward the Easter mystery.

Taken together with the other readings, the transfiguration offers inspiration for the disciple's radical trust in God's promises. Abraham's obedience is born of that absolute trust and is rewarded in due time. The apostle Paul is confident that God, who has given us his own Son, will provide for our every other need and permit nothing to condemn or defeat us. The disciples who witness the transfiguration see in their suffering Master the strange fulfillment of the law and the prophets. Their questions will be answered in due time, and that answer will transform their own lives and deaths into a share in Christ's risen glory. The Preface for the Second Sunday of Lent echoes the gospel, reminding all who approach the saving waters that the way to resurrection leads through suffering and death. How does this speak to the elect who experience a radical death and birth this Easter? To all of us who are joined with the elect in dying to self that we may live in Christ? The invitation is frightening and glorious at one and the same time!

■ PENITENTIAL RITE FOR CANDIDATES: Today a special penitential rite may be celebrated for the candidates, similar to the scrutinies for the elect, which will take place on the next three Sundays. This rite (see RCIA, #459) is for

FEBRUARY

baptized but uncatechized Catholics and baptized people joining the Catholic Church from other Christian communities. For an important discussion on distinguishing between baptized candidates and the elect, see Ron Oakham's *One at the Table* (LTP, 1996).

MON 24 — Lenten Weekday
#230 [231] (LMC, #176–184) violet

The prophet Daniel's eloquent and lengthy prayer for forgiveness is a model act of contrition in its honesty and sincerity. The gospel, interestingly, is as brief as Daniel's prayer is long. Its message is clear: For those who renounce judgment of others, forego condemnation and forgive from the heart, pardon for their own sins is there for the asking!

TUE 25 — Lenten Weekday
#231 [232] (LMC, #176–184) violet

Hypocrisy is the first deadly sin for religiously observant people! Both readings castigate a pious observance devoid of practical consequences. Isaiah bids us come to the immediate and practical aid of the community's least powerful, if we would see our scarlet sins become white as snow! Jesus, too, points to the frequent link between ostentation in religious practice and thoughtless neglect of others' basic needs. Jesus implies that the humility of knowing how much we still need to learn can keep us open to serving those who can best reveal God's face to us.

WED 26 — Lenten Weekday
#232 [233] (LMC, #176–184) violet

Jeremiah, Jesus and every true prophet have faced a similar response from those to whom they preach: rejection and unjust suffering. There is a twofold challenge in today's readings. The waters of baptism lead us to the oil of prophetic anointing! Are we willing to share the prophets' fate as part of our baptism into Christ? And how do we respond to the prophetic voices in church and society that trouble our comfortable certainties?

THU 27 — Lenten Weekday
#233 [234] (LMC, #176–184) violet

Jesus' parable is addressed to religiously observant people "who loved money" and clearly trusted the security it promised. The parable is joined to the Jeremiah reading, about human instability and unreliability. Part of our lenten journey involves a serious assessment of priorities and principles. But we have to live in the real world, we are fond of saying, whenever the gospel challenges the presuppositions we've come to take for granted. But the "deviousness of the human heart" on which Jeremiah muses sounds pretty real.

FRI 28 — Lenten Weekday
#234 [235] (LMC, #176–184) violet

Day of abstinence. ▪ One of the Bible's greatest stories, and an age-old lenten epic, is told in the first reading and psalm today. It is a tale of human treachery, but more than that, it is a story of human sin transformed by God's providence into salvation for the very brothers who betrayed their own flesh and blood! So Christ's rejection and execution will become, in God's saving purpose, a harvest beyond anything the appointed tenants could have produced.

March

SAT 1 — Lenten Weekday
#235 [236] (LMC, #176–184) violet

Spendthrift is another word for *prodigal*. It is the father in the story who is prodigal, wasteful with his love. The younger son is just foolish! Micah sings of the God whose "passover" includes passing over our sins, who actually gets a kick out of showing mercy. It's all summarized in a wonderful new hymn by Thomas H. Troeger and Carol Doran that ought to be part of every parish's lenten repertoire (*Worship*, #597). The first few lines read: A spendthrift lover is the Lord/Who never counts the cost/Or asks if heaven can afford/To woo a world that's lost.

2 — Third Sunday of Lent
Year B #29 or Year A #28 (LMC, #25) violet

▪ MASS: Year A's scriptures may be used today. This decision determines the choice of other texts.

- Year A scriptures: Preface of the Third Sunday of Lent (P14)
- Year B scriptures: Preface for Lent I (P8) or II (P9)
- Celebration without scrutiny: all texts from Third Sunday of Lent.
- Celebration with scrutiny: opening prayer, prayer over the gifts, prayer after communion and insert for Eucharistic Prayer I from the ritual Masses in the back of the sacramentary.

See *The Sacristy Manual*, pages 201–2, for notes on today's liturgy.

▪ FIRST SCRUTINY: Paragraph numbers refer to the *Rite of Christian Initiation of Adults*:

MARCH

- *Invitation to Prayer (#152):* After the homily, elect and godparents gather before presider and the assembly. Position them to face the congregation, perhaps with presider in center aisle or position pairs of elect and sponsors throughout the assembly.

    Presider directs elect to bow their heads or kneel and pray. A noticeable period of silence is observed.

- *Intercessions for the elect (#153):* Godparents place their right hands on the shoulders of the elect during the intercessions.

    These are prayers for the elect, not the usual general intercessions. Many consider them to be too general and too weak as given. Some parishes adapt them to pray for the power of Christ to overcome what is sinful in the elect and in the community.

- *Exorcism (#154):* Presider, with hands joined, offers first prayer; he then lays both hands on the head of each of the elect in silence (in many parishes, catechists and godparents also lay on hands). The silence is to be unhurried and complete, not covered over by instrumental music or congregational singing. Presider, with hands outstretched over all the elect, offers second prayer (in some parishes, the whole assembly joins in this gesture).

The exorcism may conclude with an appropriate psalm (#154 has an extensive list) or song. Select one and sing it at each scrutiny. Since the scrutinies are meant to uncover and heal what is weak and sinful, a hymn that speaks of healing might be appropriate. Some suggestions:

- First scrutiny: "O Healing River," arranged by J. Michael Joncas (GIA, G-2594)
- Second scrutiny: "Amazing Grace" ("blind but now I see"); Marty Haugen's "Awake, O sleeper" (text echoes second reading, Year A)
- Third scrutiny: refrain of "I am the Bread of Life" (Susanne Toolan), repeated several times; "God is our fortress and our rock" (translation by Michael Perry in *Worship*); "Now the green blade rises"

■ DISMISSAL (#155): An optional text is provided if the elect are not dismissed, but this option is by way of concession. The dismissal should take place!

■ AFTER THE SCRUTINY (#156): Note that the position of the general intercessions and the Creed is reversed after the scrutiny. The introduction to the general intercessions might link them to the prior prayers for the elect. ("We now continue our ministry of intercession, praying for the needs of all.") Resist the rubric that permits omission of these elements "for pastoral necessity."

■ PRESENTATION OF THE CREED: The RCIA (#157) provides for the ancient *traditio,* or handing on, of two of the community's most precious treasures to the elect: the Creed this week and the Lord's Prayer during the fifth week. If this practice is to be observed, the announcement of it should be made, perhaps before the dismissal of the elect, and the community should be invited to it.

MON 3 — #237 [238] (LMC, #176–184) violet
Lenten Weekday

Blessed Katherine Drexel, virgin, religious founder / optional memorial. ■ The gift of salvation is given so simply, when you think about it. Neither the waters of the Jordan nor the waters of the parish font seem extraordinary enough to work miracles. Yet that is exactly what happened for the Syrian commander and what is about to happen for the community's elect. Meanwhile, those of us already baptized have Christ in our midst, in his word, in the eucharist, in the elect of the community. Can we hear what Christ is telling us about ourselves through these several "voices"?

Katherine Drexel died just as the civil rights struggle was about to emerge into long overdue legislation and erupt in long-repressed confrontation. Yet her life and ministry, dedicated to the needs of native and black Americans, did much to pave the way for human development and to set the stage for mutual enrichment. Could the leprosy of racism that still marks this land, long after legislation and confrontation, be attributable, at least in part, to our rejection of the prophetic Christ who still challenges our complacency?

TUE 4 — #238 [239] (LMC, #176–184) violet
Lenten Weekday

Casimir / optional memorial. ■ Whenever the first reading in Lent pleads for mercy, forgiveness, acceptance of our offering, notice that the gospel chosen always challenges us to forgiveness of others. Is the church trying to tell us something here? Poor Peter! He thinks he is being generous by doubling the threefold forgiveness, recommended by the rabbis of his day, and adding one extra pardon for good measure! Jesus multiplies Peter's proposal to infinity and makes the point crystal clear: We can stop forgiving others only when we want God to stop forgiving us!

Whatever did a late medieval court make of a peace-loving prince and his celibate lifestyle? Whatever they made of him, he clearly took no notice of them. The account of Casimir's life in the Office of Readings for his memorial makes it clear that he was too busy being "father, son

MARCH

and brother" to all who were in need. And isn't that the point of celibacy for the sake of the kingdom and of the lenten observance for all of us?

WED 5 Lenten Weekday
#239 [240] (LMC, #176–184)   violet

Liturgical historians remind us that today's Mass was once part of an ancient catechumenal scrutiny in which the elect were examined on the Ten Commandments. The First Testament reminds us that the commandments are the gift of a God who has chosen to come near his people. Jesus reminds his disciples that far from abolishing the law or the prophets, he has come to make them complete in spirit and in truth. How much of our Christianity is a matter of legal fulfillment only, and how much of it the loving gift of self in service to God and neighbor?

THU 6 Lenten Weekday
#240 [241] (LMC, #176–184)   violet

By some reckonings today is a midpoint of Lent, and ICEL's revised translation of the day's prayer gives a hint of the expectancy that awakens in the hearts of both the elect and the penitent:

God of majesty, we make this
   heartfelt prayer:
that the nearer we come to the
   great feast of our salvation,
the more fervently we may
   prepare ourselves
to celebrate the paschal mystery.

The responsorial psalm sounds the keynote of the readings: "If today you hear God's voice, harden not your hearts."

FRI 7 Lenten Weekday
#241 [242] (LMC, #176–184)   violet

Day of abstinence / Perpetua and Felicity, martyrs / optional memorial. ▪ The tender and personal love of God for each creature: This image was the prophet Hosea's gift to his people. How hard should it be to renounce dead idols and return to a God whose love is so alive and forever abiding? Jesus reminds the scribe that above and beyond all theological intricacies, love of God and love of neighbor says it all and surpasses every sacrifice.

Perpetua, a young woman with a newborn son, and Felicity, a pregnant slave, were arrested with their catechist and several other African catechumens. While in prison they were baptized and Felicity gave birth to a daughter. Thrown to wild beasts and then put to the sword, they died in the embrace of the sign of peace at Carthage about the year 203.

That was some catechumenate! The story is too wonderful to pass by on this lenten weekday in the midst of the scrutiny Sundays. Here is a living inspiration across two millennia to those about to be immersed in the waters of new life. How beautiful, too, that they should have died celebrating their own liturgy of sorts: embracing each other in the sign of peace, which, as newly baptized, it was now their privilege to share!

SAT 8 Lenten Weekday
#242 [243] (LMC, #176–184)   violet

John of God, religious founder / optional memorial. ▪ A love as flimsy as morning dew and prayer offered pridefully: How often we have offered just those gifts! How compellingly today's scriptures summon us to better things!

God's healing power was manifested, physically and spiritually, to the sick of John of God's age through his loving ministry and the family of brothers (the Order of Brothers Hospitallers of Saint John of God) he left behind. Today would be a good day to pray in the general intercessions for the sick of our community, especially for any health or hospice programs specially aided by the community's prayer and labor during the lenten season.

9 Fourth Sunday of Lent
Year B #32 or Year A #31
(LMC, #28)   violet or rose

Laetare, Jerusalem! The ancient entrance chant gives this Sunday both its title and its mood.

Rejoice, Jerusalem and all who
   love her;
mourners, rejoice and be consoled,
blissful as babies at the breast
   (see Isaiah 66:10–11).

Rose vestments, floral arrangements (the custom of bringing spring roses to church this day led to the vestment color) and instrumental music: These should mark Laetare Sunday in the parish's liturgical life, a harbinger of the paschal spring about to blossom forth (in the Northern Hemisphere). If an a capella chant ("Attende, Domine") has begun the liturgy so far this Lent, the glorious hymn "Lift high the cross" (CRUCIFER) makes a distinctive and fitting opening today. For instrumental and choral parts see settings by Carl Schalk (Concordia) and Richard Hillert (GIA). This anthem provides a foretaste of the Triduum, since it is a perfect entrance song for Holy Thursday and even Good Friday's veneration.

▪ MASS: See preparation notes in *The Sacristy Manual,* pages 201–2. Last week's decisions form the pattern for today.

- Year A scriptures: Preface of the Fourth Sunday of Lent (P15)
- Year B scriptures: Preface for Lent I (P8), especially appropriate for

MARCH

Laetare Sunday with its note of "joy" or Preface for Lent II (P9)
- Celebration without scrutiny: all texts from Fourth Sunday of Lent.
- Celebration with scrutiny: opening prayer, prayer over the gifts, prayer after communion and insert for Eucharistic Prayer I from the ritual Masses in the back of the sacramentary.

■ SECOND SCRUTINY: See the outline for last week's first scrutiny.

MON 10 — #244 [245] (LMC, #176–184) violet
Lenten Weekday

Scripturally speaking, the first "phase" of Lent is over. With today's liturgy the lectionary abandons its "couplet" approach. In the first weeks of Lent a daily First Testament and gospel reading joined to communicate a more-or-less unified lesson. Today, however, begins a semicontinuous proclamation of John's gospel, leading through Wednesday of Holy Week into the Johannine passion of Good Friday. These passages will necessarily involve treachery, pain, the passion. But this is a life-giving passion. So the first two days celebrate the gift of new life in the healing of the Gentile's child and of the paralyzed man by the pool of Bethsaida. Isaiah's prophecy celebrates the imminent creation of a new heaven and a new earth. The church's longing intensifies as we draw near to the sacraments of initiation!

TUE 11 — #245 [246] (LMC, #176–184) violet
Lenten Weekday

Ezekiel's vision provides the church with an age-old Eastertime chant that may still be used to accompany the sprinkling with water at Sunday eucharist: *Vidi aquam,* I saw water flowing forth from the temple. The new life in abundance that thrives where that water flows both heals and nourishes, as does the new life bestowed in baptismal immersion. The healing of the paralyzed man in Bethsaida's water was long ago taken as an image of the risen life given in baptism or restored in penance, and a number of ancient baptistry mosaics testify to this association.

WED 12 — #246 [247] (LMC, #176–184) violet
Lenten Weekday

Isaiah's reading is unmatched for the tenderness of the image it offers us of God's abiding love for each one of us. This sets the context for the judgment the Father has enabled the Son to pass on the world. A judgment of mercy and forgiveness is the judgment Jesus has come to pass, one that leads to a new passover from death to life.

THU 13 — #247 [248] (LMC, #176–184) violet
Lenten Weekday

The first reading presents Moses, Israel's great lawgiver and liberator and also the great priest who intercedes before an angry God to turn God's wrath from the people. Jesus invokes the witness of John and the authority of Moses as a joint witness on his own behalf. Ironically, the Moses who once mediated their deliverance, says Jesus, could now become their accuser. In light of the passion, however, Jesus will become, in a way, a new Moses: lawgiver, liberator, intercessor par excellence. The religiously observant must always beware: We who have knowledge of the message and who venerate the messenger are thus bound to heed his warnings and live the way of life he points out!

FRI 14 — #248 [249] (LMC, #176–184) violet
Lenten Weekday

Day of abstinence. ▪ Two weeks before Good Friday, both scriptures point to that day's passion. It is far too easy to apply the Wisdom reading to the leaders of another faith in another age! For each disciple in every age, Jesus must be "the reproof of our thoughts," the silent and living reproach to our established prejudices, our comfortable lifestyle, our cherished sins. More than that, his prophetic challenge can echo in the voices of those who, in our own day and age, challenge the established order and question the status quo. By whom are we believers challenged today? How do we deal with prophets in our midst? As George Bernard Shaw's Saint Joan asked at play's end, "When will your earth be ready to receive your saints?"

SAT 15 — #249 [250] (LMC, #176–184) violet
Lenten Weekday

Jeremiah's sorrowful reflections on rejection and betrayal by his own have long been applied, liturgically, to the experiences of Jesus. The gospel shows undeniably religious people trying to arrive at truth simply by interpreting the received scriptures. Nicodemus prescinds from that discussion to appeal, in vain, to reason and justice. Scripture can be used to justify almost anything! It is the Catholic approach to enlist revelation and reason, head and heart, in searching out the ways of God in the mysteries of life. Yet think of some of our failures in that regard! Saint Paulinus of Nola, reflecting on a friend's suffering at the hand of fellow believers, remarked: "Christ suffers his passion over and over again in everyone who

MARCH

has suffered, from the beginning of time until now."

☀ 16 Fifth Sunday of Lent
Year B #35 or Year A #34 (LMC, #31) violet

■ LENT'S PASSION PHASE: Although the miniseason of Passiontide was wisely suppressed in the calendar reform of 1969, there is a subtle change in the liturgy's mood as Holy Week draws near. The passion of the Lord comes into clearer focus. This is still the season of baptismal preparation and penitential discipline, but both appear more clearly in scriptures and prayer, for two weeks ahead, as a participation in the paschal mystery of Christ, a mystery that includes sacrificial death, a redemption whose price is the blood of Christ. The official entrance chant of the sacramentary gives the signal: Psalm 42, *Judica Me:* Give me justice, O God! Defend my cause against the wicked! Rescue me! Last week's "Lift high the cross" is thus again an excellent gathering song. More passion-oriented hymns might also make an appearance today.

■ MASS: See the preparation notes in *The Sacristy Manual,* pages 201–2. The liturgical pattern of the last two Sundays continues today.

- Year A scriptures: use Preface of the Fifth Sunday of Lent (P15)
- Year B scriptures: use Preface for Lent I (P8) or Preface for Lent II (P9)
- Celebration without scrutiny: all texts from Fifth Sunday of Lent.
- Celebration with scrutiny: opening prayer, prayer over the gifts, prayer after communion and insert for Eucharistic Prayer I from the ritual Masses in the back of the sacramentary.

■ THIRD SCRUTINY: The order is that of the previous two scrutiny celebrations.

■ PRESENTATION OF THE LORD'S PRAYER: The RCIA (#178) has a rite for the *traditio,* handing on, of the Lord's Prayer during this week. If this rite is to be celebrated, an announcement should be made before the dismissal of the elect, and the community should be invited to participate.

■ HOLY WEEK PREPARATIONS: Today's bulletin and bulletin board, an early-in-the-week parish mailing, media announcements and other means of communication need to alert the community, and those beyond it, about the upcoming paschal celebrations. Without being too commercial, the information needs to invite and inspire. See LTP's prepared bulletin insert, *Three Days to Save,* as a possibility.

MON 17 Lenten Weekday
#251 [252] (LMC, #176–184) violet

Saint Patrick, bishop, missionary / optional memorial. ▪ The story of Susanna is beautiful and moving, too good to be omitted, too interesting to be presented in its "abbreviated" version. The liturgy does well to pair it with Christ's encounter with the adulterous woman.

Saint Patrick's Day is celebrated easily in relationship to Lent, especially with regard to Christian initiation. Some legends claim that one of his first liturgical actions was to kindle (and "christen") the Celtic May Day bonfire as part of the service of light for the Easter Vigil. The shamrock was a helpful "visual" aid for teaching the catechumens preparing to be baptized at Easter in the name of the Trinity. Patrick's chasing the snakes out of Ireland was a dramatic form of exorcism! Green became the ritual color associated with penitents returning to the church at Easter, as white is associated with the newly baptized. And Patrick's *Confessions* makes good lenten reading (a portion is in the Office of Readings for his memorial).

TUE 18 Lenten Weekday
#252 [253] (LMC, #176–184) violet

Saint Cyril of Jerusalem, bishop, doctor of the church / optional memorial. ▪ The serpent in the desert and the Son of Man on the cross: The First Testament scriptures present the image of healing, John's gospel the image of glory, and both are accomplished through a lifting up. As our celebration of the passion draws near, we should keep in mind the Johannine perspective, which never loses sight of the glory.

■ SAINT FOR THE ELECT: Be sure to go to Cyril's writing in the Office of Readings, if not for the actual homily of today's liturgy, then for spiritual reading. Ambrose, John Chrysostom, Augustine and Cyril have so much to teach the elect and us, the penitent faithful, journeying with them to the font.

MARCH

WED 19 #543 (LMC, #272) white
Joseph, husband of the Virgin Mary
SOLEMNITY

A carpenter, though born of the royal house of David, Joseph was an upright man who, as husband of the Virgin Mary and head of the holy family, cared for Mary and the child Jesus. He was venerated in the East after the fourth century, and his cult flowered in the West during the fifteenth, following the development of medieval nativity plays, the Christmas crib and increasing devotion to Mary (© ICEL).

▪ LITURGY: Joseph is patron of the universal church, of fathers and of a happy death. The insertion of his name into the Canon of the Mass (Eucharistic Prayer I) by Pope John XXIII marked the first formal alteration of that text in centuries.

- Lenten elements: the sung acclamations, most of the decor, a passion chant or hymn
- Festal elements: white vesture (perhaps the Christmas set), floral arrangements, instrumental music, the Gloria and suitable decoration or lighting for Joseph's window, statue or shrine. Good hymns in honor of Joseph are few and far between. "By all your saints still striving" (*Worship*, #706) has a verse in his honor, and G.W. Williams's "Come now, and praise the humble saint" is matched to the well-known and singable American tune, LAND OF REST. The *Collegeville Hymnal* also has selections for this solemnity.

▪ SAINT JOSEPH'S TABLE: This Italian tradition began as a meal to which all, especially the poor, were welcomed without cost. It was given often as a thanks-offering to Saint Joseph "for a favor received." This is a perfect lenten custom, since it combines in one event the three lenten disciplines of prayer, fasting and almsgiving. Prayer and song, both for Joseph and Lent, are customary. The table features meatless dishes, and a collection is taken for the poor. See *Book of Blessings,* "Order for the Blessing of St. Joseph's Table" (chapter 53) and *Catholic Household Blessings and Prayers* for domestic prayer (page 165) and Saint Joseph's litany (page 346).

THU 20 #254 [255] (LMC, #176–184) violet
Lenten Weekday

As he has already invoked the memory of Moses, now Jesus goes to Israel's "father in faith," patriarch Abraham to bear witness to his authority. The first reading portrays God's initiative in making covenant with Abraham. That covenant would be lived out in testing and trial before it could issue in glory. So the renewal of that covenant that Jesus is about to inaugurate will involve the passion and cross before the glory of resurrection.

FRI 21 #255 [256] (LMC, #176–184) violet
Lenten Weekday

Day of abstinence. ▪ A week before Good Friday, Jeremiah appears again as the image of the prophet forsaken by mortals but accompanied by God, in whose abiding care the prophet both trusts and exults. The gospel's ending is particularly poignant: Jesus returns to where it all began, to the Jordan where John had been baptizing, where Jesus had been anointed with the Spirit for the mission he is now about to accomplish.

SAT 22 #256 [257] (LMC, #176–184) violet
Lenten Weekday

Before beginning Holy Week, the lectionary provides us with an exultant prophecy of Ezekiel: The nation is gathered from dispersion, established as a covenant people on a land restored, sin cleansed and age-old wounds healed. Jesus is at Bethany, scene of the raising of Lazarus, which prefigures his own resurrection. And a new prophecy is pronounced by an unlikely spokesman: Jesus will die and gather into a covenanted people not only his nation but the dispersed of every land.

☉ 23 #37–38 (LMC, #34) red
Palm Sunday of the Lord's Passion

▪ HOLY WEEK: This unique name, which our ancestors used for this one week of all the year, should cause us to enter it with reverence, embrace its considerable demands with delight, and celebrate its multiple rites with all the care, devotion and energy they deserve. To celebrate Holy Week is, after all, to celebrate who we have become through Christ's paschal mystery. It should go without saying that those who serve the community's prayer must now lay

aside all other cares. All parish activities should cease, all regular business be suspended and the community's best efforts and fullest attention be focused entirely on all the details that constitute these "days of salvation."

THE COMMEMORATION OF THE LORD'S ENTRANCE INTO JERUSALEM

The commemoration of the Lord's entrance takes place at every Mass. In practice there is at least a modified procession (presider, ministers, at least some of the faithful) from the door of the church, where the palms are blessed, to the sanctuary. At the principal Mass, however, a solemn blessing in a separate place should end in a great procession to the church. Rubrics, in fact, restrict this procession to the principal Mass not to restrict the parishioners' experience of the rite but to call for one grand liturgy for all parish members — just as during the Triduum (for preparation notes for Palm Sunday, see *The Sacristy Manual*, pages 203–4).

- GATHERING: Quotes without reference are from the sacramentary; others from the *Ceremonial of Bishops* (CB).
  - Assembly gathers in a place "distinct from the church to which the procession will move."
  - Branches of sufficient size are distributed in generous quantity. They are already in the hands of the assembly before the presider and other ministers arrive.
  - Red vesture: presider in cope or chasuble; deacon in dalmatic
  - Song: "Hosanna to the Son of David" is the traditional antiphon (mode VII, adapted by Richard Proulx, *Worship*. See also Proulx's choral setting titled "Fanfare for Palm Sunday," GIA, G-2829).

- BLESSING OF THE BRANCHES:
  - Sign of the cross (CB, #266)
  - Greeting: Use that chosen for the other lenten Sundays.
  - Introduction: The sacramentary text is concise and coherent. It may be given by the deacon or by a concelebrant (CB, #266).
  - Blessing: Presider offers prayer of blessing (sacramentary says "with hands joined"; ICEL's revision: "with hands outstretched").
  - Sprinkling: Presider silently sprinkles branches held by the people.
  - Presider and other ministers who have not carried branches from the beginning take them from table or pedestal. Incense is placed in the censer. The deacon who is to proclaim the gospel is blessed.
  - Gospel: Deacon, concelebrant or presider proclaims the gospel of the entry into Jerusalem.
  - "A brief homily may be given."

- PROCESSION:
  - Invitation to the procession: Deacon (or presider) invites assembly to join in the procession.
  - Order of the procession:
    - thurifer
    - cross bearer (with cross "suitably adorned") flanked by two candle bearers
    - deacon with book of gospels
    - lectors
    - concelebrants
    - presider and assistants
    - choir
    - assembly

  The procession can move directly toward the church or take a longer route around the parish property. Be sure that thurifer and cross bearer walk slowly enough to keep the procession together.

  The route may require the cooperation of the police or the obtaining of a permit. Some cities require permission for the use of audio systems outdoors (even on private property). Walk the processional route beforehand, looking for trouble spots as you go: Will banners and cross fit through tight places? Will the head of the procession (cross and its decorations) be clearly visible? Are there places where part of the procession can bog down, where people can trip easily, become confused or take shortcuts?

- PROCESSIONAL MUSIC: "All glory, laud and honor" was specially written for this procession by Bishop Theodulph of Orleans around the year 800 (and translated beautifully by John Mason Neale).

LITURGY OF THE WORD

- THE SCRIPTURES: The following notes are from ICEL's Pastoral Introduction: Palm Sunday, #2:

  Introduced by brief texts from the prophet Isaiah and Paul's letter to the Philippians, the reading of the passion is at the heart of the liturgy on this first day of Holy Week. Because of the importance of these texts of scripture for the spiritual good of the faithful, the passion should be read in its entirety and the readings which precede it should not be omitted unless there is some overriding pastoral reason that compels it. A brief homily helps to unfold their riches.

  The proclamation of the passion needs to be carefully prepared. Traditionally it is read by three persons taking the parts of Christ, the narrator and others. Conferences of bishops may wish to indicate other forms for the proclamation of the passion. It may be helpful, for example, to divide the narrative into sections, with different readers and some variation in the posture of the assembly for each part. The sections may be separated with periods of silent reflection and acclamations which all can sing. While it has a dramatic quality, the passion is not so much enacted as proclaimed solemnly and simply, without candles, incense, greeting or signs of the cross.

- PSALM 22 is available in a variety of settings:
  - C. Alexander Peloquin, *Songs of Israel* (GIA, G-1666)
  - Christopher Willcock, *Psalms for Feasts and Seasons* (Liturgical Press)
  - Marty Haugen in *Gather*
  - David Isele, *Psalms for the Church Year* (GIA, G-2262)
  - Christopher Walker in *Out of Darkness* (OCP)

- GOSPEL ACCLAMATION: Whatever the acclamation is, make sure that the traditional verse (Christ became obedient for us) is sung in full, perhaps by a cantor using a simple chant formula, the *tonus peregrinus* or tone IV are especially appropriate.

- THE PASSION: Consider singing some of the passion-oriented chants the congregation already knows during the proclamation of the passion. Especially suitable would be "O sacred head surrounded," "My song is love unknown" and "What wondrous love is this."

After the verse about the death of the Lord, all kneel for a time of complete silence (CB, #273).

At the end of the passion the gospel book is not kissed.

- BRIEF HOMILY: That the homily should be brief, because the passion says so much, is understandable. That the homily should simply be omitted here is unconscionable, in light of the sacred days about to unfold. Gabe Huck has a fine model of such a homily in *The Three Days* (LTP, 1992 [revised edition], appendix: part three) and Raymond Brown provides a moving insight into Mark's gospel and into the diversity among the passion narratives in *A Crucified Christ in Holy Week* (Liturgical Press, 1986). Whenever anti-Semitism is a danger in the hearing of Holy Week's texts, consult the Bishops' Committee on the Liturgy's *God's Mercy Endures Forever*, #21–25.

- DISMISSAL OF CATECHUMENS AND ELECT: Continue to use one of the lenten dismissal formulas.

- PROFESSION OF FAITH AND GENERAL INTERCESSIONS: These follow in the usual lenten way. In the sacramentary's appendix, the intercessions for Monday, Tuesday and Wednesday of Holy Week are suitable also for today.

LITURGY OF THE EUCHARIST AND CONCLUDING RITES

- EUCHARISTIC PRAYER: Special texts for today:
  - Preface for Passion (Palm) Sunday (P19)
  - Eucharistic Prayer for Reconciliation I is especially appropriate for today.

- CONCLUDING RITE:
  - The solemn blessing "Passion of the Lord" is appropriate.
  - Some parishes end the celebration on a great note of triumph with a rousing recessional hymn as people bear their palms homeward. Other communities chant the blessing and dismissal but then have the ministers leave quietly to the "Vexilla Regis" chant, a melody at once triumphant yet reflective.

TAKING IT HOME

- DOMESTIC RITUAL AND PRAYER: *Catholic Household Blessings and Prayers* provides prayers for Placing of Branches in the Home on Palm Sunday (page 140) and Prayers of the Triduum (page 143). This would be an excellent time to make this important book available for purchase. It is a treasury of domestic prayer and family customs and a good reminder about the importance of observing our special days outside the church building, too.

- DAYLIGHT SAVING TIME: In those parts of the country that switch to Daylight Saving Time, next Saturday night is the time for everyone's clock to "spring up" an hour—after the Vigil, of course.

MON 24 — Monday of Holy Week
#257 [258] (LMC, #176–184)
violet

The first of the "Suffering Servant" songs shows the servant who does not break the bruised reed or extinguish the flickering flame, just as Jesus graciously receives the anointing of Mary and gently deflects Judas' criticism.

Special intercessions are in the appendix to the sacramentary. The Preface of the Passion II (P18) is specifically appropriate to these days. And the Prayer over the People will surely be the traditional Holy Week text (#17).

On this day in 1980, Archbishop Oscar Romero of San Salvador was martyred as he presided at the eucharistic liturgy, repeating a sacrilege that is part of our history: for example, Stanislaus of Cracow, Thomas Becket of Canterbury. They were both canonized almost immediately! Though strangely Romero has not been so honored by the official church, his icon is venerated throughout the Americas. Pray for justice and peace in El Salvador and throughout the earth.

MARCH

TUE 25 — Tuesday of Holy Week
#258 [259] (LMC, #176–184)
violet

The ingathering of the dispersed children of God is the servant's mission and canticle. The canticles of praise that accompany a sacred meal among friends are interrupted by the discordant notes of betrayal. And it is night. See the Office of Readings for Basil's beautiful meditation on our baptism into Christ's death and resurrection.

WED 26 — Wednesday of Holy Week
#259 [260] (LMC, #176–184)
violet

Face set like flint . . . the price of betrayal fixed and delivered. It is almost the Triduum. Until recently, today was called "Spy Wednesday" and known to Christians as early as 250 by the title "day of betrayal." The new lectionary continues the custom.

THU 27 — Holy Thursday
white for the Chrism Mass
(#260) [39]

■ NO MORNING MASS: Only with the explicit permission of the diocesan bishop, for the most grave pastoral necessity, may a Mass other than the Evening Mass of the Lord's Supper be offered. That concession given, however, the sacramentary and lectionary provide no texts. The texts surely cannot be those of Thursday evening, for there is a specific prohibition about anticipating the Triduum. Nor are funeral Masses permitted. The message is clear: Everyone, including mourners, commuters, senior citizens, school children—the whole assembly—is to be present this evening for the solemn inauguration of the Christian Passover.

■ NO COMMUNION CALLS: While communion may be brought to the sick at any hour of the day if necessary, the 1988 *Circular Letter* of the Congregation for Divine Worship is quite correct in suggesting that communion be borne to such persons directly after the celebration of the Lord's Supper.

■ MORNING PRAYER: At the same time of the morning that the daily lenten Mass has been held, why not celebrate Morning Prayer, perhaps with augmented readings: the Letter to the Hebrews on the high priesthood of Jesus and the beautiful Easter homily of Melito of Sardis, both in the *Liturgy of the Hours*.

■ SCHOOL PRAYER: Because Catholic schools are often still in session today, various prayer customs have developed for the students. Mass is out of the question, but a prayer service that is an extended prelude or "call to worship" for the Triduum would be fitting. Students should be expected and encouraged to attend the Triduum liturgies. These liturgies will help form them in the Catholic way of life, and most young people respond instinctively and movingly to the mystical beauty of these sacred rites. See an outline of ideas for prayer today in the *Leader's Manual of the Hymnal for Catholic Students* (page 90).

■ CHRISM MASS: This celebration should draw representatives from every area, even every parish of the diocese. The *Sacramentary Supplement* (1994) considers it appropriate that the oils be formally received by the parish at the Evening Mass of the Lord's Supper, especially since these will be used at the Easter Vigil's celebration of initiation.

TEXTS FOR THE EUCHARISTIC ASSEMBLY

INTRODUCTORY RITES

Greeting

The grace and love of Jesus Christ, who calls us to conversion, be with you all.

The bishops of the United States have recently approved a simplification of the introductory rites (awaiting Roman confirmation). The numbers and arrangements below reflect that simplification.

I. Blessing and Sprinkling with Holy Water

(This form is more appropriate during Eastertime)

II. Penitential Rite

INVITATION TO THE PENITENTIAL RITE
Weeks 1 to 4:
As we begin this eucharist, let us heed the lenten call to conversion of heart and, by acknowledging our sins, seek reconciliation and communion with God and our neighbor.

Week 5 and Weekdays of Holy Week:
Acknowledging that we are all sinners cleansed by the blood of Christ, let us pardon one another from the depths of our hearts and ask forgiveness from God who is merciful and just.

CONFESSION OF SIN
The Confiteor (I confess) with absolution.

III. Litany of Praise

INVITATION
Rich in mercy is our Savior
and great in kindness.
Praise the Lord Jesus Christ.

INVOCATIONS TO CHRIST
A. Focusing on Initiation
By water and the Holy Spirit, you give us
    a new birth in your image:
Lord, have mercy.

You send your Spirit to create a new heart
    within us:
Christ, have mercy.

You call us to your supper to partake
    of your body and blood:
Lord, have mercy.

B. Focusing on Reconciliation
You command us to forgive each other
    before we come to your altar:
Lord, have mercy.

You asked your Father to forgive sinners
    as you hung upon the cross:
Christ, have mercy.

You have entrusted your church with the
    ministry of reconciliation:
Lord, have mercy.

"Let us pray" and the opening prayer follow.

IV. Kyrie

LITURGY OF THE WORD

Dismissal of the Catechumens and the Elect

My dear friends: With the assurance of our loving support this community sends you forth to reflect more deeply upon the word of God we have shared. May Christ who is the power and wisdom of God challenge you to be one with us in the disciplines of prayer, fasting and almsgiving, that you may be one with us at last in the paschal feast of the Lord's table.

General Intercessions

INVITATION TO PRAYER
In this, the acceptable time, the lenten spring, the Lord invites us to be renewed in mind, purified in spirit and more responsive to the needs of others. Let us ask God to accompany us on our journey to conversion and to draw all the human family to the waters of life and the paschal feast.

LITURGY OF THE EUCHARIST

Invitation to the Sign of Peace

If the sign of peace takes place before the presentation of the gifts:

Mindful of the Lord's admonition not to bring
    our gifts to the altar unless we are at
    peace with our brothers and sisters,
let us offer each other now a sign of
    reconciliation and of the Lord's peace.
—*Messale Ambrosiano*

LENT: TEXTS FOR THE EUCHARISTIC ASSEMBLY **117**

Invitation to Communion

Behold the Lamb of God, who takes away
　　the sins of the world:
our Passover sacrificed for us, our peace and
　　reconciliation.
Happy are those who are called to his supper.
(*or:* Blessed are those called to the banquet
　　of the Lamb.)

CONCLUDING RITE

Dismissal of Eucharistic Ministers

Go forth in peace to the sick and homebound members of our community, bearing the word of life and the body of Christ, together with the assurance of our love and concern. May these gifts strengthen our absent brothers and sisters in their communion with us through the pilgrimage of Lent to the paschal feast of the kingdom.

Dismissal

As a people called to conversion on a journey
　　to new life,
go in peace to love and serve the Lord.

A PENITENTIAL PROCESSION FOR THE FIRST SUNDAY OF LENT

The *Circular Letter Concerning the Preparation and Celebration of the Easter Feasts* suggests that an appropriate way to mark the First Sunday of Lent with penitential solemnity would be to begin the liturgy with a procession during which the litany of the saints is chanted. Reference is made to #261 of the *Ceremonial of Bishops,* which describes how the procession is held.

- The community assembles in a place apart from the place where Mass will be celebrated.
- While a gathering song is sung, the presider and ministers go to that place.
- The presider (who may be vested in a cope) greets the assembly with the sign of the cross and then the seasonal liturgical greeting.
- The presider or a deacon or other minister offers a brief introduction, for example:

　　We have come to the beginning of our lenten spring, the season to prepare the holy Passover that will bring our catechumens to the saving waters of rebirth, the Passover that will be, for those of us already initiated, a pilgrimage of conversion.

　　Lent is a journey with the Lord who longs to draw us more closely to himself that he might speak to our hearts. Along the way we will be challenged to recognize Christ in the scriptures we read, in those we love and serve, and in those whom we so often neglect to love and serve—for surely Christ is most specially present in them.

　　Therefore, let us begin the journey!

　　Our procession is in the spirit of the pilgrimage of the Israelites, our forebears in faith. We call upon the saints, our holy ancestors, who remind us that we do not journey alone.

　　Let us move forward in joy, keeping our eyes fixed on Jesus and the goal of our lenten journey, Jerusalem, the holy city of God.

- The presider offers a collect.

Suggestion: opening prayer for Feast of the Triumph of the Cross, September 14, with modifications.

or:

　　Almighty God, whose most dear Son went
　　　　not up to joy
　　but first he suffered pain,
　　and entered not into glory before he was
　　　　crucified:
　　Mercifully grant that we, walking in the
　　　　way of the cross,
　　may find it none other than the way of life
　　　　and peace;
　　through Jesus Christ our Lord.
　　　—*Book of Common Prayer 1979*

NOTES

NOTES

TRIDUUM

The Season
Perspective on the Triduum / 123
Presentation of the Season / 124
Preparing the Parish / 126
Taking It Home / 126
Other Ritual Prayers and Sacraments / 127
The Calendar
March 27 – March 30 / 128
ICEL PASTORAL INTRODUCTIONS
Holy Thursday / 128
Good Friday / 132
Holy Saturday / 137
Easter Vigil / 138
Liturgical Texts
The Reception of the Holy Oils / 149
Hymns for the Liturgy of the Hours / 149

Perspective on the Triduum

The Easter Triduum of the passion and resurrection of Christ is the culmination of the entire liturgical year. In this festival, Christ's saving work is commemorated by the church with the utmost solemnity. Through the liturgy of the Triduum, the church is intimately united with Christ and shares in his passage from death to life (Pastoral Introduction: Easter Triduum, 1).

A friend, who is a professional sociologist, calls them "uh-oh's": the signals that indicate, often early into an event, that perhaps the entire enterprise is about to go wrong. While not an official sociological construct that has been accepted in the professional literature, "uh-oh's," claims this friend, are found in every occupation, across every dimension of society.

For instance, airline personnel can frequently sense indications, quite apart from mechanical problems, that a flight is getting off to a bad start. Business people sometimes know early in a conference or presentation that things aren't "clicking," participants just aren't pleased. Politicians say they can often intuit, in the opening phases of a campaign, that their fortunes are just not going to "pan out." Coaches can sometimes tell, right at the beginning of the big game, that Lady Luck is not going to smile on their side of the field. A friend's son says he can tell, 30 seconds into a date, whether the evening is going to be "awesome" or "bogus." And what homilist doesn't know — in about the same amount of time — whether the assembly is with the message or heading, mentally at least, back to the parking lot! For each of us there are "uh-oh's" that send a clear signal: Something is wrong.

What are some Triduum "uh-oh's"? "Lord, who at that first eucharist" as the gathering song on Holy Thursday evening is an "uh-oh," a sure sign that this opening movement of the Triduum has been disconnected from the whole and turned into a celebration focused only on the eucharist's institution. Other "uh-oh's" on Holy Thursday are bowls for a "hand washing" (Pilate's action!) to replace the footwashing mandated by Jesus, parish "seders" and Mass turned into reenactments of the Last Supper. The sound effects of a distant hammer, coldly pounding against a nail, while a mournful choir sings "Were you there?" on Good Friday is another "uh-oh," indicating that this celebration of the Lord's triumphant witness is being approached as a kind of "passion play" or funeral service for Jesus. A church filled all day Holy Saturday with people loudly and busily decorating for Easter is another "uh-oh," the quiet watch-keeping, the church's official mood for the day, simply by-passed for the feverish activity of getting things ready for the Vigil. The same church locked up by noon on Easter is an "uh-oh" signaling that paschal Vespers may not be held.

Of course, what these "uh-oh's" never indicate is bad will or an intentional decision not to do the right thing. Often, they signal just the opposite: a sincere desire to make the Triduum special, an attempt to be creative with what can seem to be a disconnected series of complex ceremonies. But enough "uh-oh's" piling up around the Triduum liturgies, even if the result of good intentions, can empty the community's paschal mystery of much of its power by turning living sacrament into dead history, ritual celebration into dramatic reenactment, and Christ's saving presence among us here and now into an attempt to kindle feelings and create an emotional rush.

The best cure for the "uh-oh's" is a therapy in three parts: 1) get a sense of the ways in which the Triduum has developed and been approached over the centuries; 2) reflect on the selected paragraphs from ICEL's Pastoral Introduction: Easter Triduum presented here; 3) work through *Sourcebook*'s presentation of the Triduum in its fullness, giving first priority to the principal celebrations. The new Pastoral Introduction to each of the Triduum's central liturgies is reproduced in the proper place in the calendar section. Always be ready, of course, for new "uh-oh's" to show up each year! But at least these will just be signals that various elements may need some fine tuning, not indications that the orientation of the whole enterprise has somehow gone astray!

Presentation of the Season

Since the Easter Triduum is the high point of the whole liturgical year, the liturgy of these days demands careful, thoughtful preparation and sensitive celebration. The liturgical symbols and gestures need to be well made and done if they are to bear the weight of the profound mysteries they express (Pastoral Introduction: Easter Triduum, 3).

To this end, the Pastoral Introduction (#4–7) highlights several requirements:

1. Sufficient numbers of well-prepared ministers: Besides presiders and deacons, the assembly will need lectors who can translate skillfully the awe-inspiring words of these days from page to sound; cantors who can exalt the chant of the psalms and draw the assembly into the church's song; choirs and servers and sacristans, too!

2. Good eucharistic practices: What *should* be normative all year *must* be normative at this time of the year: eucharist consecrated at and for each celebration (except Good Friday, of course); bread that can be broken; the cup offered to all.

3. Good music: In contrast to the antiphons that the Roman rite relies on most of the year, specific hymns are prescribed at various points in the Triduum liturgies.

4. Unity in celebration: One church, one celebration is the norm throughout the Triduum. Religious and lay communities "should take part in the common worship of their local parish church." Small parishes might well consider teaming up with larger ones. Where multiple celebrations of a particular liturgy are contemplated, convenience must never be the norm "nor should the quality of celebration suffer on this account."

DECORATING FOR THE TRIDUUM

■ OVERVIEW: Early in Lent the planning team will have met to draw up a chart of priorities, necessities and a "wish" list. Some items that need early and detailed planning:

- Vesture: What will be needed for presiders, ministers, the elect?

- Flowers: How much is to be spent, how many will be needed, how soon to be delivered?

- Lights and sound: All burned out bulbs should be replaced, spot and track lighting aligned if necessary, any "bugs" in the sound system taken care of, if not in advance of the long lenten Sunday gospels, certainly before Palm Sunday.

- Grounds and church: Before Palm Sunday all places of gathering and processional routes should be thoroughly cleaned and spruced up.

Beyond the preliminary notes offered here, essential information for the decorating/sacristy teams is found in *To Crown the Year* (pages 74–119) and *The Sacristy Manual* (pages 207–19).

■ VESSELS AND OTHER OBJECTS: Special materials to get ready:

Holy Thursday

- Processional materials: cross, banners, incense, candles

- Altar materials: cloths, purificators, corporals, festive garments

- Communion vessels: distribution, procession, reservation

- Oil vessels: containers, ambry
- Footwashing items: pitchers, bowls, towels

Good Friday

- Cross for veneration, incense vessels

Easter Vigil

- Fire and light: paschal candle, assembly candles, material for the fire, baptismal candles
- Initiation materials: baptismal needs, chrism vessels, towels, robes

■ VESTURE

- Holy Thursday: simple white Mass vestments; humeral veil(s)
- Good Friday: red (non-Pentecost) as on Palm Sunday
- Holy Saturday: violet for the Liturgy of the Hours and preparatory rites for initiation
- Easter Vigil and onward: the finest paschal vesture used only during the Fifty Days
- Albs for singer of Exsultet, neophytes, lectors and cantors (for greater solemnity).

■ LITURGICAL BOOKS:

- Usual books: sacramentary (special presider's book may be desired), lectionary, book of gospels
- Book (or scroll) of the Exsultet
- Ritual books assembled for Liturgy of the Hours

It will be necessary to coordinate cues for lighting, movement and song with musicians, ministers and servers.

■ SPECIAL TIMES

Thursday evening (before Mass)

- Tabernacle entirely empty. Veil removed. Vigil light removed. Doors left open.
- Church stripped and cleaned. Only materials needed for the eucharistic celebration are present.

Thursday evening

- When elect and catechumens are dismissed, they go to the catechumeneon, a space apart suitably appointed and conducive to gathering and prayer.
- Chapel suitably (i.e., moderately, tastefully) decorated for reservation, conducive to prayer and meditation (*Circular Letter,* #49), not a side altar or the usual tabernacle (*Bishops' Committee on the Liturgy,* March 1993)

Thursday evening (after Mass)

- "Stripping" of altar and church carried out in an orderly and reverent way
- Furniture not part of the building itself removed: credence table, kneelers, chairs, etc.
- Oriental or festive carpeting rolled up and removed
- Crosses removed from church or veiled
- Holy water removed from fonts

Thursday midnight (after Night Prayer)

- All candles extinguished, except one near the tabernacle in chapel of reservation
- All other decorations taken from eucharistic chapel before first hour of prayer on Friday

Friday (before the Celebration of the Passion)

- Only furniture needed for the rite is set out
- Candles ready near cross for solemn entrance
- Altar cloth kept to side for later use
- All else bare

Friday (after communion rite)

- Remaining eucharist brought to separate, private place to be kept for viaticum (not eucharistic chapel; reservation is not provided for visitation or private prayer)

Friday (after the celebration)

- Altar and sanctuary again completely stripped, except perhaps for the cross
- Cross carried in during the celebration is placed with lighted candles in a place conducive to quiet prayer and veneration. The *Circular Letter* (#71) suggests the now-empty eucharistic chapel. If the cross is a stationary one (for example, suspended over the sanctuary), candles (and perhaps a spotlight) might grace it.

Saturday in general

- Church is bare for Liturgy of the Hours, preparatory rites, any other assembly
- Cross, enshrined, remains in its place of honor
- Church should be decorated for the Vigil as late as possible (see Mazar, page 127)

Saturday morning

Circular Letter (#74) suggests an image or two be introduced into the space for the whole day:

- Image of Christ crucified or lying in the tomb (see catalog from Holy Protection Monastery, Geneva NE 68361. 800-729-4952 for veneration cloth of the Byzantine rite and icons the *Letter* suggests)
- Icon of the descent into (or "harrowing of") hell, which mystery Holy Saturday recalls in the Office of Readings
- Image of the sorrowful Virgin Mary

Saturday night (Vigil)

Rubrics in the *Ceremonial of Bishops* (#48) ban the use of flowers from "Ash Wednesday until the Gloria at the Easter Vigil."

- Immersion font is called for. A temporary font large enough for an adult to kneel in while water is poured over the head (a graceful position for baptism) is devised easily. See the article "Testing the Waters," *Environment & Art Letter* (LTP, April 1992).

Preparing the Parish

THE Easter Triduum and the rest of the liturgical year have an effect on each other. On one hand, a powerfully beautiful experience of celebrating—not watching or "attending"—the Three Days often draws the marginally active worshiper back to recapture something of the grace of those moments. On the other hand, a parish whose Sunday liturgies feature well-prepared ministers, a strong tradition of sung liturgy, good communion practice, thoughtful presiding and sensitive preaching, is likely to find that all these efforts blossom—and all that prayer comes to fruition—in a reverent and moving celebration of the Triduum. It is unlikely that a parish careless about its Sunday liturgy, or negligent of its ministries year round, will have the commitment and energy to celebrate a very prayerful Triduum. Nor is it likely that a poor experience of the Triduum is the result of a sudden breakdown of worship that generally goes right week by week!

■ PARISH STAFF AND MINISTRIES: There is no substitute for prayerful and serious study together. It is hoped that this *Sourcebook* provides some materials for such a concerted, common endeavor. Other materials that will be helpful: Gabe Huck, *The Three Days* (LTP; revised edition, 1992); Kenneth Stevenson, *Jerusalem Revisited: The Liturgical Meaning of Holy Week* (Pastoral Press, 1988); Raymond Brown, *A Crucified Christ in Holy Week* (Liturgical Press, 1986).

■ PARISHIONERS IN GENERAL: Why not supplement Bible study with liturgical study? Ministers are frequently surprised at the number of people who will be happy to make this kind of lenten commitment, or even a one-afternoon concentrated study, perhaps on Palm Sunday afternoon before or after Evening Prayer. For this group, the texts of the rites themselves are the primary workbook on which to focus, and perhaps even the music that will weave the days together. If those who plan and preside at the Triduum find the rites sometimes a tangle of ceremonies, imagine how these days must strike the church's "general populace"! Many people are truly grateful to sit down together and explore the "road map" of the Christian Passover. From their own study, parish ministers can bring biblical and historical insights to these sessions, which should be primarily pastoral and practical in nature.

Taking It Home

PASCHAL FAST: Steady and patient catechesis helps people to embrace this new, though old, discipline. In the recent past, our juridical, "Roman" way of looking at fasting has been reinforced by the virtual elimination of any meaningful practice of this discipline.

■ TRIDUUM SOURCEBOOK: This first of LTP's "Sourcebook" series has been revised. It is a wealth of prayer and scripture, a compendium of texts from around the churches that stands as a sure and steadfast companion for personal prayer year after year during the Triduum. There is so much in this new edition that it is published as a three-volume set.

■ CATHOLIC HOUSEHOLD BLESSINGS AND PRAYERS: Our oft-recommended friend contains many texts for observing the Triduum (pages 143–52): meditations, an antiphon to echo through the days, texts of the baptismal renewal and a blessing of Easter foods.

■ TAKE ME HOME: This educational resource from LTP has a fine page on the Triduum, with simple and practical things to do at home during these holy days, and an "eggciting" way to keep the holy day that helps young people relate the ancient custom of Easter eggs to the resurrection of Christ.

■ EASTER CANDLES: Some parishes encourage families to make and/or decorate their own Easter candles. These candles are brought to church and used during the Vigil in place of the individual tapers, then brought home and lighted during prayer through the Fifty Days of Easter at home.

Other Ritual Prayers and Sacraments

According to the church's ancient tradition, the sacraments are not celebrated today or tomorrow (sacramentary, Good Friday rubric).

WEDDINGS are not celebrated from Holy Thursday through Easter. Weddings are allowed on Easter (with the texts of the day) but are clearly inappropriate.

■ PENANCE may be celebrated, but it properly belongs in Lent as a preparation for the Triduum. Communal penance services certainly should not be scheduled during the Triduum, and many parishes and dioceses avoid scheduling individual confessions after Wednesday of this week.

■ ANOINTING OF THE SICK may be celebrated in cases of emergency, but normally this sacrament would not be scheduled during the Triduum.

■ COMMUNION TO THE HOMEBOUND: On Holy Thursday, this most appropriately takes place following the parish's evening celebration. On Good Friday, communion outside the Celebration of the Lord's Passion may be given only to the sick; this means, for example, that communion may not be distributed at Stations of the Cross. On Holy Saturday, communion may be given only as viaticum.

■ FUNERAL MASSES are not celebrated during the Triduum. Funerals that cannot be delayed until Monday are conducted without Mass, music or flowers. The *Order of Christian Funerals* (#179) allows for funeral rites to take place at sites other than church. The rite used during the Triduum begins at #183.

C A L E N D A R

March

27 #39 [40] white
Holy Thursday

ICEL PASTORAL INTRODUCTION

1 The Mass of the Lord's Supper is fittingly the first liturgical action of the Easter Triduum. It is celebrated in the evening at a time convenient for the full participation of all the people.

> At the Last Supper, on the night when he was betrayed, our Savior instituted the eucharistic sacrifice of his body and blood. He did this in order to perpetuate the sacrifice of the cross throughout the centuries until he should come again and in this way to entrust to his beloved bride, the church, a memorial of his death and resurrection: a sacrament of love, a sign of unity, a bond of charity, a paschal banquet "in which Christ is eaten, the heart is filled with grace and a pledge of future glory given to us" (*Constitution on the Sacred Liturgy*, 47).

2 Christ prayed at the Last Supper that all might be one (see John 17:21–23). In a new commandment, he urged his disciples to love one another: There is no greater love, he said, than to lay down one's life for a friend (see John 15:12–13). As a sign of this love, Christ, the servant destined to suffer and so to enter into glory, performed an act of love and service in washing the feet of his disciples. It is this gospel text that is proclaimed at the Mass of the Lord's Supper. It is followed by the ritual washing of feet in the midst of the assembly, unless there are serious pastoral reasons for omitting it.

- Because of the Last Supper themes of unity and love, special efforts are made on Holy Thursday to gather the whole people of God to share in the one parish celebration with all priests concelebrating and with the full participation of the whole local community and its various ministers. According to the church's most ancient tradition, all Masses in the absence of the people are prohibited and no other Mass is celebrated in the parish on Holy Thursday, except where permitted by the bishop in cases of genuine necessity. When such a Mass is allowed for those in no way able to take part in the common parish eucharist, it must not prejudice the principal Mass or be celebrated for the advantage of private persons, nor should it anticipate the beginning of the Triduum. The priest who, out of necessity, has celebrated such a Mass (or who concelebrated at the Chrism Mass if this took place earlier on Holy Thursday) may still concelebrate the Mass of the Lord's Supper.

- The unity of the Lord's table is extended to those who are sick and unable to be present. While communion may be brought to them at any hour of the day, it is more fitting that the eucharist be taken directly from the parish celebration.

- The eucharist itself already draws together the whole Easter mystery of Jesus' death and resurrection. Other liturgical signs reinforce the unity of Holy Thursday with the Triduum as a whole: The solemn reservation of the eucharist for communion the next day and the service of washing feet both look forward to Good Friday. Since the washing of the feet also has links with baptism in significant parts of the Christian tradition, this gesture looks to the initiation rites of Easter night, as does the dismissal of the elect from the Mass of the Lord's Supper. If the bells are rung during the singing of the Gloria, they anticipate the joy of the Easter Vigil, when the same custom may be followed.

- The rite of washing feet is more than a mime in which the washing of the disciples' feet is reenacted. It is a rite in which the presiding priest assisted by other leaders of the community himself performs an act of service, an act which reveals the true nature of Christian love and discipleship. This is not just any act of service but is specifically a gospel sign. Through this gesture, the community is encouraged to follow more closely the one who "came not to be served but to serve and to give his life as a ransom for many" (Matthew 20:28). The sign may be strengthened if the ministers perform this act of service for a representative group of the faithful. So that the gesture will be seen by all, it may be desirable to place those whose feet are to be washed at various points throughout the church.

- The mutual service typical of Christian love is further expressed by bringing to church gifts for the poor, especially if they are the fruit of lenten penance. These contributions are set aside for the poor at the preparation of the gifts.

- The Mass of the Lord's Supper is the first ritual moment in the celebration of the Easter Triduum. Its focus is the unity of the baptized in the sacrifice of Jesus' death and resurrection. The rites should be noble in their simplicity and unencumbered by added or secondary elements. Any other rites should be in harmony with the paschal character of the celebration and contribute to the unity of the gathered community.

3 With the solemn transfer of the consecrated elements to the blessed sacrament chapel, the Mass of the Lord's Supper ends simply, without a dismissal. The time for private adoration afterward can help the faithful to experience the presence of the risen Lord in the three days of the paschal feast. The Triduum of waiting and praying has begun.

- Holy Thursday evening makes particularly clear the meaning of eucharistic reservation. It is derived from the celebration of the sacrifice: Thus, previously reserved elements will have been consumed and the tabernacle is empty when the Mass of the Lord's Supper begins. The primary purpose of eucharistic reservation is the reception of communion in special situations outside the eucharistic celebration: usually viaticum for the dying, in this case communion on Good Friday. Its secondary purpose is to allow for the adoration of the Lord present in the sacrament: thus, the faithful are encouraged to continue adoration before the reserved sacrament for a suitable period of time after the Mass of the Lord's Supper until midnight.

- The rites presume that the eucharist is normally reserved in churches in a separate blessed sacrament chapel. The procession with the eucharist therefore leaves from the altar and goes to the reservation chapel where the liturgy ends. If a church does not have a blessed sacrament chapel, one should be set up for the occasion in the best way possible. Decorations are to be suitable and in due proportion.

- After Mass, the altar is stripped, crosses are removed from the church or covered, votive lights are extinguished. If it has not already been done, the baptismal font and holy water fonts are emptied.

- Prayer in the blessed sacrament chapel at this time is usually personal in nature and done in silence. If circumstances suggest, a portion of the Gospel of John, for example, chapters 13–17, may be read. Evening Prayer is not said by those who participate in the evening Mass.

HOLY THURSDAY CHECKLIST

Sacristans and planners may find a list similar to the following helpful from year to year:

- Get holy oils
- Prepare pitcher(s), bowl(s), towels
- Clean censer, fill boat with incense
- Clean cups for both species
- Measure wine needed
- Prepare sufficient bread for Thursday and Friday
- Prepare baskets or other receptacles for gifts for the poor at Mass
- Use white altar paraments and vestments
- Prepare humeral veil(s)
- Prepare altar of reservation
- Empty tabernacle, doors open
- Tell server about bells during Glory to God
- Train servers for procession
- Prepare inserts for eucharistic prayer
- Arrange for stripping of altar and church after Mass
- Announce adoration until midnight

MASS OF THE LORD'S SUPPER

Introductory Rites

■ OPENING HYMN: The first note of the liturgy in the sacramentary's official antiphon sounds the keynote of the whole Triduum and signals the unity of the Three Days:

We should glory in the cross
of our Lord Jesus Christ,
in whom is our resurrection,
our salvation and our life (see Galatians 6:14).

Anything chosen as an alternative should likewise reflect the unity of the whole paschal mystery. The ancient text by Venantius Fortunatus, "Sing my tongue," not the eucharistic "Pange lingua" (which Aquinas based on Fortunatus) but the passion-oriented one prescribed for the veneration of the cross on Good Friday (*Worship*, #437; *The Hymnal 1982*, #166) is most suitable. Other gathering songs: "Lift high the cross," "Praise to you, O Christ our Savior" (Farrell, OCP, 7126).

■ RECEPTION OF HOLY OILS: The *Sacramentary Supplement* (1994) directs that the holy oils be carried up at the preparation rite as gifts, before the bread and wine. But on this night alone, the sacramentary directs that "bread and wine and gifts for the poor" be the elements borne in that procession, while even the hymn is prescribed "Where charity and love are" ("Ubi caritas"). This chant hardly seems appropriate to a presentation of oils, and the words appointed for their presentation (along with an optional response by the people) will surely eclipse the presentation of the bread, wine and gifts for the poor. The Italian sacramentary, in contrast, places the reception of the oils at the beginning of the liturgy, where they will not overshadow anything else. The suggested order is as follows:

- Three ministers (including those who minister to the sick and to the catechumens) carry the oils blessed at the Chrism Mass, in suitable vessels in the entrance procession, placing them on the altar (because these are blessed and consecrated, this is appropriate).

MARCH

- The ministers step to one side so that as the entrance hymn continues the presider may incense the holy oils as he incenses the altar.
- After the greeting, the presider speaks in these or similar words: On this holy night, we enter into the Three Days of the Lord's Pasch, the sacred Triduum, the paschal mystery of the Lord's passion, death and resurrection, into which the elect of our community (of the church) will be initiated. As we begin, therefore, we receive from our bishop N., of the church of N., the holy oils blessed and consecrated for the sacramental life of our parish community.
- Each presenter may announce the oil being carried.
- The presider responds with appropriate words.
- Then the oils are taken to the repository near the font, where they are reserved. A good musical accompaniment to this rite is "Rite for Receiving the Holy Oils" (John Schiavone, OCP, 9120).

■ GLORIA: Either of Richard Proulx's "Two Plainsong Gloria Settings with Handbells" (GIA, G-3638) is suitable this evening, since neither will overshadow the festivity of the Vigil's version. The first is a setting of John Lee's "Gloria" *(Worship)*, the other from Chant Mass VIII ("Missa de Angelis"). If the parish's Gloria has a refrain, consider a random handbell ring during the refrain. Tradition calls for church bells to be rung during tonight's Gloria. If the church has tower bells, these should be rung at this time.

Liturgy of the Word

■ CHILDREN'S LITURGY OF THE WORD: Tonight the whole community gathers together at the only eucharist permitted. Since this liturgy celebrates our unity in Christ, children should not be sent to a separate liturgy of the word (see the introduction to the *Lectionary for Masses with Children*, 30). The readings are straightforward, and the washing of the feet is a powerful ritual in which the children should be included. It is for the homilist to preach in a manner accessible to all ages on this special night.

■ FOR PSALM 116: Michael Joncas' setting (NALR, JO 07-JON-SM) is a wonderful choice, though material for some verses is taken from outside the psalm. Marty Haugen's setting in *Gather* is also a fine choice as is Marcy Weckler's "Our blessing cup" (WLP, 6201). A highly skilled cantor is needed for Charles Conley's setting with the refrain "What return can I make to the Lord?" (GIA, G-2528) and for the lovely refrain and challenging verses of Stephen Dean's "How can I repay the Lord" (OCP, 7119).

Washing of Feet

■ THE MANDATUM: What "serious pastoral reasons" could justify disobeying this command, ignoring this example of the Lord? What discomfort or embarrassment with intimacy could justify replacing this imitation of Jesus with a handwashing more reminiscent of Pontius Pilate! The footwashing is a powerful symbol of our identity as a servant people, a visual homily. It calls for real humility on the part of both those who do it and those who have it done to them. Peter, remember, was the first to find the gesture a bit too much!

No words of introduction are provided in the ritual, so the spoken homily should lead naturally into the washing of feet (see the Episcopal Church's *Book of Occasional Services* for eloquent words). If not carried in the entrance procession, adequate washbasins, pitchers of warm water and ample towels can be brought from the sacristy as the singing begins and as participants move to their places. This singing continues throughout the washing and during any follow-up washing of the hands of the ministers, ending just before the intercessions.

The Pastoral Introduction makes several points that bear attention: *First,* the presider is not alone but is "assisted by other leaders of the community."

Second, "twelve" is not the specified number but "a representative group of the faithful." This reminds us that this is not historical reenactment but sacramental-liturgical ritual. In fact, there is nothing to prevent a larger number, or even the whole assembly taking part, depending on circumstances. Parishes might also ask whether the poor, the homeless or people with AIDS might be invited to have their feet washed as a sign of the community's commitment to serve.

Third, visual participation by the assembly requires careful positioning, perhaps "at various points throughout the church."

■ MUSIC: Music for the mandatum should be chosen carefully to complement the ritual. The entire assembly should be able to watch or participate in the foot washing. A hymn, by its complexity of text, may force the assembly to choose between participating in singing or participating in the ritual action. Good responsorial pieces for this annual moment are readily available: Steve Janco's "Whenever you serve me" (WLP, 6210); Taizé, "Mandatum novum" (GIA, G-2433); Michael Ward's "A new commandment" (WLP, 7579); Steve Warner's "The garment of love" (WLP, 7211); Chrysogonus Waddell's "Jesus took a towel"

MARCH

(*Worship,* #432). "Jesu, Jesu" (*Worship,* #431) is a song from Ghana that speaks in concrete terms of our "mandatum" to serve as Jesus did. Christopher Walker's "Faith, hope and love" is based on the mandatum text with alternate verses derived from "Ubi caritas" (OCP, 7149).

- DISMISSAL OF CATECHUMENS AND ELECT: Catechumens and elect are sent forth following the washing of feet. At this stage, the elect and catechumens may be able to continue reflection and discussion on their own, perhaps with some prepared questions as a guide. This would allow the catechists to stay for the entire liturgy. A catechist who accompanies the catechumens and the elect may, however, see this as another way of following the Lord's command to wash feet.

- GENERAL INTERCESSIONS: See intercessions from tonight's Evening Prayer in the *Liturgy of the Hours*. In accord with the usual scope of general intercessions, however, recast these as invitations to pray to the Father rather than to Christ.

LITURGY OF THE EUCHARIST

Preparation Rites

"At the beginning of the liturgy of the eucharist, there may be a procession of the faithful with gifts for the poor" (sacramentary). The *Circular Letter* (#52) adds that these might be "especially those collected as the fruit of lenten penance." Canned goods for a food bank, "rice bowls" for Catholic Relief Services or similar gifts could be collected in this procession, which ends with those bringing up the bread and wine for the eucharist.

In a rare directive, the church prescribes the song for this moment. "Ubi caritas," from Reichenau Abbey in the year 800, is accessible to every congregation in many chant adaptations. Few hymns have such a venerable history. Do not let another Triduum planning season go by without having the assembly learn and sing this chant. Richard Proulx offers two versions, one in *Worship* (#598) and a second, "God is love" (GIA, G-3010) for unison choir, cantor and congregation. Taizé's mantra "Ubi caritas" (*Worship,* #604) establishes a calm, prayerful environment and lends itself to embellishment for use throughout the ritual. A well-known and worthy survivor from the 1960s is "Where charity and love prevail," now with inclusive language in the *People's Mass Book* (World Library Publications) and *Gather*. Due to its brevity, musicians may call on an instrument (flute or oboe) for interludes between verses. World Library also offers a new, contemporary-style setting of "Where charity and love prevail" by Mark Hill (WLP, 8593).

- EUCHARISTIC PRAYER:
  - Preface: Holy Eucharist I is prescribed.
  - Three special inserts are provided for tonight.

- ACCLAMATIONS: The simplicity of Richard Proulx's "Corpus Christi Mass" (for unaccompanied choir, cantor and congregation), based on the familiar tune "Adoro Te," perfectly suits this evening. The familiar tune provides for optimal participation by the assembly.

- BREAKING OF BREAD: Even if the parish does not yet use loaves or hosts large enough to break for the community at every Mass, tonight truly requires such bread. Breaking the one bread is an important symbol of the eucharist's meaning. Bread for tomorrow is also broken tonight. See LTP's *The Three Days* for a good recipe.

- COMMUNION PROCESSION: Psalm 34 is most appropriate. Settings include James Moore's "Taste and see" (GIA, G-2802), which needs a cantor who can do justice to the wonderful gospel-style verses; Stephen Dean's "Taste and see" (OCP, 7114); Michael Joncas' "Take and eat" (GIA, G-3435); J. Gerald Phillips' "O taste and see" (WLP, 8613); Richard Hillert's "Taste and see" (in *Service Music for the Mass,* vol. 1; WLP, 6611); and Alan Hommerding's "Taste and see," which uses the "Adoro te devote" melody (in *Sing Out! A Children's Psalter,* WLP, 7910).

Robert Hutmacher's "Love is his word" (*Worship,* #599) gathers the evening's several images in a graceful musical setting. Lucien Deiss' "Song of my love" (WLP, 2561) contains particularly beautiful language about the eucharist. Alan Hommerding's "Litany for the Holy Eucharist" (*We Celebrate,* #29) is based on the Agnus Dei from the "Jubilate Deo" Mass. Musicians might consider repeating tonight's song for the communion procession at the Vigil.

- DISMISSAL OF EUCHARISTIC MINISTERS: The Pastoral Introduction echoes the *Circular Letter* (#53), reminding us that the hospitality of the Lord's table should be extended to the homebound by bringing them communion directly from this evening's celebration.

- AFTER COMMUNION: The vessel with eucharistic bread for Good Friday's communion is left on the

MARCH

altar. After a period of silence, the prayer after communion is sung or said. The procession follows immediately.

Transfer of the Holy Eucharist

■ PREPARATION: The presider stands before the altar and places incense in the thurible. Kneeling, he incenses the eucharist three times. Assisting ministers and all others also kneel. Presider then puts on humeral veil, takes vessel with eucharist and covers it with the ends of the veil. Meanwhile, ministers who will lead the procession gather in correct order. If the largest vessel available cannot contain the bread for Good Friday, a second vessel should be carried by a deacon or concelebrant also wearing a humeral veil.

■ PROCESSION: The cross bearer and two acolytes lead the procession. Deacons, concelebrants, two censer bearers and presider with eucharist follow. Other ministers and members of assembly follow presider to reservation chapel, if room permits.

"Pange lingua/Sing my tongue" (Aquinas' eucharistic text) is the classic chant for this ritual. Verses can be sung in Latin, English or alternate between the two. Musicians should coordinate with planners so that the first four verses may be repeated or so that the procession lasts until the final two verses ("Tantum ergo").

■ CONCLUSION OF PROCESSION: The presider sets vessel down in tabernacle (leaving door open) or just in front of it. He then removes the humeral veil, kneels and incenses vessel with one of the thuribles. All then sing the last two verses of the "Pange lingua" ("Tantum ergo"). The deacon places eucharist in tabernacle (if the presider did not) and closes the door. A period of silent adoration follows. Then altar is stripped in silence. People may stay for prayer and leave when they choose. Note that there is no dismissal, no real "ending" of this liturgy, which thus forms one movement of a liturgy that ends only at the Vigil. People simply disperse to continue prayer and fasting at home.

EUCHARISTIC ADORATION

From the transfer of the eucharist to midnight, all should be encouraged to continue in prayer. The *Circular Letter* (#56) calls for John 13—17 to be read as part of this prayer time. Many parishes encourage participation by involving different groups in vocal prayer and singing—religious communities, prayer groups, Bible-study groups or others. With coordination and division of time, the chapel can be filled for hours with public prayer (it should be parish prayer, not the devotions of any particular group or of individuals). See *To Crown the Year*, pages 94–97, for good ideas on preparing the place of reservation.

NIGHT PRAYER

Many parishes conclude the period of adoration by singing Night Prayer together just before midnight, then quietly extinguishing the candles and dispersing in silence. In place of the usual responsory, "Into your hands," the church uses "Christ became obedient" throughout the hours of the Triduum, adding a phrase each day.

28 #40 [41] red
Good Friday

ICEL PASTORAL INTRODUCTION

1 On the afternoon of this day, the Christian faithful assemble to recall devoutly the death of Jesus "in the sure hope of the resurrection" (Prayer over the People, Good Friday). It is a *celebration* of the Lord's passion because the resurrection is not separated from Jesus' death. On this day the community of faith with full heart worships God, who chose to redeem us by the cross, "that Satan, who conquered through a tree, might on a tree be overcome" (Preface, Triumph of the Cross).

2 The afternoon celebration of the Lord's passion is the center of Good Friday's worship. It may take place around three o'clock unless pastoral reasons suggest a later hour. In addition, it is recommended that the Office of Readings and Morning Prayer be celebrated publicly with the people; Evening Prayer, however, is not said by those who participate in the afternoon liturgical service. Devotions such as the Stations of the Cross may find a place on Good Friday, but the liturgical celebration of the Lord's passion by its very nature far surpasses them in importance. These devotions should be so fashioned

MARCH

that they accord with the sacred liturgy, are in some way derived from it and lead the people to it.

3 Since, according to the church's most ancient tradition, the eucharist itself is not celebrated, the celebration of other sacraments is normally out of place on Good Friday. Even the sacrament of penance is better celebrated by the end of Lent, that is, before the Easter Triduum, since the penitential season of Lent and the sacrament of penance prepare one to celebrate the Triduum.

4 As the first day of the Easter fast, Good Friday is a day of fast and abstinence. The ancient forms of today's liturgy are likewise marked by an austere solemnity. Silence plays a significant role: the afternoon liturgy begins and ends in silence. Music is simple and decorations very sparse. The altar should be completely bare, without cross, candles or cloths. Only the number of ministers necessary to the celebration should be present in the sanctuary. Red Mass vestments are worn by priest and deacon.

- The liturgy begins starkly with a profound act of adoration. Prostrating or kneeling, participants may wish to adopt an ancient posture for prayer by extending their arms in a cruciform gesture.

- The first part of the liturgy is the proclamation of the word. After two readings and a psalm, the narrative of the passion from the Gospel of Saint John is read or sung. It is followed by a homily, silence and the general intercessions. The solemn proclamation of the passion on Good Friday lies at the heart of the celebration.

- In preaching on the passion, special care should be taken not to show the Jewish people in an unfavorable way. The crimes during the passion of Christ cannot be attributed indiscriminately to all Jews of that time, nor to Jews today. The Jewish people should not be referred to as though rejected or cursed, as if this view followed from scripture. As the church has always held, Christ freely suffered his passion and death because of the sins of all, that all might be saved. Likewise, the "reproaches," when used, are to be understood as directed to ourselves and our lack of gratitude for the gift of salvation.

- In response to its meditation on the passion of Christ, the church cries out for the needs of the world. The general intercessions, traditionally sung, cover a variety of intentions which signify the universal effect of Christ's triumphant death. In case of serious public need, the bishop may add a special intention. Those prayers most appropriate to local circumstances may be chosen provided the series follows the usual scope and sequence of the general intercessions. Acclamations sung by the people will enhance their participation in this ancient form of prayer. The conference of bishops may provide such acclamations for the people to replace the invitation to kneel and pray silently. If there is no deacon, the invitation to each prayer may be sung or said by another minister.

- The veneration, which follows the liturgy of the word, focuses not so much on a figure of the crucified as on the cross itself; with lighted candles on each side, it is a symbol of victory and salvation. A large, well-crafted cross solemnly shown to the people provides a moving climax to the liturgy of Good Friday. Each person comes forward after the showing to kiss or touch the cross in an individual gesture of veneration. Only one cross is used. If it is large enough and is set up in the midst of the assembly, processions of the faithful will be able to approach it from several directions at once. This personal act of participation is an important feature of the liturgy. Simultaneous veneration by all should be used only when this individual gesture is impossible. The antiphons, "reproaches" or other songs that are sung during the veneration view the cross within the whole story of salvation and look to the light of the resurrection. They may be sung antiphonally with the people.

- The simple communion rite that concludes the Good Friday liturgy is a proclamation of the Lord's death until he comes (see 1 Corinthians 12:26) and a testimony to the presence of the risen Lord. The elements consecrated and reserved on Holy Thursday are brought from the chapel of reservation and shared among the faithful. Only what is required for communion of the sick should be reserved for the rest of the Triduum. Holy communion is not given to the faithful outside this celebration of the Lord's passion, though it may be brought at any hour of the day to the sick who are unable to participate in the liturgy. After a final prayer over the people, all depart in silence, leaving the cross in the church in order to encourage meditation on the paschal mystery.

- The altar is stripped at a convenient time after the service.

OFFICE OF READINGS AND MORNING PRAYER: TENEBRAE

■ **TENEBRAE:** The "Office of Shadows" or "Darkness" was the title used before Vatican II for the Office of Readings combined with Morning Prayer, during which candles, arranged on an elaborate triangular "hearse" were extinguished one by one as the liturgy progressed and the morning light came in. In recent centuries, despite the early-morning images, this was sometimes moved to Wednesday night, a sort of prelude to the Triduum, which led to the creation of various meanings to explain the diminishing candles. The *Ceremonial of Bishops* (#296), the

TRIDUUM: GOOD FRIDAY 133

Liturgy of the Hours (#210) and the *Circular Letter* (#40, 62) all call for a return of the original Tenebrae. While more permanent rites for combining these hours are prepared, parishes should choose between the Office of Readings and Morning Prayer, or combine the two liturgies using the *General Instruction of the Liturgy of the Hours* (#99) for structural guidance. The combined office follows this outline:

- invitatory antiphon and psalm (Office of Readings [OR]); chant these "recto tono" (on one note) to add a distinctive and sober sound to the celebration.
- hymn: Fortunatus' "Pange lingua" is prescribed.
- antiphons and psalms: OR
- verse: OR
- scripture: Hebrews 9:11–28.
- silent reflection and responsory: OR
- patristic reading: from *Catecheses* of John Chrysostom: "The power of Christ's blood."
- silent reflection and responsory follows: OR
- antiphons, psalms and Old Testament canticle: Morning Prayer (MP)
- scripture: Isaiah 52:13–15
- response: Triduum antiphon: "Christ became obedient for us even unto death," adding today, "even unto death on a cross": MP; see note for Thursday Night Prayer, page 132
- antiphon and Canticle of Zechariah: MP
- intercessions, Lord's Prayer and concluding prayer: MP
- blessing and dismissal

CHILDREN AND THE TRIDUUM

Those who prepare the Triduum liturgy must consider how best to include the community's children in the prayer of the church. Childcare should be provided for the youngest ones, at least for the main celebrations on these Triduum days. Ways to involve preschool and older children should be planned carefully. Possibilities include:

- Midday Prayer (or Stations of the Cross), with some music taught during religious education classes.
- References to the faith life of children as part of the Triduum homilies.
- Participation of children in preparing the church building for the Triduum.
- Catechetical assemblies for all children of the parish Good Friday and Holy Saturday mornings.

■ CATECHETICAL ASSEMBLIES: One way to encourage active participation of young people in the liturgies may be to hold catechetical assemblies for parish youth on Good Friday and Holy Saturday mornings. Parents will appreciate this attempt to draw their children into the great mystery of faith, and children will enjoy the gatherings if the assemblies are planned well. Such events could involve youth from preschool through grade six or so. They would gather each day for an hourlong event organized more or less as a celebration of the word. What distinguishes this from a children's liturgy that competes with the principal liturgy is that it must clearly point to the parish assembly — a kind of rehearsal and orientation to enable children to participate fully in the principal liturgies.

Good Friday's catechetical assembly might include:

- Music that speaks of the passion and cross and that will be used at the celebration of the Lord's passion.
- A reading or two from the day's Liturgy of the Hours, using images with which children can identify.
- Instructions given by one or more catechists, introducing the liturgy that the children will take part in later today. Instructions may be given in smaller groups by age level.
- Rehearsal and explanation for the solemn actions they will perform with the adults later on (passion reading, prayers and especially veneration of the cross).
- Some preparation of the physical requirements for the principal liturgy: For example, children can see the stripped-down church and reflect on it, help prepare a resting place for the cross, or get the cross out of storage and bring it to the place from which it will be carried in solemn entrance.
- Pray some of the general intercessions from the celebration of the passion.

GOOD FRIDAY CHECKLIST

A list similar to what follows may be helpful for sacristans and planners:

- Practice singing intercessions
- Arrange microphones for passion
- Cross, candles, matches in back (incense materials, too, if used for veneration)
- Altar cloth and corporal on credence table
- Arrange for collection for Holy Land
- Be sure the holy water fonts are emptied
- Prepare red vestments
- Private place prepared for reservation of any remaining consecrated bread after service
- Place prepared for "enshrinement" of the cross after the service

CELEBRATION OF THE LORD'S PASSION

Introductory Rites

■ SILENCE: "Silence plays a significant role" in this liturgy (PI, 4). The liturgy begins in absolute silence and ends in absolute silence. No cross, no candles, no great procession. No gathering song. No solo instruments. Only those ministers necessary for the liturgy sit in the sanctuary. Except for a bookbearer, even the servers could be seated in the assembly, with the lectors and ministers of communion, coming forward only when needed.

■ FALLING PROSTRATE: Presider and assistants reverence the bare altar, then fully prostrate themselves. The *Circular Letter* (#65) stresses the importance of this ritual gesture:

> This act of prostration, which is proper to the rite of the day, should be strictly observed, for it signifies both the abasement of "earthly man" [sic] and also the grief and sorrow of the church.

The Pastoral Introduction heightens the posture's importance by suggesting that "participants may wish to adopt an ancient posture for prayer by extending their arms in a cruciform gesture" (PI, 4). The plural *participants* (after suggesting minimal presence of ministers) implies that all in the assembly may wish to join in this gesture of prayer. If the physical arrangement of the room allows this (a rare thing), the whole assembly should join in the prostration. Otherwise the assembly kneels, while the few in the sanctuary prostrate. All pray silently, as the sacramentary suggests "for a while," which means long enough for the power of this gesture to sink in and long enough for this first and, therefore, crucial time of silence to become prayer.

■ OPENING PRAYER: At the chair, the presider omits both greeting and "Let us pray." This signals that today's liturgy is really a continuation of the liturgy we began last night, the whole Triduum is one integral celebration. With hands extended, the presider offers the opening prayer and sits down for the liturgy of the word.

LITURGY OF THE WORD

■ LITURGY OF THE WORD FOR CHILDREN: Again, it is best to let the children remain as part of the main assembly rather than leaving for a separate liturgy of the word.

■ PSALM 31 is the first music of this liturgy. Let it be sung a cappella. In fact, the absence of musical instrumentation throughout this celebration can be a remarkably powerful experience. Choose music that is easy to sing without accompaniment. Chant always serves well. Notice that Psalm 31, rather than last Sunday's Psalm 22, has been chosen for today. This is in keeping with the majestic image of Christ that shines through the Johannine passion. *Worship*'s setting (#814) is effective and simple. Francis V. Strahan's simple refrain, "Father, Father" *(People's Mass Book)* is a fine alternative.

■ PASSION ACCORDING TO JOHN: Several approaches are possible for this proclamation. It may be chanted by three strong singers, to the time-honored melody of the Roman rite (GIA, G-1795). Deacons, presbyters, cantors or capable lectors chant the parts of Christ, narrator, speaker.

Or, a single, well-trained lector may provide a strong proclamation.

Or, several lectors may each take a section of the story, with musical refrain by assembly between each section. An appropriate refrain would be the parish's usual setting of the memorial acclamation "Lord, by your cross." This text is fitting, since John's passion focuses on the triumph of the cross.

However it is proclaimed, the passion is read in an atmosphere of simple austerity:

- No incense or candles
- No greeting or signs of the cross
- After the verse of the Lord's death, all kneel and a brief silence is observed.

■ HOMILY: Today's homily should avoid any language that even hints at blaming the Jewish people for Christ's death. In fact, the homily should correct any such impression left by John's passion.

■ DISMISSAL OF ELECT AND CATECHUMENS: The general intercessions are prayers of the baptized faithful, so the elect and catechumens are dismissed before they begin. They may leave with a catechist or on their own to continue their reflection on the passion, perhaps returning after the liturgy to venerate the cross.

■ GENERAL INTERCESSIONS: These are an important part of the ministry of the baptized on this day. The ancient form of the prayers at this liturgy can help all of us learn to see these prayers as part of a priestly ministry through which we share in the high priestly, intercessory role of Christ.

Veneration of the Cross

■ THE CROSS: According to the Pastoral Introduction, the object of veneration is not the figure of the crucified, but the cross, set up

as a symbol of victory and salvation (PI, 4). Beyond that, the Pastoral Introduction says that the cross should be "large and well-crafted" and that only one cross should be used. Processions may approach the cross simultaneously from several directions, as ushers direct the flow. Using several little crosses is absurd after bringing one large cross in with solemn reverence. The other alternative permitted, holding the cross up for communal worship by a silent assembly in place, loses all the power of the ritual. There is surely no need to rush today. Let the veneration take whatever time is necessary.

Peter Mazar devotes a number of pages to the finest treatment available on the subject of the cross and its veneration (*To Crown the Year*, pages 98–103).

■ BEHOLD THE WOOD OF THE CROSS: Two options are given in the sacramentary: "uncovering" and "bringing in." The "uncovering" form is necessary if the cross is suspended or otherwise stationary. Even here, architects or interior designers should have planned for lowering it for this rite. Note carefully what the rubrics say: The veiled cross is not carried in and unveiled in stages along the way. Rather, the gradual unveiling occurs entirely in one place.

■ VENERATING THE CROSS: See Mazar for interesting ideas on how to place the cross for veneration. Some parishes make sure the cross is always held by people during the veneration. Some parishes simply lay it flat or on the steps before the altar. The cross should never be propped up on furniture, much less on the altar.

An ancient custom calls for all ministers—indeed all the people—to come to the cross barefoot or in stocking feet. While this custom is not mentioned in the sacramentary, the *Ceremonial of Bishops* (#322) tells the presider to leave his chasuble—and shoes—at the chair! They should be taken off before the entrance of the cross, so that the procession flows into the veneration. This tradition, still observed by many monastic orders and frequently mentioned by ancient homilists, catches on quickly if the presider and other assisting ministers handle it with grace. Announce it in the participation booklet. If the presider is seen taking his shoes off while others in the sanctuary do the same, the assembly may feel comfortable removing theirs.

■ MUSIC FOR THE VENERATION: When selecting veneration music, keep in mind the unity of the Triduum. Even today is "a celebration of the Lord's passion," says the Pastoral Introduction (#1), "austere but never sad" (#3). One way to establish this mood is an invitation to come and adore sung by the cantor near the cross followed by a strong proclamation of praise such as the traditional Good Friday trisagion, "Holy is God." Three settings, by Howard Hughes, David Isele and Michael Joncas, appear in *Praise God in Song* (GIA, G-2270).

This procession will take time and cannot be rushed. Prepare plenty of music. Vary styles and participants, congregational singing and pieces by the choir. Using cantor or soloist in either case adds further variety and increases participation. Begin and end with music that involves the assembly. "Sing, my tongue" (the passion "Pange, lingua") is most ancient and most appropriate. Marty Haugen's, "Tree of life" (GIA, G-2944) is suitable throughout the Triduum, as are the Taizé (GIA, G-3719) "Crucem tuam," "Adoramus te Domine I" (*Gather*, #221) and "Jesus, remember me" (*Gather*, #167). Owen Alstot's "Wood of the cross" for choir and congregation (OCP, 8826) combines the refrain "Behold the wood of the cross" with Psalm 22, providing strong and moving music for this rite. The "Lamentations of Jeremiah" are coupled with a haunting chant melody in Gabe Huck's book *The Three Days* (LTP). The refrain "Jerusalem, Jerusalem, return to the Lord your God" can be sung by the assembly after the cantor without any rehearsal.

The Reproaches still appear as an option in the official Roman books and in many missalettes. Their danger is the potential misreading of texts as directed toward all the Jewish people of Jesus' time—or even our own. A striking revision of the verses, clearly directed to the Christian church of today, appears in the *United Methodist Book of Worship*, with the trisagion ("Holy is God") mentioned above.

Communion Rite

■ COMMUNION: A simple transfer rite brings the eucharist to the altar, where altar cloth, corporal and book have been placed. Candles carried with the cross are arranged near the altar. The order is simple: Lord's Prayer, embolism, invitation to communion. The music from last night may be repeated. Haas' "Now we remain" (*Gather*, GIA) is also appropriate.

■ AFTER COMMUNION: Any remaining eucharist (for Holy Saturday viaticum) is carried without ceremony by an assisting minister to a suitable place outside the church. Then the prayer after communion is said.

MARCH

- **PRAYER OVER THE PEOPLE:** The traditional greeting is omitted. The presider extends hands over the assembly and offers this prayer, which, like all of the official texts, is particularly positive and focused on eternal life and glory. Like last night, there is no dismissal or formal ending to this liturgy. All simply depart in silence.

NIGHT PRAYER

This liturgical prayer, perhaps after a simple fasting meal, follows the format of last night and includes the same proper antiphon but with the same addition that was added this morning: Christ became obedient for us even unto death, even unto death on a cross.

29 violet — Holy Saturday

ICEL PASTORAL INTRODUCTION

On Holy Saturday the church waits at the tomb of Jesus, meditating on his suffering and death and looking forward to the holy night of the Easter Vigil. This day is characterized by fasting, waiting and alertness in prayer. Thus the community assembles for the Vigil to begin the Easter celebrations with a heightened sense of expectation and joy.

- As on Good Friday, the celebration of the Office of Readings and Morning Prayer with the people is recommended. The celebration of marriage and the other sacraments is forbidden; although exception is made for the sacraments of penance and the anointing of the sick, these are better celebrated before the Easter Triduum. The altar is left bare, the eucharist is not celebrated and holy communion may be given only as viaticum for the dying.

- For the elect it is a day of retreat in final preparation for the sacraments of initiation. When it is possible, they come together with some of the faithful for reflection and prayer and to celebrate some or all of the preparation rites: the presentation of the Lord's Prayer, the "return" or recitation of the Creed, which was presented to them solemnly during Lent, the ephphetha rite, the choosing of a baptismal name and the anointing with the oil of catechumens. If the anointing is celebrated, it may be a suitable occasion to receive in the parish the oils newly blessed by the bishop.

OFFICE OF READINGS AND MORNING PRAYER: TENEBRAE

The outline for this service given under the entry for Good Friday (page 133) is used. The official morning hymn, "Christ Jesus, Savior of the World" appears in the revised *Triduum Sourcebook* (LTP), page 199.

After the scripture reading of Morning Prayer, the special Triduum antiphon is chanted or recited again, "Christ became obedient for us even unto death, even unto death on a cross," with the final phrase of glorification added: "Therefore God raised him on high and gave him the name above all other names."

Many parishes combine some or all of Morning Prayer with the preparation rites for the elect or with the rite of reception of children (before infant baptism) on this day. Notes regarding such a service are given below in the next section.

PREPARATION FOR INITIATION

- **PREPARATION RITES FOR THE ELECT:** The *Rite of Christian Initiation of Adults* (starting at #185) situates the preparation rites on Holy Saturday: song and greeting, reading the word of God and homily, celebrating certain rites (presentation of the Lord's Prayer, if deferred, the "return" of the Creed, and/or the ephphetha rite).

These rites can be celebrated on their own, with full participation of the parish community encouraged. They could also be joined to an hour of prayer from the Liturgy of the Hours. In this case, the preparation rites follow the proper psalmody and scripture reading (and perhaps the patristic homily).

Note that the anointing with the oil of catechumens is no longer part of these preparation rites. The current edition of the rite prescribes this anointing as a repeatable rite for the period of the catechumenate.

- **RITE OF RECEPTION OF CHILDREN:** If infants will be baptized at the Vigil, the *Rite of Baptism for Children* (#28) calls for preparatory rites with infants, parents, sponsors and community.

A preparatory rite for the infants to be baptized involves the rite of receiving the children (at the door), the prayer of exorcism and anointing with the oil of catechumens. This may be celebrated before a "fasting lunch" or in conjunction with one of the hours of the Liturgy of the Hours.

TRIDUUM: HOLY SATURDAY **137**

MARCH

- **COMBINED PREPARATION RITE:** A service combining reception of infants with preparation of the elect is possible, uniting in one assembly the prayers and expectation of the elect, the parents, the sponsors and the catechists. The format is as follows:

  - Gathering hymn, with entire assembly at the entrance way. An appropriate text is found on page 170 of the revised *Triduum Sourcebook*.
  - Reception of infants (*Rite of Baptism for Children* [RBC], #35–41)
  - Procession of all to seating near ambo; refrain or hymn sung by all
  - Liturgy of the Hours option: psalms, antiphon, scripture of the appropriate hour

  or

  Liturgy of the word option: reading(s) related to preparatory rites, followed by psalm (possible rites listed in RCIA, #185.2; readings at #179–180, 194, 198)
  - Homily
  - Preparation rites for infants: exorcism (RBC, #49), anointing with oil of catechumens (RBC, #50)
  - One or more preparation rites for adults and children of catechetical age: presentation of Lord's Prayer (RCIA, #180), recitation of Creed (RCIA, #195) or ephphetha (RCIA, #199)
  - Hymn or gospel canticle (if part of Morning or Evening Prayer)
  - Intercessions from Morning or Evening Prayer of Holy Saturday, supplemented with prayers for baptized candidates for full communion
  - Prayer of blessing (RCIA, #204)
  - Dismissal (RCIA, #205)

CATECHETICAL ASSEMBLY FOR CHILDREN

See the introduction given under this heading on Good Friday, page 134. Today's catechetical session may include any of these items:

- Participation of children in preparation of the elect, especially if children of catechetical age will be prepared
- Participation of children in any of the hours of the Liturgy of the Hours
- Painting of Easter eggs to be distributed to all after the Vigil
- Hearing (and dramatizing) scriptures from the Vigil
- Preparing the worship space for the Vigil

These activities are meant to prepare the children for the Vigil and presume their participation in it.

EVENING PRAYER

Depending on the time of the Vigil, this hour may be best for the preparatory rites for the elect. It also may be the best prayer hour to link to a fasting meal. If the Vigil is very late or just before dawn, those in the habit of coming to church for early evening Mass may appreciate the scheduling of Evening Prayer at that time.

29 / 30
#41 [42]   white
Easter Vigil

ICEL PASTORAL INTRODUCTION

1 On this holy night, called the "mother of all vigils," the church keeps watch, celebrating the resurrection of Christ in the sacraments and awaiting his return in glory. It is the turning point of the Triduum, the passover of the new covenant which marks Christ's passage from death to life. **2** This paschal mystery, already celebrated in various ways since the Mass of the Lord's Supper, is clearly and joyfully announced from the very beginning of the Vigil liturgy. The service of light, culminating in the great Easter proclamation of the resurrection, establishes from the outset the meaning of the celebration. It is in the light of the Easter candle that the scriptures are read, understood and received. They unfold the wonderful story of God's work of creation and re-creation. Then, those chosen for Christian initiation are plunged into the waters of Jesus' death and resurrection and are anointed by the Spirit. The whole assembly of the faithful renew the promises of their baptism, and, finally, gathered at the table of the Lord, all

celebrate Christ's triumphant sacrifice and share the sacrament of his body and blood.

3 In this way, in accord with most ancient traditions, this night is kept as a vigil for the Lord (see Exodus 12:42). The Gospel of Luke (see Luke 12:35ff.) reminds the faithful to have their lamps burning, to be like servants awaiting the return of the head of the household who, on arriving, will find them awake and will seat them at the family table.

- The entire celebration of the Easter Vigil takes place at night, beginning after nightfall or ending before daybreak on Sunday. It occupies the main part of the night and it does not correspond to the usual Saturday evening Mass in time or duration; its character is unique in the liturgical cycle.

- The people assemble around a bonfire. Its flames dispel the darkness and light up the night. The beauty of the fire, its warmth and its light, draw the liturgical assembly together as the people arrive. Assistance should be provided for the infirm. Sound amplification equipment may be necessary to enable all to hear. After a while, the ministers, in white Mass vestments, come to the fire. It is blessed and the large Easter candle is prepared.

- Circumstances where it is impossible to light a large fire call for careful adaptation of the rite so that the power of this first sign is not destroyed. In this instance, after the people have assembled inside the church, the priest goes with the ministers (carrying the Easter candle) to the door of the church or another place best suited to the participation of the people. If necessary, the people turn to face the priest.

- The various rites provided for the preparation of the candle are optional. The conference of bishops, in keeping with the culture of the people, may determine special rites for this preparation.

- Having taken time to gather around the fire, the community sets off in a solemn procession of light into the church. This procession will have its full effect if the church is in darkness. The large Easter candle, a "pillar of fire" symbolizing the risen Christ who conquers sin and death, leads the procession. The best time and method for distributing and lighting the candles of the people will depend on circumstances, but it should not disrupt the procession. Those to be baptized do not yet carry candles. Sung acclamations are provided for the procession, and others in honor of Christ may be added.

- On arrival in the church, the Easter proclamation is sung by the deacon, the priest or a cantor. The participation of the people may be enhanced by inserting approved acclamations. The Easter proclamation is sung standing in the holy light of the Easter candle and the candles held by the people. For good effect, electric lighting may be left off until the service of light is finished. Then it could be used throughout the Easter Vigil, focusing first on the ambo, then on the font and finally on the altar.

- The character of this night as a vigil is demonstrated most clearly in the liturgy of the word, when the church meditates on all the wonderful things God has done for us from the beginning. The nine readings trace the outstanding events of the history of salvation, understood in the light of the Easter proclamation, which has just been heard. The sung Gloria points toward the proclamation of the good news about Jesus; it should not be so elaborate that it overshadows what it is meant to introduce. The gospel of the resurrection, with which the account of salvation history culminates, is greeted with greatest solemnity in the joyful Easter Alleluias. The faithful reflect calmly on each reading by singing the responsorial psalm, by silence, and by listening and responding to the prayer proclaimed by the priest. The prayer after each reading helps to place the reading within the context of the paschal mystery. The homily, an integral part of the liturgy, draws these elements together and leads the people into the celebration of the Easter sacraments, which will follow. A variety of ways of proclaiming the lessons and singing the responses will sustain the attention of all. Time is unimportant on this holy night, haste is unseemly, and abbreviation of the liturgy of the word is unnecessary except when pastoral conditions genuinely require it. (At least three readings from the Old Testament should be read, although for very serious reasons the number may be reduced to two. The reading of Exodus 14, however, is never omitted.)

- In the third part of the Vigil, new members of the church are reborn in the celebration of the sacraments of initiation as the day of resurrection approaches. Baptism recalls and makes present the paschal mystery of Jesus' death, burial and resurrection because in baptism we pass from the death of sin into life (see Romans 6:1–11). Easter, especially the Easter Vigil, is therefore the best time for the celebration of baptism. It is highly desirable that baptism by immersion be used on this night, since it is more suitable as a symbol of participation in the death and resurrection of Christ. Without the celebration of baptism at the Vigil, the blessing of water, the renewal of baptismal promises and the sprinkling lose some of their significance. In a parish, therefore, it ought to be quite exceptional to celebrate the Vigil without baptism, at least the baptism of infants in those instances where there are no adult candidates. The bishop, in particular, chief steward of the mysteries of God and leader of the entire liturgical life in the church, should personally celebrate baptism at the Easter Vigil.

- If the blessing of the baptismal water does not take place at the baptistry, the vessel of water is reverently carried to the font after the renewal of baptismal promises. If the blessing of baptismal water does not take place, the water blessed for the renewal of baptismal promises is put in a suitable place after the renewal.

- Adults and children of catechetical age who are baptized at the Vigil are normally also confirmed before sharing in the eucharist. In addition, there may be baptized adults who, after a period of catechesis, are ready for confirmation and first eucharist. In this case, some restructuring of the rites of the Easter Vigil may be necessary, and help can be found in the chapter of the *Rite of Christian Initiation of Adults* titled "Preparation of Uncatechized Adults for Confirmation and Eucharist." The candidates for baptism are presented first, the litany is sung and the water of the font is blessed. After their profession of faith, they are baptized and presented with a lighted candle. Confirmation is celebrated with the laying on of hands and the anointing with chrism. Then all the faithful also light their candles, and they renew their baptismal promises. They are sprinkled with the baptismal water. The initiation liturgy concludes with the general intercessions, that is, the prayer of the faithful, in which the neophytes take part for the first time.

- If infants are to be baptized during the Easter Vigil, the following is done. First, the rite of reception of the infants is celebrated at a convenient time and place before the Vigil. In this separate celebration the liturgy of the word may be omitted. The prayer of exorcism is said, followed by the anointing with the oil of catechumens. During the Easter Vigil itself, the infants are presented by the parents and godparents after the presentation of the adult candidates. The parents and godparents make the profession of faith with the elect. After all the infants have been baptized, they are anointed with chrism. Following the presentation of the lighted candles, the parents and godparents return to their places with the infants. The celebration then continues with the confirmation of the adults.

- Pastoral considerations may suggest that along with the celebration of the sacraments of Christian initiation, the Easter Vigil should include the rite of reception of already baptized Christians into the full communion of the Catholic Church. This will necessitate some restructuring of the rites of the Easter Vigil. Provision is made for this in the chapter of the *Rite of Christian Initiation of Adults* titled "Celebration at the Easter Vigil of the Sacraments of Initiation and of the Rite of Reception into the Full Communion of the Catholic Church."

- The Vigil culminates with the liturgy of the eucharist, when the whole church is called to the table that the Lord has prepared for his people through his death and resurrection. It is the high point of the night's liturgy because it is in the fullest sense the Easter sacrament: the commemoration of the sacrifice of the cross, the presence of the risen Christ, the completion of Christian initiation and the foretaste of the eternal pasch. Therefore it should not appear as an appendix to the Vigil liturgy nor should it be overshadowed in its solemnity by the eucharist of Holy Thursday evening. Before being welcomed to the supper of the Lord's body and blood, the newly initiated share for the first time in the faithful's holy kiss of peace.

EASTER VIGIL CHECKLIST

This list is offered to bring order to some of the Vigil's ceremonial complexities. It needs adaptation to the local situation and should be used together with *The Sacristy Manual* (pages 215–17) and *To Crown the Year* (pages 104–17).

Items to be in place:

- Fire, matches, wood
- Paschal candle, stylus, nails, incense
- Censer, charcoal (one or two at base of fire), incense, tongs
- Wooden tapers to light paschal candle from fire
- Sacramentary or presider's book
- Small penlight
- People's candles (bobeches, windguards)
- Water container, for emergency
- Aspergillum and bucket (or branches and bowls)
- Holy-water-font fillers
- Chrism
- Baptismal candles
- Towels for baptized and for floor around font
- Baptismal garments
- Exsultet music in suitably decorated book or on scroll
- Hymnals where needed
- Bells for the Gloria
- Wine, chalice, cups for assembly's communion, purificators
- Bread and additional patens for distribution
- Music for eucharistic prayer; sheet for concelebrant

SERVICE OF LIGHT

■ DARKNESS: The Pastoral Introduction reiterates the very clear instructions of all the liturgical books. The Easter Vigil takes place at night: after nightfall, before daybreak.

The power of darkness is to be experienced before the light of the Risen One can be experienced fully in the contrast of the Easter candle. Almanac tables and weather services need to be consulted to determine what is the earliest time to begin the Vigil.

- **EASTER FIRE:** What: *Rogus*, in Latin, correctly translated in the Pastoral Introduction as "bonfire." Why: To "draw the liturgical assembly together" by its "warmth and light" (PI, 3). Where: On a lawn, if a thick tarp is put down and ten inches of sand laid over it, or a large trough for watering livestock can be used to contain the wood, sand or cinder blocks underneath for insulation. Who: Everyone meets around the fire, which may be lighted even before most arrive. Bad weather (short of blizzard or downpour) should not deter us. Those who do not gather outside should be asked to move to the sides of the church, so as not to impede the procession in the center aisle. And the church remains in total darkness.

- **SAFETY CONSIDERATIONS:** Dried hardwood is safer than pine or quickly consumed woods. Consult the fire department or fire marshal's office. Many communities have regulations about fires, even if set up on private property. But officials are generally respectful of people's religious customs. On the other hand, no responsible pastor would allow anyone to strip away one of the central instruments of this service of light: the lighted candle in every person's hand. Ushers should be alert and prepared to snuff out a fire using a thick blanket. One should be kept on hand along with fire extinguishers.

- **BLESSING THE FIRE AND LIGHTING THE CANDLE:** A paschal candle made of wax, new every year and sufficiently large, is mandatory. Artificial candles with inserts and liquid wax in a plastic cylinder are prohibited. Order:
  - No cross or other candles are carried.
  - Unlit paschal candle is carried by acolyte or deacon. Deacon may also read introduction, so this may determine who candle bearer is.
  - Censer bearer carries empty censer.
  - ICEL's revision suggests, as the liturgical greeting: "Grace, mercy and peace in abundance from our loving God and Christ Jesus our Lord be with you all." In older usage, no greeting is given.
  - Deacon, presider or concelebrant gives instruction, using sacramentary text or similar words.
  - Fire is blessed.
  - Paschal candle is prepared and lit.

- **PROCESSION:** The censer is prepared by lighting coals from the fire and adding incense at this point. Because it takes time for the coals to be ready for incense, the charcoal can be placed in the fire before the liturgy begins and removed at the appropriate time with long-handled tongs.

  The deacon carries the candle high, preceded only by censer bearer, followed immediately by presider: These three lead the whole procession into church. Everyone's candles should be lit early in this procession. Careful planning with several acolytes passing the flame avoids lengthy delays.

  The one who will chant the Exsultet (perhaps wearing a cope) carries a fine book or scroll with the text and music. If a deacon is to sing the Exsultet, an assisting minister becomes the book or scroll bearer.

  If the fire is some distance from church, use a glass windguard for the candle. People's candles can be lit before the procession if windguards are provided. Paper cones are available; Orthodox church goods stores offer red plastic windguards designed to be placed on the substantial candles used in their processions.

  "Light of Christ! Thanks be to God!" is the processional song. It may be augmented by fuller acclamations in honor of Christ. One recommendation is to intersperse verses of the classic evening hymn "O Radiant Light" *(Phos hilaron)* set to the chant "Jesu, dulcis memoria" between these brief acclamations.

  Coordination of movement, music and ministers cannot be left to chance. Be sure the acclamation pitch is clear and matches the key of the hymn. If each acclamation or hymn verse will be sung at a higher pitch, carefully prepare and rehearse transitions.

  The candle is honored with incense when placed in the stand, normally near the ambo where the Exsultet is sung. The censer bearer stands nearby. If the deacon sings the Exsultet, he asks for and receives the presider's blessing in a low voice.

- **EASTER PROCLAMATION:** Despite the suggestion in the sacramentary, do not turn on the electric lights until after the Exsultet. Some parishes, in fact, conduct the whole liturgy of the word by candlelight, turning the lights on only at the Gloria.

  Robert Batastini's adaptation of the Exsultet (GIA, G-2351) is a smooth working of the English text to the traditional chant melody for single cantor. Christopher Walker has a setting for cantor and SATB choir, with assembly's concluding Amens (St. Thomas More, OCP, 7175). J. Michael Thompson's arrangement of the sacramentary setting is available from World Library (#5716) and well worth exploring. Everett Frese's setting (Pastoral Press) also respects the integrity of the text for cantor, successfully incorporates the assembly in brief opening and closing sections.

MARCH

LITURGY OF THE WORD

- CHILDREN AND THE LITURGY OF THE WORD: Tonight's assembly is the gathering of the whole church, including children and the parents of infants to be baptized. No separation of age groups is desirable.

- NUMBER OF READINGS: "Time is unimportant on this holy night, haste is unseemly and abbreviation of the liturgy of the word is unnecessary" (PI, 3).

To "sustain the attention of all," try "a variety of ways of proclaiming the lessons and singing the responses" (PI, 3). Though one well-prepared lector proclaiming a long reading all the way through is quite effective, consider the approach suggested for Lent's lengthy Johannine gospels. The Genesis and Exodus readings lend themselves to reading by several lectors stationed throughout the worship space, accompanied by acolytes if the liturgy of the word is conducted by candlelight. If the long form of the creation story is chosen, chant "Evening came and morning followed, and God saw that all this was good" after the proclamation of each day of creation.

See LTP's *Triduum Sourcebook* with Easter Vigil readings from the various Christian traditions, if your parish is ready to add to the nine readings in the lectionary (e.g., Noah and the flood, strangely omitted from the current Roman lectionary). If the parish has done minimal readings in the past, gradually restore the full celebration by adding one reading each year until the parish regains the riches of this full liturgy of the word, by which "the character of this night as a vigil is demonstrated most clearly" (PI, 3).

- PSALMODY: "The faithful reflect calmly on each reading by singing the responsorial psalm, by silence and by listening and responding to the prayer proclaimed by the priest" (PI, 3). A wide variety of settings is available to provide a worthy rendering of the Vigil's psalmody.

The canticle response to Exodus is incorporated into the reading. The lector could end the reading with the previous line: "Then Moses and the Israelites sang this song to the Lord." The lector turns, at this point, in the direction of the cantor. This great song of the Israelites must be rhythmic and lively, and may be accompanied by percussion instruments. Tambourine lends an Eastern flare.

For the response to Isaiah 55, see Robert Batastini's "You will draw water" (GIA, G-2443), with a handbell accompaniment effectively suggesting water imagery.

- GLORIA: The sung Gloria points toward the proclamation of the gospel of the resurrection and "should not be so elaborate that it overshadows what it is meant to introduce" (PI, 3). A Gloria with a repeated refrain is an appropriate choice, especially where there are many visitors. Some of these are by: Peter Jones, "Glory to God" (OCP); Richard Proulx, "Gloria for Eastertime," based on "O filii et filiae" (GIA, G-3086 or choral version G-3087); C. Alexander Peloquin, "Gloria of the bells" (*Worship*, #258).

- DURING THE GLORIA: Candles on or near the altar are lit. If all the lights in the church were not put on after the Exsultet, they are turned on now. Church bells are rung now, as on Holy Thursday. The procedure of the two nights should parallel each other, as a public announcement of good news to the neighborhood.

The worship place may be decorated at this point. (See Mazar, pages 111–112). A "decoration procession" of flowers and other items is the most orderly way. Ask volunteers and ministers for the Triduum, certain groups (confirmation class or altar guild) to come to a brief rehearsal sometime on Holy Saturday after the flowers are delivered. Participants can help place the flowers (and other things) where they should end up at the Gloria, assign zones to different clusters of volunteers, then bring the materials to a side room (or rear pew). During the last reading and psalm before the Gloria, bearers quietly and unobtrusively join in their clusters near their materials and form one or more double lines. As the Gloria begins, the groups each go in procession to the correct places for their flowers or material.

- GOSPEL ACCLAMATION: An ancient custom, revived in the *Ceremonial of Bishops*, says that before the gospel acclamation, "the deacon or the reader goes to the bishop [presbyter] and says to him, '[Most] Reverend Father, I bring you a message of great joy, the message of 'Alleluia''" (*Ceremonial of Bishops*, #352). If this ancient custom is followed it must be proclaimed or even chanted clearly and well. The minister chanting may do so *recto tono* and then intone the solemn, once-a-year only, three-times repeated Alleluia (see the official Mode VIII chant, *Worship*, #826). All repeat the Alleluia each time on a higher pitch. The cantor then sings the verses of Psalm 118. All sing the same Alleluia after each verse. Other very effective settings of this psalm can be found in many resources.

The gospel acclamation must be selected carefully and executed in light of tonight's full procession: incense, perhaps banners, gospel book held high. No candles are carried tonight because the Easter candle is the symbol of light, enthroned most appropriately near the ambo from which the Exsultet and gospel are both proclaimed. Choir, bells, brass, organ, with music that does not require the assembly to have heads buried in hymnals, will best welcome the Alleluia back into our worship.

Other possibilities for the re-introduction of the Alleluia include "Celtic Alleluia" (*Gather*; OCP, 7106) with handbells, if possible; "Easter Alleluia" (*Gather*), based on "O filii et filiae," verse by Marty Haugen; Richard Proulx's "Alleluia and Psalm for Easter" (GIA, G-1965), specifically written for this night, with familiar three-fold Mode VI Alleluia (congregation, choir, cantor, organ and handbells) and Donald Reagan's "Fanfare and Alleluia" (WLP, 7959).

The gospel passage, or at least the greeting and conclusion, may be chanted.

■ HOMILY: Any preacher would be overwhelmed at being called on to offer reflections in a context of actions and mysteries as powerful and awesome as those of the Vigil. See the paschal homilies in the Office of Readings through the Easter octave. Look also at LTP's *Triduum Sourcebook* for John Chrysostom's classic Vigil homily, and other excellent reflections, as well as at its companion volume, *Easter Sourcebook*.

INITIATION AT THE VIGIL

The liturgy of baptism takes one of several forms, depending on the parish situation.

- *Parishes with elect to be baptized and candidates to be received into the full communion of the Catholic Church:* This outline is followed in the commentary that follows and in the *Rite of Christian Initiation of Adults* (RCIA), appendix I, 4. Some parishes of these also baptize infants at the same assembly.

- *Parishes with elect to be baptized but without candidates for reception into full communion:* Follow RCIA, part I and elements commented on in the following section. Note that these are arranged in a different order. See the note on page 145. Some of these parishes also baptize infants at the Vigil.

- *Parishes with only infants to be baptized and with candidates for full communion:* Same outline as previously for parishes with both elect and candidates. Note rubrics for infant baptism at the vigil at #28 of the *Rite of Baptism for Children* (RBC).

- *Parishes with only infants to be baptized and with no candidates to be received into full communion:* Follow the RBC, noting the rubric at #28. Although that rubric notes that the presentation of the lighted candle is omitted, it may be appropriate to keep it.

- *Parishes without baptisms but with candidates to be received into full communion:* Use RCIA, appendix I, 4, beginning with #580.

- *No one to be baptized or received:* Follow the order given in the sacramentary. The renewal of baptismal promises may be enhanced with some of the following elements of the rite of baptism.

Initiation: Celebration of Baptism

■ PRESENTATION: The RCIA outlines three methods of presentation for those to be baptized (#219, 568). This presentation is connected with the procession to the baptistry. Almost every parish can use form B, regardless of the placement of the font. The summoning of the elect and godparents (infants and parents) is done solemnly, with names called out loudly and slowly.

■ PROCESSION TO THE BAPTISTRY: Those to be baptized process to the baptistry, following the paschal candle carried by the deacon or an acolyte. The elect, godparents and parents of infants are followed by the deacon, presider and assisting ministers. If the baptistry is outside the main assembly area, others can process as well. This procession should take a long route through the church to the baptismal font.

■ LITANY OF THE SAINTS: This chant accompanies the procession, calling those gone before us to accompany this most important part of the community's pilgrimage. Names may be added to the standard litany (see RCIA, #221, 570; sacramentary, #41): the titular of the church (if saint or blessed), patron saints of the area (diocese, city), patrons of those to be baptized and received.

Several settings of the litany are available: John Becker's "Litany of the Saints" (OCP); David Haas' "Litany of the Saints" in *Who Calls You by Name*, vol. I; Matthew Nagi's setting, #A40 in *We Celebrate*, vol. 2, cycle A, and Paul Page's setting (#165) in volume 1 of the same resource.

■ INVITATION TO PRAYER: In form B (RCIA, #219 or 568), when all are at the font and the litany ended, the invitatory (RCIA, #220 or 569) follows.

■ BLESSING OF WATER: This blessing may include repeated sung acclamations, even Alleluias. David Haas' "Blessing of the Water" (*Who Calls You by Name*, vol. II (GIA) with the "Springs of water" refrain that concludes it, is set to the familiar "O filii et filiae" chant and is learned easily.

By tradition, the candle is plunged into the font once or three times, an archetypal symbol that needs no explanation. If the font is visible from the assembly area, keep the sight lines clear.

The blessing ends with an acclamation by the people. The suggested text is "Springs of water." Suitable music at this point includes:

- Thomas Savory, "Springs of water "(GIA, G-2549); cantor verses use Psalm 118
- Donald Fellows, "Springs of water" (GIA, G-3639); cantor verses use text from the sprinkling rite, "I saw water flowing . . ."
- Mike Hay, "Springs of water" (#108, *We Celebrate,* volume 1)
- Richard Proulx, "Rite of Sprinkling" (GIA, G-3097)

■ PROFESSION OF FAITH: This profession of faith is at the heart of baptism, the immediate prelude to the water bath.

Follow the rite closely; ignore the options given "if there are a great many to be baptized." While the rite may be done with a group or individually, questions of profession of faith are asked of each individual, who is then baptized immediately. Parents and godparents of infants to be baptized are then addressed and questioned as in the RBC (#58, 60–61).

■ BAPTISM: Immersion is the preferred method of baptism in the Roman Catholic Church. If the permanent font does not allow for that, consider temporary arrangements until full renovation is possible.

As each person rises from the waters, the acclamation is sung by the assembly. Keep the assembly free to watch the ritual and sing an acclamation by using the "call and response" form: cantor sings the line, assembly repeats it. Some suggestions:

- Howard Hughes, "You have put on Christ" (GIA, G-2283)
- Arthur Hutchings, "Rejoice, you newly baptized" (ICEL Resource Collection, GIA, G-2514)
- Marty Haugen, "Song over the waters" *(Gather)*
- Lynn Trapp, "Rite of Christian Initiation of Adults" (Morning Star MSM-80-907A)
- John Olivier, "You have put on Christ" *(People's Mass Book)*

A lively sung Alleluia also works well. Whatever is chosen should be the "standard" acclamation, each time the community celebrates baptism, at the Vigil and throughout the year.

■ EXPLANATORY RITES: Infants are anointed with chrism after the prayer (RCIA, #228 or 577; or RBC, #62).

The newly baptized (adults and children) are dressed in their baptismal garments. A room for parents to diaper and dress infants should be prepared with enough dressing tables for the number of babies to be dressed (diapers, powder, lotions could be left there by parents before the liturgy). Separate rooms for adult men and women should be prepared with extra towels.

Godparents assist adult neophytes in drying off as they emerge from the font and in robing while other professions of faith and baptisms continue. The words at the robing (RCIA, #229 or 578) may be omitted, or said by parents and godparents as the newly baptized are clothed.

The presentation of the baptismal candle is described in the RCIA, #230 or 579. The presider and godparents pass light to the neophytes. Plain small paschal candles, with candle followers, make good baptismal candles, if the parish paschal candle is sufficiently larger. Some candlemakers offer smaller versions of their paschal candle designs for this purpose (e.g., Marklin Candle Design, PO Box 1001, Nashua NH 03061; 603-595-2981).

Parishes with baptisms but without receptions into full communion should read "Initiation: Rites after Baptism when There Are No Receptions," page 145 before the next three sections of commentary.

INITIATION: RENEWAL OF BAPTISMAL PROMISES

■ RENEWAL: Baptismal promises are spoken from the font, and the water for the sprinkling comes from the font. If the font is in a separate place, renewal follows a procession back to the assembly area. Candidates for reception join in the renewal at this point (RCIA, #580), so that their reception flows from it.

All stand. The candles of the assembly are relit (neophytes may share the flame from their baptismal candles). The renewal formula may be sung, to avoid the anticlimactic, bland "I do" to momentous questions!

When renewal is completed, water is drawn from the font (if it has not already been brought from the font). During the sprinkling or signing, parents and godparents of newly baptized infants bring them back to their places in the assembly.

■ SPRINKLING: This important ritual gesture should be as full as possible. People should feel the water. Assisting ministers may sprinkle side aisles while the presider takes the main section of the assembly. Branches from evergreen bushes or trees make excellent sprinkling implements. Tie several together to form a full, generous surface. Tape the stems at the bottom to form a handle and to keep sap off people's hands. Colorful ribbons may be added. Each person who sprinkles might be accompanied by an assistant who carries the bowl of water.

During the sprinkling, acolytes take water to all the holy water fonts in church.

- SIGNING: Instead of sprinkling, everyone may come to the font (if it is in the worship space) or to bowls filled with water drawn from the font. People may approach the font or bowls in lines from all sides and sign themselves or others with water.

- MUSIC FOR SPRINKLING OR SIGNING: Music used at end of blessing of water (see page 143) may be repeated here, unifying the use of water tonight. Richard Hillert's "Lord Jesus, from your wounded side" *(Worship)* and Michael Joncas' adaptation of the Baptist hymn "O Healing River" (GIA) would serve well.

INITIATION: CELEBRATION OF RECEPTION

- PROCESSION: If the font is in a separate building, the procession occurs before the renewal of promises. If neophytes and ministers are in the main church building, they now return in procession from the font to the front of the main worship space. Following the paschal candle, the neophytes carry their lit baptismal candles.

The RCIA, #584, suggests a hymn at this time. The *Ceremonial of Bishops* (#366) suggests "You have put on Christ." Another appropriate text is Michael Saward's "Baptized in water" found in *Worship*. The Taizé ostinato "Beati in domo Domini," is another good choice, particularly if the procession is not lengthy.

- ACT OF RECEPTION: The rite of reception (RCIA, #584) is brief but solemn and deliberate. Neophytes and godparents should be nearby but not blocking the assembly's vision of this act. Those being received, and sponsors, stand so that the congregation can see their faces. Consider concluding the receptions with a repeat of an earlier acclamation. An Alleluia is appropriate.

INITIATION: CELEBRATION OF CONFIRMATION

If there are both neophytes and newly received to be confirmed, use the introduction at RCIA, #589. Confirmation is the same both for newly baptized and those received into the church. They are not anointed in any particular order.

The music to be sung during the laying-on of hands, prayer and chrismation must be chosen carefully. A Taizé ostinato ("Veni, Sancte Spiritus" or "Confitemini Domino") serves well; the song may be continued quietly or be hummed during prayer. Christopher Walker's "Veni, Sancte Spiritus" (St. Thomas More/OCP, 7116) also is effective. The refrain repeats the text several times and is graceful and easily singable; omit overlaid cantor verses for this occasion, unless the number to be confirmed is large. The traditional "Come, Holy Ghost" may, of course, be used.

INITIATION: RITES AFTER BAPTISM WHEN THERE ARE NO RECEPTIONS

If there are baptisms but no receptions, the procession from the font to the front of the assembly takes place after the explanatory rites (RCIA, #231). Confirmation follows (#233), using musical suggestions highlighted previously. The renewal of baptismal promises (#237) leads to signing or sprinkling of all, as described above. During the signing or sprinkling, the neophytes return to their places in the assembly.

INITIATION: GENERAL INTERCESSIONS

For the first time the neophytes, now members of the order of the faithful, join in the church's priestly ministry of intercession for the needs to the world. All the languages of the community should be represented in the petitions.

LITURGY OF THE EUCHARIST

- PREPARATION RITES: The neophytes bring up the bread and wine for the eucharistic meal in which they will share for the first time.

After the lengthy rites of initiation, the choir and musicians may show their artistry by offering the community any selection from the wide array of Easter anthems and instrumental music, with full instrumentation restored for Easter.

- EUCHARISTIC PRAYER: Preface of Easter I includes the words "on this Easter night." Eucharistic Prayer I has several inclusions:

  - "Remember . . ." from ritual Mass of baptism if there were baptisms (post godparents' names into the sacramentary)

  - "In union . . ." for Vigil and octave (printed under the prayer in the sacramentary)

  - "Father, accept . . ." from the ritual Mass of baptism if there were baptisms *or* for the Vigil and octave (printed under the prayer in the sacramentary) if there were no baptisms. The two versions of this insert start the same, but the initiation text is richer.

- COMMUNION RITE: "Before saying "This is the Lamb of God," the presider may briefly remind the neophytes of the preeminence of the eucharist, which is the climax of their initiation and the center of the whole Christian life" (RCIA, #243). A similar note for the newly received appears at #594.

Music for the communion procession might include Tom Parker's "Praise the Lord, my soul" (GIA, *Gather* or G-2395); a setting of Psalm 34 with the refrain "Taste and see the goodness of the Lord"; Paul Hillenbrand's "Eucharistic Litany" (WLP, 5200); "I received the living God" (*Worship* and GIA, G-3071; choral setting is one step higher than hymnal) by Richard Proulx (a beautiful concertato version, by Ellen Doerrfeld-Coman, is available from World Library, #7215); Taizé's "Eat this bread" (GIA, G-2840); Michael Joncas' "Take and eat" (GIA), especially if it was sung on Thursday evening.

CONCLUDING RITE

The dismissal with double Alleluia might be sung to the Gregorian melody associated with it from time immemorial. Note that this distinctive dismissal is sung at every day of the octave, at Mass and at the Liturgy of the Hours, including next Sunday and again on Pentecost. The Episcopal Church prescribes this dismissal throughout the entire Fifty Days, a tradition Roman Catholics should consider adopting.

BLESSING OF FOOD AND FOOD FOR ALL

The blessing of food on Holy Saturday is no longer practiced, because it predates the revision of Holy Week and hearkens back to a time when "Lent ended" at noon on Holy Saturday.

The *Book of Blessings* (chapter 54) provides texts and outlines for tonight's blessing of food for the first meal of Easter. See the discussion of this custom on page 147.

If Easter eggs are distributed or a parish Easter breakfast held tonight, include these foods in the blessing. This breakfast, a hallowed tradition among the Orthodox and many ethnic groups, is a grand celebration for all the baptized, and a kind of "reception" that welcomes the neophytes to share Easter joy for the first time as fully initiated members of the household of faith. See the recipe for "Pascha" in the revised *Triduum Sourcebook*, page 477.

Easter water should be available for people to take home tonight and tomorrow. Easter eggs (and fresh flowers) may be given to all as they leave or during breakfast. The eggs may have been colored at the catechetical assembly of children earlier or prepared and distributed by the candidates to be confirmed during Easter's Fifty Days.

#41 [42] Evening: #46 [47]
white

30 Easter Sunday

The joy of the resurrection, proclaimed and celebrated during the Easter Vigil, overflows into the Masses of Easter day. The Easter candle is alight in the sanctuary, Alleluias are sung. It is important to sustain the celebration of the resurrection during this festival day, so that its place as the last day of the Triduum is evident (ICEL Pastoral Introduction: Easter Sunday).

■ SUSTAINING THE CELEBRATION: Accomplish this through a schedule that gradually moves the parish toward including a number of festive celebrations through the course of the day. First among these are Morning Prayer and Paschal Baptismal Vespers in addition to Easter Sunday Mass(es). Other possibilities are suggested below.

MORNING PRAYER

This is the Catholic version of the "sunrise service" popular among the many Protestant churches that have yet to recover the Easter Vigil. A growing number of parishes have found that a surprising number of folks welcome the opportunity to greet Easter dawn with Morning Prayer or at least to celebrate Morning Prayer at some point on Easter morning. This early morning celebration may be a good ecumenical prayer, if the community would like to join with non-Catholics in celebrating the risen Christ who is Lord of us all. See GIA's *Worship: Liturgy of the Hours*, leader's edition.

MORNING MASS

While elements proper to the Easter Vigil should not be repeated, it is appropriate for the faithful to renew their baptismal promises at Masses on Easter day. . . . This renewal replaces the profession of faith and is accompanied by the sprinkling of the people with water from the baptismal font. A song having a baptismal character is sung (ICEL Pastoral Introduction: Easter Sunday).

MARCH

- **INTRODUCTORY RITES:** The forthcoming revision of the American edition of the sacramentary will suggest adapting the Orthodox/Episcopal Easter greeting:

   V. Alleluia, Christ is risen.
   R. The Lord is risen indeed. Alleluia.

   If this would require practice or an announcement (a real mood-breaker after a joyous gathering anthem) the presider could simply add an Easter touch to a standard greeting: "Alleluia! The Lord is truly risen! His grace and peace be with you all!"

   The sprinkling takes place at the renewal of baptismal promises after the homily, so water is not used in the introductory rites. The Gloria follows the greeting immediately.

- **LITURGY OF THE WORD:** The Acts of the Apostles replaces the readings from the First Testament scriptures for the Great Fifty Days of Easter.

   The Eastertime responsorial psalm may begin this morning. Throughout Eastertime the antiphon for the responsorial psalm can always be Alleluia.

   The beloved sequence hymn, "Victimae Paschali Laudes," follows the reading from Paul. Some settings: chant, Mode I, in Latin and English translation by Peter Scagnelli (*Worship*, #837); Richard Proulx (arr.), "Easter Sequence" (GIA, G-3088), lively, rhythmic setting of chant with congregational refrain. Ann Colleen Dohns has set both Easter and Pentcost sequences with responses for the assembly (WLP, 5718).

- **GOSPEL ACCLAMATION AND PROCESSION:** Today's gospel procession should be in proportion to the day's solemnity and the greater-than-usual size of the assembly.

- **HOMILY:** Gracious hospitality and a real desire to share the community's joy with anyone and everyone who has chosen to join us at worship: This was John Chrysostom's approach (see *Triduum Sourcebook*).

- **RENEWAL OF BAPTISMAL PROMISES:** Repeat the Vigil's procedure: several buckets and sprinklers, or instead of sprinkling, the entire congregation comes to the font for ritual signing with the Easter water. Buckets or bowls (if used) should be filled from the font for this rite.

- **LITURGY OF THE EUCHARIST:** Preface of Easter I is prescribed. Eucharistic Prayer I has two inserts.

   Use the Eastertime acclamations, which debuted at the Vigil.

- **CONCLUDING RITE:** As on Christmas, beware of seasonal greetings and gratitude that mean well but make it sound as if "the priests and staff thank you for helping them with Mass!"

   Use the distinctive Easter dismissal with double paschal Alleluia, sung to Gregorian melody. See note on page 146.

- **HOSPITALITY:** A spring flower may be given to all as they leave Mass today. Easter eggs, too, are a traditional gift with sacred significance.

   Parishes that have a weekly coffee hour should keep the custom today, despite the crowds and even if many will be going out for an Easter brunch.

   An Easter egg hunt can be held for adults and children alike, either after Mass or in the afternoon before Paschal Vespers.

BLESSING FOODS AT THE END OF MASS

Blessing Easter food is not simply the pious custom of some ethnic groups but a part of Christian tradition that should be part of a parish's liturgical life. It provides a fine and prayerful link between the Lord's table and the household meal. Remind people toward the end of Lent to bring baskets of food as well as children's Easter baskets to any Mass on Easter, including the Vigil. Tables may be set up for the baskets, and ushers should be prepared to direct people to place their baskets on these tables, especially at the Vigil when people arrive in the dark. Or household members may keep baskets with them in their places and raise them up for the blessing prayer and sprinkling.

According to the *Book of Blessings*, the Order of the Blessing of Food for the First Meal of Easter takes place after the prayer after communion (#1723) or before post-Mass refreshments. The water sprinkled on the food baskets is drawn from the font.

MIDDAY PRAYER AND EASTER DINNER

Midday Prayer helps the parish to observe the entire Triduum ritually, "sustaining the spirit of celebration" that should mark this whole solemnity. Some suggestions for celebration:

- Introduction: V. Christ our Light. R. Thanks be to God.
- Hymn
- Psalmody: Psalm 118
- Scripture: Ephesians 2:4–6
- Response: "This is the day"
- Prayer: of Easter Day in sacramentary or conclude with blessing of food

MARCH

Alternatively, the blessing of food may be celebrated on its own (*Book of Blessings*, #1707–1719). This blessing is especially meaningful if the parish holds a festive Easter dinner for homeless or elderly folks, for anyone who would otherwise eat alone and for those who prefer to eat their meal and sing their songs in a community bigger than the domestic one.

AFTERNOON MASS

Parishes with a regular Sunday afternoon or evening Mass should probably have one today, too. There is a special gospel for this evening (#46) [47]. There is a hymn based on the Emmaus gospel in *Worship*, "Daylight Fades" (#448), which may be appropriate.

PASCHAL VESPERS

To conclude the sacred Triduum, Evening Prayer may be celebrated solemnly together with the newly baptized (ICEL Pastoral Introduction to Easter Sunday).

The restoration of "Baptismal Vespers" to complete the Triduum is recommended in several official liturgical documents: the ICEL Pastoral Introduction, the *Circular Letter* (#98), the *Ceremonial of Bishops* (#371) and the *General Instruction of the Liturgy of the Hours* (#213). This is the traditional and appropriate way for the community and its neophytes to continue delighting in the joy of the Vigil, a kind of reconvening to celebrate after catching our breath!

This liturgy is stational: Its various components are celebrated in different locations ("stations") in the church complex. The pattern is that of early and medieval Christians who, celebrating this Vespers at their cathedrals, went from the eucharistic space to the baptismal space to the chrismation space. A suggested order:

- Gathering: Assembly gathers near the paschal candle.
- Service of Light: Assembly's candles and all church candles are lit from the paschal candle.
- Opening dialogue: V. Christ our light. R. Thanks be to God.
- Hymn: "At the Lamb's high feast"
- Thanksgiving for light, sung by cantor or presider. For Easter texts: see GIA's *Praise God in Song* or *Worship: Liturgy of the Hours* (Leader's Edition). The assembly's candles may be extinguished as the lights needed for the psalmody are turned on.
- Psalms: Sunday, Evening Prayer II, Week I
- During the canticle from Revelation, the congregational Alleluia is repeated as cantors sing verses, assembly processes to font: incense bearer, minister with paschal candle and presider lead. Take the longest route, preferably that used to and from the font last night.
- Depending on the size and location of the baptistry, all remain there until after the baptismal commemoration or until the end of the service.
- Reading: Hebrews 10:12–14 or Emmaus gospel
- A patristic selection from Easter octave texts in the *Liturgy of the Hours* may be read, *or* brief homily on symbols of Easter, *or* forgo preaching, beyond patristic words, and enjoy a brief moment of silent prayer and reflection.
- Sung response to reading as at Morning Prayer: "This is the day"
- Prayer over blessed Easter water (adapt RCIA, #222 D or E); or rite of sprinkling, form C, sacramentary
- All approach the font to sign themselves or each other while all sing the antiphon as at the blessing of water at the Vigil.
- Canticle of Mary (Magnificat): sung with proper antiphon, while all are honored with incense. Procession to the altar may take place before or during this canticle.
- Intercessions from *Liturgy of the Hours*
- Lord's Prayer
- Concluding prayer of Easter Day
- Solemn blessing
- Dismissal: Easter tone with traditional double Alleluia
- Closing hymn suggestion: "Come ye faithful, raise the strain" (*Worship*, #456) or "The day of resurrection" (*The Hymnal 1982*, #210)

TEXTS FOR THE RECEPTION OF THE HOLY OILS

The "Order for the Reception of the Holy Oils," now recommended for use at the Evening Mass of the Lord's Supper on Holy Thursday, will appear in future editions of the sacramentary. Its ceremonial is described on page 129. These texts are to be adapted as needed (e.g., the presenter may proclaim the entire formulary).

Oil of the Sick

PRESENTER OF THE OIL OF THE SICK:
The oil of the sick.

PRIEST:
May the sick who are anointed with this oil
experience the compassion of Christ and his saving love, in body, mind and soul.

Oil of Catechumens

PRESENTER OF THE OIL OF CATECHUMENS:
The oil of catechumens.

PRIEST:
Through anointing with this oil may our catechumens
who are preparing for the saving waters of baptism
be strengthened by Christ to resist the power of Satan
and reject evil in all its forms.

Holy Chrism

PRESENTER OF THE HOLY CHRISM:
The holy chrism.

PRIEST:
Through anointing with this perfumed chrism
may children and adults, who are baptized and confirmed,
presbyters and bishops, who are ordained,
and assemblies, whose altars and churches are dedicated,
receive the gracious gift of the Holy Spirit.
—© USCC

HYMNS FOR THE LITURGY OF THE HOURS

These hymn texts may be sung to any appropriate Long Meter (88 88) tune.

GOOD FRIDAY

Midday Prayer

"Crux mundi benedictio"
Peter Damian (+ 1072)
Liturgia Horarum, 1971
Translation and verse 3: Peter J. Scagnelli, 1992

1. O Cross, the world's true blessing sign,
   redemption sure and hope divine!
   Grim standard once of hell's despair,
   now heaven's portal bright and fair.

2. The Victim lifted up on you
   unto himself all peoples drew;
   While this world's Prince who sought his life
   himself was conquered in that strife.

3. To God the blessed Three-in-One
   be praise while endless ages run;
   And in this Pasch be glorified
   the Lord victorious, crucified.

   Amen.

—*© Peter J. Scagnelli. All rights reserved. Permission to reprint this text is given to users of* Sourcebook 1997.

HOLY SATURDAY

Morning Prayer

"Christe, caelorum Domine"
Author unknown (5th or 6th century)
vv. 1, 4, 5 (in Latin and below)
"Tibi, Redemptor omnium"
Author unknown (5th or 6th century)
vv. 2, 4 in Latin (below in English as 2 and 3)
Liturgia Horarum, 1971
Tr. Peter J. Scagnelli, 1992

1. Christ Jesus, Savior of the world,
   and heaven's Lord enthroned on high,
   Your death upon the cross set free
   those doomed by death's decree to die.

2. Your cross destroyed the deadly force
   our age-old Foe was strong to wield:
   That cross, faith's banner, now we bear,
   your Sign upon our foreheads sealed.

3. Descending to death's dark abode
   where dwelt just souls from ages past,
   You led them forth, a vict'ry march,
   to glory in new life at last.

4. Their ransom paid in your own flesh,
   from endless vigil giv'n release:
   With you they rose to know in heav'n
   eternal praise, enduring peace.

5. Count us among that countless throng
   from ev'ry land, of ev'ry race:
   A kingdom for the Father formed
   and hallowed by the Spirit's grace.

   Amen.

—© *Peter J. Scagnelli. All rights reserved. Permission to reprint this text is given to users of* Sourcebook 1997.

Midday Prayer

Based on *Missale Romanum,* Holy Saturday, rubric, and *Office of Readings,* second reading, ancient homily for Great and Holy Saturday
Peter J. Scagnelli, 1993

1. O Jesus, Lord of life and death,
   with peaceful hearts we come to pray,
   While stillness solemn and sublime
   reigns over all the earth this day.

2. The church keeps watch beside your tomb
   throughout this day of quiet pray'r,
   Until the paschal vigil bids us
   rise reborn, your life to share.

3. In this, the Sacred Triduum,
   we praise you, Holy Trinity,
   For Christ our Pasch is sacrificed
   to give us life eternally.

   Amen.

—© *Peter J. Scagnelli. All rights reserved. Permission to reprint this text is given to users of* Sourcebook 1997.

Evening Prayer

"Auctor salutis unice"
Author unknown (10th century)
Liturgia Horarum, 1971
Tr. Peter J. Scagnelli, 1992

1. Sole Author of salvation's grace,
   Redeemer of a world brought low,
   Upon us, who acclaim you King,
   the glory of the cross bestow.

2. True life, you ransomed life itself;
   your death became our death's defeat;
   The devil's work you overthrew,
   his deadly mission of deceit.

3. Devoted friends laid you to rest
   within the tomb's tranquility,
   But you descended to the dead
   to grant their longed-for liberty.

4. Now at the Father's right enthroned,
   you reign, O Victim glorified,
   Hear pray'rs poured forth by those redeemed
   in blood that flowed from your pierced side:

5. Grant us to follow in your steps,
   walking the pathway you have shown,
   confronting every evil force
   armed with your mighty cross alone!

6. To Father, Son and Paraclete
   coequal praise your servants give,
   And by the vict'ry of the cross
   life everlasting hope to live.

   Amen.

—© *Peter J. Scagnelli. All rights reserved. Permission to reprint this text is given to users of* Sourcebook 1997.

NOTES

NOTES

EASTER

period of postbaptismal catechesis. For all the faithful, it is a waiting for the ultimate completion of the paschal mystery when the Spirit will unite the peoples and nations on earth to proclaim the glory of God with one voice and one song.

Perspective on Eastertime

THE first fact to keep in perspective about Eastertime is that it can be a difficult season to keep in perspective! For one thing, Eastertime follows Lent, a season of intense and well-focused preparation. After such an extensive commitment of energy, there follows, inevitably, a sense of relief that makes immediate and subsequent refocusing extremely difficult. Moreover, Lent is a season to which we all bring a well-established institutional memory and personal history. Even when the church had no weekday lectionary (for the 400 years after Trent!), there was at least a daily lectionary for the lenten season. For the long generations during which the liturgy was, for the most part, the property of the clergy and theirs alone to "perform," Lent belonged to the individual lay person in a way that was very personal and participatory.

In contrast, what memories, institutional or personal, attach to Eastertime? Where's the focus? It is true that as a church, especially in North America, we've traditionally done some things during the Easter season. April, May and June are popular months for first communion and confirmation, even ordination and marriage. The Pastoral Introduction points out the suitability of the sacraments of initiation occurring during this time for those baptized in infancy (PI, 2). But was it Eastertime that led us to choose these months for those sacraments — or springtime? Confirmation (and ordination) were almost like graduations — and graduations traditionally happen at this general time of the year. First communion was celebrated on Mother's Day weekend in many places, among various ethnic groups, connected usually to the crowning of a statue of the Blessed Virgin Mary. But, again, is that Eastertime at work or another ecclesial association?

Another problem with keeping Eastertime — it's just plain *long!* The "winter pascha" is of almost perfect length: four weeks of Advent preparation, the Christmas octave (or maybe its 12 days), Epiphany and the Lord's baptism. Here is a slice of time we patrons of the "short attention-span theater" can handle! But look at spring: Lent (40 days) + Triduum (3 days) + Eastertime (50 days): 93 days. That's a long time! Once we've kept a vigorous Lent and celebrated an intense Triduum, 50 days turns into an especially long period of time in which to keep an "unbroken celebration" (PI, 1). So it may help to "break it up" just a little!

■ I. EASTER: THE SOLEMNITY OF SOLEMNITIES: "The Lord of life who died reigns glorified" (Easter sequence), walks in our midst and makes himself known in the scriptures we read, the bread we break and the companions with whom we share the journey.

■ II. EASTER OCTAVE: AN EIGHT-DAY SOLEMNITY: Bringing forth the community's finest stories of discipleship's witness and our experience of the risen Lord, the church feasts the neophytes — and the faithful — on the heart of the Easter mystery.

■ III. FROM THE OCTAVE TO THE FORTIETH DAY: Christian life then is presented in memory, even as that past memory becomes a lived experience now. The church's experience of the risen Christ compels the believers to witness, which in turn brings about development and expansion. It is a time of ministry and shepherding, of becoming an inclusive community that serves in mutual and self-sacrificing love.

■ IV. NINE DAYS FROM ASCENSION TO PENTECOST: Though this is the original "novena," numbers are always relative in liturgical celebration. Differing days for Ascension will change the enumeration. No matter. The important thing is that the Spirit, already bestowed on the day of resurrection in John's gospel, is, in Luke's chronology (which gives the liturgical calendar its numbering system), particularly associated with the fiftieth day. As the season of intense resurrection celebration (octave) flowed into a season of joyful peace (the Forty Days), so these final days of Eastertime are appropriately marked by an intensification of prayer as the paschal mystery draws to its culmination.

■ V. PENTECOST: The whole cycle of Fifty Days is "the pentecost," but tradition gives this day the title in an entirely singular way. An extended vigil on Pentecost Eve appropriately marks the

beginning of this special solemnity (PI, 2). Special texts appear in this *Sourcebook* at page 177.

Purpose of the Season

LITURGICALLY, the risen Christ and "the powerful gift of the Spirit" have "been celebrated by the community without ceasing" since the initiation rites of baptism, confirmation and eucharist at the Easter Vigil (PI, 2). This experience gives the season its special sacramental identity and liturgical character. Eastertime is a time for several things.

A TIME FOR MYSTAGOGY

By the extraordinarily esoteric term, *mystagogical catechesis,* the Pastoral Introduction means this: "unpacking" the mystery of Christ's death and resurrection, not as something remembered but as something experienced, shared in, lived out.

The custom is an ancient one. The famous fourth-century pilgrim to the Holy Land, Egeria, sat in on the Easter octave mystagogy given to the neophytes and faithful in Jerusalem's Church of the Holy Sepulcher. She describes the experience:

> The newly baptized come into the Anastasis [church of the resurrection], and any of the faithful who wish to hear the mysteries. . . . The bishop relates all that has been done [at the Easter Vigil] and interprets it, and, as he does so, the applause is so loud that it can be heard outside the church. Indeed the way he expounds the mysteries and interprets them cannot fail to move his hearers (quoted in *Preaching about the Mass,* LTP, 1992, XVI-XVI).

Imagine that kind of response!

Texts and audiovisuals are explored in this "school of the Lord." Our "book" is the Sunday and weekday lectionary, a gift most immediately from Vatican II but compiled according to the traditions of East and West across the centuries. From this same gracious donor comes another treasury of words known now as the Office of Readings. In the *Liturgy of the Hours* (volume II) we find teachers without peer. Some of them are anonymous, their names lost to history, hidden with Christ in God. Others are names we should get to know: Melito of Sardis, Cyril of Jerusalem (and the others who first preached the *Jerusalem Catecheses*), Augustine of Hippo, Ambrose of Milan, John Chrysostom, Justin, Bede and a host of others.

But some of our "discussion questions" go beyond the text to focus on the sacramental choreography of this dance of life: the rites we have celebrated in saving mystery. Other focal points are the elements that have mediated Christ to us: water and oil, bread and wine, the touch of hands laid upon us, shining garments and myriad candles alight.

Like the liturgy, Eastertime's mystagogy is not something done to or for the neophytes. It is something done by "the community and the neophytes together," as we strive "to deepen [our] grasp of the paschal mystery and to make it part of [our] lives" (PI, 2). There is action and contemplation here: "meditation . . . and personal experience." And if the effort is a joint one, the positive effects are enjoyed mutually: "The community of faith helps them . . . and, in turn, is inspired by their fervor" (PI, 2).

A TIME FOR INITIATION

The Pastoral Introduction mentions specifically the appropriateness of initiation rites being associated with and celebrated during Eastertime's Fifty Days: infant baptism, confirmation of children baptized as infants, first reception of the eucharist.

In most communities it would be an easy matter, perhaps over the course of a couple of years, and with due sensitivity to local feelings, to establish or redirect parish custom in this direction. Diocesan confirmation scheduling focuses frequently on either fall or spring, according to parish request and episcopal availability. An early enough request ought to be able to secure a date within Eastertime. First communion may already be associated with a Saturday in May or with Mother's Day. Homiletic catechesis, bulletin announcements and musical selections, together with the renewal of baptismal vows around the font, can link the liturgical celebration to Easter. Scheduling should aim toward a principal Lord's Day Mass, making the event a community-wide celebration rather than a semiprivate ceremony. In any event, just as this year's elect and candidates, together with those continuing in the catechumenate, have been the object of the parish's prayerful attention, so might the youngsters preparing for these initiatory rites and their families and sponsors have pictures posted and names recommended for intercession and hospitality.

Presentation of the Season

IN seeking to capture the mood of Eastertime as succinctly as possible, the Pastoral Introduction focuses on sound and decor: "Alleluias are sung and the Easter candle stands in the midst of the assembly" (PI, 2). Consider for a moment, then, the "sounds of the season," and the "look of the season," and add to that, as *Sourcebook* has done with other seasons, our "ritual entrance" into the season's liturgies.

MUSIC

"Let our joyful voices resound this night! Let God's people shake these walls with shouts of praise!" (*Exsultet,* revised translation) Let our instruments, too, join the earthquake of exultation! Musicians across the centuries have given their best efforts to providing what is an already available—and constantly growing—feast for ear and voice and heart. The fast is over; now let us delight in the rich fare their talent provides!

■ PRELUDES: Eastertime is a season for our gatherings to be blessed with an abundance of instrumental riches. In preparation for the Fifty Days, all church musicians, and organists especially, should review their repertoire of preludes and postludes. This music is "participatory" in its own unique way: setting a festive mood as the assembly gathers, sending the community forth to its mission of witness on a wave of joyful praise.

The Episcopal and Lutheran churches, with their venerable traditions of tastefully appropriate instrumental music, can offer us help in this area; write to the Church Hymnal Corporation (Episcopal) and Augsburg/Fortress (Lutheran) for catalogs (see page xv).

■ DURING THE SPRINKLING WITH HOLY WATER: This "most suitable opening rite" (PI, 2) is highly recommended, at least at the principal Masses, on all the Sundays of Eastertime. Choose a good, strong setting, melodic yet interesting enough, to be the parish's Eastertime "theme" song.

Among the possibilities: Howard Hughes' "You have put on Christ" (GIA, G-2283); David Hurd's "Vidi aquam" (in English; GIA, G-2512); Michael Ward's "I saw water flowing" (WLP, 8548). Also, see the music suggested for the blessing of the water at the Vigil, page 143.

■ GLORIA: On all Eastertime Sundays (and on each day of the octave, too, if resources permit), the Gloria should be sung. Perhaps a simple, yet festive unison setting could be used for most Masses, and a more ornate version for the Mass at which the choir participates. Some simple versions are provided with choral enhancement to permit both continuity and embellishment. See the suggestions for the Gloria at the Vigil on page 142. Other suggestions: Christopher Walker, "St. Augustine's Gloria" (OCP, 7107); Marty Haugen, "Mass of Creation" Gloria (*Gather);* John Rutter, "Gloria" (*Worship,* #276).

■ RESPONSORIAL PSALM: Psalm 118 is the Eastertime psalm, the core of the Easter Vigil gospel procession, the proper psalm for Easter Sunday and its octave. Numerous settings make it an easy addition to every community's repertoire: Michael Joncas' setting in *Psalms for the Cantor,* vol. I (World Library) is rhythmic and delightful for cantor and congregation; Richard Proulx has a classic setting, joyful in tone, embellished easily by canonic singing of refrain and descant (GIA G-1964); Christopher Willcock's composition in *Psalms for Feasts and Seasons* (Liturgical Press) has strong 7/8 time refrain and lively verses for cantor; Christopher Walker's "This day was made by the Lord" is lively, dance-like and the assembly's "echo" within the verses is delightful; Scott Soper's "This is the day" (OCP), a new setting, is easily sung; Hal H. Hopson's "Psalm 118" in *10 Psalms* (Hope, HH 3930) is for SATB, congregation, organ; Bob Hurd's "This is the day" (OCP, 9458) is arranged for SATB, congregation, piano, guitar and two trumpets.

■ SEQUENCE HYMNS: Remember that Eastertime is "bracketed" with a unique enhancement of the liturgy of the word known as sequence hymns. Do *not* let these be recited! See page 147 for settings.

■ GOSPEL ACCLAMATION: Appropriate and exuberant settings of the gospel acclamation abound. The threefold Alleluia refrain of "O filii et filiae" ("Ye sons and daughters") is particularly appropriate for Eastertime; see John Schiavone's version for Easter, Ascension, Pentecost (GIA

G-2162). Robert Hutmacher's "Gospel Processional" (GIA G-2450) is more gently moving. J. Biery's arrangement of Vulpius' "Gelobt sei Gott" provides a "Gospel Fanfare for Easter Morning" (GIA G-2719), with option of trumpets, trombone, horn and timpani. Jeremy Young's "Easter Alleluia" (GIA, G-3175) has verses for each Sunday of Easter. See page 142 for other suggestions.

■ EUCHARISTIC ACCLAMATIONS: For festive settings of the eucharistic acclamations that work well, and have brass and percussion parts available for enhancement, see: Richard Proulx's "Festival Eucharist" (*Worship* or G-1960), in which the cantor suffices if choir is absent; Paul Inwood's "Coventry Acclamations" (OCP, 7117); Christopher Walker's "Festival Mass" (OCP, 7154).

By no means as fancy, but with a nice blend of Easter tunes, is Carrol T. Andrews' "Easter Carol Mass," (G-1398) which may be enhanced using the 2-equal or 4-mixed voices versions.

■ COMMUNION RITE: In place of the Roman rite's Lamb of God, the Episcopal eucharist chants "Christ our passover is sacrificed for us; therefore let us keep the feast." During Eastertime, an Alleluia is added to both verse and response. Some settings of this anthem may be useful as a communion processional during Eastertime. Other possibilities include Suzanne Toolan's "I am the bread of life" and Richard Hillert's "Worthy is Christ."

Some Taizé ostinato refrain settings include "Surrexit Christus" and "Christus Resurrexit" (*Music from Taizé*, vol. II; GIA, G-2778), with segments of Psalm 118 by the cantor answered by short acclamation responses by the assembly. Bob Hurd's "In the breaking of the bread" (*Gather*) and Michael Ward's piece by the same name (WLP, 7950) recall the Emmaus appearance. See page 146 for other suggestions.

■ EASTERTIME HYMNS: Strong, familiar hymns, the "keynotes" of the season, should be repeated each year. "The strife is o'er"; "Hail thee, festival day"; "Come, ye faithful, raise the strain"; and "At the Lamb's high feast," to name but a few, are found in many hymnals. To this familiar and majestic repertoire, try adding a few carol-style Easter hymns, many of them found in readily available collections: "Now the green blade rises" (NOEL NOUVELET); "This joyful Eastertide" (VRUCHTEN); "That Easter Day with joy was bright" (PUER NOBIS).

From the new Lutheran collection, *With One Voice* (Augsburg/Fortress, 1995), come some interesting possibilities: "There in God's garden," and a beautiful *Kentucky Harmony* tune with Charles Wesley's words "Come away to the skies, my beloved arise." Though listed for "The Three Days," both are appropriate Eastertide hymns. Also in this collection are Brian Wren's "Christ is risen! Shout Hosanna!" and Herbert Brokering's "Alleluia! Jesus is risen."

Two new "Emmaus" hymns might also be useful: In GIA's *Hymnal for the Hours*, find "Sing of one who walks beside us" (text by Ralph Wright, American folk melody HOLY MANNA) and "Daylight fades" (text: Peter Scagnelli; Gaelic melody DOMHNACH TRIONOIDE), also in *Worship*.

DECOR

The Pastoral Introduction calls attention to the Easter candle, the baptismal font and to the "living symbols" of Easter's rebirth, the neophytes and their sponsors (PI, 2). These, not flowers or banners, are the principal focal points of our Fifty Days, though flowers are important elements of festivity and banners can add beauty and meaning to the assembly's many gatherings between Easter and Pentecost. For every dimension of Eastertime's decorations, see page 220 of G. Thomas Ryan's *The Sacristy Manual* and Peter Mazar's *To Crown the Year* (pages 122–52).

■ THE EASTER CANDLE: The Easter candle needs to be large enough for its function as principal symbol of the risen Christ in our midst and for the worship space in which it is displayed. The candle stand, likewise, needs to be proportionate to both candle and room. Even in parishes where a suitably sized candle and a new stand have to go on the wish list for next year, four simple but inflexible "rules of procedure" can be implemented immediately and go a long way toward ensuring the silent Easter candle's effectiveness at the assembly's every liturgical gathering:

1) Light the Easter candle for every service held during the Fifty Days.

2) Light it long before the first worshipers arrive.

3) When worshipers have arrived, if other candles need to be lighted (e.g., altar or processional candles for Mass or the hours), let it be obvious to the whole assembly that these are being lighted from the flame of the Easter candle.

4) Never extinguish the Easter candle until every worshiper has left.

The Easter candle is enthroned near the ambo so that the Exsultet can be sung and the Vigil scriptures proclaimed by its light. This, then, is its proper place throughout Eastertime, even during funerals; and it is moved only after Evening Prayer of Pentecost, and then to the baptistry.

■ THE FONT: Making the font a focal point for Eastertime can be a real challenge, depending on its location, construction and appearance. Newer (or newly renovated) churches ought to have an easy time of it, especially if the font is appropriate to its purpose and true to its biblical roots: large enough for adult baptism and alive with flowing water.

Constructing a whole new area for a makeshift font is especially tempting if the parish's real font is not in clear view. Then, too, old fonts that are not works of art or that are clearly inappropriate now even for infant baptism may be renewable only by replacement. If this seems unthinkable, remember all the work done on altars and sanctuaries since Vatican II! This may need to be a parish priority for the coming year. At the same time, remember all the mistakes that were made! Some parishes have found it possible to construct new fonts and to "recycle" the older fonts.

Beware of moveable punch bowls in Easter "displays" in the sanctuary or ugly electric water circulators in make-believe fountains. Better to decorate and honor the real font wherever it is located.

■ THE NEOPHYTES: Make sure to attend to the living symbols of Eastertime, the neophytes baptized at the Vigil. In them the Lord's death and resurrection is most clearly visible this year. The Pastoral Introduction reminds us that, according to the RCIA, they, "their godparents and those who have assisted them in their preparation" have a special place reserved for them in the Sunday assemblies of Eastertime (PI, 2). Specifics will depend on the architecture of the worship space, but perhaps there will be room near the ambo and Easter candle, or near the font. If this cannot be done, it will certainly be possible to honor their reserved seats with floral decorations and, of course, to honor them with incense at some point in the liturgy.

■ FLOWERS: "Discouraged in Lent, demanded by Easter," is the way Mazar begins "Easter Flowers" in *To Crown the Year* (pages 149–52). Here is another area in which we have not been used to considering Eastertime as one great fifty-day celebration. The common practice was to blanket the altar and sanctuary area (and perhaps the paschal candle) with lilies for Easter itself. As glorious as lilies look at their opening, hardly any plant looks as sad in its demise! Usually by the fourth week of Eastertide, all that remained of Easter's splendor were a few pots of sadly limping, slowly browning lilies.

Many parishes now plan their floral displays and adjust their flower budgets to cover the entire season. Mazar mentions a number of suitable plants that can enhance the church's Eastertide decor: forsythia, flowering plum, apple and pear blossom, for instance. The mood to create is sustained festivity and steadily growing anticipation: "The use of indigenous materials can help foster a sense of the progression of the season and its building toward Pentecost" (page 149).

This year, for the last two and a half weeks, the Easter season coincides with May, traditionally the month dedicated in a special way to Mary. This, too, will have an effect on the planning of the church's floral decorations.

■ ALTAR, VESSELS, VESTURE: Every parish brings forth its finest treasures for the season of the Lord's resurrection, as for Christmas and its brief season of celebration. In times past, even the most beautiful of altars, with the most extravagant frontispieces, were adorned with a finely embroidered antependium on Easter. While the noble simplicity of the altar table is rightly emphasized during most of the year, for the Fifty Days a full covering of fine fabric or tapestry might be appropriate. If the altar has a resurrection motif carved into it, however, there might be a way to highlight or enhance this, encircling it with a wreath, for instance.

ENTRANCES

■ OUTDOORS, DOORWAYS, VESTIBULE: As with Christmastime, so with Eastertime: To those arriving for worship (or business, for that matter) and to neighbors who may never come inside, the common "home" of God's people should proclaim visually that we have entered into our

most solemn season of matchless joy. Bunting and banners, maypoles and streamers: There are all kinds of possibilities. Eastertime wreathes adorning every doorway leading into the worship space will silently but beautifully communicate the springtime of nature and grace we are celebrating.

■ ENTRANCE RITE: Everything about the opening rites, silent and spoken, should signal that this gathering takes place within the wider gathering of the universal church into the Fifty Days of unbroken celebration (PI, 1).

Procession: The procession and reverencing of the principal focal points might take on a special character for the Fifty Days. Some parishes carry in and ritually "place" the processional cross, as in the other liturgical seasons, but the cross is adorned festively, perhaps with flowers and fabric, for Eastertime. Other communities leave the cross in place, suitably adorned but not so much as to compete with the paschal candle. Its participation in the procession is omitted during Eastertime precisely to avoid any "ritual competition" with the candle. Whatever decision is made and whatever ritual approach seems to work should then become the parish's standard seasonal approach.

Incense, the specially chosen "Easter scent," would, of course, lead the procession throughout Eastertime. If the font is at some distance from the altar area, there may need to be a pause there, to reverence the font with incense and to draw water to carry to the chair for the blessing that will open the liturgy. Once at the front (or center) of the worship space, altar and candle should also be reverenced with incense.

Greeting: The forthcoming sacramentary incorporates the Episcopalian adaptation of the popular greeting used by Orthodox Christians and Eastern rite Catholics:

V. Alleluia. Christ is risen.

R. The Lord is risen indeed. Alleluia.

—© USCC

Blessing and sprinkling of water: At least at the principal Sunday liturgies, the blessing and sprinkling of water should replace the penitential rite. In fact, according to the new sacramentary, the penitential rite may be omitted throughout the Easter season at all Sunday Masses even when the sprinkling is not done. In this case, the Gloria is sung instead. The sacramentary contains a special Eastertime prayer for the blessing of water.

Gloria: Suggested appropriate Eastertime versions are mentioned on page 159. As is always the case when a strongly engaging entrance song has been followed by an equally powerful sprinkling chant, the Gloria becomes something of a problem. The proposed ritual simplification of the entrance rites suggests omitting the Gloria when the sprinkling takes place! Some communities sing the Gloria (or in Eastertime, Richard Hillert's "This is the feast") during the sprinkling itself.

Opening Prayers: The new scripture-oriented opening prayers by ICEL, which have appeared in previous years' *Sourcebook*s, are a particularly helpful way of focusing the community's attention to the word about to be proclaimed. They are especially sensitive to incorporating the themes of initiation and baptismal renewal associated with the season, as well as the concept of mission appropriate to the latter part of the season. Their conclusions incorporate Easter motifs in a subtle and effective way. On the other hand, the translated opening prayers of Eastertide are classic texts drawn from the ancient sacramentaries. Whichever text is not used as the opening prayer might well become the concluding prayer to the general intercessions (with the shorter ending, of course).

LITURGY OF THE WORD

■ HOMILY: Since the mystagogy proper to Eastertime is destined to assist the renewal of all, the RCIA's point is well taken: The homily "should take into account the presence and needs of the neophytes" (#248). Scan the classic texts in the Office of Readings. Those great fourth-century preachers took their communities, newly and not so newly baptized, back to the water, the oil and the table, and then "unpacked" the words and actions that had happened. Next, in light of that sacramental encounter with the risen Christ, they challenged their listeners' perceptions of the world and its "wisdom." Finally, they pointed the whole assembly toward the kingdom's dawning yet to be, not only in the world to come beyond the grave but even in this world, progressively transformed by the presence of Christ's gospel incarnated in the lives of his disciples.

■ DISMISSAL OF THE CATECHUMENS: While the community rejoices in the radiant presence of the neophytes in its midst, there may yet be catechumens who will be among next Lent's elect, next Easter's neophytes. These should still be dismissed after the homily to continue their own prayer and reflection on the word.

■ GENERAL INTERCESSIONS: *Seasonal* and *sacramental:* These words might capture what the authors of Eastertime's intercessions should be striving for. Reflect the scriptural words and images of the season, but don't forget the sacraments whose celebration initiated the season and give it a unique character, the sacraments of initiation. Some examples for the season may be found in LTP's new *Prayers for Sundays and Seasons*.

LITURGY OF THE EUCHARIST

■ PREFACES: Five prefaces bear the designation "Easter." The former prescription that Easter I alone be used throughout the octave has been removed. Each preface has a title, and this should encourage a thoughtful rotation of prefaces according to the spirit of the day's readings or the part of Eastertime being celebrated.

For Ascension, two prefaces are provided. The second of these is quite brief. The first is more lengthy but considerably richer both theologically and poetically. There is an almost litanic celebration of the exalted Christ's titles: Lord, King of glory, mediator between God and humankind, judge of the world, Lord of heavenly powers, beginning and head.

■ EUCHARISTIC PRAYER: For Eucharistic Prayer I, the sacramentary provides three inserts: Easter and its octave, Ascension and Pentecost. The new sacramentary will provide alternate inserts for use with Eucharistic Prayer III.

■ COMMUNION RITE: Thoughtful use of appropriate variations in the communion rite can help sustain the assembly's Eastertime spirit. As ritual texts designed to form a community in prayer, these should not be left to ad-libbing or be new every week. The best variations parallel the official texts in style and spirit.

CONCLUDING RITE

■ BLESSING: The current edition of the sacramentary alternates the threefold solemn blessing with a randomly chosen prayer over the people on all the Sundays of Eastertime. This is an editorial decision by the publisher, and one might question its wisdom. Would it not be better to use

(sing?) a threefold solemn blessing throughout the season, perhaps according to this schema:

Blessing 6: Easter Sunday, throughout the octave, Second Sunday of Easter
Blessing 7: Sundays 3–6
Blessing 8: Ascension and Sunday 7 (changing the reference to "on this day")
Blessing 9: Pentecost

If the prayer over the people is used on the weekdays of Eastertime, the most appropriate would seem to be #3, 14 and 18 in early Eastertime; #20, 23 and 24 in later Eastertime.

■ DISMISSAL: A double Alleluia, in a beautiful, age-old Gregorian melody, graces the words of the deacon's dismissal and the assembly's response: on Easter, throughout the octave (including the Second Sunday of Easter), on Pentecost (Mass and Evening Prayer). Some traditions wisely suggest continuing the practice for all Fifty Days.

Preparing the Parish

A well-constructed, liturgically based catechesis (for instance, LTP's *Paschal Mission*) will always speak of one season in conjunction with another, of a preparatory season in light of its celebration and fulfillment in the season ahead. During Lent, for example, it is entirely appropriate to refer frequently in bulletin and homiletic material to the springtime flowering of the Forty Days in the splendor of the Fifty Days. The lenten lectionary's fine selection from the First Testament finds a fitting complement in Eastertime's continuous readings from the Acts of the Apostles. Those who exercise a public ministry of teaching and preaching, and those whose ministry is less public but just as influential, might well suggest that if friends have found nourishment in Lent's fasting and prayer, then they ought not to miss the feasting and praise of Eastertime. Of course, the best possible preparation for an exuberant Eastertime is a well-celebrated Triduum, preceded by an intensely kept, spiritually engaging Lent.

Taking It Home

DOMESTIC PRAYER: Whatever good practices were tried or begun at other seasons should find a complement or contrast during Eastertime. Some communities find it helpful to propose a single possibility for daily prayer to households for each season and to provide the practical necessities to help it happen. For example, across the seasons the parish could offer for sale Advent wreath materials; a simple outline for daily prayer (LTP's pocket prayerbooks or *Proclaim Praise* are perfect); simple wooden crosses made by the youth group; a selection of pillar candles, perhaps decorated by a parish craft group with the year's numerals in a style that parallels that of the parish's Easter candle; Lent-Eastertime prayer cards and so forth.

Liturgy Training Publication's *Take Me Home* resource book contains pages for each week of the season through Pentecost. Eggs, grain, water, animals, fruits and gardens all appear in these pages and offer a perfect link between Sunday worship and daily living.

See *Catholic Household Blessings and Prayers* for a blessing at table (page 84), blessing of the home (page 153), blessing of children before confirmation (page 230) or first eucharist (page 231), blessing for Mother's Day (page 197), intercessory prayers for the blessing of fields and gardens (page 166), and a prayer to complete Eastertime on the Solemnity of Pentecost (page 157).

Other Ritual Prayers and Sacraments

LITURGY OF THE HOURS: If lenten Sundays were crowned by the communal celebration of Evening Prayer or if at least some of the hours were prayed during the Triduum, then Eastertime's seven Sundays provide a perfect opportunity to keep the custom alive. This is another lenten custom that can find its exuberant counterpart and complement for the Easter season, even if such is not the parish custom during the rest of the year. It is a simple and prayerful way of saying that Eastertime is at least as important at Lent. The celebration includes, of course, the lighting of the assembly's candles from the already and seemingly continuously burning paschal candle, perhaps repeating the Vigil's "Light of Christ"/"Thanks be to God."

Whatever is done on the other Sundays, the season's completion ought to be ushered in with a special Vigil on the eve of Pentecost. It parallels the Easter Vigil, though its character is not baptismal but rather evocative of the prayerful expectancy of Mary and the Apostles at the first Pentecost (PI, 2). See special texts on page 177.

■ COMMUNAL ANOINTING OF THE SICK: Rites celebrated with the community's sick, anointing or holy communion for the homebound, appropriately use the scriptural passages in these rites selected from the Acts of the Apostles or the Johannine selection on the Good Shepherd. If offered communally on an Eastertime Sunday, the scriptures of the Sunday should be used.

■ MARRIAGES: On the Sundays of Eastertime one of the scripture selections given in the marriage rite can be substituted for the Eastertime readings, but on Easter Sunday, Ascension and Pentecost, no such substitution is permitted—the church's polite way of suggesting that no rite as important as marriage should distract from solemnities as important as these!

■ FUNERALS: In many parishes, people who buried their loved ones at noneucharistic services during the Triduum will return to celebrate Mass during the octave. On these days it will be appropriate to use the Acts readings and gospels already assigned, perhaps choosing a second reading from the New Testament selections of the funeral lectionary. Remember that the presidential prayers of the funeral Mass, form C are specially provided for use in the Easter season. Because these liturgies are not concluded by a procession to the cemetery, the parish should take the opportunity to provide food and hospitality following the liturgy.

At funeral Masses after the octave, the first reading is appropriately chosen from among the Acts of the Apostles selections in the funeral lectionary or from Revelation. The Emmaus gospel is also appropriate. Funeral Masses are not celebrated on Sundays of the season or on Ascension Thursday.

■ HOUSE BLESSINGS: The *Book of Blessings* (chapter 50) speaks of Christmas and Easter as traditional times for blessing homes. Despite the awesome amount of work involved in coordinating such an effort, the results can be wonderful in terms of community-building and faith-sharing. The texts situate "visitation" squarely in the context of prayer, the minister's presence as a form of evangelization, sharing the good news of God's reconciling love made known in Christ. In the reformed rite, all pastoral ministers may be involved and forms for blessings offered by lay ministers are provided.

■ NATURE BLESSINGS: Springtime has always been blessing time in agriculturally based Christian communities. In the medieval and post-Tridentine church, rogation days (April 25 and the three days before Ascension Thursday) were set apart for fervent prayer for growth and fruitfulness. The *Book of Blessings* contains orders of blessing for fields and flocks (chapter 26) and for seeds at planting time (chapter 27). For other materials contact the National Catholic Rural Life Conference, 4625 N.W. Beaver Drive, Des Moines IA 50310.

MARIAN DEVOTION

This year, midway through the Fifth Week of Easter, the month of May begins, and in this "fairest of seasons" as the old hymn says, the church traditionally honors her whom the angel hailed as "fairest among women." With careful planning and sensitive coordination, there need be no conflict between maintaining Eastertime's focus on the risen Lord and the community's instinctive veneration for the mother of the Lord.

■ THE MARIAN SHRINE: Most Catholic churches fittingly reserve a special space for a statue or icon of the Virgin Mary. Moving such an image front and center is hardly ever the best approach: Too frequently such a setup competes with the Easter candle for attention. As with the font, better to honor the image of Mary wherever it happens to be. If the parish's Easter finery has been kept up to par throughout these first five weeks, surely an appropriate and proportional decoration of our Lady's image will not detract from either the font or Easter candle!

■ MARIAN PRAYER: There are several good Marian hymns specifically for use during Eastertime. The most traditional is "Regina coeli." Its simple chant setting is lovely and singable, in both Latin and English (*Worship*, #443) and the subject of several fine polyphonic settings as well. "Be joyful Mary, heav'nly queen" is another good choice, and there is a verse for Mary in "Ye watchers and ye holy ones." Of course, the Magnificat is always a good selection. It is available in several translations, and the old Gelineau solemn setting resounds with glorious Alleluias.

It is a fact that most sanctoral devotions do not mix well with the eucharistic liturgy. Simply inserting Marian devotions such as the litany or a decade of the rosary after the homily or after communion does not do justice to the eucharist or to our Lady! But these prayers can become the core of a noneucharistic devotional gathering. Recent recordings or televising of the pope praying the rosary demonstrate how easy and beautiful it is to enhance this devotion with the proclamation of scripture and the solemnity of song. The traditional May crowning can thus be a service unto itself, or in connection with the celebration of Evening Prayer, or even after Mass concludes, as a procession journeys to the indoor or outdoor Lady shrine to carry out this ritual much beloved in many communities.

The Common of the Blessed Virgin Mary in *The Liturgy of the Hours* provides good resources for such prayer. Explore, too, the fine material in *Collection of Masses of the Blessed Virgin Mary: volume I, Sacramentary* (Catholic Book and Liturgical Press). Note that none of these Mass formularies, which are intended primarily for use in Marian shrines and on Saturdays of Ordinary Time, may replace the proper Masses of Eastertime (introduction, #21, 28).

March

MON 31 #261 (LMC, #185–192) white
Easter Monday
SOLEMNITY

"My little children in Christ, new offspring of the church, gift of the Father, proof of Mother Church's fertility, a holy seed, a new colony of bees, the very flower of our ministry, the fruit of our toil, my joy and my crown!" That's the opening line of one of Saint Augustine's Easter octave homilies! Maybe we couldn't use some of those expressions today, but Augustine certainly was enthusiastic about having those neophytes around. In his church, they gathered each day of the octave for mystagogical catechesis. We moderns fancy ourselves extremely busy, but was it any easier or more practical for our forebears? At any rate, here are some contemporary possibilities to consider:

- Eucharist on one or several evenings of the week, with extended mystagogical sharing.
- One of these could be followed by refreshments and socializing. Many people like to watch videos of big moments they've celebrated. What could be more important than rebirth? If initiation was unobtrusively and tastefully videotaped at the Vigil, why not put that up on the screen of the parish hall and maybe give a tape to each neophyte as a remembrance?
- Invite the neophytes to dinner with the ministry staff, or with families in different sections of the parish. A perfect time for gifts and personal welcomes.
- Be sure to invite this year's neophytes to celebrate with those from the previous years who are celebrating their anniversary of initiation.

Let there be rejoicing, too, in parishes without neophytes. The octave is a perfect time for a gathering of those involved in the liturgical planning and celebration of Lent and the Triduum to swap stories, critique the experience (constructively) and make notes for next year, sing Easter songs and treat each other to the Easter feasting that has now replaced the lenten fast.

▪ AN EIGHT-DAY SOLEMNITY: Each eucharist is celebrated as on Easter Day (though without the profession of faith). Although only the Preface for Easter I gives this rubric, whichever Easter preface is used should begin "on this Easter day when Christ became our paschal sacrifice." Each day the gospel acclamation repeats the refrain "This is the day the Lord has made!" The sprinkling rite should take place (if possible), as should a sung Gloria and sequence hymn and the double Alleluia at the dismissal. Each day's gospel acclamation repeats the refrain. At Morning Prayer and Evening Prayer, Easter Sunday's psalms, canticles and antiphons are used all through the week. Every liturgical element is designed to remind the assembly that this octave is an extended Easter day. Let everything look and sound and feel like Easter Sunday all week long!

April

TUE 1 #262 (LMC, #185–192) white
Easter Tuesday
SOLEMNITY

Peter's sermon in Acts is a wonderful model for preachers today, straightforward and filled with truth. His goal is not to stir up guilt but to move his listeners to the choice for a new direction. We are known to Jesus by name, the gospel reminds us, and it is in the personal call—even today—that people are most likely to respond to the Lord and to the community of his disciples. If there were no neophytes at the Vigil, does the community need to get a bit more personal?

WED 2 #263 (LMC, #185–192) white
Easter Wednesday
SOLEMNITY

Time and movement are in both readings today. At three o'clock, Peter and John go to the temple for midday prayer. On a journey that takes them till nightfall, two disciples head for Emmaus. Jesus is manifested each time in both places: in the making whole of a sick man and in the breaking of the bread. So we are reminded that, to the eyes of faith, Christ is visible everywhere: in the "sacred space" of worship and along the dusty or busy roads of our lives; in all of our breaking and in the making whole again. Two beautiful "Emmaus collects," prepared by ICEL, are appropriate today:

> O God, worker of wonders,
> you made this day for joy
>   and gladness.
> Let the risen Lord abide with us
>   (this evening),
> opening the scriptures to us
> and revealing their meaning.
>
> Set our hearts aflame and open
>   our eyes,
> that we may see in his sufferings
> all that the prophets spoke
> and recognize him in our midst,
> the Christ now entered into glory,
> firstborn from the dead,
> who lives with you now
>   and always
> in the unity of the Holy Spirit,
> God for ever and ever.

or

> O God of mystery,
> out of death you delivered
>   Christ Jesus,
> and he walked in hidden glory
>   with his disciples.
>
> Stir up our faith,
> that our hearts may burn
>   within us
> at the sound of his word,
> and our eyes be opened to
>   recognize him
> in the breaking of the bread.

APRIL

Grant this through Jesus Christ,
the firstborn from the dead,
who lives and reigns with you
   now and always
in the unity of the Holy Spirit,
God for ever and ever.

THU 3 — #264 (LMC, #185–192) white
Easter Thursday
SOLEMNITY

Throughout the octave, the second reading from the Office of Readings provides both model and material for mystagogical homilies. Today's selection, from the *Jerusalem Catecheses* of the fourth century, addresses the neophytes and us: "You were led into the font. . . ." Peter's words are, again, a model of Christlike approach to past mistakes: "I know you acted in ignorance. . . ." Both he and we know that from personal experience. However did we Christians forget that in our relationships with the Jewish people?

FRI 4 — #265 (LMC, #185–192) white
Easter Friday
SOLEMNITY

A wonderful day for singing Easter's Psalm 118 and that strong, compelling hymn "At the name of Jesus!" On the lakeshore, Jesus manifests himself and provides in abundance for the little, broken community, when they take him at his word and give their fishing one more try — even after an "all nighter" that produced nothing. A wonderful lesson here for neophytes and baptized: Jesus always seems to call us to push just beyond what we think we're capable of. With him guiding the community, the results will come in time — or at least in eternity!

SAT 5 — #266 (LMC, #185–192) white
Easter Saturday
SOLEMNITY

Disbelief yielding to faith and leading to witness: Today's gospel summarizes three postresurrection appearances and offers us the pattern by which we move, sometimes more than once in the course of a lifetime! The selection from Acts reminds us to whom we owe our heart's first allegiance.

Today is a solemnity, so the Mass of the day is used at wedding celebrations. To the two prescribed readings may be added a reading from the epistle selections in the *Rite of Marriage*.

6 — #44 [45] (LMC, #38) white
Second Sunday of Easter

Dominica in albis, "Sunday in whites," was today's name in the old liturgical books. The name reflects the fact that the neophytes wore their baptismal garments for the whole octave, laying them aside only today, after Vespers.

Today is still the *today* of Easter Day! Sing it in the hymns and in the preface; reinforce it with the sequence and the double Alleluia at the dismissal! Continue Easter Sunday's joy and splendor throughout the whole Fifty Days! Parishes with strong ethnic traditions observe this "Second Easter Sunday" as a day for a parish potluck supper where folks bring ethnic specialties for a parish Easter feast.

In many parts of the world, this Sunday is the traditional day for children to receive their first communion.

MON 7 — #545 (LMC, #274) white
The Annunciation of the Lord
SOLEMNITY

This feast originated in the East during the sixth century and gained universal observance in the West during the eighth. It is a feast of the Lord, commemorating the announcement to the Virgin Mary of the Word made flesh, Mary's acceptance of God's will and the conception of Christ nine months before Christmas. Its occurrence close to Easter links the incarnation with the whole mystery of human redemption in Christ (© ICEL).

The first "free day" after the octave features, this year, one more solemnity, transferred from March 25, which fell during Holy Week. Today, at the profession of faith, all should be invited to genuflect (this needs a pause) at the phrase that commemorates the incarnation.

TUE 8 — #268 (LMC, #185–192) white
Easter Weekday

The beginning of Nicodemus' dialogue with Christ was replaced by the solemnity's gospel yesterday. It might be helpful, therefore, to combine yesterday's and today's selection. Acts presents, yet again, the early community's sharing of goods. While few would hand over lands or houses today, we can all lay our talents at the community's feet and put something of our time at its disposal.

APRIL

WED 9 — Easter Weekday
#269 (LMC, #185–192) white

Living the faith today rarely results in imprisonment, but there is sometimes a price to be paid socially for publicly taking the whole message seriously. The "cost of discipleship" might be a good topic of discussion for the neophytes or for the young people preparing for confirmation.

THU 10 — Easter Weekday
#270 (LMC, #185–192) white

To obey God rather than human authority: This principle, asserted by Peter and the apostles today in Acts, sounds simple enough, but what happens when that human authority claims to speak for God? What the church really does and does not teach, who in the church speaks definitively and when, are important topics for the neophytes to discuss and for the whole community to reflect on from time to time. In the midst of the church's trials and tribulations over the centuries, we can rest secure on the promise Jesus presents in his discussion with Nicodemus: "The Father loves the Son and has placed all things in his hands"—and that includes us!

FRI 11 — Stanislaus, bishop, martyr
#271 (LMC, #185–192) white
MEMORIAL

A few years ago this optional memorial became obligatory. Before John Paul II became Peter's successor in Rome, he had been Stanislaus' successor in Cracow. He felt, with good reason, that the whole church should celebrate Stanislaus' example of preaching the truth, no matter how powerful the target and how severe the consequences. The warning is given clearly in today's reading from Acts. The gospel of loaves and fishes points toward the eucharist as one of the initiation sacraments in which we meet the Risen One.

SAT 12 — Easter Weekday
#272 (LMC, #185–192) white

We're only in chapter 6 of Acts: How quickly the idyllic picture of "all things in common" has changed to one of grumbling complaint. Human nature is ever the same! The crisis becomes an opportunity for change, growth and development of ministry, always the pattern in a church led by the Spirit and sure of the presence of the risen Christ! The gospel story confirms that trust: With Jesus in the boat (often a symbol of the church) we will survive the storms and reach shore sooner than we dreamed!

13 — Third Sunday of Easter
#47 [48] (LMC, #41) white

The gospel presents the "aftermath" of the Emmaus story. Recognized in the breaking of the bread and seeming to confine his appearances to fleeting glimpses, Jesus is forever present to and within the community. Note the emotions of the assembled disciples: fright, disbelief, wonder, joy. Are any of us strangers to these? Yet Jesus is here—not in spite of but in the midst of whatever we are feeling. 1 John reminds us to rejoice in the sure knowledge that we have an "advocate with the Father, Jesus Christ the righteous." It is the message celebrated especially in Easter Preface III.

MON 14 — Easter Weekday
#273 (LMC, #185–192) white

Though preaching was Stephen's forte, winning friends and influencing people surely was not. The passages today and tomorrow give only a brief summary of his long and confrontational witness before the Jewish authorities. In contrast, how often we prefer to sugarcoat the difficult truths of the gospel! The gospel asks us, and perhaps especially the neophytes, to reflect on what exactly we hope to find in the following of Jesus. For that matter, what goals are we pursuing in all areas of life: career, finance, possessions, achievement? With limited energies to invest, the followers of Christ need to ask how many of our goals are perishable and how many will endure?

TUE 15 — Easter Weekday
#274 (LMC, #185–192) white

Stephen's death is described today as an imitation of the pattern set down by Jesus, proclaiming two qualities all Christians need, not only in death but perhaps most especially in life. One is confident trust: "Into your hands . . . Receive my spirit"; the other is unconditional forgiveness: "Father, forgive them . . . Lord, do not count this against them." The gospel reminds us that only in Jesus, the living bread come down from heaven, can we find the strength so to live.

WED 16 — Easter Weekday
#275 (LMC, #185–192) white

Acts presents Stephen's martyrdom not only as the beginning of a time of trial for the early church in Jerusalem but as a time of incredible expansion far beyond that narrowly defined space. Even Saul's cameo appearance yesterday and today brings joy to

APRIL

us who know how his story ends. Indeed, as he himself would later write, God makes all things work together for good for those who love him. Jesus' promise in the gospel holds true even now: He will lose nothing of all that the Father has given him.

THU 17 — Easter Weekday
#276 (LMC, #185–192) white

The wonderful story of Philip and the Ethiopian eunuch reminds us that for the disciple of Jesus, no encounter is a chance meeting and the most unlikely settings may present an unexpected opportunity for evangelization. The gospel continues our extended meditation on the bread of life, one that will be repeated this year on the Sundays of July and August. These passages present a perfect opportunity for eucharist-centered mystagogy.

FRI 18 — Easter Weekday
#277 (LMC, #185–192) white

As Philip finds an unlikely place for evangelization, Ananias meets the world's most unlikely candidate! Acts relates the conversion of Saul (Paul), a classic description of the complete reversal of one's life.

SAT 19 — Easter Weekday
#278 (LMC, #185–192) white

Persecution has yielded to peace, though trials will surely come again. The ebb and flow of church life has continued steadily from that day to this. Healing still happens all around us, though not often as dramatically as in today's reading from Acts. Acts is wonderful for the detail of persons and places it presents, a living history of the young community which, in these weeks, has been made young again in our neophytes.

20 — Fourth Sunday of Easter
#50 [51] (LMC, #44) white

Every year the beautiful image of Christ as Good Shepherd appears on the Fourth Sunday of Easter. Far from a gentle herdsman, the Good Shepherd we meet in today's gospel defends his sheep against the wolf and is in complete command of his self-sacrificing vocation: "I have power to lay down my life and to take it up again." Preface for Easter II pictures Christ as leading his people back into the kingdom.

■ WORLD DAY OF PRAYER FOR VOCATIONS: Since the days of Vatican II, this Sunday has been designated Vocation Sunday. Use the Fourth Sunday texts and maintain the ritual patterns established for the season. Prayers and readings for vocations in the back of the liturgical books are not for use today. A context of prayer for vocations should neither ignore the church's need for ordained and religious servants, nor devalue lay ministry or marriage.

MON 21 — Easter Weekday
#279 (LMC, #185–192) white

Anselm, bishop, religious, doctor of the church, optional memorial/white. ▪ Today's liturgy of the word celebrates the inclusivity of Jesus' mission. Acts recounts Peter's personal development in appreciating how boundless the Christian community is meant to be. The gospel continues yesterday's Good Shepherd imagery, stressing that Jesus has opened the gates of salvation for all.

TUE 22 — Easter Weekday
#280 (LMC, #185–192) white

Some of the rousing spirituals in many of today's hymnals are perfect on days when the music needs to be a cappella. Today's reading from Acts celebrates the first use of the designation "Christian" for the disciples. "Lord, I want to be a Christian in my heart" and "I have decided to follow Jesus" would be perfect. The gospel keeps Sunday's reflection on Christ as the Good Shepherd present to the community's mind. The question for today: Do we who bear his name truly hear and follow his voice?

WED 23 — Easter Weekday
#281 (LMC, #185–192) white

George, martyr, optional memorial/red. ▪ The gospel presents Jesus' own comforting testimony that he has come "not to judge the world but to save it." Acts presents a brief ministry roster from the church in Antioch and shows the disciples guided by the Spirit in the designation of people for ministry, an ongoing concern for today's communities.

Today's saint is a wonderful Eastertime saint. George slays the dragon; Christ slays death. *Geoergos* means "earth-worker" — gardener, vinedresser, farmer, all Easter images for Jesus.

THU 24 — Easter Weekday
#282 (LMC, #185–192) white

Fidelis of Simaringen, presbyter, religious, martyr, optional memorial/red. ▪ Today and tomorrow the first reading presents Paul's "history of salvation" delivered in the synagogue at Antioch in Pisidia. Tomorrow's conclusion to today's reading will be preempted by the proper readings of the feast, so (omitting the repetition of the introduction) some may

APRIL

wish to combine the two selections. Paul covers from Exodus through Jesus, and the gospel reminds us that our principal imitation of Christ expresses itself in self-sacrificing service of our brothers and sisters.

Fidelis, a Capuchin known for his care of the sick, was martyred in 1622 for his preaching in Protestant Switzerland. His memorial recalls a less happy time than ours in ecumenical relations.

FRI 25 — Mark, evangelist
#555 (LMC, #284) red
FEAST

▪ YEAR B'S EVANGELIST: Our evangelist for 1997 is today's saint, and today's celebration should take grateful and festive note of that fact with appropriate reflections on this earliest and briefest of gospels and this most elusive of evangelists.

Who is Mark? An early second-century source calls Mark "Peter's interpreter," and his ministry has long been linked to Peter's two sees: Antioch, where a church contains a spring from which (the legend goes) Mark made his ink and, more commonly accepted, Rome, where Peter was martyred in the early 60s, when Mark's gospel is thought to have been put together. Alexandria claims Mark as its first evangelizer. Venice adorns its principal piazza with the lion that symbolizes him (Mark's gospel begins with John the Baptist in the desert). And Aquileia, not far from Venice, claims that Peter sent him there to be the city's first bishop. An impressive list of credits for one of whom we know, officially and verifiably, very little!

How do we keep his day? The scriptures celebrate Mark's link to Peter's preaching (first reading) and present Mark's postresurrection missioning of the first disciples. Especially beautiful are Mark's closing lines: "The Lord worked with them . . . ." How reassuring that must have been to Mark's often persecuted communities and how important for our own communities to hear and believe today! The Episcopal *Hymnal 1982* has two strong hymns in honor of evangelists, both translations from the Roman, Latin tradition: "Come sing, ye choirs exultant" and "Come, pure hearts, in joyful measure." "By all your saints still striving" (*Worship*, #706) has a special verse for Mark's feast day.

SAT 26 — Easter Weekday
#284 (LMC, #185–192) white

Today's selection from Acts reminds us of the sometimes bitter conflict between early Christians and the Jewish community as the gospel spread to the Gentiles. Jesus speaks of his unity with the Father and of his disciples' unity with him in doing the work of God, one of which, surely, is to promote reconciliation and mutual respect among peoples of all faiths. His words are spoken as "the hour was at hand for him to depart." Such will be the setting of the gospel selections over the next three weeks.

27 — Fifth Sunday of Easter
#53 [54] (LMC, #47) white

For the next three Sundays, the gospel passages are from the "Final Discourse" spoken at the Last Supper in the Gospel of John. In the Canadian lectionary, almost each weekday reading for the next three weeks begins, "When the hour had come for him to depart from this world to the Father." This sets the daily passage clearly within its scriptural context.

Today's first reading recounts the gradual introduction of Saul (Paul) to the Jerusalem church and the peace and expansion that church enjoyed. 1 John's text reminds us how to translate Jesus' words about abiding in him and bearing fruit into practical reality: by loving one another.

MON 28 — Easter Weekday
#285 (LMC, #185–192) white

Peter Chanel, presbyter, religious, missionary, martyr, optional memorial/red. ▪ The gospel today begins a three-week continuous reading from the Last Supper discourse, with the promise of Jesus that the community will always be assisted by the Paraclete in its ongoing growth in the truth. In Acts, Paul and Barnabas, in a classic case of missionary misunderstanding, have to insist to the Lycaonians that they are human, not divine.

TUE 29 — Catherine of Siena, virgin, doctor of the church
#286 (LMC, #185–192) white
MEMORIAL

Peace is Jesus' farewell bequest and promise in today's gospel—but not the peace the world gives. The first reading from Acts illustrates the truth of that promise!

Today's saint knew both the peace of contemplative prayer and the persecution that comes with any public involvement. Catherine figured prominently in the life of church and state during a period of rival popes and contentious princes.

WED 30 — Easter Weekday
#287 (LMC, #185–192) white

Pius V, pope, religious, optional memorial/white. ▪ The next three days' readings from Acts chronicle a crisis of interpretation in

MAY

the early church and the peaceful resolution that eventually ensued. This reminds us that disagreement is normal in the church and that anything and anyone who is alive is, by definition, growing, changing, developing. Meanwhile the gospel challenges us always to be united as living branches grafted onto one vine. Separation inevitably means the end of fruitfulness.

The readings are especially appropriate as we remember Pius V, whose special ministry was to translate the reforms of Trent from proposals on paper to a reality in the church's life. Of special note were the liturgical reforms implemented under his jurisdiction, upon which the reforms of Vatican II built, as the *General Instruction of the Roman Missal* reminds us (introduction, #2–15).

May

THU 1 #288 or 559 (LMC, #185–192) white
Easter Weekday

Joseph the Worker, optional memorial/white. ▪ Today's first reading records the discussion at the first council of the church in Jerusalem. Despite strong feelings on both sides of the issue, the council made a courageous and farsighted decision to move beyond the Judaism in which most of the participants had been raised, so as not to burden Gentile converts with more than was truly necessary for shared faith. This is a practical translation of Jesus' command in the gospel to keep his commandments and live in his love. In its finest hours, usually in council, the church has been guided by the Spirit in similar paths of courage and foresight.

In the midst of the Cold War, today's memorial was instituted to "baptize" workers' celebrations frequently sponsored by groups or governments indifferent or hostile to the church. From Leo XIII's *Rerum Novarum* (1898) onward, of course, the church had been an outspoken champion of working people, as it still is. In the United States, our Labor Day occurs in September and may be a better occasion to celebrate this memorial or a votive Mass for the blessing of human labor.

FRI 2 #289 (LMC, #185–192) white
Athanasius, bishop, doctor of the church
MEMORIAL

Acts shows the decision of the community's elders as partaking of the Spirit's presence in a special and powerful way: "It is the decision of the Holy Spirit, and ours too. . . ." The result of the deliberations is joy among the Gentiles awaiting word. Surely the decisions to suppress customs that were deeply a part of the religious training of many at the council must have been a true "laying down of one's life for one's friends," as Jesus counsels in the gospel. Life in community can progress and be sustained in no other way than the path of self-sacrificing love.

Today's saint knew well the price of truth. To the Arians of his time, as to many of our own contemporaries, the concept of God becoming our brother in the flesh was a possibility too difficult to accept. "Athanasius against the world!" was the cry, as he stood firm in this faith: Jesus Christ, truly God, truly human.

SAT 3 #561 (LMC, #452–455) red
Philip and James, apostles
FEAST

The celebration of apostles fits in naturally with the Easter season. The first reading gives us the opportunity to reflect on the fact that our faith is none other than the faith of the first disciples, handed down faithfully, ever the same, yet ever new, from generation to generation. In the gospel Jesus counsels Philip to see the Father in him; as we must learn to see and serve the living God in the neighbor who is before our eyes.

4 #56 [57] (LMC, #50) white
Sixth Sunday of Easter

In the archdioceses and dioceses of Canada, and in the archdioceses and dioceses of Alaska, California, Hawaii, Idaho, Montana, Nevada, Oregon, Utah and Washington, the Ascension of the Lord is transferred to the following Sunday, May 11. The second reading and gospel of the Seventh Sunday of Easter (#60 [61]) may be read on the Sixth Sunday of Easter.

The work of the Spirit lives and breathes through readings of the Sixth Sunday, gently turning us toward the Pentecost mystery. In Cornelius' household, for instance, not only does the Spirit descend on Gentiles, to Peter's surprise, but the gift is given even before the folks are baptized! The selection from 1 John is that letter's ode to the love for one another that is born of God's love for each of us, revealed in Christ. Reinforcing this is the gospel's challenge to love one another.

MON 5 #291 (LMC, #185–192) white
Easter Weekday

There is a wonderful intimacy and immediacy about today's first reading. Haven't we all — and especially in spring — sought out

MAY

a place designed by nature for prayer to nature's God? And haven't we all been surprised and delighted by the kindness and hospitality of the sisters and brothers the Lord has sent our way? In the gospel the inevitability of persecution is matched by the firm assurance of the Spirit's unfailing presence and aid.

■ ROGATION DAYS: These three days before Ascension were formerly days designated *rogare,* to make intense prayer and supplication. This was marked by processions through fields and gardens, with litanies and holy water, on behalf of the fruits of the earth. In some places, there was intercession for the fruitfulness of the ministry in those preparing for orders.

TUE 6 — #292 (LMC, #185–192) white
Easter Weekday

Another of the Spirit's gifts is celebrated in today's selection from Acts: reconciliation. An all-night vigil of song and prayer doesn't convert the jailer. But the sensitivity and concern of the Christian prisoners for the jailer's plight makes their witness authentic to the man. The threat of suicide yields to rebirth in Christ. As Jesus says in the gospel, when it comes to sin and righteousness and judgment, worldly standards yield to the Spirit's truth.

WED 7 — #293 (LMC, #185–192) white
Easter Weekday

Paul does a wonderful job trying to meet the Athenians "where they're at"—a model homily in many ways. But it doesn't work. In the end, Paul will learn to temper his eloquence with a straightforward proclamation of Christ crucified. Jesus reminds us in the gospel that, although the word deserves and demands our best efforts, the work of conversion is, ultimately, the Spirit's to accomplish.

THU 8 — #58 [59] (LMC, #53) white
The Ascension of the Lord
SOLEMNITY

In the archdioceses and dioceses of Canada, and in the archdioceses and dioceses of Alaska, California, Hawaii, Idaho, Montana, Nevada, Oregon, Utah and Washington, the Ascension of the Lord is transferred to the following Sunday, May 11. May 8 is kept as an Easter weekday. Readings for today are found at #294 in the lectionary.

■ AN EASTERTIME MASS: Keep the Eastertime patterns, with the changes of text required by the liturgy and subtle modifications of decor suggested by the feast (see Mazar, *To Crown the Year,* pages 143–44).

■ PASCHAL CANDLE: Formerly extinguished after today's gospel, the candle now stays in its Easter location and is lighted until the Fifty Days are completed.

■ INTRODUCTORY RITES: Set the tone with a strong opening hymn, such as "Hail the day that sees him rise" (LLANFAIR) or "A hymn of glory let us sing" (LASS UN EFREUEN). Link the day to Easter with a repeat of the Eastertime Gloria.

■ LITURGY OF THE WORD: The new lectionary offers an alternative second reading for Year B, especially good for celebrating the community's increase in its new members: Ephesians 4:1–13 (or 4:1–7, 11–13), building up the body of Christ to full stature. The exultant responsorial psalm (Psalm 47) would be used from Ascension to the Saturday before Pentecost. Many fine settings, of varying complexity, abound; choose one worthy of the solemnity and use it every year. Proulx's setting in *Worship* fits these criteria admirably. Other possibilities: Hal Hopson's "Sing out your praise to God" in *Psalms for All Seasons* (NPM); Angelo della Pica's setting in *Psalms for the Cantor,* vol. V (WLP); Christopher Willcock's "God mounts his throne" in *Psalms for Feasts and Seasons* (Liturgical Press); and Marty Haugen's "God mounts his throne *(Gather).*

■ LITURGY OF THE EUCHARIST: As noted above, Ascension I is the richer preface, a fine resource for a bulletin summary the week before, orienting the community to this solemnity. Eucharistic Prayer I has its proper insert in the sacramentary.

■ OTHER CELEBRATIONS: Funerals, weddings and anointings are not celebrated today. For school liturgies, see page 96 of the Leader's Manual of the *Hymnal for Catholic Students.*

FRI 9 — #295 (LMC, #185–192) white
Easter Weekday

The Lord's words to Paul in today's first reading might be addressed to all of our communities, wherever they may be: "Do not be afraid; speak; do not be silent: there are many of my people in this city."

MAY

SAT 10 #296 (LMC, #185–192) white
Easter Weekday

Acts relates Paul's journeys to proclaim the gospel and to give strength to the disciples, and Apollos putting his native eloquence at the service of the gospel. Surely the gospel's promise that God will provide the community with what it needs is fulfilled through those, in every generation, who offer their time and talent for the building up of the body.

SUN 11 #60 [61] (LMC, #56) white
Seventh Sunday of Easter

In the archdioceses and dioceses of Canada, and in the archdioceses and dioceses of Alaska, California, Hawaii, Idaho, Montana, Nevada, Oregon, Utah and Washington, the Ascension of the Lord is celebrated on the Seventh Sunday of Easter. The readings and prayers are those of that solemnity.

This Sunday situates us chronologically between Ascension and Pentecost, a reminder, like Advent, of our spiritual location: between the "already" and the "not yet." This is not a place to escape from ("I am not asking you to take them out of the world") but a space to live trustfully ("but to protect them from the evil one"), purposefully ("I have sent them into the world") and even happily ("that their joy may be complete")!

■ COME, HOLY SPIRIT: Let this Sunday's music also point us to Pentecost. While keeping the familiar Eastertime patterns, use a new gathering song, Psalm 47 from Ascension, and perhaps both "Alleluia, sing to Jesus" (a reference both to Christ's Ascension and to his promise to remain with us) and "Come down, O Love divine" or the parish's favorite Holy Spirit hymn.

■ MOTHER'S DAY: The dominant motif of the liturgy must remain a paschal joy that anticipates Pentecost's promise and fulfillment. But the Mother's Day tradition can be integrated gracefully into that motif.

■ PRAYER IN THE ASSEMBLY: Sample intercessions and a prayer over the people are in the *Book of Blessings,* #1727–1728. Following the liturgy's closing procession and hymn, the blessing of mothers might take place at Mary's shrine.

■ DOMESTIC PRAYER: See *Catholic Household Blessings and Prayers* (page 197) for prayer appropriate at home.

MON 12 #297 (LMC, #185–192) white
Easter Weekday

Nereus and Achilleus, martyrs; Pancras, martyr, optional memorial / red. ■ Baptism and the gift of the Holy Spirit appropriately grace this week's first selection from Acts. Christ nevertheless predicts persecution and dispersal, but this will not be the last word. After all, Christ has conquered the world. The courage he enjoins is not a human creation but the Spirit's gift.

TUE 13 #298 (LMC, #185–192) white
Easter Weekday

The first reading is rich indeed. Paul's ministry is yet a model: tireless preaching, practical service. The Spirit was not, for him, a theological concept but an abiding and directive friend. This gives us courage, whose place, according to Christ's gospel word, is not in detached contemplation or quiet safety but in the midst of the world with his work to do.

WED 14 #564 (LMC, #293) red
Matthias, apostle
FEAST

Paul's farewell speech in Acts offers good guidance not only for church leaders but for all of us. Jesus' prayer in the gospel also applies to all members of the church as well as the apostles.

The story of Matthias' election is one we have heard already this Eastertime, but in the context of today's celebration it affords the opportunity to rejoice at the Spirit's guidance of the church and provision for its continuity.

THU 15 #300 (LMC, #185–192) white
Easter Weekday

Isidore the farmer, and his wife, Maria, married couple, optional memorial / white. ■ Acts is a wonderfully human document: Paul gives quite a good (and clever) account of himself in today's first reading, managing to reduce his accusers to arguing with each other. Always a masterful ploy! But in the midst of the humanity, the Spirit is present: Paul must go on to Rome. The event should give us courage, for today's gospel reminds that we, too, are to be evangelizers.

FRI 16 #301 (LMC, #185–192) white
Easter Weekday

Today's passage from Acts explains the legalities by which the Spirit's will was accomplished: Paul will be sent to Rome. If there is no morning Mass tomorrow, it would be a good idea to add tomorrow's reading to this one, thus bringing the reading of Acts. In Rome, of course, both Peter and Paul will offer their lives' definitive answer to Jesus' question in today's gospel: "Do you love me?"

M A Y

SAT 17 Easter Weekday
#302 (LMC, #185–192) white

The Acts reading concludes Eastertime's presentation of the young church alive in the Spirit. John's gospel concludes with the reminder that in the witness of martyrdom or of lively witness the call is to proclaim Christ faithfully, to the end. Though the written canon of scripture is concluded, the story of Christ continues to be told on the living pages of disciples' lives.

18 Pentecost SOLEMNITY
#62–63 [63–64] (LMC, #58) red

This, the fiftieth day, concludes the season of Easter, the continuous single festival of the risen Christ. Pentecost, the Jewish feast of harvest, which also commemorates the giving of the Law of Moses, was the day when the Holy Spirit came upon the apostles (see Acts 2:1ff.); the event has been celebrated on this day at least since the third century. The joy of Pentecost is that the risen Christ breathes upon the church and says, "Receive the Holy Spirit" (John 20:22) (© ICEL).

A good sense of the richness of today's solemnity shines through its history. More than the birthday of the church, Pentecost is a day to recapitulate all that Eastertime has been for this community in which "the powerful gift of the Spirit has been celebrated . . . without ceasing since the baptisms and confirmations at the Easter Vigil" (PI, 2). The intimate relationship of Pentecost to Easter should be manifested ritually, in sprinkling with water and Eastertime's fragrant and floral incense, and musically in the Eastertime Gloria, a special sequence, the resounding Alleluias that mark the gospel acclamation, and the unique dismissal melody with its double Alleluia that closes Mass and echoes again in the final verse and response of Evening Prayer.

■ DECORATIONS: Peter Mazar (*To Crown the Year*, pages 145–48) derives wonderful suggestions from the link of this day to the Jewish titles of Shavuout (harvest) and Yom Habikkurim (day of first fruits).

■ NEOPHYTES: The neophytes, dressed for the last time in their white robes, should be present in their special places: honored, perhaps in a homiletic reference and with a special incensation at the preparation rite (just before the whole assembly is); prayed for in the intercessions; and toasted in posteucharist or post-vespers hospitality.

Babies baptized at Easter and throughout the past year can be brought to church in their baptismal gowns, accompanied by parents, godparents, families and friends.

Those received into full communion should be included in the intercessions and might have special seating.

The newly confirmed and first communicants should also be in our prayers. They, too, might have special seating and be dressed in what they wore at confirmation or first communion.

SATURDAY VIGIL MASS

The extended vigil described below is the preferred form of celebration this evening (PI, 2). Where circumstances make this impossible, and the regular Saturday vigil Mass is celebrated, there are special texts in both the sacramentary and lectionary.

EXTENDED PENTECOST VIGIL

As with all solemnities, the church taps into its Jewish roots, computing time from sundown to sundown. Quoting the challenging *Circular Letter* (1988) from the Vatican's Congregation for Divine Worship, the Pastoral Introduction (PI, 2) suggests for this evening an extended vigil whose character is not baptismal but one of intensive common prayer modeled on Acts 1. Using the Old Testament readings indicated in the lectionary, this vigil provides a suitable way of closing the period of postbaptismal catechesis. It may be enhanced by combining evening prayer with Mass. See the order of worship on page 177.

MORNING PRAYER

Christmas and Easter mornings will have provided the precedent and pattern for this morning. Scheduled at a time when at least the principal members of the Sunday morning "team" can be present, the celebration of this hour today will signal the holiness of the whole day.

MASS DURING THE DAY

■ INTRODUCTORY RITES: A quietly expectant atmosphere can be established as the community

gathers through the use of special instrumental music or the Taizé ostinato "Veni, Sancte Spiritus." Once the actual liturgy begins, continue the Eastertime ritual patterns.

■ LITURGY OF THE WORD: On this last day of Eastertime, the assembly responds to the mighty proclamation of the Pentecost event in Acts with Psalm 104. Three settings are offered by GIA: C. Alexander Peloquin (GIA, G-1662) and Robert Edward Smith's (G-2122) "Lord, send out your Spirit"; and Paul Lisicky's "Psalm 104," in *Gather*. World Library offers several settings of this psalm: Angelo della Pica's in *Psalms for the Cantor*, vol. v; Vern Pat Nelson's "Spirit Psalm" (#2616) which has more elaborate verses for the cantor; Dan Tucker's fine "Lord, send out your Spirit" (#7994); and two bilingual settings, "Renueve la Tierra Madre" by Charlotte Struckhoff, and "Ven, O Espiritu" by Lorenza Florian, which is particularly good for children.

Don't fail to sing the sequence. The traditional chant melody, called the "Golden Sequence," with Latin or English text, can be found in *Worship* (#857). Alternately, Ann Colleen Dohns has set this sequence with responses for the assembly (WLP, 5718). The sequence text might well appear beforehand, in a bulletin insert orienting the community toward Pentecost, and maybe even as part of a take-home brochure for the novena of prayer between Ascension and Pentecost.

■ LITURGY OF THE EUCHARIST: See today's proper preface and the inserts for eucharistic prayer I. Repeat the acclamations used throughout the Fifty Days, perhaps enhancing them with more instrumentation and harmonies.

■ CONCLUDING RITE: There is a beautiful solemn blessing for today (which may be repeated at Evening Prayer II). Even if you haven't done it since the Easter octave, today's dismissal includes the double Alleluia, a final reminder (at Mass and vespers) that this is still the Easter feast.

■ HYMNODY: The hymn of the day, in addition to the Golden Sequence, is "Veni Creator Spiritus," found in many forms, including Richard Wojcik's "O Holy Spirit, by whose breath, (*Worship*, #4750); Ralph Wright's translation in *Hymnal for the Hours* (GIA), which can be sung to the traditional chant or to an 88.88 meter tune (e.g. Puer Nobis); and Mike Hay's "Holy Spirit, Creator's breath" (*We Celebrate*, #940).

DOMESTIC PRAYER

Today's mealtime prayer might be celebrated at a dining table graced with a fiery assortment of spring's brightest blossoms, and perhaps red dinner candles. Prayers for home use are in *Catholic Household Blessings and Prayers* (page 157), and the outline for Eastertime table prayer still is appropriate today (page 84).

EVENING PRAYER II

This liturgical hour marks the end of Eastertime and merits attention and celebration. The double Alleluia dismissal signifies the formal end of the Fifty Days. A procession accompanies the transfer of the Easter candle from its place of honor near the ambo to its year-round place of importance at the font. Use the best of Easter's songs for the procession or one with plenty of Alleluia refrains for people to sing by heart (maybe the Alleluia from the Easter Vigil gospel). As when entering the church at the Easter Vigil, so now the whole assembly follows the candle—this time to the font. As the candle is placed there, let the music continue, while all come to the font to sign themselves with the living and life-giving waters.

TEXTS FOR THE EUCHARISTIC ASSEMBLY

INTRODUCTORY RITES

Greeting

A *Presider:* Alleluia. Christ is risen.
  People: The Lord is risen indeed. Alleluia.

B The God of life, who broke the bonds of death and raised Jesus from the tomb, be with you.

According to the order proposed in the revised sacramentary, only one form of the opening rite is used at any celebration. Form II, the penitential rite, is not used during Eastertime.

I. RITE OF BLESSING AND SPRINKLING OF WATER

The special Eastertime form given in the sacramentary may be used.

III. LITANY OF PRAISE

When the Gloria is not prescribed, the litany of praise may be used. After an Invitation, invocations V or VI of Penitential Rite, form C in present sacramentary may be used. The absolution prayer is omitted, and the opening prayer follows immediately.

IV. KYRIE

When the Gloria is not prescribed, the litany of praise may be used.

Invitation

God is making all things new.
Acclaim Christ, the first fruits of the
    new creation.

The Kyrie, in English or Greek, follows; the absolution is omitted, the opening prayer is offered.

LITURGY OF THE WORD

Dismissal of the Catechumens

My dear friends: With the assurance of our loving support, this community sends you forth to reflect more deeply on the word of God we have shared. May Christ who is risen from the dead, and who shines with special radiance among us in this Easter's newly baptized, fill you with joyful hope and steadfast perseverance, so that in the beauty of an Easter yet to come, you, too, may be one with us in the paschal feast of the Lord's table.

General Intercessions

Invitation

God has given us a new birth unto a living hope by raising Christ from the dead. Let our Easter prayer embrace the needs of all, as we offer it through Christ who for ever intercedes for us before the Father.

LITURGY OF THE EUCHARIST

Dismissal of Eucharistic Ministers

Go forth in peace to the sick and homebound of our community, bearing the word of life and the body of Christ, together with the assurance of our love and concern. By your presence and the holy gifts you share, remind them of the communion that is ours in the risen Lord whose paschal mystery has made us one body and one spirit, in the one baptism by which we have been born to new life.

EXTENDED VIGIL FOR PENTECOST EVE

INTRODUCTORY RITES

Mass begins with an entrance antiphon or song, sign of the cross and the Eastertime greeting. If an additional opening rite is desired it should be Kyrie or Litany of Praise, page 176.

Opening Prayer

Let us pray.

Pause for silent prayer.

God of power,
let the splendor of your glory come upon us,
and through the radiance of the Holy Spirit
let the brightness of Christ,
who is light from light,
shine in the hearts of those born again
    by grace.

Grant this through our Lord Jesus Christ,
    your Son,
who lives and reigns with you in the unity
    of the Holy Spirit,
God for ever and ever.

or:

God of majesty and glory,
you bring us to the day
that crowns our joyful Easter feast.

Open for us the fountain of living waters
promised to the faithful,
that the outpouring of the Spirit
may reveal Christ's glory
and enlighten all who wait in hope
for the glorious day of redemption.

We ask this through Jesus Christ,
    the resurrection and the life,
who lives and reigns with you in the unity
    of the Holy Spirit,
God for ever and ever.

— © ICEL

EXPANDED LITURGY OF THE WORD

Invitation

Presider addresses the assembly in the following or similar words.

We have begun the vigil of Pentecost,
my dear friends,
after the example of the apostles and
    disciples,
who, with Mary, the Mother of Jesus,
devoted themselves to prayer as they
    awaited the Spirit promised by the Lord.

Let us now listen with quiet hearts to the
    word of God.

Let us reflect on the great deeds the Lord
    has done for his people and pray that
    the Holy Spirit, whom the Father sent
    as the first fruits to those who believe,
    may complete God's work in the world.

Reading 1

Genesis 11:1–9: *It was named Babel because there the Lord confused the language of the whole earth (lectionary, #63.1).*

Responsorial Psalm

Psalm 33:10–11, 12–13, 14–15.
    R. Happy the people the Lord has
    chosen to be his own.

Prayer

Let us pray.

Pause for silent prayer.

Almighty God,
preserve your church as that holy people
united by the oneness of Father, Son and
    Holy Spirit;
let it be for all the sacrament of holiness
    and unity
and lead the world to the perfection
    of your love.

We ask this through Jesus Christ our Lord.

Reading 2

Exodus 19:3–8, 16–20: *The Lord God appeared before all the people on Mount Sinai (lectionary, #63.2).*

Responsorial Psalm

Canticle of Daniel 3:52, 53, 54, 55, 56.
    R. (52b): Glory and praise for ever.

or:

Psalm 19:8, 9, 10, 11
    R. (John 6:68c): Lord, you have the
    words of everlasting life.

Prayer

Let us pray.

Pause for silent prayer.

O God,
you once gave the ancient law to Moses
amid fire and lightning on Mount Sinai;
and on this day you revealed a new covenant
in the fire of the Holy Spirit.
Let the Spirit you poured out on your apostles
burn within us always,
and let the new Israel, gathered from
    every people,
welcome with joy your eternal commandment
    of love.
We ask this through Jesus Christ our Lord.

Reading 3

Ezekiel 37:1–14: *Dry bones of Israel, I shall put my Spirit in you, and you will live (lectionary, #63.3).*

Responsorial Psalm

Psalm 107: 2–3, 4–5, 6–7, 8–9
    R. (1b): Give thanks to the Lord, God's love is everlasting.

or:

    R. Alleluia.

Prayer

Let us pray.

Pause for silent prayer.

Lord God of hosts,
you restore the fallen
and preserve what you have restored.
Increase the number of people to be
    renewed and made holy in your name,
that all who are cleansed by baptism
may be guided always by your inspiration.
We ask this through Jesus Christ our Lord.

Reading 4

Joel 3:1–5: *I will pour out my spirit on all humankind (lectionary, #63.4).*

Responsorial Psalm

Psalm 104: 1–2a, 24 and 35c, 27–28, 29bc–30.
    R. (See 30): Lord, send out your Spirit, and renew the face of the earth.

or:

    R. Alleluia

Prayer

Let us pray.

Pause for silent prayer.

Lord, in your mercy
fulfill your promise to us,
that the Holy Spirit who is to come
may make us witnesses before the world
to the gospel of our Lord, Jesus Christ,
who lives and reigns for ever and ever.

The priest then intones the Gloria.

Collect

Let us pray.

Pause for silent prayer.

Almighty and ever-living God,
whose will it was
to encompass the paschal mystery within
    a season of Fifty Days,
grant that the people once scattered over
    the face of the earth
and divided by many tongues
may be gathered together by your heavenly
    Spirit
to confess your name with a single voice.
We ask this through our Lord Jesus Christ,
    your Son,
who lives and reigns with you in the unity
    of the Holy Spirit,
God for ever and ever.

Epistle Reading

Romans 8: 22–27: *The Spirit intercedes for us with sighs too deep for words.*

Gospel Acclamation

This verse may accompany the singing of the Alleluia.

Come, Holy Spirit, fill the hearts of your
    faithful
and kindle in them the fire of your love.

Gospel

John 7:37–39: *Out of the believer's heart shall flow rivers of living water.*

DISMISSAL

In dismissing the people, the deacon or presider adds the double Alleluia to the invitation, as do the people to their response.

NOTES

SUMMER AND FALL ORDINARY TIME

The Season
Perspective / 183
Purpose / 184
ICEL Pastoral Introduction: Order of Mass / 185
Taking It Home / 198
The Calendar
May 19 – November 29 / 199

Perspective

As we begin an almost half-year stretch of Sundays, this would be a good time to revisit the reflections concerning this "season of Sundays" in the Winter Ordinary Time section of this *Sourcebook*.

■ SOLEMNITIES ON SUNDAY: This year only a few solemnities interrupt the flow of "Sunday as Sunday." Ordinary Time begins with two solemnities known among liturgists as "idea feasts," that is, celebrations not focused on events but on doctrines, not from the events presented by the scriptures but from the living faith born of the community's reflection over the centuries: Holy Trinity (May 25) and the Body and Blood of Christ (June 1).

Two other solemnities occur around the points that mark the beginning and end of summertime in the lives of most communities, Saints Peter and Paul (June 29) and the Holy Cross, usually called the Exaltation or Triumph of the Holy Cross (September 14).

Finally, two more celebrations (one technically not a solemnity but replacing Sunday liturgy nonetheless) occur during November when, fortunately, they fit in quite well with the several "eschatological" motifs associated with late Ordinary Time: the Commemoration of All the Faithful Departed (All Souls, November 2) and the Dedication of the Lateran Basilica in Rome (November 9).

SEASON OF MARK (AND A BIT OF JOHN!)

Lectors and homilists will benefit immeasurably from at least some familiarity with the many fine commentaries now available on Mark's gospel. They range in content and style from the very scholarly to the very popular, but all of them are designed to make this deceptively simple text more accessible, and therefore more compelling, to contemporary Christians. The *Anchor Bible* series from Doubleday is renowned for its detailed scholarship. C.S. Mann's volume on Mark and Raymond Brown's multivolume commentary on John are considered the classics in English. The *New Jerome Biblical Commentary* (Prentice Hall, 1990) remains the standard Catholic, one-volume commentary, while *The Collegeville Bible Commentary* (Liturgical Press, 1983) is a far more accessible presentation of the same contemporary biblical scholarship. The same publisher offers the more technical *Sacra Pagina* series, single-volume commentaries on the New Testament books; and the new *Berit Olam* ("The Everlasting Covenant"): *Studies in Hebrew Narrative and Poetry,* a similar series for the First Testament.

A Bible with a built-in commentary, as well as helpful notes on the arrangement and use of the lectionary, is *The Catholic Study Bible* (Oxford University Press, 1990). Donald Senior and Pheme

Perkins provide a concise and highly readable guide to Mark and the other gospels. There is even a very interesting Buddhist approach to this year's gospel! John P. Keenan's *The Gospel of Mark: A Mahayan Reading* (Maryknoll: Orbis, 1995) provides a wealth of fascinating insights for homiletic preparation and personal prayer, and offers additional testimony that we have never really finished reading even the most basic of scriptural texts!

A SEASON OF SHIFTS AND SHADINGS

When planning the celebration of this vast expanse of time, those who prepare the liturgy will find it helpful to determine the several "blocks" of time within it. Sunday as Sunday, the original feast day unique in itself and without seasonal coloring, is still our ideal in Ordinary Time. Moreover, planners must resist the temptation to divide Ordinary Time into several artificial or overly thematic "miniseasons." But, handled carefully and subtly, charting the several shifts and varied shadings prevents an unfocused drift through these long weeks and guards against each Sunday appearing as a discrete unit, related to nothing but itself.

The most fruitful way to discern the shading that occurs in the mosaic of Ordinary Time is to align the several categories of shifts that occur in these weeks between Holy Trinity and Christ the King. *Sourcebook* suggests a multifaceted approach that looks to several "stars" for guidance:

■ THE LECTIONARY AND LITURGICAL TEXTS: Several commentaries referred to offer various ways of systematizing the Ordinary Time block of gospel readings. In the calendar entries, some ideas are offered on choosing liturgical texts and music that will paint each phase of Ordinary Time with a particular but subtle shade suggested, in great part, by the lectionary.

■ SOCIAL LIFE AND CALENDAR PATTERNS: This long stretch of Ordinary Time embraces a wide variety of activities on most people's social calendars. At one end, school's out and parish activities are winding down. There is a burst of social activity in late May and early June: graduations and weddings, cookouts and parties. Then much of the world eases into the activities of high summer: reunions, picnics, parades and day trips to the beach or lakes. Later, summer can be a bit more mellow; scheduled events may be few and far between as people move in and out of the community on vacation. Eventually school reconvenes, and parish, civic and social programs start after Labor Day. Then it's football season again, and homecoming dances and Halloween costumes; then time to remember saints and souls and to make plans for Thanksgiving travels and gatherings.

■ NATURE AND THE ENVIRONMENT OF WORSHIP: In many parts of the U.S. and Canada, late May and early June explode into the sights and smells, colors and contrasts of late spring. Soon enough, though, the light greens of early growth yield to the deeper greens of summer's humid weeks. In many places, flowers, grains and first fruits begin to mature, and, over the centuries, several liturgical feasts of August and September have been associated with their harvesting and blessing.

In these same areas, a spate of unexpected warmth is frequently a gracious surprise in late September or even mid-October, but the changing leaves announce clearly the changing of seasons. Soon branches are bare, and the pumpkins are carved into jack-o-lanterns. For many, it's a time to decorate the graves of the family saints and souls no longer physically with us, and to plan the yearly gathering together with family and friends in happy thanksgiving for the bounty of earth.

When all three considerations are taken together, this pattern emerges:

Summer I: Ordinary Time, Weeks 7–14
Summer II: Ordinary Time, Weeks 15–23
Autumn: Ordinary Time, Weeks 24–30
November: Ordinary Time, Weeks 31–34

Purpose

WITH no particular aspect of the Christian mystery to claim our focused attention, ICEL's Pastoral Introduction: Ordinary Time [PIOT] suggests that this may be the perfect time of the liturgical year "to develop consistent patterns for both ministers and the assembly as they fulfill their respective roles in the celebration of the eucharist" (PIOT, 7). During Winter Ordinary Time, *Sourcebook* presented some reflections from the Pastoral Introduction: Order of Mass (PIOM). These centered on carrying out the "transitional" rites (introductory, preparation and concluding rites) and on the overall ritual structure and ministries of the liturgy of the word and liturgy of the eucharist. Here are further sections of that Pastoral Introduction for reflection, discussion and action. Besides the points noted by the *Sourcebook,* each community will surely find in this Pastoral Introduction its own "examination of conscience" and program for local refinement and revision.

ICEL Pastoral Introduction: Order of Mass

LITURGY OF THE WORD

82 The lectionary for Mass, revised at the direction of the Second Vatican Council, has opened up the treasures of the Bible, so that richer fare might be provided for the faithful at the table of God's word. The introduction to the lectionary speaks extensively of the word of God in the plan of salvation and in the life of the church. All who share in the ministry of the word will want to study this introduction and take its teaching to heart.

83 The functions of the various ministers, and guidelines for their service, are given in the introduction to the lectionary and in the first part of this introduction.

■ COMMENTARY: The PIOM makes it clear that those who serve in the ministry of reader ought to be thoroughly familiar not only with the specific texts they are to proclaim but with the book in which these are enshrined and with the foundational documents that introduce that book. Sadly, the 1970 edition of the lectionary, which has been used in the United States until now, does not contain the very fine and extensive introduction prepared for the 1981 Latin edition of the lectionary. Revised editions will, of course, provide this. In the meantime, LTP has published the introduction to the new edition in *The Liturgy Documents: A Parish Resource* (third edition).

BIBLICAL READINGS

84 In the word of God handed down in the scriptures the community of faith even now hears God speaking to it. For this reason the biblical readings and their accompanying scripture chants may not be omitted, shortened or replaced by nonbiblical texts.

85 The proclamation of the gospel reading is the high point of the liturgy of the word. The other readings in their established sequence from the Old and New Testaments prepare the assembly for this proclamation.

86 The principles governing the selection and distribution of these readings are explained in the introduction to the lectionary.

- When a prayerful silence is observed before or after a reading, the whole assembly is to take part in it. The reader does not move to or from the ambo during the period of silence.

- The liturgy of the word may, when it would be helpful, be introduced by a brief word on the background of the readings. Such comments, whether from the priest or another minister, should always be succinct and well prepared.

- The readings may be sung, provided the form of singing respects the rhythms and genius of the language and does not obscure the words.

- The conclusion to the first and second readings, "The word of the Lord," may be sung, even by someone other than the reader, so as to elicit from the faithful a sung response of gratitude for the word of God.

■ COMMENTARY: Several "housekeeping" chores, perfect for attending to during Ordinary Time, are mentioned here. They involve these various ministers:

■ LECTOR: Reading an excerpt intelligently requires knowing the context in which it occurs. Lectors are well advised to look at what comes before and what follows the passage entrusted to their ministry. General principles for the seasons and for Ordinary Time are spelled out in the lectionary. The annual *Workbook for Lectors and Gospel Readers* (LTP) provides commentary in the margin to orient lectors to the context of each reading.

■ ASSEMBLY: Sacred silence doesn't just happen. Our aural environment is provided by the media, and TV and radio stations fear few things more than "dead air"—the sound of silence that signals nothing is happening! Developing a communal comfort with an appropriate length

of reflective silence is something that the community—presider, lector, assembly—has to work on together. So important is this reflective pause that the new Canadian lectionary includes a rubric regarding silence after every first and second reading!

■ PRESIDER OR OTHER MINISTER: Introducing the readings is a topic about which people generally have strong feelings. Some bemoan the verbosity of the usual comments: more verbiage added to an already wordy liturgy of the word. Others feel strongly that, pastorally, a family struggling to get from the breakfast table to the car through the parking lot and into church needs a moment of orientation to be able to "hear" an obscure passage from Ezekiel. The PIOM spells out the criteria: when helpful (not a constant feature); succinct (not a minihomily); well prepared (never off the top of the head: write it out!).

■ MUSIC MINISTRY: While chanted readings have all but vanished from current usage, there is a long tradition for this. The new Episcopal service books (New York: Church Hymnal Corporation) provide an extensive orientation to the old Roman tones, and GIA still publishes Joseph Kush's adaptation of more ornate chants for the festal readings. As the PIOM notes, however, many communities find it an enhancement on solemnities to chant the introductory dialogue and the concluding verse and response.

RESPONSORIAL PSALM

87 The responsorial psalm follows the first reading and is an integral part of the liturgy of the word. After hearing and taking to heart God's word, the assembly responds with words which are themselves God-given. Words which have expressed the faith and feelings of God's people over the centuries are selected by the church to express the appropriate response, whether of wonder and praise, repentance and sorrow, hope and trust, or joy and exultation.

88 The assembly is to be helped and encouraged to discern God's word in the psalms, to adopt them as their own prayer and to experience them as the prayer of the church.

- The psalms, the songs and hymns of Israel, are normally sung. This may be done in a variety of ways. The preferred form is responsorial, in which the cantor or psalmist sings the verses and the whole assembly takes up the response. In the direct form, which is also permitted, there is no intervening response and the cantor, or the whole assembly together, sings the verses consecutively.

- But if other ways of singing or sharing the psalms are appropriate to the particular language or culture, they, too, are used, so that the people's participation may be facilitated by every means.

- Even when it is impossible to sing the psalm, it may be possible to support and enrich its recitation with instrumental music. Psalms should always be recited in a manner conducive to meditation.

- The common responsorial psalms, provided in the lectionary for various seasons, may be used instead of the one assigned for the day, if that choice would facilitate sung participation.

■ COMMENTARY: Many communities still find the weekly chanting of the responsorial psalm a challenging prospect. But anyone who has experienced the power of this part of the liturgy celebrated properly will testify that every effort ought to be expended to achieve it. There is nothing quite so moving as hearing the word proclaimed powerfully, reverently and well, then to reflect in prayerful silence, and to feel the assembly around you and the presider before you doing the same. Finally, to repeat a refrain after the cantor helps the reading just heard to echo in the assembly and, beyond the celebration, to reecho in one's heart as the refrain returns to mind off and on during the week.

GOSPEL ACCLAMATION

89 The Alleluia, or, according to the season, the gospel acclamation, is an acclamation which expresses the people's greeting of the Lord and their faith in his presence as he addresses them in the gospel reading.

90 The gospel acclamation has traditionally accompanied the gospel procession, in which the book of the gospels is carried to the ambo accompanied by lights and incense.

- The Alleluia or gospel acclamation looks forward to the gospel reading. It does not respond to the previous reading, from which it is separated by a distinct pause.

- If incense is to be used at the gospel reading, it is prepared after the second reading and before the gospel procession.

- The deacon who is to proclaim the gospel reading bows before the priest celebrant and asks for a blessing. If a priest reads the gospel, he bows before the altar and silently recites the prescribed prayer.

- The assembly stands while the procession moves to the ambo and the Alleluia is sung.
- As an acclamation, the Alleluia is sung by everyone present. The verse may be sung by cantor or choir (or even recited). If the Alleluia cannot be sung, it is omitted.

GOSPEL READING

91 Because the proclamation of the gospel reading is the high point of the liturgy of the word, it is distinguished from the other readings by special marks of honor. Its proclamation is reserved to a deacon or, in his absence, a priest. The one who proclaims the gospel reading prepares himself, the deacon by receiving a blessing, the priest by prayer. The people stand to hear the gospel reading and acclaim Christ present and speaking to them. Servers with candles may stand on each side of the ambo, and the book may be incensed before the text is proclaimed. If the book of the gospels is used, it is carried in procession from the altar to the ambo.

- The proclamation of the gospel reading is never omitted, even at Masses with children at which an abbreviated liturgy of the word is permitted.
- The gospel reading is proclaimed by a deacon. If no deacon is present, it is proclaimed by a priest other than the one presiding. Only if no deacon or other priest is present is it to be read by the priest who presides.

    The deacon (or priest) greets the people with "The Lord be with you," and while announcing the gospel passage he makes the sign of the cross first on the book, then on his forehead, lips and breast. The faithful also sign themselves in this way and then respond, "Glory to you, Lord."
- Even if the gospel reading itself is not sung, it may be helpful to sing the greeting and title of the gospel reading at the beginning and "The gospel of the Lord" at the end, so as to allow the people to sing their acclamation. On more solemn occasions, it may be appropriate to repeat the sung Alleluia at the end of the gospel reading.

■ COMMENTARY: Reflection on this segment of the PIOM provides the community with the resources for combining ritual action, musical possibilities, visual elements and even an olfactory dimension, into a powerful celebration of Christ's presence in the gospel proclamation. Questions to consider:

- On what days, or in which seasons, does (or should!) our community employ a solemn gospel procession?
- What does the Ordinary Time movement from silence after the second reading to gospel proclamation look like? Even without incense and candles, movement and ritual are possible (see the Ordinary Time Sunday featured in the LTP video *The Word of the Lord*).
- Have the familiar gestures (signing the book, the forehead, lips and breast) become too familiar? Like all nonverbal ritual, this one can become perfunctory and meaningless. Might not Ordinary Time provide an opportunity for some homiletic reflections linking this gesture to the sign of the cross and the shaping of our Christian lives, and thus suggesting a more thoughtful execution?
- What role does (or should) music play in "bracketing" the proclamation with sung praise?

HOMILY

92 The homily is an integral part of the liturgy and a necessary source of nourishment for the Christian life. By means of it the mysteries of the faith and the guiding principles of Christian living are expounded, most often from the scriptures proclaimed but also from the other texts and rites of the liturgy.

93 In the readings God's word is accessible to people of every age and condition, but the homily as a living explanation of the word increases its impact by assisting the faithful to assimilate it and apply it in their lives. It leads them from contemplation of the word to profound appropriation of the mystery of Christ and his sacrifice in a more wholehearted celebration of the eucharist and in their daily lives.

94 If it is to fulfill its purpose, the homily must be the fruit of meditation, carefully prepared, and in length, style and content sensitively adapted to the needs and capacities of all present. This may well be more easily achieved if the priest prepares the homily in shared reflection and prayer with members or representatives of the congregation.

- On Sundays and holy days there must be a homily at all Masses celebrated with a congregation; it may not be omitted without a serious reason.
- A homily is strongly recommended on the weekdays of Advent, Christmas, Lent and Easter and on other occasions when people come in considerable numbers. For the benefit of those people who are regular participants, and because it is indeed an integral part of the liturgy, a homily is appropriate at almost all Masses with a congregation.
- The homily is ordinarily given by the priest who presides. A deacon or, at a concelebration, one of the concelebrating priests may be invited to preach.

- On particular occasions someone besides a priest or deacon may be invited to preach the word of God. At Masses for children, for example, one of the adults better able to communicate with children may be asked to speak after the gospel reading. Such preaching has its own importance, though it is not a homily. The one who gives the homily or speaks at this point should be a participant in the entire celebration and so experience the proclamation of the word on which the preaching is based and the consummation of the celebration in eucharistic communion.

- The priest celebrant gives the homily while standing or sitting at his chair or from the ambo. Other homilists use the ambo. In particular circumstances, such as in an unrenovated church or at a celebration with children, the homilist may need to approach closer to the congregation in order to communicate effectively.

- The custom of beginning and ending the homily with the sign of the cross arose when the sermon was somewhat detached from the liturgy of the Mass. The practice is now inadvisable.

- It is most appropriate that a period of silence follow the homily, so that the people may take the word of God to heart and prepare a response to it in prayer.

- If catechumens are present, they may be kindly dismissed before the profession of faith in order to go and reflect together on the word proclaimed. Texts for this dismissal are provided in the *Rite of Christian Initiation of Adults*.

■ COMMENTARY: Some technical matters surface immediately. The homily begins with the gospel and ends with a period of silent reflection! Separated from it no longer by the parish announcements or even the devotional gestures of the former rite, the homily is integral to the liturgy of the word. Style and content reflect this integrity. The liturgical (euchological) texts enjoy an authority in the Catholic tradition that places them close to the scriptures as appropriate materials to inspire preaching. Ordinary Time might well be a time in which to plan a homiletic series that reflects the scriptures of the day but helps the community grow in appreciation of the liturgy. *Preaching About the Mass* (LTP) is an excellent resource, presenting a complete program of sample homilies, bulletin inserts and reflection questions.

The quality of preaching is an ongoing concern, not just to congregations but to preachers themselves. A number of parishes and homilists have instituted a postliturgy reflection group. After the assembly's coffee hour, a small group (perhaps a different one each month) meets within a strict time frame, for a two-part session. With or, in some cases, without the homilist, these questions are answered:

- What was the bad news confronted by this week's homily?
- What good news did the homily propose in response to the bad news?
- What difference will that make in my life this week?

Other concerns and questions may be surfaced and noted for sharing with the homilist. For the second part, the homilist, if not already present, joins the group, and similar questions are raised regarding the next week's readings. Thus the homilist leaves with some concrete idea as to what at least one group of parishioners is wondering about regarding next week's readings, and parishioners have a sense that they are assisting in the preparation of the homily they hope will assist them in living the Christian life.

For more help with homilies, see LTP's *Preaching the Just Word* video series.

PROFESSION OF FAITH

95 In the profession of faith, the people respond and give their assent to the word of God heard in the readings and the homily. And before they celebrate the mystery of faith in the eucharist, they call to mind the rule of faith in a formulary approved by the church.

- The profession of faith is recited by priest and people together on Sundays and solemnities. It may also be said at other solemn celebrations.

- The form customarily to be used is the Nicene Creed. At Masses with children, and in countries where it is authorized at Masses with adults, the Apostles' Creed may be used. The Apostles' Creed is provided in two forms, one for recitation straight through, the other in the form of question and response.

- At the Easter Vigil, and at Masses in which baptism or confirmation is celebrated, the Creed is replaced by the baptismal profession of faith. In Masses that include acceptance into the order of catechumens and in ritual Masses for the election or enrollment of names or for the scrutinies, the profession of faith may be omitted.

- The origin and nature of the Creed indicate that it is more naturally recited than sung. If it is sung, it should be in a way that involves the entire assembly.

- A profound bow is made by all at the phrase that begins "was incarnate of the Holy Spirit." [This refers to the revised translation to be used in the new sacramentary.]

■ COMMENTARY: Where permission has been given for the use of the Apostles' Creed, some order should be determined for parish usage, so that the community has the opportunity to learn both Creeds and the Apostles' Creed in both forms. The Advent-Christmas-Epiphany season would seem especially appropriate for the Nicene Creed, as would the feasts of the Presentation, Annunciation, Holy Trinity and Christ the King. The Apostles' Creed would seem good for the Easter season, since it is the ancient baptismal profession of faith. Ordinary Time might be suitable for the question/answer format that will appear in the revised sacramentary.

GENERAL INTERCESSIONS

96 Enlightened and moved by God's word, the assembly exercises its priestly function by interceding for all humanity. Because "the joy and hope, the struggle and anguish of the people of this age and especially of the poor and those suffering in any way are the joy and hope, the struggle and anguish of Christ's disciples" (*Pastoral Constitution on the Church in the Modern World*, 1), the church prays not just for its own needs but for the salvation of the world, for civil authorities, for those oppressed by any burden, and for the local community, particularly those who are sick or who have died.

97 Thus, even though the intercessions may be quite concrete or particular in content, they should always look beyond the concerns of the local assembly to the needs of the whole church and of the wider world. As such, they are a sign of the communion of the particular assembly with all other assemblies and with the universal church.

98 The priest celebrant directs the prayer from the chair. He briefly invites the people to pray, and at the end he draws their intercessions together in a brief concluding prayer. The intentions are proposed by a deacon, another minister or members of the assembly at the ambo or another suitable place. After each intention, the faithful respond by silent prayer or a common response or both. They affirm the concluding prayer of the priest with their Amen.

- The general intercessions are ordinarily included in all Masses.
- Both the priest's introduction and the proposed intentions are addressed to the assembly, not to God. They are invitations or biddings to the faithful, who then pray for the suggested intention in the silence of their hearts and in a common petition.

- These intentions should be short, clear and objective enough for the faithful to comprehend and respond to them without difficulty.
- The response they are to evoke is petition rather than praise, thanksgiving or repentance.
- On particular occasions, when other sacraments or particular rites are celebrated in conjunction with the Mass, the range of intentions may be more closely concerned with the occasion; but even so, the intercessions should always include some general or universal intentions.
- For each intention, the invitation to pray and the response may be sung or the entire intention may be sung or even spoken while music is played.
- Those who propose the intentions return to their place only after the completion of the concluding prayer.

■ COMMENTARY: Though the PIOM does not specifically offer this direction, presiders should be aware that the collect concluding the general intercessions, as words addressed to God on behalf of the community, ought to be no less carefully prepared than the homily or the introduction to the liturgy or readings. If the alternative opening prayer found in the sacramentary was used earlier, perhaps the regular opening prayer (with short conclusion, e.g., "we ask this through Christ our Lord") could end the general intercessions. If the regular opening prayer was used earlier, then consider the alternative prayer (with short conclusion) as a perfect way to recap and conclude the liturgy of the word. Presiders who are used to ad-libbing this concluding prayer should analyze the style and content of what they usually say. The richness of our collect tradition provides plenty of texts to serve as prayers or at least as models. *Prayers for Sundays and Seasons* (LTP) offers examples of scripturally inspired general intercessions for each week.

LITURGY OF THE EUCHARIST

III The eucharistic prayer, the center and summit of the entire celebration, sums up what it means for the church to celebrate the eucharist. It is a memorial proclamation of praise and thanksgiving for God's work of salvation, a proclamation in which the body and blood of Christ are made present by the power of the Holy Spirit and the people are joined to Christ

in offering his sacrifice to the Father. The eucharistic prayer is proclaimed by the priest celebrant in the name of Christ and on behalf of the whole assembly, which professes its faith and gives its assent through dialogue, acclamations and the Amen. Since the eucharistic prayer is the summit of the Mass, its solemn nature and importance are enhanced when it is sung.

112 The eucharistic prayer is proclaimed over the people's gifts. In the rich and varied tradition of this prayer, the church gives praise and thanks for God's holiness and justice and for all God's mighty deeds in creating and redeeming the human race, deeds which reached their climax in the incarnation, life, death and resurrection of Jesus Christ. In the eucharistic prayer the mystery of Christ's saving death and resurrection is recalled; the Last Supper is recounted; the memorial sacrifice of his body and blood is presented to the Father; and the Holy Spirit is invoked to sanctify the gifts and transform those who partake of them into the body of Christ, uniting the assembly and the whole church and family of God, living and dead, into one communion of love, service and praise to the glory of the Father.

113 The following eucharistic prayers are provided in the sacramentary.

- Eucharistic Prayers I–IV are the principal prayers and are for use throughout the liturgical year.

- Eucharistic Prayers for Masses of Reconciliation I and II express thanksgiving in the context of the reconciliation won by Christ. They are particularly appropriate for use during the season of Lent and may be used at other times when the mystery of reconciliation is reflected in the readings or other texts of the Mass or is the reason for a particular gathering of the faithful.

- Eucharistic Prayers for Masses with Children I–III may be used at Masses when children constitute a significant proportion of the assembly. These texts are for the purpose of enhancing the participation of children in this central prayer of the Mass and of preparing them to take full part in Masses with adults. The eucharistic prayers for children, with their variety of acclamations, will be most effective in engaging the children when sung. The three prayers use different levels of language. Prayer I may be more suitable for those only recently introduced to the eucharist, Prayers II and III more appropriate as children grow in sacramental awareness and in familiarity with the eucharistic liturgy. The texts are rich in catechetical themes which may be drawn upon when preparing children for the eucharistic celebration and as the basis for reflecting with them afterward on, for example, the nature of the eucharist as thanksgiving for creation and salvation, the role of the Spirit and the real presence of Christ in the eucharist and the church, the concepts of sacrifice, sacrament and meal.

■ **COMMENTARY:** The Pastoral Introduction suggests some questions about our eucharistic praying: Are the eucharistic prayers chosen according to any reflective pattern or solely at the presider's discretion? How frequently is time the principal factor? Or is there a conscious effort to be sensitive to season, feast or scripture passage? Is there a good balance between variety and repetition? Some parishes find it helpful to chart a pattern of use throughout the seasons, solemnities, feasts and blocks of Ordinary Time on which planners and presiders can agree.

114 The following elements may be recognized as characteristic of the eucharistic prayer. They do not all appear with equal force in every eucharistic prayer.

Dialogue

115 Since the celebration of Mass is a communal action, the dialogue between priest celebrant and the assembly is of special value. It is not only an external sign of communal celebration but also the means of greater interchange between priest and people. The dialogue establishes at the outset that the eucharistic prayer is prayed in the person and power of the Lord who is with the church, and in the name of the whole assembly and indeed of the whole church in heaven and on earth. All are invited, in biblical terms, to lift up their hearts, that is, to raise up and place in God's presence their entire being, thoughts, memories, emotions and expectations, in grateful attention and anticipation.

- The voice, the gestures, the stance and entire demeanor of the priest celebrant help to convey the importance and the urgency of this movement, lifting the assembly and stimulating it to gratitude and wonder. This may be most effectively achieved by singing.

- Before the dialogue, the priest may introduce the eucharistic prayer by suggesting very briefly particular motives for thanksgiving.

Preface

116 The praise and thanksgiving from which the entire eucharist takes its name is especially concentrated in the "preface," which proclaims the church's thanks for the saving work of God. In the Eastern tradition this is a fixed part of the eucharistic prayer, beginning the praise of God and the rehearsal of God's mighty deeds that continue throughout the prayer. In the Roman tradition the preface has been a variable element, stressing one aspect of God's saving work according to the day, the feast or the season. Over 80 such prefaces from ancient and more recent sources are provided for use with Eucharistic Prayers I, II and III.

- The preface is not a preliminary to the eucharistic prayer but the first part of it. It indicates a proclamation, a speaking out before God and the faithful, rather than a foreword or prelude. For this reason it is most appropriately sung.
- The eucharistic prayer is always expressed in the first person plural. It is the whole assembly of the faithful which makes eucharist, even when one voice speaks in the name of all. It is the responsibility of the priest, speaking for Christ the head of the church, to proclaim the prayer with and for the people, to engage their attention and to elicit their involvement throughout.
- Eucharistic Prayer II has a proper preface, based like the rest of the prayer on an ancient Roman model, but other prefaces may be substituted for it, especially those which similarly present the mystery of salvation.
- Eucharistic Prayer IV is constructed on an Eastern model. Its preface is a fixed and integral part of the prayer, whose themes continue beyond the Sanctus. For this reason, it is always to be used with its own preface. This is also true of the Eucharistic Prayers for Masses with Children and for Masses of Reconciliation.

■ COMMENTARY: As with the eucharistic prayer, the preface text should be chosen thoughtfully. Try striking a balance. There should be sufficient variety so that the riches of this treasury of texts get heard. There must be sufficient repetition if words of prayer spoken by one person on behalf of the assembly are to become words the assembly knows almost "by heart." It may be helpful, for instance, to stick with one preface throughout a block of Sundays; suitable choices are suggested in the Calendar section. One variation in what the PIOM says: When Eucharistic Prayer for Reconciliation is used in Advent or Lent, seasonal prefaces may be used.

Sanctus Acclamation

117 In this acclamation the assembly joins its voice to that of all creation in giving glory to God, with words inspired by the vision of Isaiah (6:3). In each celebration of the eucharist, the church is taken up into the eternal liturgy in which the entire communion of saints, the heavenly powers and all of creation give praise to the God of the universe.

- This acclamation is an integral part of the eucharistic prayer. It belongs to priest and people together. Of its very nature it is a song and is meant to be sung, even if the preface is not. Choir or cantor parts may also be sung if they facilitate and enhance the congregation's participation.

Epiclesis

118 In these sections of the prayer, before and after the narrative of institution, the church invokes God's Spirit to hallow the gifts and make them the body and blood of Christ and to gather those who receive them into a true communion of faith and love. Through the sanctifying power of the Holy Spirit the repetition of the Lord's words of institution is efficacious, the memorial of Christ's death and resurrection is effected, and the church is built up again as the body of Christ in the world.

- The life-giving power of the Spirit, who moved over the waters in the first days of creation and overshadowed Mary in the moment of the incarnation, is vividly expressed by the ancient gesture of the bringing together of the hands with the palms downward and extended over the elements to be consecrated. When done with great gravity and deliberation, this gesture can reinforce powerfully the understanding of the words and of the Spirit's action. This is a laying on of the hands and is the same sacramental gesture used in ordination, confirmation, the anointing of the sick and the sacrament of reconciliation.
- In accord with ancient tradition, if there are concelebrating priests, they stretch out both their hands toward the elements. The full impact of this gesture can be achieved if the concelebrants adopt the same gesture as the presiding priest.

Institution Narrative and Consecration

119 At the heart of the eucharistic prayer the account of the Last Supper is recited. Everything for which God has been thanked and praised, all that was accomplished in the history of salvation, is summed up and made present in the person of the crucified and risen Lord. The words of Jesus, in which he gave himself to his disciples as their food and drink, are repeated in the context of praise. In the power of the Spirit, these words achieve what they promise and express: the presence of Christ and his sacrifice among his people assembled.

- This narrative is an integral part of the one continuous prayer of thanksgiving and blessing. It

should be proclaimed in a manner which does not separate it from its context of praise and thanksgiving.

- As a narrative it is also recited for the benefit of the assembly. It should therefore be proclaimed reverently, audibly and intelligibly.

- On concluding the words over the bread, the priest shows the consecrated bread to the people and subsequently does the same with the cup. The scale of the gesture will be indicated by the size and situation of the assembly. The gesture should be deliberate and reverent but not prolonged; this would affect the unity and continuity of the eucharistic prayer.

Memorial Acclamation

120 The memorial acclamation of the people in the eucharistic prayer confesses the church's belief in the central mystery of our faith, the paschal mystery of Christ's death, resurrection and presence among his people.

- The four memorial acclamations provided are not specific to the four eucharistic prayers; each may be used with any of the prayers.

- Each of the acclamations has a particular invitation. This invitation is directed to the assembly and helps indicate which acclamation is to follow. The invitation may be given by the priest celebrant or the deacon.

- As acclamations they are intended to be sung.

[The invitations referred to here will appear in the revised sacramentary. They are:

   A. Great is the mystery of faith.
      R. Christ has died, etc.
   B. Praise to you, Lord Jesus.
      R. Dying, you destroyed our death . . .
   C. Christ is the bread of life.
      R. When we eat this bread . . .
   D. Jesus Christ is Lord.
      R. Lord, by your cross and resurrection . . .]

Anamnesis and Offering

121 The whole action of the eucharist is done in obedience to the Lord's command, as a memorial of him. The church understands this memorial as a living representation before God of the saving deeds which God has accomplished in Christ, so that their fullness and power may be effective here and now. In this memorial representation, the church offers the one sacrifice of praise and thanksgiving, a sacramental offering of the sacrifice made "once for all" by Christ, the "holy and living sacrifice" that "brings salvation to the whole world." It is an offering made by the whole church but especially by those here and now assembled who, in the power of the Holy Spirit, offer themselves with and through Christ, the Victim and Priest who joins the church's offering to his own.

Intercessions

122 By the grace of the Holy Spirit, the church has become a single offering in Christ to the glory of God the Father. It now prays that the fruits of this sacrifice may be experienced throughout the church and the world. (In Eucharistic Prayer I, the intercessions are divided, some before, some after the institution narrative.) The Blessed Virgin Mary and the saints are named as the prime examples of the fruits of this redemptive sacrifice and as forerunners in the communion of the living and the dead. Praying in communion with Mary and the other saints of God, the assembly now intercedes for the living and the dead in union with the Lord, who for ever lives to make intercession (see Hebrews 7:25).

- The saints enumerated in Eucharistic Prayer I are, besides the outstanding figures of the apostolic church, the heroes and martyrs of the local church of Rome who do not necessarily enjoy universal significance or particular devotion elsewhere in the church. Their names may be omitted from Eucharistic Prayer I. On the other hand, local patrons or saints whose feast or memory is being celebrated may be mentioned in the intercessions of Eucharistic Prayer III.

- If all the bracketed saints in Eucharistic Prayer I are omitted, the commemoration becomes restricted to male saints only, with the exception of Mary the Mother of God. The names should be selected in such a way that male and female saints are included.

■ COMMENTARY: Again, the PIOM's approach is to point us toward thoughtfulness in making textual choices. How and when the patronal saint and saint of the day are named should be a matter of conscious choice and not simply left to chance. Consistency among presiders, within seasons, and on saints' days is a subtle element that establishes itself as a ritual pattern and becomes a feature of the community's prayer life only by repetition.

Doxology

123 Faithful to the Jewish pattern of prayer known and used by Jesus and his disciples, the eucharistic prayer concludes where it began, with an ascription of praise and glory to God, which is endorsed and ratified by all present in their acclamation Amen. Saint Paul considered this ratification by the assembly to be essential to the thanksgiving prayer (see 1 Corinthians 14:15–16), and early Christian writers laid great stress on it as the people's confirmation of all that was proclaimed on their behalf by the priest.

124 Through Christ, with him and in him, all is turned to the Father's glory by the action of the Holy Spirit. At this climax of the prayer the consecrated elements are raised high in a gesture that vividly expresses the true nature of the eucharistic sacrifice as the offering of the church through Christ the High Priest, with Christ, who is really present in the church, in Christ, who has incorporated his people into himself by the action of the Holy Spirit.

- The profound importance of the assembly's ratification and acclamation can be difficult to bring out in the one short word Amen. At the very least it should be sung or spoken loudly both at the Sunday celebration and at simpler weekday celebrations. Musical settings which prolong the Amen or repeat it or even intersperse it between the phrases of the doxology sung by the priest can all help the assembly to experience and express its true power.

- At the conclusion of the eucharistic prayer, the priest should make a distinct pause to make clear that the eucharistic prayer (the "giving thanks") is complete and that the communion rite (the "breaking and sharing") is about to begin.

COMMUNION RITE

125 The eating and drinking together of the Lord's body and blood in a paschal meal is the culmination of the eucharist. The assembly is made ready to share in this banquet by a series of rites that lead from the eucharistic prayer directly to the communion. The themes underlying these rites are the mutual love and reconciliation that are both the condition and the fruit of worthy communion and the unity of the many in the one symbolized at both the natural and the sacramental level in the elements of bread and wine.

- Though each of these rites (the Lord's Prayer, sign of peace, breaking of the bread) is important in itself, in the context of the whole celebration they constitute together a transition from one high point, the eucharistic prayer, to another, the sharing in communion. Their musical treatment should not be so elaborate as to give the impression that they are of greater significance than the giving thanks which precedes them or the eating and drinking which follows them and which is accompanied by communal song.

■ COMMENTARY: The PIOM points here to the need planners and presiders have to step back now and then for a broad perspective on our celebrations. What is the balance of time among the various parts or movements of the liturgy? It is a point well taken! If the heart of the liturgy of the eucharist, the eucharistic prayer, is dwarfed in time and musical adornment to a long preparation of the gifts (and multiple collections) on one side and by an intensely musical communion rite on the other, then the eucharistic prayer looks and sounds far less important than it ought to be. Thus it becomes clear that bracketing the eucharistic prayer with a distinct pause before the preface dialogue and after the doxology is no mere rubrical fussiness. It is, rather, the careful attention to detail on which ritual celebrations stand or fall.

THE LORD'S PRAYER

126 The community of the baptized is constituted as the family of God by the Spirit of adoption. In the fullness of this Spirit, who has once again been invoked upon it, the assembly calls on God as Father. Because of its themes of daily bread and mutual forgiveness, the Lord's Prayer has been used in all liturgical traditions as a most appropriate preparation for communion, "so that what is holy may be given to those who are holy" (*General Instruction of the Roman Missal*, 1). The final petition is expanded into a prayer that concludes with the congregational doxology or acclamation "For the kingdom," which was appended to the Lord's Prayer in some of the earliest liturgical texts and in texts of the New Testament.

- As the family prayer of all God's children, the Lord's Prayer belongs to the whole assembly. When sung, it is sung by everyone together. In this case, it will normally be desirable for the priest to sing the embolism that follows and for the priest and people together to sing the concluding acclamation "For the kingdom."

■ COMMENTARY: The United States adaptations, following the lead of several other countries, suggests the *orans* position of hands extended for the entire assembly during the Lord's Prayer. This is surely the most ancient posture of prayer, depicted in ancient icons and mosaics through-

out the Christian world, long before it became the preserve of the clergy. But it faces stiff competition in some quarters from a more recent innovation: holding hands. Proponents of hand-holding point to the warmth and unity this bespeaks. Opponents label it typically American and superficial, an attempt to impose artificial intimacy on a whole assembly. Where hand-holding is not the custom, the *orans* posture deserves serious consideration. Even where hand-holding is established, communities might want to reflect, with sensitivity toward all and openness on the part of all, on the appropriateness of this more recent gesture in contrast to the more ancient, traditional posture of prayer.

SIGN OF PEACE

127 A ritual kiss is mentioned in the oldest writings of the New Testament and is found in the eucharistic liturgy from the earliest days of the church (see Romans 16:16). In most traditions it occurs before the presentation of gifts and is understood as a manifestation of that mutual love and reconciliation that Jesus called for before the offering of sacrifice (see Matthew 5:23). Eventually in the Roman tradition it found its place after the Lord's Prayer, whose themes of mutual forgiveness it echoes. In the early church it was described as a "seal" placed on prayer.

128 The biblical concept of peace includes total well-being, a life in harmony with God and with ourselves, with our neighbors and with the whole of creation. Such peace can only be the pure gift of God. It is won for us by the risen Christ, present in the midst of the assembly, and so it is the peace of Christ that is exchanged.

129 The exchange of peace prior to the reception of communion is an acknowledgment that Christ whom we receive in the sacrament is already present in our neighbor. In this exchange the assembly acknowledges the insistent gospel truth that communion with God in Christ is enjoyed in communion with our sisters and brothers in Christ. The rite of peace is not an expression merely of human solidarity or good will; it is rather an opening of ourselves and our neighbors to a challenge and a gift from beyond ourselves. Like the Amen at communion, it is the acceptance of a challenge, a profession of faith that we are members, one with another, in the body of Christ.

- The peace is always exchanged, though the invitation which introduces it is optional, and the gesture by which it is exchanged may be determined by the conference of bishops in accordance with the culture and customs of the people.
- All the members of the assembly, ministers and people, turn to those immediately around them. It is not transmitted in sequence, as it were from a single source. Christ, who is its only source, is present and active in the assembly.
- The sign is sufficiently strong and expressive in itself not to need explanatory song or commentary.

■ COMMENTARY: Three important points are made here, and need to be, in light of the continuing misuse (and disuse) of this ancient ritual gesture.

1. *The sign of peace is not optional.* However, the invitation to it might well be omitted during Ordinary Time. Although "similar words" of invitation are always permitted, ICEL's new alternatives are perfect for Lent and Eastertime: "As children of the God of peace, let us offer one another a sign of reconciliation and peace," or "Brothers and sisters, let us offer one another the peace of the risen Christ."

These provide models, in length and style, for local compositions attuned to the other seasons. Memorize one formula and use it throughout a particular season or block of Ordinary Sundays.

2. *The presider does not make his way through the assembly.* This is for a good reason (beyond not leaving the eucharist unattended at the altar): "Christ is among us," our Eastern rite Catholic and Orthodox friends say at the sign of peace, with the response, "He is and will be!" Moving through the assembly, though motivated by the desire to share the sign with many, unwittingly connotes a kind of subtle clericalism.

3. *The gesture is to speak for itself.* Move the suitable "peace songs" to communion time, and, if any instrumentation is desired, let it be an introduction to the Agnus Dei litany.

BREAKING OF THE BREAD

130 This characteristic action of Christ at the feeding of the multitude, at the Last Supper and at his meals with the disciples after his resurrection was so central to the eucharist that it seems to have given its name to the entire celebration in the days of the apostles. The natural, the practical, the symbolic and the spiritual are all inextricably linked in this most powerful symbol. Just as many grains of wheat are ground, kneaded and baked together to become one loaf, which is then broken and shared out among many to bring them into one table-fellowship, so those gathered are made one body in the one bread of life which is Christ (see 1 Corinthians 10:17).

131 In order for the meaning of this symbolism to be perceived, both the bread and the breaking must be truly authentic and recognizable. The eucharistic bread is to "have the appearance of food" and is made so that it is able to be broken and distributed to at least some of the members of the assembly.

- The faithful are not ordinarily to be given communion from the tabernacle with bread consecrated at a previous Mass.
- When, for genuine pastoral reasons, for example, the late arrival of unexpected numbers, the bread consecrated at the Mass must be supplemented with reserved consecrated bread from the tabernacle, this may be brought reverently but without ceremony from the tabernacle to the altar at the breaking of the bread.
- The breaking of the bread is done with dignity and deliberation. It begins after the exchange of peace is completely finished, and the attention of the assembly is again focused on the action taking place at the holy table.
- The regular use of larger breads will foster an awareness of the fundamental eucharistic symbolism in which the whole assembly, priest and people, share in the same bread. At every Mass at least one large bread is broken into several portions. One of these portions is consumed by the priest, the rest are distributed to at least some other members of the assembly.
- During the breaking of the bread, the Agnus Dei is sung or said. It calls on Jesus as the Lamb of God (see John 1:29, 36) who has conquered sin and death (see 1 Peter 1:18; Book of Revelation 5:6, 13:8). The Agnus Dei is a litany-song intended to accompany the action of breaking and may therefore be prolonged by repetition or by the insertion of invocations to Christ. It loses its entire purpose if a perfunctory breaking of bread is already completed before the Agnus Dei has even begun.
- If additional vessels are needed for the distribution of communion, they may be brought to the altar at this point. The consecrated bread is then divided among the plates or dishes, and the consecrated wine is poured into the cups.
- If special ministers are to assist at communion, it is desirable that they come to the altar after the exchange of peace, in order to assist with the preparation of the vessels and the eucharistic elements.

■ COMMENTARY: There is abundant material here for a communal, liturgical examination of conscience! One recurring question is finally, definitively answered: Who goes to the tabernacle to get the ciboria: priest, deacon or eucharistic minister? Answer: none of the above! No communion from the tabernacle, at least not ordinarily.

Real and decent bread, reverently prepared and not mass produced is still the ideal. And Ordinary Time is the ideal time to work toward it!

COMMUNION

132 The prayer for the private preparation of the priest is recited inaudibly. At this time the faithful prepare themselves quietly and in their own way for communion.

133 The consecrated elements are extended toward the congregation, whose members are invited to communion with a formulary that expresses the confidence of the baptized and to which they respond with the humility of the centurion (see Matthew 8:9).

- Several formularies are provided for the invitation. Like all other introductions and invitations, these may be adapted for particular feasts or occasions but should always end with a recognizable cue to elicit the people's response "Lord, I am not worthy...."
- The priest celebrant holds out the consecrated bread and wine to the people in a gesture that is inviting but dignified.

■ COMMENTARY: The new ICEL translation of the single Latin formulary is closer to the original and presents more clearly the scriptural verse from Revelation. The image is the eschatological wedding feast of the kingdom. For the sake of fidelity to that scripture, presiders need to be careful about changing "those" to "we." The former is guaranteed by scripture, the latter signals not only a bit of presumption, but even exclusivity, on our part!

> Behold, the Lamb of God,
> who takes away the sin of the world.
> Blessed are those called
>   to the banquet of the Lamb.

DISTRIBUTION OF COMMUNION

134 Faithful to the Lord's command to his disciples to "take and eat," "take and drink," the assembly completes the eucharistic action by eating and drinking together the elements consecrated during the celebration. It is for this reason that the faithful should not ordinarily

be given communion from the tabernacle. Also for this reason, it is most desirable that the faithful share the cup. Drinking at the eucharist is a sharing in the sign of the new covenant (see Luke 22:20), a foretaste of the heavenly banquet (see Matthew 26:29), a sign of participation in the suffering Christ (see Mark 10:38–39). Provision should be made for this fullest form of participation in accord with the conditions laid down by the conference of bishops.

135 Although a communion procession is not obligatory or always possible, it should be the normal arrangement for both practical and symbolic reasons. It expresses the humble patience of the poor moving forward to be fed, the alert expectancy of God's people sharing the paschal meal in readiness for their journey, the joyful confidence of God's people on the march toward the promised land.

136 All signs of discrimination or distinctions among persons at the Lord's table are to be avoided.

- There should be a sufficient number of ministers to assist in the distribution of communion. This will normally mean two ministers of the cup to each minister of the bread.

- It is desirable that all who minister the eucharist take full part in the entire liturgy and thus experience the proclamation of the word, the eucharistic prayer and the consummation of the celebration in eucharistic communion.

- When communion is administered under both kinds, the deacon who ministers the cup is to receive from it after the assembly. This expression of eucharistic hospitality and service may also be followed by all other communion ministers in order to facilitate the distribution of communion in a timely and orderly manner. If there are many concelebrating priests, the communion of the assembly should not be delayed but should be begun after the presiding celebrant has communicated. There is no need for all the concelebrating priests to finish receiving communion before distribution to the assembly can commence.

- When the conference of bishops allows the reception of the consecrated bread in the hand, the choice whether to do so is the prerogative of the communicant.

- When the conference of bishops and the local bishop have determined that communion under both kinds may be given, the pastor or priest celebrant should see to its full and proper implementation. Even when communion is given under both kinds, however, the communicant may refrain from drinking from the cup.

- Should communion under both kinds sometimes be given in the form of intinction, the communicant may choose to receive under the form of bread only. When communion in the form of intinction is given, the following formula is said, "The body and blood of Christ," and the communicant responds, "Amen."

- Communion may be received standing or kneeling, in accord with the decision of the conference of bishops. The manner of reception customary in the community is followed so that communion may truly be a sign of familial union between all who share in the same table of the Lord.

- By tradition the deacon ministers the cup. Beyond this, no distinctions are made in the assignment of the consecrated elements to particular ministers for distribution. Therefore when a concelebrating priest or priests and other ministers share in the distribution, the elements are not assigned on the basis of any distinction between the ministers, cleric or lay, male or female. All may minister either element. This avoids any seeming depreciation of one or other of the consecrated elements or of a particular ministry.

■ COMMENTARY: Who does what? How do we do it? And who decides? The PIOM draws out some important considerations about the rights of the communicant, the roles of ministers, cleric and lay, and suggests a thoughtful reevaluation of local practice in light of these reflections.

COMMUNION SONG

137 The communion of priest and people is traditionally accompanied by the singing of a psalm with a simple congregational refrain. Any psalm or other song is appropriate which expresses the spiritual unity of the communicants, shows the joy of all, and makes the communion procession an act of union of brothers and sisters in Christ. In its structure and its simplicity, it should encourage the participation of the entire assembly.

- The communion song begins immediately after the common recital of "Lord, I am not worthy."

- So as not to encumber the assembly with books or scripts during the procession, the song may be led by cantor or choir and include a repeated response from the assembly.

- Although several communion songs may be sung in succession, depending on the length of communion, it may be preferable to interrupt one song with periods of silence or instrumental music and resume the singing after an interlude.

- Many traditional eucharistic hymns were composed for benediction of the blessed sacrament. They concentrate on adoration rather than on the action of communion and may not be appropriate as communion songs.

■ COMMENTARY: What kinds of things do we sing at communion time? And when do we begin—and end? How does our approach to music at this time help or hinder the processional movement of the assembly? How do we vary the musical pattern of song, silence, praise, thanksgiving from season to season?

CLEANSING OF VESSELS

138 When communion is completed, the altar table is cleared again. The cleansing of the eucharistic vessels is a functional task, appropriately described by the term "cleansing."

- Although performed with reverence, it should be done briefly and inconspicuously and is preferably left until after Mass.
- If possible, this cleansing is carried out at the side table. Only as a last resort should it be done at the altar, and if so, at the side rather than at the center.

PERIOD OF SILENCE OR SONG OF PRAISE

139 When communion is completed, the whole assembly may observe a period of total silence. In the absence of all words, actions, music or movement, a moment of deep corporate stillness and contemplation may be experienced. Such silence is important to the rhythm of the whole celebration and is welcome in a busy and restless world.

- Silence and true stillness can be achieved if all, the assembly and its ministers, take part in it.
- This period of deep and tranquil communion is not to be interrupted by parish announcements, which if needed come correctly in the concluding rite, or by the taking of a collection. Nor should this silence be broken or overlaid by the public reading of devotional material.
- As an alternative or addition to silent contemplation, however, a psalm or song of praise may be sung. Since there has already been singing during communion, the opportunity for silence may be more desirable.

■ COMMENTARY: While we instinctively attend to silence after the readings and after the homily, the time of silence after communion frequently becomes a waiting period while various ministers conclude their tasks and return to their places. Here again the PIOM calls for thoughtful and reflective ritual behavior by the whole assembly. And again we see how the various elements support each other. The communion rite needs to be truly communal: a communion refrain with full participation by all, and the movement necessary for all to eat and drink at the Lord's table together, will make us grateful for a brief period of peaceful and purposeful silence, when each of us can be alone, together, in the Lord's presence.

The miracle of the copy machine should have eliminated, by now, the need for anything but the most necessary of announcements. Pastoral judgment will determine when invitations are appropriate so that visitors and guests may join the assembly afterward for fellowship. On occasion, there may need to be a special announcement about blessings to be conferred after the liturgy (e.g., for birthdays or travelers).

PRAYER AFTER COMMUNION

140 In a final presidential prayer that brings to a close the communion rite, the community of faith asks that the spiritual effects of the eucharist be experienced in its members' lives.

- The prayer may be sung or said; the assembly responds, "Amen."

FURTHER POSSIBILITIES

■ A SEASON OF SAINTS: Ordinary Time provides numerous opportunities to celebrate Christ's paschal mystery in a particularly lively, diverse and interesting way. As the Epiphany Proclamation puts it:

> Likewise the pilgrim church proclaims
>   the passover of Christ
> in the feasts of the holy Mother of God,
> in the feasts of the apostles and saints,
> and in the commemoration of
>   the faithful departed.

Saints whose days are ranked as solemnities, feasts and obligatory memorials are observed by all communities throughout the church. These are the brothers and sisters gone before us whose witness to the gospel is deemed to have a significance for the universal church. From among the optional memorials each community should thoughtfully select those that resonate in some way with the community's particular character or spirituality.

- MAINTAIN THE LECTIONARY: Except on solemnities and feasts, the weekday lectionary's assigned selections, drawn in semicontinuous portions from various books, are proclaimed. Each week the Calendar section of *Sourcebook* notes when this is to be interrupted by a solemnity or feast, so that planners may employ the option of adding to a "free" weekday's reading the selection displaced by the feast.

- KNOW THE BIOGRAPHY: A few well-chosen words about the day's saint prevents him or her from becoming a kind of "Unidentified Liturgical Object" that appears suddenly during the opening prayer! Have on hand the new edition of the classic *Butler's Lives of the Saints* (Liturgical Press, 1995). An additional, excellent resource, which contains many of the saints in the Roman calendar and many contemporary figures, is *For All the Saints: Prayers and Readings for Saints' Days* (Toronto: Anglican Book Centre, 1994; 800 pages of material!).

Taking It Home

AN indispensable manual for home use during this long Ordinary Time and all year long is *Catholic Household Blessings and Prayers*. Parishes can help families celebrate special days and feasts at home by making copies of this book widely available and then calling attention to prayers and rituals available in it. *Catholic Household Blessings and Prayers* has prayers for Father's Day, Independence Day, Labor Day and Thanksgiving. It has blessings for Rogation Days, Assumption, St. Francis; prayers for visiting a grave, and for November. Bulletin reminders should suggest use of the other blessings in the book at appropriate times: blessing before a journey (and returning); blessing before leaving for school, employment or ministry; blessing for those moving.

- TAKE ME HOME: This resource from LTP has pages the parish could copy and distribute throughout Ordinary Time: Trinity Sunday, Body and Blood of Christ, Father's Day, Birth of John the Baptist, Peter and Paul, Independence Day, Blessed Kateri, Mary Magdalene, James, Martha, Transfiguration, Assumption, Bartholomew, Labor Day, Moses (September 4 in the Eastern calendar), Birth of Mary, Holy Cross, Matthew, Vincent de Paul, Michael and the Archangels, Francis of Assisi, the Jewish Festival of Sukkot, Luke, Halloween, All Saints and All Souls, Martin, Thanksgiving Day and Christ the King.

- I WILL LIE DOWN THIS NIGHT: Ordinary Time frequently provides a bit more leisure for quiet prayer and even family prayer in common. Parishes would do a great service by making these inexpensive resources available for summer reading and prayer. For those who wish to do more, *Psalms for Morning and Evening Prayer* and, indeed, the whole *Psalter*, make fine summer books with which to spend reflective time.

- SUMMER READING/FALL STUDY: A fine ministry is to assemble and coordinate a borrowing library well stocked with some of the scripture commentary referred to in these notes and some liturgical materials the parish may have on hand. Next year's lectionary evangelist is Luke; in preparation for the fall, someone may want to begin researching and assembling good materials that focus on Luke's gospel, so that when Bible study groups reconvene, appropriate resources will be on hand to prepare for a new liturgical year.

CALENDAR

May

MON 19   #341 (LMC, #193–227)   green
Weekday (Seventh Week in Ordinary Time)

Unadorned ritual, simple acclamations, brief forms of greeting and invitation, intercessory and eucharistic prayer: These signal in a subtle way the passage from Easter's high festivity to the gentler pace of Ordinary Time. An atmosphere of simplicity permits the assembly to experience liturgy's basic shape: word, silence, song; taking, blessing, breaking, sharing.

■ READINGS: From two centuries before Christ come two weeks of Jesus ben Sirach's wisdom, beginning today. There is much practical help in Sirach for living in community; indeed, Sirach's other name is "Ecclesiasticus," the church's book. It may be a real discovery for the neophytes if they have come to us from churches where this book is seldom if ever read. And today we rejoin the Gospel of Mark, with Jesus drawing near to Jerusalem.

TUE 20   #342 (LMC, #193–227)   green
Weekday

Bernardine of Siena, presbyter, religious, missionary, optional memorial/white. ■ "Prepare for trials" may sound like good advice before any secular undertaking but what about when coming to the Lord's service? It usually doesn't take long to see how well advised the warning is! But so is Sirach's litany of counsel: Be patient and persevering, humble and hopeful. The reading asks if anyone has trusted in the Lord and been forsaken. The gospel answers: Yes, and points to the cross! But Christian optimism is realism: Jesus was not ultimately forsaken nor will his disciples be.

WED 21   #343 (LMC, #193–227)   green
Weekday

As the weather warms up, weekend athletes and even casual joggers and walkers realize that getting back into shape takes time after winter's hibernation. No less does spiritual shaping up! Jesus reminds the disciples that no one, no matter how close (as John legendarily was) has a monopoly on him. Do we offer joyful thanks for truth and goodness wherever and in whomever we find it?

THU 22   #344 (LMC, #193–227)   green
Weekday

Presumption and procrastination: Sirach warns us to stay clear of these. Least of all should we put our faith in something that was as unstable in the dusty alleys of the biblical world as in the columned halls of Wall Street!

FRI 23   #345 (LMC, #193–227)   green
Weekday

Sirach's comforting words on the gift of friendship and Jesus' challenging words on the relationship of marriage should turn our prayer today toward those nearest and dearest to us. How are our relationships going? Are they a separate "department" from our spiritual lives? Do we intercede for friends and coworkers, spouse and children? Do we offer thanks for those gracious presences that reveal the Presence? Might not summertime present at least some opportunities to voice our gratitude, show our love, maybe even heal old wounds?

SAT 24   #346 (LMC, #193–227)   green
Weekday

Commemoration of the Blessed Virgin Mary/white. ■ It sometimes takes childlike trust to remember that everyone we meet is formed in the Lord's own image and likeness. Just imagine what a challenge we present to others! "Becoming a child" might inspire us to reflect on the beautiful qualities of children: openness to wonder, willingness to learn, an almost inexhaustible capacity to forgive, which goes hand-in-hand with a seeming unwillingness to keep an accurate score of injuries received. We could learn a lot from the kids!

■ MARY ON SATURDAY: See *Collection of Masses of the Blessed Virgin Mary* (CMBVM) #16, Mary, Fountain of Life and Light. Directives permit use of formularies not officially part of the current season. This one, from the Eastertime set, relates Mary to our recent celebration of the sacraments of initiation. As the neophytes grow in a Catholic devotional life, this resource is a fine way of relating Marian piety to scripture and liturgy.

25   #165 [166] (LMC, #159)   white
The Holy Trinity
SOLEMNITY

This feast, first celebrated in monastic communities in the ninth century as an expression of praise to the triune God, was extended to the entire Western church in the fourteenth. It celebrates the mystery of God's self-revelation through the experiences of the people of Israel, the disciples of Jesus and the Christian people since Pentecost (© ICEL).

MAY

This (and next) week's decorations, musical selections and ritual patterns should not convey the impression that Eastertime has been extended two more weeks. Simplicity may involve omitting the sprinkling and the festive incensations that were so much a part of those Sundays. The Gloria should not be Eastertime's melody, the gospel acclamation should be an Alleluia not heard in the season just past. Eucharistic Prayer III incorporates the mystery of the Trinity's saving work into its opening lines and is a fitting choice today. When doing standard trinitarian hymns, be sure not to omit the Holy Spirit by mistakenly omitting the final verse!

■ BLESSING OF MARRIED COUPLES: *Book of Blessings,* chapter 1, III. Today's feast and doctrine celebrate God as a God of relationships, so today may be far more appropriate for a blessing than an annual renewal of vows on Valentine's Day (sometimes in Lent) or the feast of the Holy Family (a potentially painful reminder at that time of year to families in difficulty).

MON 26 — Philip Neri, presbyter, religious founder
#347 (LMC, #193–227) white
MEMORIAL

Memorial Day (U. S.) ▪ Sirach praises the God who happily welcomes back the repentant. The young man who goes away sad presents a striking contrast to today's saint, who found such joy in the service of God and neighbor. Nor was the age in which Philip Neri lived a very happy time in the church. The reformations, Protestant and Catholic, had rent the Christian community asunder and caused widespread disillusionment and abandonment of faith. But Philip dared to have faith, hope, love and a sense of humor! How do we deal with turmoil and trouble in the church, local and universal? Does our joy attract others to the community in which we live and serve?

■ MEMORIAL DAY: Many parishes celebrate Mass in the cemetery on this day. As an alternative, today's liturgy might conclude with a procession to the cemetery (see *Book of Blessings,* chapter 57).

- Suggested texts: Mass for Independence Day and Other Civic Observances (sacramentary, appendix X, 6); Preface P-82; Eucharistic Prayer for Reconciliation II with its own preface or Eucharistic Prayer for Various Needs and Occasions D: Jesus, the Compassion of God.
- Readings: Peace and Justice (lectionary, #831–835) or Weekday (#341).
- Visit to a Cemetery: *Book of Blessings* (chapter 57) provides a formal rite; *Catholic Household Blessings and Prayers* has more simple, family-style prayer (pages 178, 280).

TUE 27 — Weekday
#348 (LMC, #193–227) green

Augustine of Canterbury, bishop, religious, missionary, optional memorial/white. ▪ Both readings remind us that God generously, and sometimes surprisingly, repays what we offer him. "Do not appear empty handed," Sirach advises; and when Peter reminds Jesus of all they had given up ("some leaky boats and torn nets," Jerome sarcastically suggested), Jesus promises a hundredfold — with persecutions! Humor and honesty on the part of Jesus! But comfort, too: Eternal life awaits the disciple in the age to come.

WED 28 — Weekday
#349 (LMC, #193–227) green

Sirach prays for mercy; James and John bid for power. The other ten are angry, possibly because James and John beat them to the punch! Jesus gives all of them a clear, straightforward orientation to the new community he is establishing and how authority and power will be exercised there. Does the picture he paints look like my household? Our parish? The church today?

THU 29 — Weekday
#350 (LMC, #193–227) green

Sirach praises the glory of God and God's creation. In one striking line he offers a particularly poignant and moving comparison: "God searches the abyss — and the human heart!" Would that we might see ourselves as clearly as we ought. With Bartimaeus we would do well to call on the Lord, who bestows sight on the baptized on a number of different levels.

FRI 30 — Weekday
#351 (LMC, #193–227) green

The Canadian lectionary wisely adds verse 8 to the Sirach 44 reading: "Some of them [the ancestors] have left behind a name, so that others declare their praise." But others . . . the addition sets up the contrast more clearly. Jesus cleanses the Temple and gets a very clear response. Who are those in our own generation who work to cleanse the temple of the world, the church, society?

SAT 31 — The Visitation of the Virgin Mary to Elizabeth
#572 (LMC, #302) white
FEAST

Two options are provided for the first reading. One matches the gospel canticle in expressing joy and expectancy. The second calls

JUNE

us to imitate Mary's concern for others. Though there are three Prefaces of Mary from which to choose in the sacramentary, there are 50 in the *Collection of Masses of the Blessed Virgin Mary*! The Visitation preface is P-3 in this collection and echoes not only the scriptures but the lesson of Mary's selfless service.

June

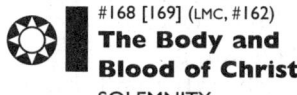

The Body and Blood of Christ
#168 [169] (LMC, #162)
SOLEMNITY

This feast, originally Corpus Christi, arose in thirteenth century Belgium in response to debates about the real presence and as a result of an upsurge in eucharistic piety. Its extension to the entire Western church was first decreed by Urban IV in 1264. The feast celebrates the mystery of the nourishing and enduring presence of the body and blood of Christ in the eucharist (© ICEL).

■ MUSIC: Classic eucharistic hymns from the Latin tradition: "Pange lingua" ("Tantum ergo"), "Adoro te," "O salutaris." Modern additions to the church's rich treasury of eucharistic hymns include Omer Westendorf's "Gift of finest wheat"; Jerry Brubaker's "O blessed Savior" (World Library); Robert Hutmacher's "Love is his word" (*Worship,* #599); J. Michael Joncas' "Song of the Lord's Supper" *(Gather);* Christopher Walker's "There is something holy here" (OCP). Bear in mind that refrains learned for the feast may fittingly be sung as communion processionals throughout the long Ordinary Time ahead.

■ LITURGY OF THE WORD: The unifying motif of the covenant sealed in blood resonates throughout the day's readings in Year B. Exodus shows Moses consecrating the people by receiving their assent to the spoken word of the book and by sprinkling with the sacrificial blood. In Hebrews, Christ is the high priest entering the holy place with his own blood of the new covenant that frees its participants from death. Mark's account of the Lord's Supper has a pronounced eschatological emphasis: Jesus speaks of one day drinking the fruit of the vine new in the kingdom.

The sequence hymn, "Lauda Sion," should be sung by all, or by the assembly in alternation with the choir. Sections of it, in an English translation set to the original chant, are in the Episcopal *Hymnal 1982* (#320). The full text in a fine new translation is in the Canadian *Catholic Book of Worship III* (#693). This version will fit any "Tantum ergo" melody and that means a melody the community already associates with eucharistic worship.

■ LITURGY OF THE EUCHARIST: Preface of the Eucharist II (P-48) stresses the effects of the eucharist in our lives and seems to be the preface of choice on this day (Eucharist I is oriented more toward Holy Thursday). If Eucharist II is used, note that in the revised version "family of mankind" becomes "the human family." Eucharistic Prayer III is a good choice today, with its references to the sacrifices of the Hebrew covenant, the Lord's command to celebrate the eucharist, and the eucharist of the church as showing forth and intimately at one with the sacrifice Christ offered.

■ COMMUNION UNDER BOTH SPECIES: In 1978 Rome formally approved the request of the United States' bishops that communion under both species be permitted on Sundays and holy days as well as on weekdays. There should be no question that this will be done today and that today's pattern is already part of the parish's eucharistic practice or soon to be so. Both the *General Instruction of the Roman Missal* (introduction, #14, 240) and ICEL's Pastoral Introduction: Order of Mass (134) strongly encourage this fuller sign of eucharistic participation. People always have the option to accept the cup or not, but it should be their option, not the presider's decision. The people of God have a right to the sacraments in their fullness. If the cup is not offered at all Masses in your parish, this is a good Sunday to begin reversing that situation, and today's readings offer an excellent opportunity to reflect on the meaning of sharing both bread and cup.

■ CONCLUDING RITES: If there is no procession, a solemn blessing may be given. Since there is no special text for this feast, signal the return to Ordinary Time by closing with the blessing that will be used throughout the next block of weeks.

■ EUCHARISTIC PROCESSION: See the order in *Holy Communion and Worship of the Eucharist outside Mass* (#101–108) and helpful notes in the *Ceremonial of Bishops* (#387–394).

JUNE

MON 2 #353 (LMC, #193–227) green
Weekday

Marcellinus, presbyter, martyr, and Peter, exorcist, martyr, optional memorial/red. ▪ (U.S.: Tobit 1:3; 2:1a–8; Canada: Tobit 1:1ad, 2a, 3, 17; 2:1–8) "At the festival of Pentecost," Tobit's adventure begins. Interesting that Tobit risks his life to bury the dead thrown "outside the wall." In the gospel, the body of the owner's son is cast "outside the wall" of the vineyard. What our tradition calls "the corporal works of mercy" are precisely the harvest for which the owner is looking. We might call it practical charity, like Tobit's, like Jesus', that acts without counting the cost or estimating the reward.

TUE 3 #354 (LMC, #193–227) red
Charles Lwanga, catechist, martyr, and his companions, martyrs
MEMORIAL

(U.S.: Tobit 2:9–14; Canada: Tobit 2:9–14 and 3:1) Tobit's response to the unexpected travails of life is prayer. Our response? Jesus challenges us to render unto God what is his: our heart's deepest loyalty and highest love.

Such a choice, in the face of apostasy and sexual exploitation, cost Charles Lwanga, a catechist, and his young friends (and many others as well) their lives in a most gruesome execution. What does our faith cost us?

WED 4 #355 (LMC, #193–227) green
Weekday

Two prayers, offered countries apart, rise to the same God. How mysteriously and wondrously the paths of our prayers, and our lives, sometimes intersect. How often do we marvel at and give thanks for these graces, which the world calls coincidences and believers call divine providence?

THU 5 #356 (LMC, #193–227) red
Boniface, bishop, religious, missionary, martyr
MEMORIAL

(U.S.: Tobit 6:11; 7:1, 9–17; 8:4–9a; Canada: Tobit 4:20; 5:4; 6:10–11; 7:1, 9–17; 8:1, 4–9) With the help of a guardian angel and the strength of heartfelt prayer, a young couple's love conquers all! The memorial of Boniface, a giant in church history, reminds us that, at times, love conquers all by giving its all, as Jesus did, laying down one's life for one's friends, and even for one's enemies.

FRI 6 #171 [172] (LMC, #165) white
The Sacred Heart of Jesus
SOLEMNITY

This devotion, which dates back to the Middle Ages, flowered in France in the seventeenth century as a result of the visions of St. Margaret Mary Alacoque (October 16). The feast was extended to the entire Western church by Pius IX in 1856. It recalls the mystery of God, who is love, and honors the heart of Jesus as the source and center of the incarnate love of God (© ICEL).

Divine compassion shines through all the readings. Through Hosea, the Lord proclaims "my compassion grows warm and tender. I will not execute my fierce anger." Paul proclaims "the boundless riches of Christ, . . . the love that surpasses knowledge." And from the pierced side of Jesus, blood and water flow; baptism and eucharist, the patristic tradition held, "the fountain of sacramental life in the church" (Sacred Heart Preface).

▪ LITURGY OF THE EUCHARIST: The special preface for today is P-45. As opposed to the sometimes "reparational" orientation of this devotion, the liturgy points us instead toward God's initiative of love for us in Christ. The exaltation of Christ on the cross is placed before us to make our hearts leap with joy at so dramatic an image of God's love and to make us hasten gladly toward the fountain of life and the springs of salvation. While Eucharistic Prayer III is standard for such solemnities, it is a shame that official directives rule out the use of the new Eucharistic Prayer for Masses for Various Needs and Occasions. Form D, Jesus, the Compassion of God, contains the beautiful lines: "Open our eyes to the needs of all; inspire us with words and deeds to comfort those who labor and are burdened; keep our service of others faithful to the example and command of Christ. Let your church be a living witness to truth and freedom, to justice and peace, that all people may be lifted up by the hope of a world made new."

▪ MUSIC: Sacred Heart hymns have been notoriously awful, most of the English texts having been written in the late 1800s and reflecting the sentimental piety of the late Victorian period. Latin texts, by contrast, were marvelously scriptural, relating the heart of Christ to the Ark of the Covenant containing the tablet of the new covenant of love. New hymnals, like *Worship* and *Hymnal for the Hours* (both GIA) steer us in the right direction and offer a sure guide to good choices,

JUNE

including "All you who seek a comfort sure" and "I heard the voice of Jesus say."

■ PRAYER OUTSIDE MASS: The beautiful and scriptural Litany of the Sacred Heart is in *Catholic Household Blessings and Prayers* (page 339) and might be part of an extended period of prayer before the blessed sacrament or before the parish's image of the Sacred Heart.

SAT 7 — Weekday
#358 or 573 (LMC, #193–227) green

The Immaculate Heart of Mary, optional memorial/white. ▪ Combine Friday's displaced reading with today's (in the longer Canadian version) for Tobit's happy ending: Tobit 11:5–15; 12:1–20. There are special texts for the observance of the Immaculate Heart, but their use is not mandatory or in this case even advisable. The weekday gospel is perfect: the widow's mite. Mary, too, gave her all, and more than her all, to the "treasury of the living Temple of the Lord." And so she is an enduring model of obedient faith and self-sacrificing love. See CMBVM, #28, for a much fuller, more scriptural formulary, complete with preface, and far superior to that provided in the sacramentary.

SUN 8 — Tenth Sunday in Ordinary Time
#89 [90] (LMC, #84) green

SUMMER 1: SUNDAYS 10–14

This block of Sundays, interrupted by the solemnity of Peter and Paul, is bracketed by stories of profound misunderstanding (Sunday 10) and sad rejection (Sunday 14). Between these brackets, however, are images as gracious and beautiful as the picture-perfect days that so often grace June and early July. Phenomenal growth, beyond all odds and expectations, is virtually unobservable while it is taking place (Sunday 11). The power of Jesus calms the storm and saves the ship, imparting peace even as he challenges our unbelief (Sunday 12).

■ LITURGICAL TEXTS: Let simplicity reign. The ancient, supremely beautiful Christian greeting, spoken with thoughtful deliberation and reverent sincerity, should begin each liturgy of Ordinary Time: "The Lord be with you." For the Litany of Praise (invocation and Kyrie), choose one set of invocations for each block of Sundays, and let their words echo the gospels of that block. A suggestion for this block:

> Lord Jesus, you sow the seeds of your kingdom in our hearts: Lord, have mercy.
> Christ Jesus, you are the Lord of life, whom heaven and earth adore: Christ, have mercy.
> Lord Jesus, you speak with authority and summon us to faith: Lord, have mercy.

The general intercessions should be simple and direct, most of them repeated throughout the block of Sundays, with one intercession each week, perhaps, changing to reflect the day's scriptures and current needs. The preparation of the gifts ought to be done simply and silently, maybe with instrumental music in the background.

■ MUSIC: The quality of responsorial psalmody appears vastly improved in recent years. Music publishers seem to be presenting refrains marked by a melodic simplicity that makes them easy to learn, yet interesting to sing. Some parishes use the proper psalm each week, even when the assembly does not have the full text before them. Common psalms are always an option, and a good one in Ordinary Time. See the lectionary, #175. Choose one common psalm for each block of Ordinary Time Sundays. In this block Psalm 63 or 23, though this is not an official "common" psalm, is a versatile favorite.

Gospel acclamations should be simple and singable; again, one version serving throughout the block of Sundays with, perhaps, the cantor's verse chosen week by week to match the gospel. The same principal applies to the eucharistic prayer acclamations. Some parishes even use one that is sung easily a cappella in case parish musicians take a well-deserved break at some point in the summer. For the communion processional, one or two refrain-style pieces might suffice. For general hymnody in this block of Sundays, focus on songs of discipleship and faith, healing and service. These will be suitable again in autumn, after the "Bread of Life" interlude, Sundays 15–23.

MON 9 — Weekday
#359 (LMC, #193–227) green

Ephrem of Syria, deacon, doctor of the church, optional memorial/white. ▪ Paul's opening lines are a hymn to that mutual strength that is the fruit of our unity in Christ. It is a good message to hear in our individualistic, self-sufficient society. In the gospel Jesus inaugurates his mission: He saw the crowds (the mission is off and running); he went up

JUNE

the mountain (like Moses); he sat down (the teacher of Torah); his disciples gathered around him (the church is assembled); and he began to teach. All the Beatitudes are addressed to the world at large, except one addressed to the church itself: "Blessed are you when people revile you. . . ."

Today's saint is a poet whose hymns are still a treasured part of the church's repertoire.

TUE 10 #360 (LMC, #193–227) green
Weekday

Paul presents Jesus as God's enduring "Yes," through whom the Christian community says "Amen." This is a good day to reflect on the Amens we pronounce as part of our worship. Affirmation of truth and commitment of self: We say Amen to what we believe; we say Amen to what we are. The gospel reminds us what we are supposed to be after saying Amen: salt for the earth, light for the world.

WED 11 #361 (first reading: 580) (LMC, #193–227) red
Barnabas, apostle
MEMORIAL

His name, we are told, means "son of encouragement" and, although the incident, diplomatically, does not show up in today's reading, Barnabas is a source of encouragement to us in a way he probably hadn't intended to be! He had such a fierce argument with Paul over John Mark's presence in the mission that he and Paul parted company. Both continued to serve the Lord and preach the gospel, but each realized that he could best serve the Lord by serving apart from the other. These things happen. Is not this one of the principal points of the Sermon on the Mount? We are to love one another, even when liking is hard or impossible. Thus do we encourage one another.

THU 12 #362 (LMC, #193–227) green
Weekday

Paul calls the Corinthians to proclaim Christ and to let the light shining in our hearts shine out from us in lives of service. In a world where acrimonious debate and bitter litigation are so often the order of the day, Jesus challenges us to be people who renounce anger, avoid insult and forego harsh language. He makes the quest for reconciliation the indispensable prerequisite for acceptable worship.

FRI 13 #363 (LMC, #193–227) white
Anthony of Padua, presbyter, religious, doctor of the church
MEMORIAL

Paul's self-description to the Corinthians is a great source of comfort to us. Clay vessels we are indeed, carrying about in our bodies the death of Jesus but with an inner joy and abiding peace that cannot be extinguished.

Every Italian American child learned early to call on Anthony for help when things were lost. Perhaps he got that reputation by "losing" his first vocation in an Augustinian classroom then "finding" his true vocation on the road with the Franciscans!

SAT 14 #364 (LMC, #193–227) green
Weekday

Blessed Virgin Mary on Saturday, optional memorial/white. ▪ Paul gives us a perfect motto: "The love of Christ urges us on . . . to live no longer for ourselves but for him."

If Mary is commemorated, look at CMBVM, #20, Mary, the New Eve. As the one who said "Yes" to God's plan, and never took it back, she is the model of words matched by deeds.

SUN 15 #92 [93] (LMC, #87) green
Eleventh Sunday in Ordinary Time

▪ FATHER'S DAY: Today is observed, as was Mother's Day, with additional intercessions and a simple blessing as provided by the Book of Blessings (chapter 56). *Catholic Household Blessings and Prayers* (page 198) has material for use at home.

MON 16 #365 (LMC, #193–227) green
Weekday

Today and tomorrow, Jesus outlines the intensive, self-sacrificial love that is the hallmark of his kingdom and that he himself will demonstrate in his own passion and death. Such a love is bound to make the Christian who makes it a life's program appear foolish, gullible and in many other ways weak and absurd in the eyes of the world (first reading). Paul, in fact, gives us a litany of apparent failures, which he transforms into a canticle of victory: having nothing, possessing everything; dying, yet we live!

TUE 17 #366 (LMC, #193–227) green
Weekday

Practice makes perfect: practicing the love Jesus outlines will make his disciples "perfect as your heavenly Father is perfect." Being like God conjures up images of omnipotence and omniscience, qualities beyond our grasp. Jesus teaches that being like God means loving the loveable and unlovable, the deserving and those we consider least deserving. Most of us have more opportunities to practice that than we care to count! To love like that is to renounce revenge and the desire to "even up the score."

JUNE

Paul reminds us that Christ made himself poor so we might become rich!

WED 18 — Weekday
#367 (LMC, #193–227) green

Paul proposes two virtues, generosity and cheerfulness. While Jesus counsels us to keep our almsgiving, personal prayer and fasting private, cheerfulness and generosity are two gifts the Christian ought freely to give a world too often lacking in both.

THU 19 — Weekday
#368 (LMC, #193–227) green

Romuald, abbot, religious founder, optional memorial/white. ▪ Paul's love gets personal and emotional with a group he did not always find it easy to like (and vice-versa, we might well imagine!). Jesus teaches his disciples how to pray but goes on to teach that without a basic commitment to the unconditional forgiveness of others no prayer, not even the one he taught us, will be acceptable to the Father.

FRI 20 — Weekday
#369 (LMC, #193–227) white

Paul's words today make him a very real flesh-and-blood person indeed! At least with Paul, we know for sure how much he treasured the gospel. It is important, Jesus reminds us, to identify exactly what our treasure is, for there, too, our hearts will be.

SAT 21 — Aloysius Gonzaga, religious
#370 (LMC, #193–227) white
MEMORIAL

Some of Paul's most beautiful and encouraging words form today's first reading: Power is made perfect in weakness. The words of Jesus are a hymn to trust in the Father's all-embracing providence.

Aloysius entered the Jesuits against his family's wishes. He died at an early age of the plague he contracted while caring for its victims. It is a good day to pray for all those who march to the beat of a different drummer, for all those who devote themselves to the victims of all our modern-day plagues.

☀ 22 — Twelfth Sunday in Ordinary Time
#95 [96] (LMC, #90) green

The Lord God speaks to Job from the whirlwind and silences his questioning. Jesus speaks to the whirlwind, silences its fury and causes his disciples to begin asking the most important question: Who is this? The old creation has passed away in the person of Christ. All is made new in Christ. What faith and love this should awaken in disciples today: to be part of the new creation means believing that God will fulfill his promises and committing ourselves to the kind of love in action that helps those promises come true.

MON 23 — Weekday
#371 (LMC, #193–227) green

Our Abraham cycle begins with God's call and Abraham's obedient response. With very few directives, Abraham takes the Lord God's word alone as the rock of faith (this is repeated in Tuesday's displaced reading). Jesus continues his teaching with a command to refrain from judgment that we might be spared judgment. Self-criticism, honestly pursued, should make us forever unwilling to offer criticism of others.

TUE 24 — The Birth of John the Baptist
#586–587 (LMC, #316) white
SOLEMNITY

This feast was observed on this date by the fourth century. It celebrates the holy birth of "the greatest of all the prophets," the one who leaped for joy in his mother's womb, who prepared the way for Christ, announced his presence and baptized him in the Jordan (© ICEL).

For most saints we celebrate the *dies natalis,* defined as the day of their "heavenly birth," which is to say, the day of their earthly death. For only three persons does the calendar also mark the date of their birth into this life: the Lord Jesus, his mother Mary and the forerunner. Indeed the conceptions of these three are noted as well: Jesus on March 25, Mary on December 8 and John the Baptist on September 24, although this feast is no longer kept in the Western church.

Noting that with today's feast, nature's daylight hours are as lengthy as they ever get (in the Northern Hemisphere) and, in fact, however imperceptibly, begin to decrease, Saint Augustine related the natural phenomenon to John's own prophecy: "Christ must increase; I must decrease" (John 3:30).

JUNE

■ VIGIL CELEBRATION: Today is one of those nonobligatory solemnities for which, nevertheless, a Vigil Mass formulary is provided. This testifies to the church's sense of the day's importance. Summer presents us with two additional vigils: Peter and Paul next week and Mary's Assumption in August. But Assumption is frequently a holy day, so the vigil Mass will probably be celebrated. With today's feast, this need not be so. But a gathering on the night of the 23rd for prayer and for festivity (after all, it is a long summer night!) would certainly be a good way to honor John. Many ethnic groups have the custom of an evening cookout with bonfires or even fireworks to honor this shining light who blazed the way for the Messiah.

■ LITURGY: Make a subtle connection of this solemnity to Christmas by using the "Christmas white" vestments and, if incense is used, bring out the "Christmas" scent. If either the vigil or day Mass is not celebrated, consider combining the two gospel passages at the Mass that is celebrated, so that the whole wondrous story can be heard.

Sing the Canticle of Zechariah in one of the many settings available. If the community is used to celebrating Morning Prayer, one of the versions familiar from that liturgy ought to be used. All major hymnals carry metrical versions. The finest hymn for today is John Mason Neale's superb translation of an eighth-century poem by Venerable Bede: "The great forerunner of the morn," in both *Worship* and the Episcopal *Hymnal 1982*. Ralph Wright has provided a fine translation of a scripturally inspired Latin poem in the hymn "O Prophet John, O man of God," found in GIA's *Hymnal for the Hours*.

The special preface for John the Baptist is a twice-yearly text. It might provide homilists with good material for preaching and those who prepare the bulletin with a handy summary of this saint's summertime commemorations to print with the schedule for today's worship and festivity.

WED 25 Weekday
#373 (LMC, #193–227) green

How can I be sure? Abram frequently asks but always believes; and so Eucharistic Prayer I designates him "our father in faith." God responds to Abram's trust by making a covenant with him. The brief gospel passage ends with Jesus' criterion for authenticity, one we ought to paraphrase if we want to shift the focus from others to ourselves: "By our fruits, others will know us."

THU 26 Weekday
#374 (LMC, #193–227) green

Either version of the first reading gets the saving point across: God fulfills his promise to Abram (and to us) in his own way, in his own time. Moreover, the contentious Ishmael is part of the saving plan, the promise's fulfillment. Jesus reminds us: We who call upon him as Lord need always to measure our words against our deeds and to check the ground beneath which we are building for the possibility of shifting sands.

FRI 27 Weekday
#375 (LMC, #193–227) green

Cyril of Alexandria, bishop, doctor of the church, optional memorial/white. ■ Abram's name is changed; Sarai's name is changed; the covenant enters a new phase, with promises so extravagant on God's part that Abraham's response is, in the shorthand of online "chat rooms," ROFL (rolling on the floor laughing)! But faith, as always, is Abraham and Sarah's definitive response: Isaac will be born.

Cyril, whose optional memorial is today, was as rough and ready a champion as the true faith ever had, though certainly not a model of diplomacy! In affirming Mary as Mother of God, he and the church were really saying something crucially profound about both Jesus and us. In Jesus we meet God-in-our-flesh. In Mary we see God's intimate bond with us. And "he whom the heavens cannot contain" encloses himself within the body of one of his creatures.

SAT 28 Irenaeus, bishop, martyr
#376 (LMC, #193–227) red
MEMORIAL

The first reading has a wonderful dialogue between the Lord and Sarah. "Why did she laugh." "I didn't laugh." "Oh, yes, you did!" What delightful familiarity: God makes himself Abraham's guest and in the gospel, the centurion gives us the words Christians have used for centuries at Mass to welcome Christ in the eucharist. Irenaeus shared in Christ's healing ministry by working toward healing the church's wounds.

JULY

#590–591 (LMC, #319) red

☉ 29 Peter and Paul, apostles
SOLEMNITY

This preeminent feast day of the city of Rome has been observed on this date since the mid-third century. It commemorates the martyrdoms at Rome under Nero, between 64–67, of Peter the "chief of the apostles" and Paul the "apostle to the Gentiles." It recalls their faith, their courage and their leadership during the difficult days of the birth of the church (© ICEL).

The church has always linked Peter and Paul in liturgy, art and preaching, finding encouragement in this partnership that should not have worked but that in Christ has formed an enduring apostolic foundation for a worldwide communion. Traditionally, Peter represents the institutional dimension of the church, Paul, the Spirit-inspired, charismatic side.

■ LITURGY: This day was once marked by the celebration of three different liturgies: Peter was remembered in his basilica on the Vatican hill, Paul at his tomb on the road to Ostia, then everyone processed to a catacomb that sheltered the remains of both during persecution. Current liturgical books provide for one celebration on the solemnity itself and a vigil liturgy the night before. Since the solemnity falls on a weekend this year, both formularies will most likely be used.

If the eve of John the Baptist was not marked by a special celebration of prayer and summertime festivities, keep the possibility in mind for the eve of this feast.

The solemn blessing printed at the day Mass is also appropriate for a vigil Mass and for the end of Evening Prayer. As always, the hymn "By all your saints still striving" has a special verse for Peter and Paul. "Two noble saints," in *Worship,* and "O Light of Lights" in *Hymnal for the Hours* are translations of Latin hymns for this feast.

MON 30 Weekday
#377 (LMC, #193–227) Green

The first martyrs of Rome, optional memorial/red. ▪ In a wonderfully lively dialogue, Abraham bargains with God on behalf of Sodom and Gomorrah. We remember that along with the simplicity of the Lord's Prayer, Jesus counseled persistence in intercession! In the gospel the week begins and ends with a vocation story. Today the would-be disciple bargains about the conditions of discipleship. On Friday Matthew rises and follows without discussion or delay.

In remembering the Roman martyrs, we ought to recall that many historians theorize that a fair number of them were catechumens, who thus received "the baptism of blood" in witness to Christ.

July

TUE 1 Weekday
#378 (LMC, #193–227) green

Blessed Junípero Serra, presbyter, religious, missionary, optional memorial/white. ▪ Sodom and Gomorrah are destroyed: So much for Abraham's hard bargain driving! But "God remembered Abraham." And this becomes one of the most frequent of prayers on the lips of prophet and psalmist: "Remember," "Be mindful," "Do not forget." In the gospel, Jesus at first sleeps through what the disciples fear is mortal danger. Responding to their anguished cry of desperation, Jesus teaches them, and us, to pray not in panic but with faith.

Franciscan Friar Junípero Serra played a decisive role in evangelizing California, though some, with the clearer perspective of hindsight, have critiqued that missionary endeavor recently. Pray in today's intercessions for the parishioners of his missions and for Native Americans. The proper opening prayer is in *Sacramentary Supplement.*

■ CANADA DAY: Include prayers for the people of Canada in today's general intercessions. Canadian parishes should use *A Supplement to the Sacramentary* (National Liturgical Office, 1991) for special Mass texts.

WED 2 Weekday
#379 (LMC, #193–227) green

God's saving plan works itself out through the very human conflict between Sarah and Hagar. No one is superfluous in that plan, no distressed soul is ultimately forsaken. There is quite a scene among the Gadarenes! Between the vocation stories of Monday and Friday is this dramatic portrayal of Jesus' sovereign authority over demons (and,

JULY

if tomorrow's is added to it, over disease and sin as well). On the lips of Jesus, the call is never coercion, always invitation.

THU 3 — Thomas, apostle — FEAST
#593 (LMC, #452–454, 322)   red

The gospel records Jesus' invitation to Thomas, "Put your finger here and see. . . . Reach out your hand, and put it in my side." But there is no record of Thomas' action in response, only his act of faith: "My Lord and my God." To this apostle, Augustine says, we should be grateful for the beatitude pronounced by Jesus on all generations of disciples: "Blessed are those who have not seen and yet have come to believe."

Pray today for the peoples of India, whom Thomas is said to have evangelized, and for all those in our families and community for whom the act of faith is a challenge.

FRI 4 — Weekday
#381 or 831–835 (LMC, #193–227)   green

Elizabeth of Portugal, married woman, queen, optional memorial/white. • *U.S.: Independence Day/civic observance/white.* • There are two sets of liturgical texts in the 1985 edition of the U.S. sacramentary: one in July and a new set in appendix X, Mass 6. Note also two Prefaces for Independence Day and other Civic Observances, both very dated by their exclusive language. Some avoid them by using the Preface for Thanksgiving Day on July 4. This text is worse, dubbed by many liturgists "Preface of Manifest Destiny," since it turns England into Egypt, the Atlantic into the Red Sea and the U.S. into the Promised Land! Look for a completely new set of prayers in the revised sacramentary.

Consider Eucharistic Prayer for Reconciliation II or the new Eucharistic Prayer for Various Needs and Occasions, especially form A (The Church on the Way to Unity) or D (Jesus, the Compassion of God).

■ LITURGY OF THE WORD: If the first reading from Thursday is shifted to today, the story of Abraham's obedient faith could fit in well with the civic observance: "The Lord will provide." The prescribed gospel makes a good point, too: At Matthew's table, at the Lord's table, all are welcome. Is this true of our community's table as well? After all, it is mercy, not sacrifice the Lord desires. Appendix X, Mass 6 lists optional scripture texts, all of them focused on peace, as is appropriate to the day.

■ PRAYER AT HOME OR AT CIVIC GATHERINGS: See *Catholic Household Blessings and Prayers* (page 199) and *Book of Blessings* (#1965).

SAT 5 — Weekday
#382 (LMC, #193–227)   green

Anthony Zaccaria, presbyter, religious founder, optional memorial/white; Blessed Virgin Mary on Saturday, optional memorial/white. • As the Jacob and Esau story illustrates, God's plan can triumph even over sibling rivalry and human deceit! The gospel question on fasting, and Jesus' answer about the guests at a wedding feast, call to mind the wedding feast at Cana. If the memorial of Mary is kept, there is an appropriate formulary in the CMBVM, #9, Our Lady at Cana.

SUN 6 — Fourteenth Sunday in Ordinary Time
#101 [102] (LMC, #96)   green

The first block of Ordinary Time Sundays closes with a definitive rejection of Jesus and his amazement at his hometown's unbelief. Brought up on images of Christ's omnipotence, we may be somewhat taken aback by Mark's bold assertion that Jesus was powerless before such a lack of faith!

■ BLESSING OF TRAVELERS: On Sundays during summer's peak travel time, those heading off for vacation in any given week might be invited to gather at the ambo or church doors for a brief order of blessing led by a pastor or lay minister (*Book of Blessings*, #635). For parish tour groups or any large, identifiable group (band, sports team) a longer order of blessing is provided (BB, chapter 9).

MON 7 — Weekday
#383 (LMC, #193–227)   green

The spiritual "We are climbing Jacob's ladder" draws its inspiration from today's first reading. The covenant with Abraham and Isaac is renewed and augmented in a new generation. Jacob discovers that any place can be holy ground; the initiative of sanctification is always God's. In the gospel, two healings take place; and while one involves the touch of Christ's garment and the other the grasp of his hand, as Jesus himself makes clear, the effective agent in both cases is faith.

JULY

TUE 8 #384 (LMC, #193–227) green
Weekday

Jacob's successful wrestling match earns him a dislocated hip and the new name, Israel. But the one who gives Jacob a name does not reveal his own name, so Jacob can only conclude that he has wrestled with God! In one way or another, haven't we all had that experience? Comforting, then, to know that in Jesus God has compassion on us who sometimes wrestle with him!

WED 9 #385 (LMC, #193–227) green
Weekday

The first part of the Joseph story, the brothers' attack on Joseph, is read during the second week of Lent. Today we begin the story of the aftermath of that deed. It may be helpful to preface today's selection with a brief reminder to the assembly of the story's set-up. In the gospel, Jesus' mission begins, in a limited way, to the lost sheep of Israel.

THU 10 #386 (LMC, #193–227) green
Weekday

The first reading needs to be proclaimed carefully to permit even a reduced assembly of "weekday regulars" to experience the depth of its emotion. The beauty of these lines reminds us that even on weekdays, the principles of good proclamation need to be observed: preparation and practice! Jesus' instructions to his disciples are appropriate for us: What you have as a gift, give as a gift; and a blessing of peace upon all whom we meet.

FRI 11 #387 (LMC, #193–227) white
Benedict, abbot, religious founder
MEMORIAL

The reunion of Israel with his beloved son Joseph brings to a happy conclusion a story of twisted relationships, violence and jealousy. Jesus warns us about these very things, painting a scene of division that reaches into political systems, religious institutions and even the family.

Fleeing the decadence of Rome, young Benedict at first sought the Lord in solitude. But God used Benedict to transform the society he had left by forming, apart from it and yet within it as a leaven, a whole new system of relationships. The solitude of Benedict's life became the Benedictine community life that still attracts so many and to which the church owes much of its recent liturgical reform.

SAT 12 #388 (LMC, #193–227) green
Weekday

Blessed Virgin Mary on Saturday, optional memorial/white. • The dying Joseph speaks a prophetic word of divine intervention and deliverance, thus setting the stage for the Exodus stories that begin next week. Jesus invites his disciples to rejoice in becoming like and in being treated like their Master. If the Saturday memorial of Mary is observed, see CMBVM, #10, which designates Mary by a beautiful title: Disciple of the Lord.

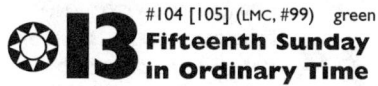

13 #104 [105] (LMC, #99) green
Fifteenth Sunday in Ordinary Time

SUMMER II: SUNDAYS 15–23

This block of Sundays begins with mission instructions (Sunday 15) and the Compassion of Jesus (Sunday 16). These selections prepare us for a lengthy digression from Mark's gospel to John's gospel, Chapter 6. The compassion expressed in the selection from Mark's gospel (Sunday 16) dovetails, in the lectionary arrangement, with a similar compassion in John's gospel, a compassion manifested by the dramatic feeding of the multitude (Sunday 17). This feeding sets up three Sundays on which Jesus teaches the crowds about himself as the living and life-giving bread come down from heaven (Sundays 18–20).

The climax of the multiple misunderstandings that occur between Jesus and his listeners comes in Jesus' direct question to the Twelve: "Do you also wish to go away?" (Sunday 21). Peter's response forms the bridge back into Mark's gospel and the final two Sundays of this block: human traditions and God's commandments (Sunday 22) and the restoration of hearing and speech, about which Jesus commands silence (Sunday 23)! In the following block of Sundays the mystery surrounding Jesus will begin to be lifted, at least for the disciples, as Peter makes a profession of faith (Sunday 24, replaced this year by The Holy Cross).

■ LITURGICAL TEXTS: Simplicity continues as the leitmotif of these Sundays. "The Lord be with you," spoken by the presider with reverence and the prescribed ritual embrace of the community (arms extended then joined in a graceful gesture) says it all. For the litany of praise in this block of Sundays:

> Lord Jesus, you are moved with compassion for those who seek you: Lord, have mercy.
> Christ Jesus, you are the living bread, come down from heaven: Christ, have mercy.
> Lord Jesus, you alone have the words of everlasting life: Lord, have mercy.

JULY

Again, consider keeping a single set of general intercessions throughout this block of Sundays, changing one intercession each week to reflect the Sunday scriptures more explicitly and to draw current needs and situations into the community's prayer.

On these Sundays it might be fitting to use Preface of the Holy Eucharist II, which includes both praise for what the eucharist is and hopes for what it should accomplish within the community. For the invitation to the Lord's Prayer, consider ICEL's new text:

> With trust in God who nourishes us in the hour of need,
> let us pray as Jesus taught us.

And this new alternative for the invitation to communion:

> This is the bread come down from heaven:
> whoever eats of it will never die.
> This is the cup of eternal life:
> whoever drinks of it will live for ever.

This is perfect for communion under both species. If this is not yet parish usage, these Sundays would be a good time to begin, since Jesus speaks explicitly of eating and drinking.

▪ MUSIC: If the proper psalm for each week is not used, consider the refrain given as the first choice from among the common psalms in the lectionary at #175: "Lord, you have the words of everlasting life." Echoed in the final climactic scene of the gospels from John 6, this refrain would tie the whole block of Sundays together well and appears in any number of settings. It would seem, however, to be more appropriately matched to the verses of Psalm 34 (#175, choice 3) than Psalm 19.

For the eucharistic prayer acclamations see Richard Proulx's *Corpus Christi Mass* (GIA, G-3693), based on the familiar "Adoro Te" melody. This could serve for the whole block and would work well a cappella, if necessary.

The most likely communion processional is any version of "O Taste and See."

General hymnody in this block of Sundays will want to draw on the large repertoire of eucharistic hymnody, both those hymns that celebrate the eucharist as the community's action and even those more commonly associated with a focus on the eucharist in itself. Look at the notes for the Solemnity of the Body and Blood of Christ (page 201). Check the liturgical and topical indices of your hymnals.

MON 14 #389 (LMC, #193–227) white

U.S.: Blessed Kateri Tekakwitha, virgin ▪ This peaceful summer day is filled, liturgically at least, with conflict. We begin reading the moving story about the bitter confrontation between Egypt and Israel, in the persons of the pharaoh and Moses. Jesus warns his disciples about the division that will inevitably be experienced, at least to some extent and in some circumstances, by those who become his disciples. And Blessed Kateri, the "Lily of the Mohawks," experiences in her own personal suffering the pain that ensues when cultures clash.

TUE 15 #390 (LMC, #193–227) white
Bonaventure, bishop, religious, doctor of the church
MEMORIAL

The compassion of pharaoh's daughter is God's providential instrument for the rescue of the boy who will become God's fiery instrument against pharaoh's rule! The reproaches of Jesus against the unreceptive cities need to be taken seriously by our own assembly.

Poor Pope Gregory X! During his famous Council of Lyons, he lost the two most famous theologians in the church! Aquinas and Bonaventure died within months of each other in 1274.

WED 16 #391 (LMC, #193–227) green
Weekday

Our Lady of Mt. Carmel, optional memorial/white. ▪ To know the Lord is the heartfelt desire of every believer in every generation. For Moses, who considers himself an inarticulate and unworthy messenger, God speaks from the burning bush with assurances of abiding presence and help. To the childlike heart, the Father reveals, in Jesus, the mysteries of the kingdom that remain hidden from "the wise and intelligent."

Prayers for the gifts of wisdom and knowledge are best preceded by prayers for the gifts of humility and openness. This certainly is the Carmelite approach to the contemplative life, evidenced in the prayerful writings of Teresa of Jesus, the mystical poetry of John of the Cross, the "little way" of Therese of Lisieux, and the witness unto death in a Nazi concentration camp of Blessed Edith Stein (Sister Teresa Benedicta).

THU 17 #392 (LMC, #193–227) green
Weekday

From the burning bush God reveals his name to Moses, the unspeakable name: I AM WHO I AM. From the heart of Jesus, God reveals his personality to us, gentle and humble, and the nature of the burden he imposes, easy and light.

JULY

FRI 18 #393 (LMC, #193–227) green
Weekday

The first reading gives the Lord's detailed instructions to Moses and Aaron about the community's observance of Passover. Jesus, our Passover and our peace, reminds the religiously observant of his day (and in our day, presumably, that means us!) that God's first desire is not sacrifice but mercy. A heart filled with judgments on others has no room left to offer praises to God.

SAT 19 #394 (LMC, #193–227) green
Weekday

Blessed Virgin Mary on Saturday, optional memorial / white. • In the first reading, Israel keeps a night of vigil, one that will be repeated in all future generations and which, in fact, we join Israel in keeping every year, under the paschal moon. Matthew looks on Jesus, whom John's gospel sees as the new paschal lamb, as fulfilling also the role of God's servant described in Isaiah.

An appropriate formulary for the Saturday Mass of Mary would be CMBVM, #22, Handmaid of the Lord. The introductory notes specifically relate that title of Mary to her Son's title "Servant of the Lord," from an Isaiah text that Jesus quotes in today's gospel.

#107 [108] (LMC, #102) green
☀ 20 Sixteenth Sunday in Ordinary Time

The beginning of today's gospel sounds like a perfect summer choice: "Come away . . . and rest awhile." But the attempted getaway quickly becomes the day off that never happened! In Jesus, the understandable quest for a bit of refreshment yields to a shepherd's heartfelt compassion. Jeremiah's picture of the good shepherd shines out in Christ, who gathers together, as Paul says, those once far from God and at odds with each other. Because the meal is provided by the One who is our peace and reconciliation, these gifts are not merely the results of our feasting together but the absolute prerequisites for our partaking of it.

MON 21 #395 (LMC, #193–227) green
Weekday

Lawrence of Brindisi, presbyter, religious, doctor of the church, optional memorial / white. • In their fear and distress, the people grumble against God and Moses. Each responds differently. Moses says: "Be still!" God commands: "Get moving!"

Today's saint valued the preaching ministry in the turbulent days that followed the Reformation.

TUE 22 #603 (LMC, #193–227) white
Mary Magdalene, disciple of the Lord
MEMORIAL

The Roman Calendar of 1969 gave Mary Magdalene no special title, but the revised ICEL version restores an ancient and beautiful designation: "disciple of the Lord." She has also been labelled "penitent," based on a long-standing, apparently erroneous, identification of her with the sinful woman of Luke's gospel. The mistake is understandable in light of Mark 16:9's unflattering description of her as one "from whom Jesus had driven out seven demons." But isn't this image of Mary Magdalene precisely what has captured the imagination and kindled the devotion of countless generations? Heroic sanctity and unblemished chastity we all admire—from a distance! In Magdalene we feel we have found a sympathetic friend, a struggling sister, in whose example we find encouragement and on whose intercession we can count.

WED 23 #397 (LMC, #193–227) green
Weekday

Bridget of Sweden, married woman, religious founder, optional memorial / white. • God sends the Israelites bread from heaven, and Jesus tells the parable of the sower. This is a good day to reflect on the "shape" of the liturgy, which stands out with great clarity after Vatican II's reform: word and eucharist; seed sown, harvest gathered; wisdom assimilated, bread broken; nourishment for us, that we might become nourishment for others. As always, the word challenges: How receptive have we been to God's gifts? What kind of soil are we?

A prayer of Bridget of Sweden, reflecting her passionate love of Christ crucified, appears in the *Liturgy of the Hours,* volume III, 1548–50.

THU 24 #398 (LMC, #193–227) green
Weekday

The Lord summons Moses to the top of the mountain to receive the Decalogue (Friday's displaced reading). If, as Jesus said, the disciples were blessed to see and hear, how much more so are we who have heard the good news of Jesus and have seen it lived out in his life and death? Not to mention in the witness of holy men and women across a span of almost 2000 years!

FRI 25 #605 (LMC, #452–455) red
James, apostle
FEAST

Paul speaks of "clay vessels," and the gospel shows us three of them: today's saint, his brother

JULY

and their very assertive mother! Self-seeking comes naturally, Jesus warns the ten, who are probably angry because those Zebedee kids tried to beat them to the top! "It will not be so among you," says the Master, who "came not to be served but to serve." This is the key to Christian hospitality — and the key to the kingdom!

SAT 26 — Joachim and Anne, parents of the Virgin Mary — MEMORIAL
#400 (LMC, #193–227) white

The weekday lectionary is used today, although optional readings are given in the proper of saints (where the gospel repeats part of Thursday's). Anyway, commemorating Joachim and Anne fits in well enough with the weekday selections. Moses inaugurates with sacrificial blood the covenant into which the human family of Jesus had been initiated just after birth. And surely the gospel image of weeds and wheat growing together is an apt image of life in the Hebrew covenant, in the Christian testament, in our parish, even in our hearts!

SUN 27 — Seventeenth Sunday in Ordinary Time
#110 [111] (LMC, #105) green

Today begins a five-Sunday reading of John 6. The weekly reading from the First Testament scriptures has been chosen not as a continuous reading from one book but according to the principle of "correspondence." Planners and homilists, therefore, will want to see what light this choice sheds on the gospel passage each week. In today's passage about Elisha, for instance, there are barley loaves and food left over, after the prophet's word. In the gospel, the loaves are of barley, Jesus' disciples echo Elisha's servant's question, there is food left over, and the crowd calls Jesus "the prophet." Jesus thus appears in continuity with Israel's prophetic tradition.

MON 28 — Weekday
#401 (LMC, #193–227) green

Remember Adam's lame excuse for his sin? "The woman whom you gave me to be with me, she gave me the fruit." Aaron sounds like Adam: "I threw the gold in the fire and out came this calf!" Little pieces of jewelry produced a big sin! But in the gospel, good and surprisingly great things come from insignificant beginnings: a barely visible seed, yeast that disappears into the flour. As with the growth of the kingdom, so with the life of the disciples. Jesus had told them early on that they had to be salt: virtually invisible on and in food but immediately noticeable when absent.

TUE 29 — Martha, disciple of the Lord — MEMORIAL
#402 and 607 (LMC, #193–227) white

What a beautiful title today has in the monastic calendar: "Martha, Mary and Lazarus of Bethany, hosts of the Lord." Another summertime feast on which to celebrate and rededicate ourselves to the practice of hospitality; a day on which to remember the homeless and reflect on our community's service of them. No one need envy Moses to whom "the Lord spoke face to face, as one speaks to a friend." In every face, we see the face of Christ. In everyone we welcome, it is Christ himself whom we serve. Today might be a good day to bless parish ministries that focus on hospitality.

WED 30 — Weekday
#403 (LMC, #193–227) green

Peter Chrysologus, bishop, doctor of the church, optional memorial / white. ▪ The radiance of Moses' face after conversing with God and the surpassing joy of those in the gospel who discover the hidden treasure, the pearl of great price: Both readings might give us pause. Have we not found Christ, the treasure, the pearl, in his word, at his table, in the community? Can people see on our faces and in our charity the joy that fills our hearts?

THU 31 — Ignatius of Loyola, presbyter, religious founder — MEMORIAL
#404 (LMC, #193–227) white

Our final selection from Exodus celebrates God's abiding presence: sometimes in the blazing clarity of fire, at other times in the dark obscurity of cloud. The kingdom's net, says Jesus, takes in all kinds! Are we not the living proof of that? If there is room for me, said the desert father, there is room for everyone! Pray today for Ignatius' family, the Jesuits, who continue to bring from the church's storehouse both the new and the old.

August

FRI 1 — Alphonsus Liguori, bishop, religious founder, doctor of the church — MEMORIAL
#405 (LMC, #193–227) white

Today and tomorrow the Leviticus passages outline the community's festivals and remind us that we who order our year of worship by readings and seasons do so in continuity with our Jewish past. Jesus' proclamation of parables ends with his hometown

AUGUST

neighbors finding him offensive and his own power to heal rendered impotent by their unbelief.

Alphonsus' devotional prayers (to Christ in the eucharist and at Stations of the Cross) are still beloved and used by many. Pray for the worldwide Redemptorist community today.

SAT 2 #406 (LMC, #193–227) green
Weekday

Eusebius of Vercelli, bishop, optional memorial/white; Blessed Virgin Mary on Saturday, optional memorial/white. ▪ As the church draws near the jubilee of 2000, we hear the scripture that inspires this practice in today's passage from Leviticus. Wouldn't it be wonderful to mark the dawn of a new millennium by implementing the biblical marks of jubilee: generosity, justice, amnesty and the canceling of debts!

The commemoration of Eusebius honors a saint who, like John, suffered for the truth of his words. If Mary is honored today, suggested formularies are CMBVM, #39: Mother of Mercy; #41: Mother of Consolation; or from the lenten season, #11 and 12: Mary at the Foot of the Cross.

☀ 3 #113 [114] (LMC, #108) green
Eighteenth Sunday in Ordinary Time

In Exodus, God's gift of bread from heaven is both gracious response to the Israelites' anguished cry and confrontational response to their continual murmuring: "In that way I will test them." They have misunderstood Moses' mission, their call, God's purpose. So profoundly did the crowd misunderstand Jesus' mission last week that he fled. Now they misunderstand the miraculous feeding. Jesus is trying to teach them that he is "bread" in two senses: Primarily as the revelation of divine wisdom, which will not disappoint or fail those who feed on his teaching. Secondarily here, and most emphatically in the passages of the next two weeks, Jesus is the living bread of the eucharist; he will give them his flesh and blood as food and drink.

MON 4 #407 (LMC, #193–227) white
John Mary Vianney, presbyter
MEMORIAL

On this memorial of a model parish priest, Moses exemplifies both a traditional priestly role and a contemporary refinement of it. He intercedes for the people he is called to serve but realizes, too, he cannot do everything alone! Note the special gospel for Year B: Matthew's version of the multiplication of the loaves.

TUE 5 #408 (LMC, #193–227) green
Weekday

Dedication of the Basilica of St. Mary in Rome, optional memorial/white. ▪ It is said that the truly great people are also the most humble, and that is the beautiful description given of Moses in today's first reading. He demonstrates this humility in responding to insult with a prayer for Miriam's healing. The gospel enjoys presenting Peter in a most human light. Even having seen so much, Peter still requests a sign. When the sign is given, Peter's faith falters once again. Jesus is now in a place of faith, unlike his hometown, and healing once again can take place.

Today's memorial, and summer leisure, presents an opportunity for every parish to research the date of its dedication and make plans to keep it as a local solemnity with grand liturgy and enjoyable festivity. The dedication of the local cathedral should also be kept as a parish feast. These days link us to the bishop of Rome, to our diocese and to the Christ who lives in the midst of our own local church.

WED 6 #614 (LMC, #344) white
The Transfiguration of the Lord
FEAST

Today highlights a horribly different manifestation of human nature's "dual" tendency. This feast that celebrates the glorious existence for which we are destined has witnessed the sad reality for which we have sometimes settled. In 1457 the pope mandated universal observance of this feast in thanksgiving for a Christian victory over Muslims near Belgrade on August 6. In our own day how the light of the Transfiguration has been eclipsed by a blinding flash of annihilation! August 6 is forever marked as the day on which Hiroshima was annihilated, a horror repeated in Nagasaki three days later. By all means keep the liturgical texts prescribed for the day, but let intercessions for peace feature prominently in Mass and in the Liturgy of the Hours, and let homiletic reflections put the feast's contrasts in sharp relief.

AUGUST

■ LITURGY: Today should celebrate Christ's glory in a way similar in tone to Easter and Christ the King. The vestments of those solemnities should be used, and candles and incense where possible. The transfiguration account from Mark repeats the gospel of the Second Sunday of Lent but is heard differently today because of the accompanying readings and chants that celebrate the "heavenly vision that will give us a share in Christ's radiance, renew our spiritual nature and transform us into Christ's own likeness" (Office of Readings). The Eastern icons (put one on a stand for veneration) picture the transfiguring light of Christ cascading from his robes onto those of the three apostles. This image, too, highlights our share in Christ's brightness. Hymns for the feast are in all major hymnals.

■ KEEPING VIGIL: On the eve of the Transfiguration, in line with the ancient Catholic tradition of the nightwatch and keeping vigil, a celebration with incense and candlelight could focus the community's intercession on the work of peace.

THU 7 Weekday
#410 (LMC, #193–227) green

Sixtus I, pope, martyr, and his companions, martyrs, optional memorial/red; Cajetan, presbyter, religious founder, optional memorial/white. ■ The Lord's response to the Israelites is blessing and punishment. Water is given from the rock, and this event will fill the memory of the church with thoughts of baptism and sacramental grace through all generations. But the waters are remembered, too, as the place of rebellion, of putting God to the test, of the divine decision that Moses will not lead the people all the way home. In the gospel, too, the word to Peter is one of both blessing and curse: You are the rock. But also: Get behind me Satan. No gift of authority, no divine revelation can release us from the obligation of following in Christ's footsteps and learning his way of self-sacrificing love.

FRI 8 Dominic, presbyter, religious founder
#411 (LMC, #193–227) white
MEMORIAL

In the eucharistic prayer, after the institution narrative, we always offer an "anamnesis," a living remembrance of God's mighty deeds in Jesus. Now, with death approaching, Moses begins a farewell discourse, a great "anamnesis" in which he celebrates God's mighty deeds for Israel. Having rebuked Peter's mistaken notion of the path Jesus should walk, the Lord outlines the journey for his disciples. In an age when the papacy would resort to military force to impose sound doctrine, Dominic and his followers became an "army of evangelizers," whose power was the truth of their preaching and the persuasive example of their common life.

SAT 9 Weekday
#412 (LMC, #193–227) green

Blessed Virgin Mary on Saturday, optional memorial/white. ■ *Shema, Israel:* "Hear, O Israel." To this day, devout Jews take this first reading with literal seriousness, binding God's commands to forehead and hand, posting them by the door to be kissed with every entrance and exit. There is a wisdom here: To obey one must remember.

For keeping the Saturday memorial of Mary, see CMBVM, #35: Mary, Pillar of Faith; or 44: Mary, Health of the Sick.

10 Nineteenth Sunday in Ordinary Time
#116 [117] (LMC, #111) green

In the desert wilderness Elijah receives as a gift from God the miraculous food as strength for his lengthy journey to God's mountain. How could Christians journeying to the kingdom through this world's desert not see an image of the eucharist? In the gospel, the new Canadian lectionary, with Vatican approval, changes "Jews" to "people." Constant repetition of "the Jews" could completely distract from the point of the passage. A thoughtful rereading of LTP's *When Catholics Speak about Jews* may be in order for planners and homilists.

MON 11 Clare, virgin, religious founder
#413 (LMC, #193–227) white
MEMORIAL

Moses reminds us that true worship expresses itself in practical charity for one's neighbor and for the stranger in our midst. Another prediction of the passion is followed by the strange money-bearing fish. Wishing not to give offense unnecessarily, Jesus pays a tax to which he is not technically bound. Then as now, there are times to bend, times to stand firm. Clare and Francis exemplified both readings, becoming one with the poor and homeless, making the Franciscan way of life flexible enough to embrace clergy and layfolk, celibates and married people, but uncompromisingly evangelical in their dedication to poverty and peace.

AUGUST

TUE 12 #414 (LMC, #193–227) green
Weekday

Moses commissions Joshua as his successor, passing on his God-given power and authority. Jesus shows the disciples, in a child, what power and authority look like in his kingdom.

WED 13 #415 (LMC, #193–227) green
Weekday

Pontian, pope, martyr, and Hippolytus, presbyter, martyr, optional memorial/red. ▪ The first reading presents Moses' final appearance: He sees but does not enter the promised land. In the gospel, Jesus outlines the community's approach to those who stray. His final advice sounds harsh at first: "Let such a one be to you as a Gentile and a tax collector." Then we remember how Jesus welcomed Gentiles and ate with tax collectors.

Although today's memorial is optional, these saints say much to us. Pontian and Hippolytus, separated by schism when authority was the issue in Rome, were reconciled in the salt mines when persecution made Christ, their one Lord, their common ground.

THU 14 #416 (LMC, #193–227)
Maximilian Mary Kolbe, presbyter, religious, martyr
MEMORIAL

The waters of the Jordan cease to flow when the ark of the Lord's covenant is carried through. In the gospel, Peter generously, he thinks, doubles the rabbinic prescription of threefold forgiveness and even adds one for good measure. But he is speaking to Jesus! And Jesus multiplies Peter's "seven times" to infinity: seventy times seven! Today's martyr, Maximilian Kolbe, caused the waters of hatred that had submerged Europe to pause for a day, as he, with forgiveness toward his executioners, offered his life on behalf of a fellow prisoner at Auschwitz.

#621–622 (LMC, #447–450, 352) white
FRI 15 **The Assumption of the Virgin Mary into Heaven**
SOLEMNITY

This feast originated in Jerusalem before the fifth century as the "Falling-Asleep of the Mother of God." It was adopted in Rome in the mid-seventh century and was renamed the "Assumption" in the eighth. It celebrates Mary's passing over, body and soul, from this world into the glory of her risen Son (© ICEL).

The multilayered meaning of this feast evolved in three stages. In its earliest form, the day focused on Christ's paschal mystery as expressed in the death of Mary. Making her entrance into God's kingdom explicit was the second stage, using the scriptural images of a victory celebration, a bridal procession and Mary's being "lifted up." The unique fact of Mary's bodily assumption later added a third layer of texts for the feast.

Pope Pius XII put it succinctly: "It is our hope that belief in Mary's bodily assumption into heaven will make our belief in our own resurrection stronger and render it more effective" (*Munificentissimus Deus*, 42).

▪ LITURGY OF THE WORD: The first reading of the day Mass begins, as do the liturgies of Eastertime, not with the First Testament but with the New Testament. The Book of Revelation presents "the woman" threatened by the dragon but giving birth to a son and rescued with him by God. Evil is foiled, God's reign is established, and in that kingdom Mary rejoices. Paul reminds us, in the second reading, that Mary's privilege will be shared by all who follow Christ.

In today's gospel, John the Baptist leaps with joy in Elizabeth's womb as Mary enters the room bearing Christ within her. All of these scriptures celebrate God's mighty power at work among his people and in Mary as the model for all believers.

▪ MUSIC: For a good setting of today's Psalm 45, see Howard Hughes' "Assumption Psalm" (GIA, G-2028), and Diana Kodner's "The queen stands at your right hand" in *Gather* (second edition). First among Marian choices should be Mary's own words. Many settings of the Magnificat abound; Owen Alstott's "My soul rejoices" (OCP) is majestic and singable; James Cepponis' "Magnificat" (*Gather*, second edition, and octavo form) has a singable refrain and lilting verses.

▪ BLESSING OF PRODUCE: For centuries, in many countries, the Assumption solemnity is inextricably linked to the blessing of the earth's bounty. The full order of blessing is in the *Book of Blessings*, chapter 26 or 28; a simple order is in *Catholic Household Blessings and Prayers* (pages 170–71), with the Litany of Mary that can be chanted to a simple tone.

A U G U S T

- VIGIL OR EVENING CELEBRATION: Whether as a longer vigil on Thursday night or as Vespers on the evening of the solemnity itself, a candlelight celebration could be held. See the *Liturgy of the Hours,* volume IV, for resources.

SAT 16 Weekday
#418 (LMC, #193–227) green

Stephen of Hungary, married man, ruler, optional memorial / white. • *Blessed Virgin Mary on Saturday, optional memorial / white.* • Joshua confronts the Israelites with a choice: Choose whom you will serve. Jesus shows the disciples again that the kingdom belongs to little ones. Today's royal saint, King Stephen, was beloved by his subjects precisely because he showed himself subject to the gospel, seeking justice for the oppressed, charity for the poor.

With yesterday's solemnity and next Friday's memorial both celebrating Mary, the Saturday Mass might be omitted this week. If celebrated, however, CMBVM, #46 would be a good choice: Mary, Gate of Heaven.

☉ 17 Twentieth Sunday in Ordinary Time
#119 [120] (LMC, #114) green

This week's gospel begins by repeating the closing verse from last week's. Raymond Brown sees verses 51–58 as an explicitly "eucharistic rewriting" of verses 35–50:

> No longer are we told that eternal life is the result of believing in Jesus; it comes from feeding on his flesh and drinking his blood (54). The Father's role in bringing [people] to Jesus or giving them to him is no longer in the limelight; Jesus himself dominates as the agent and source of salvation. Even though the verses in 51–58 are remarkably like those of 35–50, a new vocabulary runs through them: "eat," "feed," "drink," "flesh," "blood" *(Anchor Bible).*

Since there is no institution narrative in the Fourth Gospel's Last Supper scene, Brown thinks that this may well be John's version of the institution, moved and rearranged to become part of the bread of life discourse. Taken together, last week's gospel (be taught, heard, learned) and this week's (eat, drink, flesh, blood) presents the twofold way in which Christ is present to the community of believers: in word and sacrament.

MON 18 Weekday
#419 (LMC, #193–227) green

Jane Frances de Chantal, married woman, religious founder, optional memorial / white. • Election by God and guidance into the promised land are enduring guarantees of God's love but not of human fidelity. "What do I still lack?" should be not only the rich young man's question but ours as well.

The optional memorial today features a saint, Jane Frances de Chantal, whose spiritual director, Francis de Sales, interpreted spirituality creatively so as to enhance the varying vocations and lifestyles of Christians. Together they founded Congregation of the Visitation, which offered an alternative form of religious life for women.

TUE 19 Weekday
#420 (LMC, #193–227) green

John Eudes, presbyter, religious founder, educator, optional memorial / white. • Gideon's honesty is wonderfully refreshing. The angel says: "The Lord is with you," but Gideon doesn't miss a beat, "Oh yeah? Then why is all this happening to us?" If things are going to change, the Lord tells Gideon, it has to begin with you. Jesus agrees with Peter's reaction to his own challenging concept of changing the world. Humanly speaking, it is impossible but not with God. Today's saint gave the church religious families (Sisters of the Good Shepherd) that still approach humanly impossible situations with the faith that Christian love can do all things.

WED 20 Bernard, abbot, presbyter, doctor of the church
#421 (LMC, #193–227) white
MEMORIAL

Not content with the Lord's kingship, Israel relies on its own judgment: always a shortcut to disaster! Jesus' images of the kingdom, today and tomorrow, challenge our concepts of what is right and fair. The gap between our standards and God's is thrown into sharp relief, for God's ultimate standard is love, a love that does not always measure by expediency and effectiveness. Today's saint has much to teach us in this regard.

Perhaps the most "unenclosed" monk of all time, Bernard was the dominant personality, in church and state, of the twelfth century. Besides his writings on theology and spirituality, the church continues to enjoy Bernard's hymns, among them: "O Sacred Head surrounded" and "O Jesus, joy of loving hearts."

THU 21 Pius x, pope
#422 (LMC, #193–227) white
MEMORIAL

In the first reading, a rash vow leads to a tragic consequence and demonstrates a complete misunderstanding of God's will and God's ways. Jesus shows us why

AUGUST

we are at the king's wedding feast: The invited guests wouldn't come, so we were invited by default! But God's graciousness still demands a cooperative response on our part, as the man without proper attire discovered.

At the turn of the century, a pope with vast pastoral experience, Pius X, laid the groundwork for much of the liturgical reform that came to fruition in Vatican II, and we keep his memory today. The centrality of the Lord's Day and the accessibility of the Lord's table, and a liturgy with full sung participation by the assembly were among his priorities.

FRI 22 — The Queenship of the Virgin Mary
#423 (LMC, #193–227) white
MEMORIAL

Ruth's fidelity to Naomi is a fine example of Jesus' summary of the covenant in the gospel: love of God and love of neighbor. Today's memorial serves as a kind of octave of Assumption, celebrating Mary's share in her Son's glory. See CMBVM, preface 29 for a text that goes well with today's observance.

SAT 23 — Weekday
#424 (LMC, #193–227) green

Rose of Lima, virgin, optional memorial/white; Blessed Virgin Mary on Saturday, optional memorial/white. ▪ Our selections from the First Testament scriptures end today, after a brief survey of Israel's failures, with Ruth setting the stage for a new phase in salvation history, as she gives birth to Obed, father of Jesse, whose son was King David. Jesus sets the stage for a new approach to teaching authority by counseling a humility and equality unknown among the religious hierarchy of his day. With yesterday's Marian feast, today's Saturday commemoration may be omitted, but if celebrated, see CMBVM, #32: Mother and Teacher in the Spirit.

SUN 24 — Twenty-first Sunday in Ordinary Time
#122 [123] (LMC, #117) green

Notice that this week it is not "the Jews" or "the people" but the disciples who complain and who finally "turned back and no longer went about with him." The first reading is a Joshua story we heard two Saturdays ago in the weekday lectionary. Joshua confronts the people with an either/or, life or death decision: to serve the living God or to follow after alien gods. The choice of this same passage to match today's gospel intends clearly to highlight the similar either/or, life or death decision with which Jesus confronts the Twelve: Do you also wish to go away? It is interesting that, far from trying to clarify his words or modify them into a less "offensive" interpretation, Jesus lets them stand and almost invites the Twelve to leave!

The second reading is presented in the United States' calendar as being either Ephesians 5:21–32 or 25–32. The Canadian solution seems preferable: add 4:32–5:2 and then see how much better 21–32 sounds! There is a mutuality in this longer text that is not apparent in either of the other editings.

MON 25 — Weekday
#425 (LMC, #193–227) green

Louis of France, married man, ruler, optional memorial/white; Joseph Calasanz, presbyter, religious founder, educator, optional memorial/white. ▪ Among Paul's first writings, First Thessalonians manifests his "apocalyptic sense" that the end is near. Wrath is coming; the Lord Jesus is coming with all his saints, and Paul is going to praise the community's strong points and challenge them to greater progress.

TUE 26 — Weekday
#426 (LMC, #193–227) green

Paul defends and describes his ministry in terms that should inspire all who serve in any of the parish community's ministries. Jesus confronts the Pharisees and scribes in words that should cause us all to examine our consciences and refine our motives!

WED 27 — Monica, married woman
#427 (LMC, #193–227) white
MEMORIAL

Urging, encouraging, pleading: Paul to the Thessalonians, Monica to Augustine! Monica saw through the confident, sophisticated exterior of her "most likely to succeed" son and saw a heart aching with emptiness, a mind lost in a tangle of confusion. Today and tomorrow are wonderful days to pray for the community's families.

THU 28 — Augustine, bishop, doctor of the church
#428 (LMC, #193–227) white
MEMORIAL

Note that both yesterday and today, the liturgical calendar (for the United States, at least) asks us to stay with the weekday readings. First Thessalonians fits in well with the memorial, as does Jesus' praise of the wise and faithful servant. Before Augustine worked hard for the church, he did quite a bit of work on himself (his mother assisting, we hasten to add!). The *Confessions* are virtually a self psycho-spiritual analysis of his inner state,

AUGUST

and the Office of Readings has lines so beautiful that they ought to be heard in the assembly as part of the homily's reflections.

FRI 29 — The Martyrdom of John the Baptist
#429 and 634 (LMC, #193–227) red
MEMORIAL

The first of today's weekday readings presents Paul's advice on sexual morality, an interesting topic when matched to the gospel of John's demise. It often seems there is no balance where this topic is concerned: Fire and brimstone thundering from the pulpit in years gone by has yielded to deafening silence in our own day. Authentic Christian moral theology is summed up by Paul: "that no one wrong or exploit a brother or sister in this matter." Today is also a day to pray for those who suffer persecution for the sake of conscience.

SAT 30 — Weekday
#430 (LMC, #193–227) green

Blessed Virgin Mary on Saturday, optional memorial / white. ▪ Paul's brief exhortation today could become a simple rule of life for any community: love of others based on God's love for us; practical concern and love for those beyond the local community; minding our own business; quietly doing our own work! The final reading from Matthew points toward the final accounting: creativity and generosity are the economics of the kingdom, not self-centered care and selfish caution! For the optional Saturday commemoration of Mary, consider CMBVM, #33: Mother of Good Counsel.

SUN 31 — Twenty-second Sunday in Ordinary Time
#125 [126] (LMC, #120) green

Though Moses had commanded that nothing be added to the Law, innumerable prescriptions had been. Jesus rephrases the Law's demands: Singleness of purpose and purity of heart will be a full-time challenge for his community. The Letter of James begins with an enumeration of commitments more challenging than the cleansing of hands and vessels: care for orphans and widows, and preservation from the world's corruption.

September

MON 1 — Weekday
#431 or 907–911 [846–850] (LMC, #193–227) green/white

U.S.: Labor Day. ▪ This observance is the modern equivalent of blessings bestowed on flocks and fields, seedtime and planting. More than ever, the term "human labor" embraces an endless array of diverse activities and commitments.

▪ LITURGICAL TEXTS: Useful elements and their origin are given below:

Greeting:

From Christ, the Son of God,
who was pleased to be known as
    the carpenter's son:
grace and peace be with you all
    (BB, #925 adapt.).

Litany of Praise:

Lord Jesus, to do the will of your
Father was your work on earth:
Lord, have mercy.

Christ Jesus, from a variety of occupations you called your first disciples: Christ, have mercy.

Lord Jesus, to those who labor and are heavy burdened you offer rest: Lord, have mercy.

Presidential Prayers:

Various Needs and Occasions, Mass 25 (revise for inclusive language); Mass 21: Progress of Peoples; Appendix X, Mass 6: Civic Occasions; May 1: Joseph the Worker.

Intercessions:

Use BB (#932) for inspiration, making sure to "universalize" the petitions to reach beyond the needs of the local community. Prayer to end these intercessions #935.

Eucharistic Prayer:

Eucharistic Prayer for Various Needs and Occasions: form C (Jesus, Way to the Father) or form D (Jesus, the Compassion of God).

▪ LITURGY OF THE WORD: The weekday readings may be used. Paul's message to the Thessalonians regarding "those who have fallen asleep" is really a call to continue working in the world, even though the community has entered into "the latter days." The gospels begin the Lucan selections today: Jesus begins his life's work with a less than enthusiastic response from his friends and neighbors. Whatever the individual Christian's professional calling, the vocation bestowed in baptismal anointing is the same as Jesus': to bring good news to the poor, release to captives, recovery of sight to the blind, freedom for the oppressed. Alternative readings appear in the lectionary, section #846–850 "Blessing of Human Labor", or #831-835 "For Peace and Justice."

▪ OTHER LITURGIES: See the *Book of Blessings* (chapter 24): "Order for Blessing Tools or Other Equipment for Work." An ecclesial or civil gathering for the holiday might be enhanced through the use of these texts.

SEPTEMBER

TUE 2 #432 (LMC, #193–227) green
Weekday

First Thessalonians concludes on an eschatological note. Especially now, when "mainline" churches rarely preach about the End Time, we need a salutary reminder that the world is going to end and, probably sooner, our individual worlds, too. Paul urges his listeners to action: Encourage and build each other up. Unrecognized in his hometown synagogue, Jesus is recognized by the people in Capernaum — and by a demon there — as one with authority.

WED 3 #433 (LMC, #193–227) white
Gregory the Great, pope, religious, doctor of the church
MEMORIAL

Colossians begins on a note of praise for that community's faith, hope and love — a gospel life that proves its authenticity by bearing good fruit. The gospel shows Simon's mother-in-law using her restored health to be of service, while Jesus balances prayer in solitude with a ministry of preaching and healing. These are appropriate readings for the memorial of Gregory the Great, the first bishop of Rome to use a designation still used by popes today: "servant of the servants of God." This monk-pope's life of prayer and work exemplified well the balance and moderation of the Holy Rule of Saint Benedict.

THU 4 #434 (LMC, #193–227) green
Weekday

Paul outlines the basic qualities of a "life in Christ": knowledge of God's will, the fruit of good works, patient endurance in trials and a spirit of joyful thanksgiving. In the gospel, Jesus, who almost never says "No" to a request, graciously refuses Peter's request today: "Lord, leave me, for I am a sinful man."

FRI 5 #435 (LMC, #193–227) green
Weekday

Scripture scholars consider today's first reading to be Paul's quotation of a liturgical hymn known to the early Christian communities. It celebrates the centrality of Christ, God's full revelation, as opposed to erroneous approaches that we will meet in next week's Colossians readings. Luke's Jesus answers the objection to his disciples' lack of religious observance by emphasizing the newness of the good news and acknowledging the difficulty those attached to the old way will have in embracing the new.

SAT 6 #436 (LMC, #193–227) green
Weekday

Blessed Virgin Mary, optional memorial / white. ▪ Both Paul and Jesus were misunderstood and faced opposition; Paul tried to follow Christ's own example of returning blessings for insults. For a second time, Jesus asserts his authority as the Lord of the new way. For the optional Marian memorial, consider CMBVM, #14: Mother of Reconciliation.

7 #128 [129] (LMC, #123) green
Twenty-third Sunday in Ordinary Time

This Sunday concludes the second block of Ordinary Time Sundays. The conclusion is, fittingly, a dramatic manifestation of Jesus' authority, an authority that always expresses itself in service of others. Some of the gestures used in this healing were once ritual gestures in the ceremonies of the catechumenate. Even today there is an optional signing ceremony in which the whole person is marked with the cross of Christ. The first reading not only uses the same imagery as the gospel healing but also incorporates baptismal imagery: waters, streams, a pool, springs of water. Being able to hear, and especially to speak, will be most important in the next block of Sundays, in which the revelation of the mystery of Christ is highlighted. Today's installment from the semicontinuous reading of James challenges Christian communities today to consider our hospitality toward those least welcome in worldly assemblies.

▪ GRANDPARENTS' DAY: It would be good today to gather in church or in a nursing home for a brief prayer service adapting texts from the Blessing of Elderly People (*Book of Blessings,* chapter 1, XII). At parish Masses, intercessions should be offered for grandparents living and deceased.

▪ BACK TO SCHOOL: Add to the Sunday intercessions some petitions adapted from the *Book of Blessings* (#527). The presider concludes by extending hands over students and teachers and using or adapting prayer #528 or #529. The first explicitly mentions the opening of school. Incorporate somewhere the wonderful phrase in the second prayer: "Let them take delight in new discoveries." The final blessing might draw from two other parts of the *Book of Blessings:* Prayer over the People (#543) or Solemn Blessing (#741).

▪ BLESSING LITURGICAL MINISTERS: A Sunday in September is appropriate for blessing liturgical ministers or introducing new members of the pastoral staff to the parish.

SEPTEMBER

MON 8 — The Birth of the Virgin Mary
#636 (LMC, #447–451) white
FEAST

Today's readings celebrate God's loving and surprising providence in bringing the plan of salvation to fulfillment. For this reason, the Romans selection is especially fitting ("all things work together for good"). Then, in proclaiming the gospel, read the whole thing! Too often heard as an endless list of mostly unknown names, the genealogy is actually the key to the saving gospel. For one thing, women are named, not customary in Jewish genealogies! And consider which women precede Mary: Tamar, who seduced Judah; Rahab, the prostitute of Jericho; Ruth, the Gentile; and Bathsheba of Uriah and David fame. In Jesus, down come the walls between Jew and Gentile, saint and sinner, male and female. God is making all things new!

TUE 9 — Peter Claver, presbyter, religious, missionary
#438 (LMC, #193–227) green
MEMORIAL (IN U.S.)

Paul speaks to the Colossians about their freedom, in Christ, from all philosophies, traditions and legalisms that seek to enslave the human person. Jesus gathers a great crowd and lets the healing power flow before delivering his own message of spiritual freedom. The readings are appropriate on this day that honors Peter Claver and his ministry among victims of the slave trade. The proper prayer for this American memorial notes how Peter's witness can help all of us overcome racial hatreds.

WED 10 — Weekday
#439 (LMC, #193–227) green

Today's passage from Colossians celebrates the fact that baptism has made us a new creation, raised from death and clothed in Christ. Jesus' Lucan "beatitudes" consist of four blessings and four woes. Where Matthew's gospel said "Blessed are those," Luke says "Blessed are you . . . Woe to you." The "you" is "us"! Each listener must decide which words to take personally!

THU 11 — Weekday
#440 (LMC, #193–227) green

Our lectionary selections from Colossians conclude with Paul's great "charter of the Christian community." Notice the progression in this brief text: Personal holiness has repercussions for community harmony; the preaching of the word leads to wisdom; and gratitude expresses itself in the liturgical praise of psalms, hymns and spiritual songs. The gospel presents Christ's "charter of Christian love," and it is nothing less than heroic.

FRI 12 — Weekday
#441 (LMC, #193–227) green

Today we begin a week-long reading from one of the "pastoral letters," writings attributed to Paul, which give us valuable insights into the life of early Christian communities as forms of organization and models of ministry were beginning to be formalized.

On these days when the readings focus on life in community, look at the presidential prayers among the Various Needs and Occasions (for the local church, for charity, for promoting harmony). Consider using the new Eucharistic Prayer for Various Needs and Occasions, form A (The Church on the Way to Unity) or form B (God Guides the Church on the Way of Salvation).

SAT 13 — John Chrysostom, bishop, doctor of the church
#442 (LMC, #193–227) white
MEMORIAL

Paul continues praising God's grace at work in him, "foremost of sinners." Jesus bids the community of disciples he is forming to hear and do, to manifest the depth of goodness by a harvest of good fruit. Consult the Eastern rite liturgy named for today's saint (Liturgy of Saint John Chrysostom) for a fine litany of intercessions and consider adapting it for use today.

14 — The Holy Cross
#638 (LMC, #370) red
FEAST

Replacing a Sunday in Ordinary Time this year, today's liturgy for the Holy Cross might blend elements of simplicity and festivity. For instance, use the simple greeting, Ordinary Time eucharistic acclamations (perhaps enhanced with choral elaboration), the simple blessing and dismissal. Balance this simplicity with a repeat of Eastertime's Gloria, a festive gospel procession and hymns that celebrate the glorious cross of Christ. Today's liturgy of the word repeats the Philippians reading heard on Palm Sunday (but now set in the context of Numbers), the serpent of healing, and John's gospel (the Son of Man's lifting up [exaltation]).

There is a special preface for today and the eucharistic prayer

SEPTEMBER

Reconciliation I has the beautiful line, "Before he stretched out his arms between heaven and earth. . . ."

In some Eastern liturgical usages, Evening Prayer for this feast concludes with the assembly coming forward to kiss the cross, which is surrounded by fragrant herbs and flowers.

AUTUMN: SUNDAYS 24–30

The first Sunday in the block of Fall Ordinary Time Sundays is displaced by the Feast of the Holy Cross. The displaced gospel (Sunday 24) is, unfortunately, the hinge of Mark's gospel: Peter's confession of faith, his misunderstanding of the nature of Jesus' messiahship, and Jesus' proclamation of the nature and conditions of discipleship. The next Sunday's gospel picks up too far from that point to permit a joining of selections. But preaching on the Feast of the Holy Cross could certainly mention the disciples' misunderstanding and Jesus' invitation to "take up the cross and follow me."

The following Sunday (Sunday 25) is another prediction of the passion and a call to humble service. The nature of discipleship is explored further on subsequent Sundays: gentleness in judging others, strictness toward self (Sunday 26), integrity of commitment and humility (Sunday 27), complete commitment and the danger of riches (Sunday 28), the key to greatness and the nature of authority in the kingdom (Sunday 29). As with the previous section of Ordinary Time, a healing with a message takes place on the last Sunday of this block (Sunday 30).

■ LITURGICAL TEXTS: The Litany of Praise in this block of Sundays might celebrate the cross, whose feast begins this segment and whose shadow is cast over it:

Lord Jesus, you humbled yourself to accept the cross for our salvation: Lord, have mercy.
Christ Jesus, you challenge us to prefer nothing to the love of your kingdom: Christ, have mercy.
Lord Jesus, you call us to follow you on the way to salvation: Lord, have mercy.

The standard set of general intercessions throughout this block could focus on the challenges of discipleship, perhaps singling out the various general "vocations" within the community (married couples, ordained ministry, single people, senior citizens, widowed folks, the young). One variable intercession each week could relate the day's scriptures to some local or current need.

The Preface for Sundays in Ordinary Time I or II might provide a subtle link binding this block of Sundays together.

■ MUSIC: Two of the refrains given in the lectionary at #175 would be appropriate to this block of Sundays if the proper psalm for each week is not used. They are available in numerous settings of every style: For Psalm 95: "If today you hear his voice, harden not your hearts"; for Psalm 100: "We are his people, the sheep of his flock."

Change the eucharistic prayer acclamations for this block of Sundays, perhaps returning to those used during Winter Ordinary Time or the first part of this summer's Ordinary Time.

For a communion processional try using the first verse of the "Bangor Antiphonary" hymn as an easily memorized refrain. Found in many hymnals, it is #732 in *Worship*. The assembly simply sings the first verse after each verse by cantor or choir: "Draw near and take the body of your Lord, and drink with faith the blood for you outpoured."

General hymnody should emphasize discipleship and community.

■ DECORATIONS: In many places, late summer will be giving way to golden autumn over the weeks of this block of Ordinary Time. Peter Mazar's *To Crown the Year* (pages 176–91) has wonderful ideas for incorporating images of autumn and harvest time, along with a few warnings.

■ ANOINTING OF THE SICK: Some communities schedule a communal anointing during the autumn part of Ordinary Time. Maintaining, of course, the prescribed liturgical texts, today's feast might provide a perfect setting in which to reflect on the uniquely Christian appreciation of the redemptive power of suffering.

■ SCHOOL PRAYER: Excellent resources for use at a children's liturgy today or a school liturgy this week are found in LTP/GIA's *Leader's Manual of the Hymnal for Catholic Students*.

MON 15
#443 and 639 (LMC, #193–227)
white
Our Lady of Sorrows
MEMORIAL

A kind of "twin" to yesterday's observance, today's memorial links Mary in an intimate way with the saving mission of her Son. The liturgical calendar keeps the daily reading from 1 Timothy, and this is a good idea, for the text emphasizes that Christ is uniquely our mediator before the Father. Then choose the John 19 gospel for the memorial, and

SEPTEMBER

we have the picture of Christ entrusting Mary and the beloved disciple (the community) to each other's mutual care.

Proper to today's liturgy, but more frequently associated with the Stations of the Cross, is the hymn "Stabat Mater Dolorosa" ("At the cross her station keeping"). Provided as an optional sequence hymn today, it might fit into the liturgy of the word as a preparation for hearing the Johannine gospel. A more suitable place, however, might be as a reflective meditation following communion.

TUE 16 #444 (LMC, #193–227) red
Cornelius, pope, martyr, and Cyprian, bishop, martyr
MEMORIAL

These two saints exemplify how, so often in the early church, division in matters of theology and ecclesial policy was overcome by unity in bearing witness to the one Lord, one faith, one baptism. Appropriate to the day's memorial, the first reading outlines office and ministry in the early church. The gospel has been interpreted by some ancient commentators as an image of Christ healing sinners within the heart of the church. Eucharistic Prayer I includes the names of both saints.

WED 17 #445 (LMC, #193–227) green
Weekday

Robert Bellarmine, bishop, religious, doctor of the church, optional memorial/white. • The "mystery of faith" is given concise presentation in verse 16 of the first reading. In the opening episodes of his public ministry, and before Luke's version of the parable of the sower, Jesus points out that to those who do not want to hear, no messenger from God will be acceptable. A practical consideration for us: How often, in the community of faith, do we dismiss the message by finding something to criticize in the messenger?

THU 18 #446 (LMC, #193–227) green
Weekday

Paul's counsel to the young minister is sage advice to anyone of any age in any ministry.

FRI 19 #447 (LMC, #193–227) green
Weekday

Januarius, bishop, martyr, optional memorial/red. • The parable of the sower in Luke's gospel is framed by today's passage on the women who accompanied Jesus and next Tuesday's description of Jesus' true family. If there is no Saturday morning assembly, the presider or deacon may wish to join Saturday's gospel to today's or to next Monday's.

SAT 20 #448 (LMC, #193–227) red
Andrew Kim Taegon, Paul Chong Hasang, their companions, martyrs
MEMORIAL

The sacramentary's listing of proper readings is only for use in communities that keep this memorial as a feast or solemnity (Korean communities, for instance). Surely prayers for Korea are in order as its people continue to struggle for personal and political freedoms so long denied them.

SUN 21 #134 [135] (LMC, #129) green
Twenty-fifth Sunday in Ordinary Time

Today's gospel is best seen as following the gospel of the Twenty-fourth Sunday (displaced last week by the Holy Cross). But the connection with last week is still easily made: The glory of the cross comes only to those willing to embrace the Lord's passion. Mark is wonderfully realistic: "They did not understand and were afraid to ask." The passage from James fits in well: The contrast between envy and selfish ambition on one hand and wisdom from above on the other is an important consideration at all times — especially, perhaps, now just as parish programs of education, service and socializing are getting back into full swing.

▪ BLESSING FOR CATECHETICAL SUNDAY: This weekend's scriptures provide the perfect setting for the parish's blessing of its catechists. Planners should always evaluate the quality of prepackaged suggestions for Catechetical Sunday before deciding to use them. The *Book of Blessings* (chapter 4) has a fine order for blessing, and the suggestions there for inclusion in the Sunday eucharist include well-written intercessions and two prayers of blessing from which to choose.

MON 22 #449 (LMC, #193–227) green
Weekday

Rebuilding God's temple begins through the agency of an unlikely helper: the king of Persia! Do we fully appreciate how the political exigencies of the "secular" world effect and summon forth the faith community's work and

SEPTEMBER

witness? Today's gospel is Jesus' counsel to wise listening. It makes little sense if we have not heard last Saturday's parable, which might, therefore, be joined to today's passage.

TUE 23 #450 (LMC, #193–227) green
Weekday

To the official selection (Ezra 6:7–8, 12b, 14–20), the Canadian lectionary adds verses that set the story in context (Ezra 4:4–5, 6:1a, 6a–d). Last Friday, before the parable of the sower, the gospel selection listed the companions of Jesus. Today, following the parable and a warning about hearing it well, Jesus' companions are listed again. Those who hear the word and do it are his family.

WED 24 #451 (LMC, #193–227) green
Weekday

Ezra's prayer blesses God for the gift of a remnant and a new chance at worship and witness. Having formed his "family of disciples," Jesus sends the Twelve on mission.

THU 25 #452 (LMC, #193–227) green
Weekday

Haggai's challenging words have a contemporary ring to them: eating but never satisfied, drinking but never filled, earning money that seems to find a hole in the bag! How do we define and then order our own priorities?

FRI 26 #453 (LMC, #193–227) green
Weekday

Cosmas and Damian, martyrs, optional memorial / red. ▪ Haggai's questions are good meditation for any of us who may look back, from time to time, to an imagined "golden" past, either for ourselves, the nation or, especially, the church. The Lord's word stands forever: "My spirit abides among you; do not fear."

The Eastern church has a wonderful designation for a whole category of saints, of whom today's saints are prime representatives, the "unmercenary ones," in this case, physicians! Pray today for all those in the medical and health care fields who freely give of time and talent in service to those unable to repay them.

SAT 27 #454 (LMC, #193–227) white
Vincent de Paul, presbyter, religious founder
MEMORIAL

Zechariah repeats Haggai's prophecy: God will be in our midst. But what kind of God? Jesus is unrelenting: "Let these words sink into your ears" (NRSV) and then offers another prediction of the passion.

Today's saint saw God in our midst, in the poorest of the poor. More than saw—he served! What a wonderful tribute to his ministry and memory that to this day the parish organization dedicated to service and outreach bears his name.

28 #137 [138] (LMC, #132) green
Twenty-sixth Sunday in Ordinary Time

Three apparently unconnected "admonitions" form today's gospel: 1) The disciples are challenged to broaden their vision of the community. 2) Jesus emphasizes the need to avoid causing "little ones" to stumble. 3) The gospel demands absolute commitment. Some scholars see a general theme here: the disciples' misunderstanding. Christ has called them to serve, not to judge the motives of others; their service is to care first for the lowliest; they are to be ruthless in maintaining and refining their own commitment but generous and compassionate with others. In this regard, James has some blistering words for the community to ponder!

MON 29 #647 (LMC, #381) white
Michael, Gabriel, Raphael, archangels
FEAST

If anyone doubts the continuing relevance of, and the surpassing interest in angels, simply walk into the nearest bookstore! Angels have always had a special place in Catholic life, both in our reflection on scripture and in popular devotion. This week provides a wonderful opportunity to rekindle and refocus this element of our heritage and tradition. Check LTP's *Leader's Manual of the Hymnal for Catholic Students* (pages 58–62) for liturgical suggestions applicable to the whole assembly. See Gregory the Great's excellent homily in the Office of Readings.

The petitions in the Office's intercessions will provide inspiration for today's general intercessions. There is a special preface, and Eucharistic Prayer I mentions the ministry of angels in the community's eucharist. Two fine hymns for the feast are in the Episcopal *Hymnal 1982:* a translation from Latin, "Christ the fair glory of the holy angels" (#283 has an ancient and beautiful chant) and "O ye immortal throng" (#284), which is especially good at synthesizing the scriptural references to angelic ministry.

SEPTEMBER

TUE 30 #456 (LMC, #193–227) white
Jerome, presbyter, doctor of the church
MEMORIAL

The prophet tells of a day when "many nations shall seek the Lord in Jerusalem"; in the gospel, Jesus "sets his face toward Jerusalem." Jerome's wonderful quote has been quoted often since Vatican II: "Ignorance of the scriptures is ignorance of Christ!"

October

WED 1 #457 (LMC, #193–227) white
Thérèse of the Child Jesus
MEMORIAL

Nehemiah makes his daring request to the king only after he has prayed. When the request is granted, Nehemiah is quick to attribute the success to God's hand. Jesus makes clear how much the kingdom costs: everything! Today's saint, popularly known as "the Little Flower" was not as delicate as that title suggests. Ill health was the least of Thérèse's challenges. When one reads between the lines of her autobiography (still available in paperback) and looks at the actual photographs of the community in which she lived, we sense that it was the daily struggle for charity and patience that made her a saint. Fidelity in the place where one is, love toward the people one is with: No wonder she is still so popular a saint. That situation and struggle make us recognize in her an understanding friend.

THU 2 #458 and 650 (LMC, #193–227) white
The Guardian Angels
MEMORIAL

The liturgical calendar prescribes that ordinarily the first reading today will be from Nehemiah. To the day-long reading of the Law, the people respond "Amen!" The gospel for the Guardian Angels focuses on the little ones they guard and on the disciples' need to become like little children. Devotion to the Guardian Angels was traditionally a wonderful way to teach children about God's personal and abiding love for each of us.

FRI 3 #459 (LMC, #193–227) green
Weekday

The prophet Baruch sees the community's grief and tribulation as the direct result of not doing what, in yesterday's first reading, the people promised to do. In the gospel perspective, seeing is not believing, changing one's life and doing the word is.

SAT 4 #460 (LMC, #193–227) white
Francis of Assisi, religious founder
MEMORIAL

Baruch's honest contrition in yesterday's first reading blossoms today into a call for courage and a promise of restoration. In the gospel, Jesus praises the Father for revealing to "infants" the mysteries concealed from the learned and clever. How well these readings fit today's saint! The universally revered and beloved Francis of Assisi speaks across the centuries and witnesses from beyond the grave to that deepest part of every human person that longs for union with God, peace with one's neighbor, and peace and unity with God's good earth and splendid creation.

▪ BLESSING OF ANIMALS: The *Leader's Manual of the Hymnal for Catholic Students* (pages 62–64) contains excellent resources for celebrating this day with young people. See the *Book of Blessings* (chapter 25) and *Catholic Household Blessings and Prayers* (page 174).

5 #140 [141] (LMC, #135) green
Twenty-seventh Sunday in Ordinary Time

For a new appreciation of today's first reading, see *The Five Books of Moses,* translation by Everett Fox (Schocken, 1995). Remember, this part of Genesis is involved in communicating not the *what* of creation but the *why*. Briefly put, the woman is not created from dirt and is not to be treated like dirt! In the kingdom there is a mutuality of dignity and rights between the two. From now until Advent, the second reading each Sunday is from the beautiful Letter to the Hebrews. The message is always a moving one to contemplate: Jesus becomes lowly so that he might be intimately one with his brothers and sisters in the human condition and help us to see that together he and we have one Father.

MON 6 #461 (LMC, #193–227) green
Weekday

Bruno, presbyter, hermit, religious founder, optional memorial / white; U.S.: Blessed Marie-Rose Durocher, virgin, religious founder, optional memorial / white. ▪ One of the most endearing books of the First Testament, the story of Jonah begins today with the reluctant prophet fleeing God's mandate and his preaching mission. For the disciple, the question is not: "Who is my neighbor?" but "To whom can I be a neighbor?"

TUE 7 #462 (LMC, #193–227) white
Our Lady of the Rosary
MEMORIAL

The Book of Jonah gives us a beautiful image of God and one of which we don't often think: God changed his mind! And God seems as surprised as Jonah at

OCTOBER

the people's repentance. Martha and Mary illustrate (as did yesterday's saints) two complementary dimensions of a disciple's life: prayer and work. Generations of Christians have found the rosary a help to growth in contemplation and a source of strength in daily labor.

WED 8 Weekday
#463 (LMC, #193–227) green

Jonah's honesty is admirable. As he readily admitted to his shipmates that he was their problem (Monday), today he lets God know how unhappy he is at the success of his preaching! He would have been happier to see Nineveh fry! God teaches a gentle lesson, and the book concludes with as wonderful an image of God as it began: "Should I not be concerned about Nineveh. . . . More than a hundred and twenty thousand persons who don't know their right hand from their left — not to mention all those animals?" The gospel is Luke's version of the Lord's Prayer.

THU 9 Weekday
#464 (LMC, #193–227) green

Denis, bishop, martyr, and his companions, martyrs, optional memorial/red; John Leonardi, presbyter, religious founder, optional memorial/white. ▪ Malachi confronts a reality we've all faced: The arrogant seem happy, the evil appear to prosper and those who test God manage to escape! Not forever, says the Lord.

FRI 10 Weekday
#465 (LMC, #193–227) green

Joel's words repeat Malachi's: "The day of the Lord is coming!" From this point of Ordinary Time on, we might be looking at harvest hymnody and songs about Jerusalem, our happy home.

SAT 11 Weekday
#466 (LMC, #193–227) green

Blessed Virgin Mary, optional memorial/white. ▪ Joel proclaims both judgment and consolation: Jerusalem shall be the city inhabited, the mountain restored. After proclaiming the demands and difficulties of discipleship, Jesus proclaims his mother's blessedness to be not the result of her motherhood but her fidelity in hearing and obeying the word! The Saturday commemoration of Mary would be a fitting observance today, with appropriate formularies from CMBVM being #10: Disciple of the Lord; or #25–27: Image and Mother of the Church.

Remember in today's intercessions the opening of the Second Vatican Council in 1962 and the ongoing work of renewal.

12 Twenty-eighth Sunday in Ordinary Time
#143 [144] (LMC, #138) green

There is an important detail in Mark's version of the story of the rich young man: "Jesus, looking at him, loved him." There is a very personal dimension to the call to discipleship and a very stern aspect to the cost of discipleship. Responding to Christ's invitation to follow him must always involve the renunciation of some riches. What kinds of wealth might encumber this community and restrict its wholehearted following of the Lord? The choice of the first reading suggests some elements to reflect on "scepters and thrones," meaning power; "wealth and priceless gems," meaning money and material possessions; "health and beauty," two of the more venerated "idols" of our age! The Book of Wisdom does not imply that these things are evil in themselves, only that the gift of discernment will help us sort out our preferences and rightly order our priorities. The self-examination, individual and communal, that this Sunday's scriptures presents does indeed confirm Hebrews' picture of God's word as a two-edged sword.

MON 13 Weekday
#467 (LMC, #193–227) green

As Roman Catholics hear the opening of this letter, there should be some feeling of personal connection with Paul: "To all God's beloved in Rome, called to be saints." The recipients were our distant spiritual forbears, after all, and we, like they, have been called to "the obedience of faith."

▪ COLUMBUS DAY: Mass prayers could be taken from a number of places in the sacramentary. The texts for civic observances might be appropriate (July 4 and appendix X, #6). But today is also a day when immigrants celebrate citizenship: The Mass for the Progress of Peoples or for Refugees and Exiles might be suitable. Given our less than impressive record with respect for Native Americans, the Masses for peace and justice might also provide good texts. Use the new Eucharistic Prayer for Various Needs and Occasions, form C (Jesus, Way to the Father) or form D (Jesus, the Compassion of God).

TUE 14 Weekday
#468 (LMC, #193–227) green

Callistus I, pope, martyr, optional memorial/red. ▪ Paul announces the heart of his teaching: "The righteous will live by faith" but

OCTOBER

clearly does not intend this assertion to eliminate the need to show forth that faith. Knowing God and living according to that knowledge are two different things, as his examples demonstrate. The gospel passage sets the stage for Jesus' teaching on the need for inner purity of heart and right intention, while connecting inward faith with outward charity. Callistus, a slave and convict who became pope, was known for his willingness to reconcile sinners and his particular care for those preparing to marry. These few facts suggest petitions for the general intercessions if his memorial is kept.

WED 15 — Teresa of Jesus, virgin, religious, doctor of the church
#469 (LMC, #193–227) white
MEMORIAL

Paul in the first reading and Jesus in the gospel both counsel withholding judgment of others and looking first to our own motives and conduct. The path to perdition, according to Paul, is not only overt evil-doing but also what he calls "self-seeking." The Pharisees and lawyers hear Jesus' condemnation for obsessive devotion to tradition, while neglecting basic justice and love; seeking honor and respect, without living lives that correspond to that reverence; and for burdening others and not sharing their burdens. Teresa's leadership by practical example is legendary. Her writings on prayer are still in print and so many of her sayings are still to the point: "God deliver us from sour-faced saints," is one. Remember the Carmelites today.

THU 16 — Weekday
#470 (LMC, #193–227) green

Hedwig, married woman, religious, optional memorial / white; Margaret Mary Alacoque, virgin, religious, optional memorial / white. ▪ Along with justification by faith, Paul proclaims the inclusivity of God's saving plan and enduring love. Jesus' criticism of the Pharisees and lawyers is something our own age needs to take to heart. On this day in 1978, Karol Cardinal Wojtyla of Cracow, Poland, was elected the youngest pope in over a century and the first non-Italian bishop of Rome in 450 years.

FRI 17 — Ignatius of Antioch, bishop, martyr
#471 (LMC, #193–227) red
MEMORIAL

Paul presents Abraham as the premier example of one who becomes righteous (justified) by faith. Jesus warns his disciples against hypocrisy and, more importantly, bids them to remember, in the midst of inevitable persecution, how precious they are to God, whose providential care will not ultimately fail them. Today's saint, mentioned in Eucharistic Prayer I, has captured the imagination of centuries of believers through his letters to the churches, which show the life of the early church as a synthesis of worship and witness, faith and action.

SAT 18 — Luke, evangelist
#661 (LMC, #452–454, 396) red
FEAST

By early Christian tradition, Luke is named as author of the third gospel and the Acts of the Apostles. Almost certainly a Gentile and perhaps a companion of Saint Paul (June 29), he wrote to reassure those who had grown uncertain toward the end of the first century. In his gospel, the compassion of Christ is inclusive of all: Gentile and Jew, the poor and the rich, women and men, the outcast and the privileged (© ICEL).

With this liturgical year rapidly coming to a close, it is not too early to start thinking about next year, which is the Year of Luke. Those responsible for adult education and Bible-study programs will want to begin exploring some of the numerous publications devoted to an analysis of Luke's gospel.

19 — Twenty-ninth Sunday in Ordinary Time
#146 [147] (LMC, #141) green

It is hard to imagine choosing only the short form of today's gospel. The two parts of this passage go hand in hand. The cost of discipleship is: everything! The sacrifice required of those in community leadership is: everything!

▪ MISSION SUNDAY: This year's observance falls on what would have been the memorial of the North American martyrs. The proper way to work this concern of the universal church into the liturgy is through proper intercessions, a special collection and a fitting hymn whose theme is mission, service or discipleship. Some presidential prayers could be drawn from the Mass for the Spread of the Gospel, and the new eucharistic prayer for Various Needs, form C (Jesus, the Way to the Father) might be appropriate.

MON 20 — Weekday
#473 (LMC, #193–227) green

Paul of the Cross, presbyter, religious founder, optional memorial / white. ▪ Combine Saturday's displaced first reading with today's passage from Romans for a

OCTOBER

more complete picture of Abraham's faith as a model for our own. Before teaching the disciples in greater detail, Jesus warns the crowds to "avoid greed in all its forms."

Around the time of the American Revolution, today's saint was preaching another kind of revolution throughout Europe, one based on the personal response of each believer to the love of Christ crucified. Pray today for the Passionist community, still blessing lives through its work of retreats and missions.

TUE 21 #474 (LMC, #193–227) green
Weekday

Today's long and complex reading needs careful proclamation. The main and consoling point comes in the next to the last verse: "Where sin increased, grace has abounded all the more." Jesus teaches the disciples that vigilance for the Lord's return and diligence in the kingdom's service are not mutually exclusive but complementary, two sides of the same coin.

WED 22 #475 (LMC, #193–227) green
Weekday

Today's gospel repeats yesterday's message of vigilance and diligence, with the added warning that "to whom much has been entrusted, even more will be demanded." Pray in today's intercessions for one to whom many gifts of nature and grace have been given and much responsibility as well: This is the nineteenth anniversary of the installation of John Paul II as bishop of Rome.

THU 23 #476 (LMC, #193–227) green
Weekday

John of Capistrano, presbyter, religious, missionary, optional memorial/white. ▪ Having spelled out the demands of discipleship, Jesus today talks to the disciples about the division that a decision for him will inevitably involve.

FRI 24 #477 (LMC, #193–227) green
Weekday

Anthony Mary Claret, bishop, religious founder, optional memorial/white. ▪ Today's passage from Romans is one of the most quoted portions of the letter. Perhaps that is because Paul's description of the "civil war" within himself rings so true to our own experience! If the reality is discouraging, how comforting Paul's conclusion: Thanks be to God through Jesus Christ our Lord!

SAT 25 #478 (LMC, #193–227) green
Weekday

Blessed Virgin Mary on Saturday, optional memorial/white. ▪ "Flesh" and "spirit" in Paul is roughly equivalent to "world" and "above" in John. The flesh condemned by Paul, and the world whose love leaves no room for God in John, are both defined by scholars as "the world system functioning apart from God with no reference to God or to the values of God." In the gospel, Jesus continues urging the crowds to read the signs and embrace the kingdom. If the Saturday memorial of Mary is kept, see CMBVM, formulary 30, which speaks of Christ's unique mediatorship and the role of Mary as "handmaid of grace."

☼ 26 #149 [150] (LMC, #144) green
Thirtieth Sunday in Ordinary Time

The autumn block of Ordinary Time Sundays concludes as did the last one: with a miracle and, this time, a new disciple to follow on the way. The message is the good news to seekers in every age. The gospel's description of the man's movement is almost ritual and, in fact, has been interpreted as the response of a catechumen coming to faith: He threw off his cloak (cast off the old way), sprang up (an image of resurrection) and came to Jesus (embracing of the gospel).

▪ REFORMATION SUNDAY: From a day of polemics today has become a day for pulpit exchange and mutual intercession, even joy at the progress made toward that unity for which Christ prayed. There is no interfaith dialogue that does not now admit that both sides were at fault in the Reformation, and both sides have much to learn from one another. "Wherever I see a wall dividing Christians," Pope John XXIII remarked, "I try to pull out a brick." Besides the publications of the multilateral dialogues in which the Catholic Church has been involved, Pope John Paul II's excellent encyclical *Ut Unum Sint* would provide a good basis for reflection within or among the churches on this weekend.

▪ DEDICATION ANNIVERSARY: This Sunday can be a local solemnity observing the anniversary of dedication especially in parishes whose dedication date is unknown, though even if the date is known, this Sunday may be

OCTOBER

chosen (footnote, paragraph 52c, *General Norms for the Liturgical Year and Calendar*, #3818 in *Documents of the Liturgy* [Collegeville: The Liturgical Press, 1983]).

MON 27 #479 (LMC, #193–231) green
Weekday

The Canadian lectionary wisely begins today's reading by repeating verse 11 from last Saturday. Otherwise, how do the hearers understand the "So then"? The Spirit of adoption by which we call out "Abba" denotes our status as children of God. Add to today's passage tomorrow's (displaced) continuation in which the sufferings of the present are placed in the context of future glory. In the gospel, Jesus expands the obligations of the Sabbath law to embrace the care of anyone in need.

TUE 28 #666 (LMC, #452–455) red
Simon and Jude, apostles
FEAST

As we approach the month of All Saints and All Souls, today's feast invites us to reflect on our communion with those gone before us and on our place as living stones forming with them the temple of God and the household of faith.

WED 29 #481 (LMC, #193–231) green
Weekday

Today's first reading is Paul's beautiful teaching on prayer, on God's providence, and on God's choice of many brothers and sisters for glory. Jesus, in the gospel, at first deflects the question about the number to be saved, urging his listeners to look to their own behavior. To hear and to eat and drink: How could we not recognize here the liturgy of the word and of the eucharist?

THU 30 #482 (LMC, #193–231) green
Weekday

These lines from Romans are among the most comforting in the New Testament: Nothing can separate us from God's love in Christ. Jesus uses a maternal image to describe his love: the mother hen gathering, sheltering, nurturing her young in hidden safety.

FRI 31 #483 (LMC, #193–231) green
Weekday

Paul today begins his reflections on the Jewish people and their response to Christ. We need to listen carefully to the litany of blessings Paul associates, irrevocably, with Israel. Jesus again tries to expand the Pharisees' vision of the Sabbath by healing someone in need.

■ HALLOWEEN: One of the few vigils to survive in the popular mind, Halloween also has some trappings that derive from Druid festivals and other pagan customs. But without an overly negative preaching that presumes the worst (and accomplishes little), we need to emphasize the Jewish and Christian tradition that links harvest time with God's harvest, gathering in the faithful. Even ghosts and goblins, skeletons and cemeteries point toward the heavenly Jerusalem! See *Take Me Home* for fine pages both for All Hallows' Eve and All Saints' Day. The *Leader's Manual of the Hymnal for Catholic Students* provides liturgical recommendations suitable for adult and mixed assemblies as well as children's liturgies. More complete notes follow on page 230.

NOVEMBER: THE FINAL WEEKS OF ORDINARY TIME

Vatican II's reformed liturgical calendar refined and reinvigorated a long-standing Catholic tradition: November is a month-long celebration of the communion of saints, of remembrance and prayer for those gone before us, of heightened anticipation of Christ's glorious Second Coming.

Mass in November

■ INTRODUCTORY RITES: Choose an opening hymn to use throughout the month. "For all the saints" is one possibility as long as the eschatological verse is used each time: "From earth's wide bounds, from ocean's farthest coast." Another custom uses the litany of the saints (with local patrons included) as an opening processional before the principal Sunday Mass. Some communities use the All Saints hymn at the preparation of the gifts or as a recessional, and only on All Saints' Day, preferring to mark the month with a Jerusalem hymn or harvest anthem for the weekly gathering song. In this case, "Jerusalem, my happy home" or "Come, ye thankful people, come," with their eschatological verses used weekly, might be good choices.

For the greeting, note this new text from ICEL:

> Citizens with the saints and members of God's household: grace and peace be with you.

For the litany of praise, use the invocations at C*ii* in the sacramentary, or let the rite of blessing and sprinkling set a more explicitly paschal tone to these November Sundays.

■ LITURGY OF THE WORD: For the responsorial psalm, Psalm 122 (lectionary, #175) is the month's common responsorial psalm. Among numerous fine settings:

NOVEMBER

- Christopher Willcock, "Let us go rejoicing," *Psalms for Feasts and Seasons* (Liturgical Press)
- Robert Kreutz, "I rejoiced when I heard them say" *Psalms* (OCP)
- A. Gregory Murray antiphon, Gelineau tone, *Worship* (#67)
- Joseph Smith, "I rejoiced when I heard them say" (GIA, G-2775)
- Michael Joncas, "Let us go rejoicing" *(Gather)*
- David Haas, "I was glad" (GIA, *Gather*, second edition)

The gospel acclamation for these last Sundays and weekdays of Ordinary Time should come from the verses at the end of each list in the lectionary (#164, 509).

A common set of general intercessions could be used throughout the month. These should include extra petitions for the dead (see the *Order of Christian Funerals* and the sacramentary, appendix I, #11).

■ LITURGY OF THE EUCHARIST: There are proper prefaces for All Saints, the Dedication and Christ the King. On All Souls, one of the prefaces for Christian death is used, and this could be repeated on the Thirty-third Sunday and even on weekdays, especially during the last two weeks. The same set of eucharistic acclamations could be used or, at least on All Saints, All Souls and Christ the King, the Eastertime set. A good eucharistic prayer to use these days might be Reconciliation II.

■ CONCLUDING RITE: Solemn blessings are suggested for All Saints (#18), All Souls (#20) and the Dedication (#19). See the revision of the All Souls' text in the *Book of Blessings* (#1438) and use it also on Sunday 33 and perhaps on Christ the King.

■ NOVEMBER HYMNODY: A large repertoire of possibilities stands ready to serve November's worship. Survey the topical and liturgical indices of your community's hymnal for various headings that suggest this season, under such headings as "The kingdom of God" and "The church triumphant." Remember that some "Thanksgiving" hymns carry associations with the heavenly, eschatological harvest. Christ the King hymns may be suitable throughout the month.

Worship Environment in November

■ OVERALL DECORATIONS: Consult Peter Mazar's *To Crown the Year* (pages 192–97). "It's a mistake not to recognize how November 1 and 2 are clothed in the harvest — an intensely paschal image that the scriptures use over and over as a sign of the kingdom to come, as an emblem of resurrection."

■ BOOK OF THE NAMES OF THE DEAD: Liturgy Training Publication's beautifully bound blank book in which members of the assembly may inscribe the names of the deceased could be placed near the baptismal font. This book can be honored with incense at least on All Saints and All Souls, if not on all the Sundays of the month, and the Easter candle lighted.

■ CEMETERIES: The care taken of cemeteries is a sign of respect not only to the dead but also to the bereaved and to the descendants who visit. Parishes enjoying such a privilege and responsibility should think about decorating the entranceway, posting signs telling the significance of November and its feasts, and leaving special prayers in weatherproof containers along walkways. A procession and blessing could be held on All Souls.

■ DOMESTIC PRAYER IN NOVEMBER: See *Catholic Household Blessings and Prayers* (pages 178–83) for prayers for this month and a family's visit to a cemetery. Liturgy Training Publication's *Sourcebook about Death* (1989), with 30 sections for day-by-day reading, might be made available for parishioner purchase throughout the month. See, too, the entries in *Take Me Home*.

November

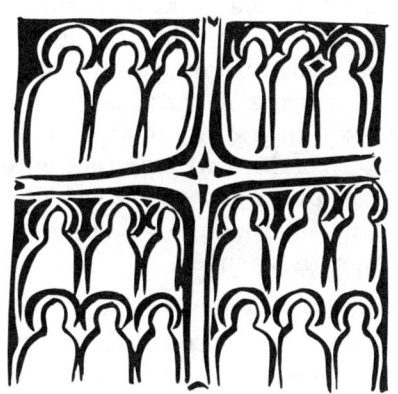

SAT #667 (LMC, #402) white
All Saints
SOLEMNITY

This feast began in the East to commemorate all martyrs and was progressively adopted in the West. In the eighth century it was celebrated in Rome on 1 November and was soon widely observed elsewhere on this day. The feast honors all holy men and women in glory with Christ: known or unknown, mighty or lowly, all whose lives were modeled on the Beatitudes and on the great commandment of love for God and neighbor (© ICEL).

As with all solemnities, this celebration begins with First Vespers. There are several All Hallows' Eve possibilities, and since this year's observance falls on a Friday, communities should plan something special that could involve a wide range of age groups.

NOVEMBER

■ HALLOWEEN MASS: An evening Mass with children, celebrated early enough to allow youngsters to go on their rounds, might be appreciated by their parents as well. Participation in costume can be fun, an eschatological sign, and pushing for "saints only" costumes is not necessary. The sung litany of the saints is a good accompaniment to a great procession, perhaps including the children, or a fine form of intercessions (include local saints). The gathering rite may include a procession that passes all the statues, windows and icons that honor the saints. Imitating the great incensation with which the Eastern rite divine liturgy begins, perhaps after the procession has passed by these images, the deacon could return to them, while the entrance song or litany continues, to honor them, and then the whole assembly, with incense.

■ VIGIL SERVICES FOR ALL HALLOWS' EVE: There are three possibilities:

1) Vigil for the eve of All Saints' Day: (*Book of Occasional Services,* Episcopal). Baptismal in nature, it calls for a service of light, three (or more) readings and psalms before the gospel, then sacraments of initiation or renewal of baptismal vows (Catholic tradition, of course, reserves initiation of adults to the Easter Vigil).

2) Service for All Hallows' Eve: (*Book of Occasional Services,* Episcopal). Combined with "suitable festivities and entertainment" or a communal visit to a cemetery, this rite begins with a service of light and continues with some very appropriate readings. The collects are wonderful and include Mary and the saints. The service concludes with a homily and the Te Deum.

3) *Liturgy of the Hours:* Use the proper texts for Evening Prayer I, the Office of Readings, and an extended vigil proper to this night.

■ MASSES ON SATURDAY: An entrance procession past the images of the saints, as described for the vigil, might be appropriate today as well.

Any readings from Masses for the Dead #1011–1016 [789–793] or #668 (LMC, #531–535) white, violet, black

2 The Commemoration of All the Faithful Departed (All Souls)

This day of commemoration began early in the Middle Ages with annual prayers for the dead in monastic communities. Fixed on this day, it spread more widely after the tenth century. Commonly known as All Souls, it expresses Christian faith in the communion of saints and our need to pray for one another in the church, especially for those in purgatory, who have died in their human imperfection (© ICEL).

■ MUSIC: Hymns from the parish funeral repertoire would make an effective beginning for today's liturgy. The gentle Taizé ostinato "Beati in domo domine" ("Happy they who dwell in God's house") would be appropriate, as would Jeremy Young's "We shall rise again" (GIA, G-2983; *Gather*). Its moving text is pastorally suited to those who have been grieving. "I heard the voice of Jesus say" is set, in *Worship,* to the comforting tune KINGSFOLD. The Episcopal *Hymnal 1982* has several beautiful and useful pieces (#354–358): the "Adoro Te" melody with the prayer "Jesus, Son of Mary"; an English version of the chant "In Paradisum"; and both a Russian chant and metrical version of the deeply moving Eastern rite *kontakion,* "Give rest, O Christ, to your servants."

■ LITURGY OF THE WORD: This year's liturgical calendar for the United States, while noting the wide variety, recommends: Daniel 12:1–3; Romans 6:3–9 or 6:3–4, 8–9; and the gospel John 6:37–40. The Canadian lectionary has a different set for Year B: Isaiah 25:6–9; 1 Corinthians 15:12–26; and either Mark 8:27–35 or John 1:1–5, 9–14.

■ CONCLUDING RITE AND CEMETERY VISIT: See the *Book of Blessings* (chapter 57) for an Order for Visiting a Cemetery on All Souls' Day.

■ OTHER ALL SOULS LITURGIES: Since All Souls is on a Sunday this year, the day could conclude with Evening Prayer from the Office of the Dead. The *Book of the Names of the Dead* could be incensed along with the altar and assembly during the Magnificat.

■ VESTURE: White, violet or black vestments may be worn. Throughout the United States, white is now the standard color for funerals, even Eastertime's white to link Christian burial with the paschal mystery. All Souls Day, however, seems to have a more emphatic note concerning our own preparation for death and judgment. Perhaps for that reason, a color more associated with quiet reflection and repentance might be appropriate: violet. This might also be the right day to bring out any black sets from storage, if they are in good condition.

NOVEMBER

MON 3 — #485 (LMC, #193–231) green
Weekday

Martin de Porres, religious, optional memorial / white. ▪ An intelligible proclamation of today's first reading almost certainly depends on hearing last Saturday's selection, which might therefore be prefixed to today's. Paul celebrates God's irrevocable call: Whatever our differences, the Jewish people and we have one overwhelming gift in common: We are both embraced by the same mercy of God. The poor, crippled, lame and blind are to be the guests of choice in the kingdom of Jesus — again, the embrace of mercy. For his service to these chosen, today's saint is revered.

TUE 4 — #486 (LMC, #193–231) white
Charles Borromeo, bishop
MEMORIAL

The first reading's list of virtues sounds alternately like one of Charles' homilies and a description of his personality. Borromeo had all the qualifications to turn out as one of the living "problems" that had caused the Reformation: a papal uncle and an early appointment to a large benefice that must surely have seemed like nepotism to his contemporaries. Yet with "Humility" as his motto, Charles set about translating the documents of Trent into a way of personal and ecclesial life. For us who live in the generation following Vatican II, his love for the Council of his day, for its liturgical and ecclesial reforms, and for its call to personal holiness provides a fine example.

WED 5 — #487 (LMC, #193–231) green
Weekday

Paul's hymn to love is today's first reading. Jesus again gives the condition for embracing the demands of discipleship: renunciation of possessions. In terms of Paul's call to love, that means renunciation of ourselves, so that our time and attention may be focused on the Christ in others.

THU 6 — #488 (LMC, #193–231) green
Weekday

We are not our own, says Paul. And Jesus shows us just how much we are worth to the One whose own we are! No business-minded shepherd would leave in jeopardy the 99 of which he was sure to look for one lost sheep; and instead of driving it home at the end of a stick, he carries it home on his shoulders. Since she still has nine silver coins, the woman's diligent search seems a bit obsessive and her eventual joy excessive. But these are beautiful images of our loving God: searching, sweeping, finding, rejoicing, extravagant in his joy over each of us.

FRI 7 — #489 (LMC, #193–231) green
Weekday

All that Paul is renowned for accomplishing he attributes to the work of Christ within him. Jesus praises not the steward's dishonesty but his prudence and creativity in the face of his impending crisis. How much time, talent and treasure the children of this age expend on frivolous, selfish and transient goals! Are we anywhere near as industrious and generous in advancing the kingdom?

SAT 8 — #490 (LMC, #193–231) green
Weekday

Blessed Virgin Mary on Saturday, optional memorial / white. ▪ Romans closes with a warm and loving roll call of Paul's personal "saints" and a doxology to God through Christ. Fidelity with the gifts entrusted to us and love of God before love of money: Jesus presents these essential qualities of disciples. In honoring Mary today, consider CMBVM, #45: Queen of Peace.

9 — #701–706 [671] (LMC, #442–446) white
The Dedication of the Lateran Basilica in Rome
FEAST

The Feast of the Dedication of the Lateran Basilica, while interrupting the sequence of Ordinary Time Sundays, fits in quite well with the eschatological thrust of the November liturgy. For the Christian, each worship space on earth is something of a reflection of the heavenly city. As the bishop of Rome's cathedral, "the Lateran" once carried the same connotations as "the Vatican" does now. The inscription over the east entrance is quite accurate: Mother and Head of All Churches in the City and Throughout the World. The observance of this feast is a token of our local church's communion with the church in Rome and with all the other churches that hold fast to similar bonds of communion.

▪ LITURGICAL ELEMENTS: It is in the liturgy of the word that the most choices need to be made. There is no need to depart markedly from the November pattern. As already noted, the dedication of any church recalls the heavenly Jerusalem that all church

NOVEMBER

buildings "symbolize" and toward which November's liturgical spirit directs us. Hymns of Jerusalem and the communion of saints are perfectly appropriate, as are "Christ is made the sure foundation" and "The church's one foundation."

In selecting sacramentary texts, remember to use those designated "Outside the Dedicated Church." There is a special preface, Dedication II, P-53 and solemn blessing (the first element of which will require some minor adaptation).

■ LITURGY OF THE WORD: Most lectionaries simply refer to the Common of Dedication but choices abound. The official liturgical calendar for the United States follows the new Canadian lectionary in specifying texts that seem to "fit" the style of November's liturgies: Ezekiel 47:1–2, 8–9, 12; 1 Corinthians 3:9c–11, 16–17; John 2:13–22.

November's common psalm, Psalm 122, is the premier "dedication psalm." Keep whatever setting of the psalm's refrain the community is using for the month: "I rejoiced when I heard them say, 'Let us go up to the house of the Lord,'" the pilgrim song of the faith community on the move across the centuries.

MON 10 — #491 (LMC, #193–231) white
Leo the Great, pope, doctor of the church
MEMORIAL

"Love righteousness, you rulers of earth," might have been Leo the Great's opening line to many a secular ruler. Surely the Spirit of the Lord's wisdom was upon this champion, whose gifts included political acumen, theological sophistication, the ability to preach clear and pastorally practical sermons, and the classical knowledge necessary to frame exquisite Latin phrases for liturgical texts of the Roman rite. These mercies of the Lord are not spent even in our own day. The gospel reminds us of the foundational gift, however: faith the size of a mustard seed but held firm and acted on.

TUE 11 — #492 (LMC, #193–231) white
Martin of Tours, bishop
MEMORIAL

Peace after suffering, the promise of Wisdom, seems appropriate on Martin's memorial. Though he surely would have considered himself a "useless servant," Martin is remembered for his nonviolent witness (together with Saints Justin and Cyprian) in the U.S. bishops' pastoral letter on peace.

■ VETERANS DAY: Martin's memorial appropriately coincides with this civil holiday, which commemorates the end of World War I. Intercessions for peace and for the dead, especially for those who died in war, would be appropriate.

WED 12 — #493 (LMC, #193–231) red
Josaphat, bishop, religious, martyr
MEMORIAL

The Book of Wisdom warns those who hold worldly power in their hands that God is not in awe of them and will judge any failure to live his law or serve his purpose. In Luke, a Samaritan returns to give thanks. Eucharist means thanksgiving: Do we balance our primary mode of prayer (petition) with a serious commitment to offer joyful thanks and praise? The memorial of Josaphat, born in Ukraine, was archbishop of Polotsk. He was killed because of his work to support the communion of the churches of the province of Kiev, with their Byzantine liturgy and customs, with the church of Rome. Today is an important day to pray for peace and communion with our Orthodox neighbors.

THU 13 — #494 (LMC, #193–231) white
Frances Xavier Cabrini, virgin, religious founder, missionary
MEMORIAL

The Spirit of wisdom surely flourished in Mother Cabrini: "She is a reflection of eternal light . . . an image of his goodness." To frightened immigrants in a confusing new world, Mother Cabrini, their fellow immigrant, was just such a beacon and benefactor. The eschatological note of Luke's gospel begins to come through clearly now as Jesus speaks of his suffering and "the Son of Man in his day."

FRI 14 — #495 (LMC, #193–231) green
Weekday

The Book of Wisdom wonders, as believers often do, how those who are wise enough to investigate the workings of the cosmos still fail to find sooner the Lord who fashioned it. For Christians waiting and watching, working and praying in these "last days" (gospels) the task is to bear witness to the imminent presence of the God who is surely coming.

SAT 15 — #496 (LMC, #193–231) green
Weekday

Albert the Great, bishop, religious, doctor of the church, optional memorial/white; Blessed Virgin Mary, optional memorial/white.
■ The Wisdom readings conclude on an eschatological note. The Word that leapt down, peacefully it seemed, at Christmas midnight now, at the other end of the liturgical year, comes as a stern warrior. Luke's gospel pictures the Son's return — quickly. Today's optional memorial honors a most comprehensive intellect placed at the service of God's people. If the Saturday memorial

NOVEMBER

of Mary is kept, look at CMBVM, #24: Seat of Wisdom.

16 Thirty-third Sunday in Ordinary Time
#158 [159] (LMC, #153) green

The end is near! But, then, so is the beginning. The lectionary omits the details of "that suffering" (v. 24 refers to vv. 14–23) and chooses to focus instead on the great harvest that will follow the cosmic cataclysm. The harvest of the elect is vast: "From the four winds, from the ends of the earth to the ends of heaven." "Know the signs," counsels Jesus, adding paradoxically, though "no one knows that day or hour." Daniel's vision is of resurrection and judgment; Hebrews' assurance: Forgiveness is ours in the all-sufficient sacrifice of Christ.

▪ FOOD COLLECTION: In many parishes, the whole month is dedicated to the "harvesting" of canned goods and cash gifts that will be transformed into food baskets for Thanksgiving and Christmas. One parish gathers these gifts at the baptismal font: We are all members of one body. If this has not been a month-long project, this Sunday's announcements ought to include a special request to bring such goods next Sunday.

MON 17 Elizabeth of Hungary, married woman, religious
#497 (LMC, #193–231) white
MEMORIAL

"Very great wrath came upon Israel." The great apostasy from the covenant culminates in the desecration of the altar of sacrifice. The gospel is Luke's version of the healing of Bartimaeus: faith leads to sight; healing to following Jesus.

Elizabeth is another of several medieval widowed folks who consecrated what could have been a lonely life into a busy time of loving service to others.

TUE 18 Weekday
#498 or 679 (LMC, #193–231) green

The Dedication of the Basilicas of the apostles Peter and Paul in Rome, optional memorial/white; Rose Philippine Duchesne, virgin, religious, missionary, educator, optional memorial/white. ▪ In his ninetieth year, Eleazar becomes a model of heroism for young Jews by his fidelity to the covenant.

Rose Philippine Duchesne was a religious of the Sacred Heart of Jesus. She served as a teacher both in her native France and in the emerging cities of the United States. Her desire to teach Native Americans was frustrated by her inability to learn their languages, but she lived a life of loving service among them and earned from them the name Woman Who Prays Much. She died in Missouri in 1852 and was canonized in 1988. Her proper prayer (in the *Sacramentary Supplement*) is joined to the weekday readings. If the anniversary of the basilicas' dedication is kept instead, there are proper readings, but it would be a shame to break the weekday cycle unnecessarily.

WED 19 Weekday
#499 (LMC, #193–231) green

Eleazar's good example bears fruit in the heroic witness of a mother and her seven sons. Deeply moving are her words of encouragement, whispered to her youngest (vv. 27–29). With a stern parable about trust and its betrayal, rejection and slaughter, Luke concludes Jesus' long journey to Jerusalem.

THU 20 Weekday
#500 (LMC, #193–231) green

Mattathias inaugurates armed resistance to the national apostasy, enlisting all who are "zealous for the Law" and "loyal to the covenant." This contrasts sharply with the "revolution" of Jesus who, at the moment of confrontation, will bid Peter sheathe his sword, and who in today's gospel weeps over Jerusalem. How clearly do we, called to be part of the new Jerusalem, recognize "those things that make for peace"?

FRI 21 The Presentation of the Virgin Mary
#501 (LMC, #193–231) white
MEMORIAL

Judas Maccabeus succeeds his father Mattathias and celebrates the rededication of the altar. This is the origin of the Jewish feast of Hanukkah.

The memorial may suggest the picture of Mary as "temple of the Lord," over whom the Spirit hovers, in whom the word becomes flesh—another November reference to the holy city.

SAT 22 Cecilia, virgin and martyr
#502 (LMC, #193–231) red
MEMORIAL

In the movies, everyone cheers when the villain gets his! The lectionary gives our rapid survey of Maccabees a happy ending in the death of the wicked King Antiochus. Jesus preaches about the new life we will enjoy in the resurrection.

Little is known of Cecilia, except that the early generations loved her and placed her name at the heart of the eucharist (Eucharistic Prayer I). In Christian lore, she joins Lucy, Agnes, Agatha and Holy Mary as the five wise virgins of the eschaton (Matthew 25:1–13).

NOVEMBER

#161 [162] (LMC, #156)
white

⊛ 23 Christ the King
SOLEMNITY

Pius XI instituted this feast in 1925 in response to the rise of totalitarianism. It celebrates Christ's reign over the human race and human hearts. The feast emphasizes God's ultimate forgiveness as well as Christ's eschatological return and final sovereignty over all creation. This last theme is continued during Advent (© ICEL).

When Pius XI established this observance, it seemed that almost apocalyptic forces had been unleashed on the world: Bolshevism in Russia, Fascism in Italy, the bloodshed of civil war in many places, ominous forebodings of new dictatorships. So the pope proclaimed: *Pax Christi in regno Christi:* "The peace of Christ in the reign of Christ!" At century's end, is the world very different?

■ ENTRANCE RITES: The gathering song should echo the glory given to the Lamb in Revelation (the original entrance antiphon): "Crown him with many crowns," "All hail the power of Jesus' name" and "To Jesus Christ our sovereign king" are but a few of such hymns. You might consider choosing a hymn that could continue into the first weeks of the coming Advent, such as "The king shall come when morning dawns."

Let the greeting, too, draw on the second reading and foreshadow the Advent greeting:

From the Christ who was,
  who is and who is to come:
grace, light and peace
  be with you all.

■ LITURGY OF THE WORD: The Ancient One who makes an awesome entrance in Daniel's night visions, is made known in Revelation as "the one who loves us and freed us from our sins by his blood and made us a kingdom." Year B ends not with Mark but with the other evangelist who has shared the year with him, John. In his gospel, Christ's official royal portrait is a king who stands bound before the powers of this world but who is supremely free as he becomes the faithful witness (martyr) to the truth.

■ LITURGY OF THE EUCHARIST: The preface of Christ the King sings a litany of qualities that should mark the life of Christ's community: truth and life; holiness and grace; justice, love and peace. Eucharistic Prayer I would be an appropriate choice.

As a communion processional, consider a Beatitudes refrain the community may already know or "Jesus, remember me" (Taizé).

■ CONCLUDING RITES: Use the solemn blessing that has been in place throughout November. Then let the community's final hymn be strong and festive, sung by all together, ministers and assembly remaining in place for the whole piece.

■ EVENING PRAYER: A fitting way to end the liturgical year and prepare for the Advent season ahead is to celebrate (or revive) Sunday Vespers. Before the Office begins, there might be a reprise of Christ the King hymns from the morning liturgy. Parishes fortunate enough to have bells should plan to have these peal out the community's joy during the singing of the Magnificat and/or at the conclusion of the celebration.

■ EMBER DAYS: In the United States, the three days before Thanksgiving are proposed as ember days in *Catholic Household Blessings and Prayers.* See page 188 for suggestions.

#503 (LMC, #193–231) green

MON 24 Andrew Dung-Lac, presbyter, martyr, and his companions, martyrs
MEMORIAL

The risk of fidelity (first reading) and the generosity that gives one's all (gospel) are mirrored in the newest saints to grace our international honor roll of martyrs. Andrew and the 116 who were canonized with him are among the thousands tortured and martyred in Vietnam between the seventeenth and nineteenth centuries.

#504 (LMC, #193–231) green

TUE 25 Weekday

The Canadian lectionary adds several verses that put the first reading in context. Consider prefixing Daniel 2:3, 9a, 10a, 27a to 31–45. The destruction of earthly kingdoms cannot help but involve turmoil. But the dream's promise is God's kingdom, which will endure. Jesus foretells destruction of cherished places and institutions, natural disasters and the destruction that we humans create on our own. In every age the signs are there.

#505 (LMC, #193–231) green

WED 26 Weekday

Daniel interprets the writing on the wall: Sacrilege and self-exaltation will bring about Belshazzar's untimely end. Jesus

NOVEMBER

speaks about persecution: Selflessness will win the disciple wisdom, perseverance, salvation. If tomorrow's civic holiday will use special readings, add Thursday's passage to today's.

THU 27 Weekday
#506 or 943–947 [881–885] (LMC, #193–231) green or white

U.S.: Thanksgiving, civic occasion/white. ▪ Some suggestions for texts:

Greeting: May the Lord, who fills you with his bounty, be with you always (BB, #1764).

Presidential Prayers: Votive Mass for Thanksgiving in sacramentary after November 30.

General Intercessions: For ideas see, *Book of Blessings,* #1760; *Book of Common Prayer* (Episcopal), Litany of Thanksgiving, #837; *Book of Common Worship* (Presbyterian), Litany of Thanksgiving, #792.

Blessing of Food: If food is to be blessed, whether for the Thanksgiving Dinner of those worshiping or for distribution to those in need, use the format and texts at BB, #1759–1761.

Eucharistic Prayer: If special preface is used, Reconciliation II (the great feast for all peoples) or Eucharistic Prayer for Masses for Various Needs and Occasions, form B (God Guides the Church on the Way of Salvation) or form D (Jesus, the Compassion of God).

▪ LITURGY OF THE WORD An appendix to the 1970 lectionary has a selection of texts for Thanksgiving Day. Of these, Joel and Zephaniah correspond to the eschatological nature of these last weeks of Ordinary Time. But Deuteronomy has a sobering warning: "Be careful not to forget." The 1 Corinthians passage speaks of being "strengthened to the end." The selection from Luke 12 might be especially fitting in communities where the "good life" struggles with the "gospel life" for equal time, while the Luke 17 passage is the classic text on God's goodness and human ingratitude.

▪ MUSIC: "Come, ye thankful people, come" is the classic American Thanksgiving text and has a fine eschatological verse about God's great harvest. "We plow the fields," "We gather together" and "For the beauty of the earth" are also hymns with long associations of this day. "Father, we thank thee" is an adaptation of the Didache prayer that can unite our civic Thanksgiving to the great thanksgiving of the eucharist. "The works of the Lord are created in wisdom" would be a nice new addition to the repertoire.

▪ DOMESTIC PRAYER ON THANKSGIVING: See *Catholic Household Blessings and Prayers* (page 200) or make available (from the resources listed above) one of the Litanies of Thanksgiving and the prayer from CHB.

FRI 28 Weekday
#507 (LMC, #193–231) green

In Daniel, beasts give way to beauty, chaos to a kingdom. Jesus calls us to attend to the signs that the kingdom is near, and the words come back to us: "He has put the signs of his coming in every generation, that every generation may expect his coming in their time" (Augustine).

SAT 29 Weekday
#508 (LMC, #193–231) green

Saturday Memorial of the Blessed Virgin Mary, optional memorial/white. ▪ If the Saturday memorial is observed, consider CMBVM, #46: Mary, Gate of Heaven. Whereas yesterday's Daniel reading spoke of God's kingdom, today's reading says that his kingdom will be ours as well "to the people of the holy ones of the Most High." The last word belongs to Jesus, who is the First and the Last, the Alpha and Omega of this and every liturgical year.

NOTES

Strong, Commanding, Refreshing

*Praise the Lord, the God of Israel,
who shepherds the people and
sets them free.*

*God raises from David's house
a child with power to save.
Through the holy prophets
God promised in ages past
to save us from enemy hands,
from the grip of all who hate us.*

*The Lord favored our ancestors
recalling the sacred covenant,
the pledge to our ancestor Abraham,
to free us from our enemies,
so we might worship without fear
and be holy and just all our days.*

*And you, child, will be called
Prophet of the Most High,
for you will come to prepare
a pathway for the Lord
by teaching the people salvation
through forgiveness of their sin.*

Luke 1:68–79 (ICEL)

Enjoy the Psalms and Canticles in your language!

THE INTERNATIONAL COMMITTEE ON ENGLISH IN THE LITURGY has produced a true translation—not a paraphrase—that employs standards of contemporary poetry and utilizes inclusive language for both human beings and God. The results are stunning!

 **NEW**

The Canticles

Sometimes the Bible breaks into song! Many of these songs scattered throughout the First Testament and the New Testament have been used in the liturgy and are called *canticles*. Poets, scripture scholars, and musicians worked together on 60 canticles from Exodus to the Book of Revelation. The results are stunning. Irene Nowell, OSB, has written an "Introduction to the Canticles," and an explanation of the translation by ICEL is found in the Afterword. Handsomely designed with two-color printing throughout in hardcover or paperback. The text is complemented by 12 monotypes by Linda Ekstrom that flow from the images of the canticles. 5 x 9, 144 pages.

Hardcover with ribbon.
Order code: **HCANT $20**
Paperback.
Order code: **PCANT $12**

The Psalter

All 150 psalms in a prayer or study book that will be a gift to anyone searching for a way to pray, a way to walk today the path that has sustained synagogue and church throughout the centuries. Introduction by the late Carroll Stuhlmueller. Printed in two-colors throughout. Complemented by 22 single-page monotypes by Linda Ekstrom. 5 x 9, 392 pages.

Hardcover with ribbon.
Order code: **C/150P $25**
Paperback.
Order code: **P/150P $16**

Psalms for Morning and Evening Prayer

The four-week cycle of psalms and canticles arranged for *Morning and Evening Prayer.* Antiphons are included, as are a selection of psalms for Daytime and Night Prayer. The pages are beautifully designed to allow the text to serve prayer and to facilitate communal recitation or chant. The psalms and canticles are pointed. Included is a set of original psalm tones by Howard Hughes. Printed in two-colors throughout with original artwork by Linda Ekstrom woven into the text.
5 x 8, 336 pages.

Hardcover with ribbon.
Order code: **C/MEP $25**
Paperback.
Order code: **P/MEP $16**

ORDER FROM YOUR RELIGIOUS BOOKSTORE OR FROM:
LITURGY TRAINING PUBLICATIONS

LITURGY OF THE HOURS IN THE PARISH

ö

Sanctify the ordinary with the daily prayer of the church.

ö

Three books to help you with Morning and Evening Prayer

ö

Introduction, History & Implementation

Leader's Manual

Participant's Booklet

ö

Morning and Evening: A Parish Celebration
By Joyce Ann Zimmerman, CPPS

Liturgy of the Hours can be an integral part of parish prayer. The long and varied history of this prayer attests to its power. This book examines the rhythm of everyday living and its relationship to daily prayer, the development of the Liturgy of the Hours, the 1971 revision of the rite, the structure and flow of morning and evening prayer, and practical ideas for celebrating Liturgy of the Hours in the parish or in other settings.

Order code: **MEPCEL** **$10**

Morning and Evening: Order of Service
By Joyce Ann Zimmerman, CPPS and Kathleen Harmon, SND DE

This manual is the perfect resource for the prayer leader, cantor and accompanist. The order of service given here has been designed as an engaging, first experience of these ancient prayers of the church. Seven forms for evening prayer and three forms for morning prayer are provided. General celebration notes guide the preparation of the worship space, the vestments, incense, music, scripture readings, intercessions and postures.

The manual is unbound, and three hole-punched for use with your own liturgical seasonal binder.

Order code: **MEPSVC** **$12**

Morning and Evening
By Joyce Ann Zimmerman, CPPS and Kathleen Harmon, SND DE N

This participant's booklet is coordinated with the leader's manual, *Morning and Evening: Order of Service*. For the same ten forms of Morning and Evening Prayer, it presents an order of service including only the participants' responses, hymns, psalms and canticles.

Order code: **MEPAID** **$20**
(per pack of twenty)

ORDER FROM YOUR RELIGIOUS BOOKSTORE OR FROM:

LITURGY TRAINING PUBLICATIONS

THE SUNDAY MASS VIDEO SERIES

THESE NEW LTP VIDEOS ARE NOT JUST FINE CATECHETICAL TOOLS. THEY WILL ACTUALLY RESTORE YOUR FAITH IN THE POWER OF LITURGY— WHEN DONE WELL—TO FORM AND TRANSFORM THE COMMUNITY. — KATHLEEN HUGHES, RSCJ

USE THESE VIDEOS
- with inquiry classes
- for mystagogy
- for a five-part adult education series
- with liturgy committees
- with liturgical ministers
- with youth
- to inspire
- to teach
- to challenge

AVAILABLE NOW

The Roman Catholic Mass Today
Introduction and Overview

Probably the finest thirty-minute look at contemporary Sunday Eucharist you can find. While introducing the Eucharist that we share in common, this overview spotlights four regionally and ethnically diverse parishes to present a breadth of ritual expression. The narrative is clear and avoids jargon. It focuses on major movements of the Mass without getting bogged down on liturgical details. You'll be proud to show this to education groups, the liturgy committee, liturgical ministers, the youth group and inquiry classes. Designed to appeal to the widest audience possible, it is even closed captioned for the hearing impaired! VHS, 30 minutes.

Order code: **RCMASS** **$39.95**

We Shall Go Up with Joy
The Entrance Rite

Through the various ways of doing processional and greeting, the song and prayer, we see how these rites take people who are isolated by their individual cares and bring them and their cares to be the church, hungry to hear God's word. VHS, 30 minutes.

Order code: **GO UP** **$39.95**

BRONZE AWARD WINNER ▲
Charleston International Film Festival — Religion and Ethics

Lift Up Your Hearts
The Eucharistic Prayer

Visit St. Peter's in Cleveland where "full, active and conscious participation" is evident in song, movement, gesture and simplicity. Filmed at Sunday Mass in October 1993. You will find yourself drawn into the prayer and community. VHS, 24 minutes.

Order code: **HEART** **$39.95**

Say Amen! to What You Are
The Communion Rite

At St. Henry Parish in Cleveland, people come on Sunday to do their liturgy. We see this as a great procession culminating in the joy and reverence of holy communion. VHS, 30 minutes.

Order code: **AMEN** **$39.95**

The Word of the Lord
The Liturgy of the Word

Those who read scriptures at liturgy and those who preach talk about their preparation and ministry. Parishioners speak about what they need and hope for from the liturgy of the word. VHS, 30 minutes.

Order code: **LITWD** **$39.95**
FINALIST — 1996 Telly Awards ▲

IMPORTANT INFORMATION
— PAL versions (*for use outside of the USA*) of most LTP videos are available. Please specify VHS or PAL when ordering.
— Study guides are included with most LTP videos. Additional copies (*pack of 20*) may be ordered.

Don't think you're up to the challenge of good liturgy? Watch The Hardest Job!

The Hardest Job: Leading a Parish to Live from Its Liturgy

You don't have to do it alone. Many people are responsible for doing liturgy well at the parishes spotlighted by our video series. Listen to the priests, staff, and parishioners at two of these parishes as they discuss what it takes to make liturgy the center of parish life. VHS, 19 minutes.

Order code: **PRESID $29.95**

ORDER FROM YOUR RELIGIOUS BOOKSTORE OR FROM:

LITURGY TRAINING PUBLICATIONS

SOLID RESOURCES
from Liturgy Training Publications

NEW FROM PETER SCAGNELLI

Prayers for Sundays and Seasons
By Peter Scagnelli

This is the first in a three-book series. It has texts for Year B (1997). Each two-page spread will offer texts for a single Sunday or feast, including new strong and memorable prayers of the faithful based on the lectionary and two collects: one is an original composition based on the day's scriptures, the other is a new translation from the Italian sacramentary. You'll find citations for the readings from both the Roman Catholic lectionary and the Revised Common lectionary, an introduction to the intercessions, an introduction to the Lord's Prayer, and an invitation to communion. This book is a companion to the *Sourcebook for Sundays and Seasons* and is intended to help all who prepare the Sunday liturgy.

Order code: **PRAYSS** **$15**

To Crown the Year: Decorating the Church through the Seasons
By Peter Mazar

Here is solid, practical advice on how to adorn the church's house for the seasons of the year and during Ordinary Time, too. Each chapter includes a section on images of the season drawn from nature, the scriptures and the liturgy. The best of the Eastern and Western liturgical traditions is at your fingertips. Illustrations will challenge your own creativity. For the liturgy committee, the sacristan and all who work with the environment of the assembly.

Order code: **CROWN** **$19**

NEWLY REVISED

A Triduum Sourcebook *(revised)*

This anthology of scripture, liturgical texts, poetry, hymns, and other literature has been revised and expanded to include more of the diversity of Christian experience throughout the world and throughout the centuries. Customs of the domestic church and a group of passages focusing on the presence of women in the resurrection narratives are among the new additions.

Sold only as a set of three volumes.

Order Code: **TRID/R** **$40**

We Watch and Pray during the Paschal Triduum

An easy way to encourage your parish to pray throughout the Triduum. On one folded card you will find an order for prayer and scripture reading for different times from Holy Thursday Evening through Easter Sunday Evening. Whether vigiling alone or with a group, whether at church or in the home, here's a way to live the three days as one celebration. Hand them out to parishioners with the bulletin or leave them in the pews to encourage parishioners to pray.

Order code: **TRIDPC** **$20** *per pack of 100*

(Sorry, we cannot break packs.)

ORDER FROM YOUR RELIGIOUS BOOKSTORE OR FROM:
LITURGY TRAINING PUBLICATIONS